Oregon Coastal Access Guide

*A mile-by-mile guide
to scenic and recreational attractions*

Oregon Coastal Access Guide

*A mile-by-mile guide
to scenic and recreational attractions*

~

Kenn Oberrecht

**Oregon State University Press
Oregon Sea Grant**

Corvallis

Dedication

To Pat, my wife and best friend,
whose contributions to this project are immeasurable.

~

The paper in this book meets the guidelines for permanence and durability of the Committee on Production Guidelines for Book Longevity of the Council on Library Resources and the minimum requirements of the American National Standard for Permanence of Paper for Printed Library Materials Z39.48-1984.

Library of Congress Cataloging-in-Publication Data
Oberrecht, Kenn.
  Oregon coastal access guide : a mile-by-mile guide to scenic and recreational attractions / Kenn Oberrecht.
       p. cm.
Includes bibliographical references and index.
  ISBN 0-87071-491-0 (alk. paper)
  1. Outdoor recreation--Oregon--Pacific Coast--Guidebooks.
  2. Recreation areas--Oregon--Pacific Coast--Guidebooks.
  3. Pacific Coast(Or.)--Guidebooks. I. Title.
  GV191.42.O7 O74 2001
  917.9504'44--dc21

                                    00-012445

Oregon State University Press
101 Waldo Hall
Corvallis OR 97331-6407
541-737-3166 • fax 541-737-3170
http://osu.orst.edu/dept/press

OREGON STATE
UNIVERSITY

Contents

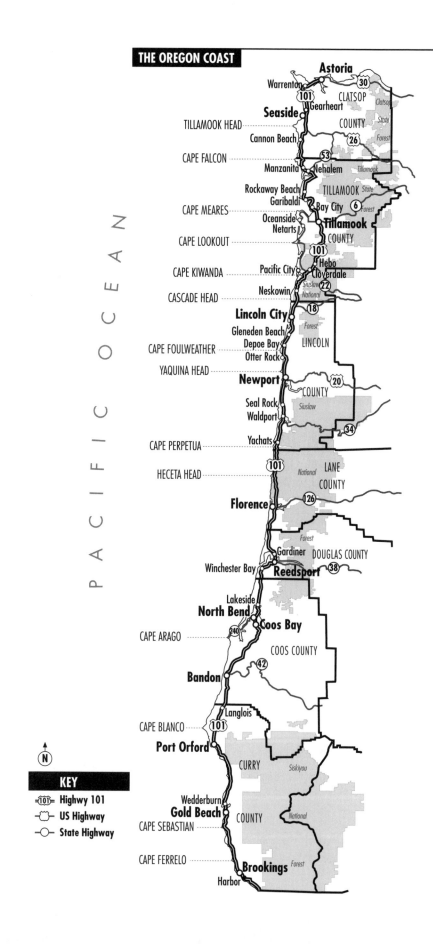

THE OREGON COAST

PACIFIC OCEAN

Astoria
Warrenton
30
CLATSOP
101
Gearheart
Clatsop
Seaside
COUNTY
State
TILLAMOOK HEAD
Cannon Beach
26
Forest
53
CAPE FALCON
Manzanita
Nehalem
Tillamook
Rockaway Beach
TILLAMOOK
State
Garibaldi
Bay City
6
CAPE MEARES
Oceanside
Tillamook
Forest
Netarts
COUNTY
CAPE LOOKOUT
101
CAPE KIWANDA
Pacific City
Hebo
Cloverdale
Siuslaw
22
CASCADE HEAD
Neskowin
National
18
Lincoln City
Gleneden Beach
Forest
Depoe Bay
LINCOLN
CAPE FOULWEATHER
Otter Rock
YAQUINA HEAD
Newport
20
COUNTY
Seal Rock
Siuslaw
Waldport
34
CAPE PERPETUA
Yachats
101
LANE
CAPE PERPETUA
National
COUNTY
HECETA HEAD
Florence
126
Forest
Gardiner
DOUGLAS COUNTY
Winchester Bay
Reedsport
38
Lakeside
North Bend
Coos Bay
240
CAPE ARAGO
COOS COUNTY
Bandon
42
Langlois
CAPE BLANCO
101
Port Orford
CURRY
Siskiyou
Wedderburn
Gold Beach
COUNTY
National
CAPE SEBASTIAN
CAPE FERRELO
Forest
Brookings
Harbor

N

Traveling the Oregon Coast

U.S. 101, Mile 0 to Mile 363.1

Oregon's seaside splendor unfolds before the traveler's eye along a ribbon of asphalt that defines the pace and essence of life in the coastal zone. The Coast Highway, U.S. Route 101, links all the coastal communities and counties and carries countless thousands of travelers north and south along Oregon's Pacific edge. It leads to beaches, sand dunes, rocky shores, forests, lakes, rivers, estuaries, trails, parks, campgrounds, waysides, wildlife refuges, and other highways and back roads. From Astoria to Brookings, Highway 101 is coastal Oregon's Main Street.

The Coastal Counties

Oregon's coastal counties have a number of similarities. They all border the Pacific Ocean, and each has stretches of sandy beach with forested hills and mountains to the east. The timber and fishing industries played major roles in their economic development. U.S. Highway 101 runs along the west end of all seven coastal counties,

Oregon's coastline ranges from sandy beaches to rocky shores and craggy headlands.

A morning fog burns off to expose the rugged Oregon coast.

connecting them with one another, and shaping them into a single entity, from the Columbia River to the California border.

Yet the counties are also very different. Clatsop County, the oldest, is home to much of the history and shares it through its fine museums, historic sites, and well-preserved buildings. Tillamook has rivers, rugged headlands, green meadows and pastures, and innumerable cows. Lincoln—with its golf courses, lighthouses, antique shops, art galleries, brew pubs, fine restaurants, casino, and more oceanfront accommodations than any other county— has naturally become the center of tourism on the Oregon coast. Forty miles of broad beach and seaside sand dunes characterize the western edge of Lane and Douglas counties. Coos County's broad shoulders and blue collars have for years concealed many of its natural treasures from the traveling public, but that will change in due course, as more people discover the charm and beauty of Oregon's south coast. Curry County, on the other hand, unabashedly displays its spectacular scenic beauty, sandy beaches, rocky shores, and lovely parks to anyone traveling along Highway 101, yet tourism is a fledgling industry here—a fraction of what it amounts to on the north and central coast.

In most coastal states, much of the coastline has been heavily developed, cutting off beaches from public access. In Oregon, all but a few miles of beaches, rocky shores, and headlands are open to the public.

In 1913, Governor Oswald West laid the groundwork for public ownership of Oregon's Pacific shores by persuading the Oregon Legislature to declare the beaches public highways. In 1967, threats of private encroachment at Cannon Beach led to widespread public outcry and resulted in House Bill 1601, the so-called Beach Bill, which Governor Tom McCall signed into law on July 6, 1967. Following is the essence of that bill:

"360.610 Policy. (1) The Legislative Assembly hereby declares it is the public policy of the State of Oregon to forever preserve and maintain the sovereignty of the state heretofore legally existing over the ocean shore of the state from the Columbia River on the north to the Oregon-California line on the south so that the public may have the free and uninterrupted use thereof.

"(2) The Legislative Assembly recognizes that over the years the public has made frequent and uninterrupted use of the ocean shore and recognizes, further, that where such use has been legally sufficient to create rights or easments in the public through dedication, prescriptions, grant or otherwise, that it is in the public interest to protect and preserve such public rights or easements as a permanent part of Oregon's recreational resources.

"(3) Accordingly, the Legislative Assembly hereby declares that all public rights or easements legally acquired in those lands described in subsection (2) of this section are confirmed and declared vested in the State of Oregon and shall be held and administered as state recreation areas.

"(4) The Legislative Assembly further declares that it is in the public interest to do whatever is necessary to preserve and protect scenic and recreational use of Oregon's ocean shore."

Oregon Pacific Coast Passport

Day-use and vehicle fees are charged at many state and federal recreation facilities along the Oregon coast. For the convenience of frequent visitors and those who may wish to stop at several fee areas on any trip, agencies began issuing short-term and annual passes. By 1998, some users of coastal recreation sites ended up needing four different passes for entrance to their favorite places, which was far from convenient.

In a joint venture among the U.S. Forest Service, Bureau of Land Management, National Park Service, and Oregon Parks and Recreation Department, these agencies now issue a single pass, called the Oregon Pacific Coast Passport, that replaces the four previous passes and costs half the total price. Five-day and annual passes are available and are valid at more than fifteen locations along the coast.

Passports may be ordered by phone from the Oregon Parks and Recreation Department at (800) 551-6949 or purchased at any of the following locations:

Astoria Welcome Center, Astoria, (503) 325-6311

Fort Clatsop National Monument, Astoria, (503) 861-2471, extension 214

Fort Stevens State Park, Warrenton, (503) 861-3170

Cape Lookout State Park, Tillamook, (503) 842-3182

Hebo Ranger District, Hebo, (503) 392-3161

Oregon Parks and Recreation Department, Lincoln City, (541) 994-8152

Beverly Beach State Park, Newport, (541) 265-4560

Yaquina Head Outstanding Natural Area, Newport, (541) 574-3100

South Beach State Park, Newport, (541) 867-7451

Siuslaw National Forest, Corvallis, (541) 750-7000

Waldport Ranger District, Waldport, (541) 563-3211

Cape Perpetua Interpretive Center, Yachats, (541) 547-3289

Mapleton Ranger District, Florence, (541) 902-8526

Honeyman State Park, Florence (541) 997-3851

Oregon Dunes National Recreation Area, Reedsport (541) 271-3611

Sunset Bay State Park, Coos Bay (541) 888-3778

Bullards Beach State Park, Bandon (541) 347-2209

Harris Beach State Park, Brookings, (541) 469-0224

Extending from the tip of Clatsop Spit at the mouth of the
Columbia River south to the Oregon-California border, the Oregon
Coast Trail is the hiker's ultimate route. Rather than a single trail, it's
a system of linked trails, beaches, and roadways, under development
since the 1970s and with a proposed final length of 400 miles.

About half its length consists of open sand beaches, connected
to trails that climb over headlands and traverse coastal rain forest.
At large rivers, bays, and places where trail segments are yet to be
added, hikers are routed alongside Highway 101 and other coastal
roadways, such as Three Capes Scenic Loop in Tillamook County
and Cape Arago Highway and Seven Devils Road in Coos County.

A number of creeks and small rivers that cross the Oregon Coast
Trail are fordable at low tide during the summer, when stream flows
are minimal. Some hikers wade them in bare feet to keep boots
dry; the tenderfoot would do well to pack along a pair of wading
sandals.

Only a few serious backpackers hike the entire trail in one trip.
Most people day-hike or backpack over the most scenic parts or
stretches of particular interest. A good way to enjoy the entire
Oregon Coast Trail is to take it section by section, as time permits,
keeping a log or journal of your experiences, until you've completed
the entire 400 miles.

The trail leads to most of coastal Oregon's state parks, the majority
of which have hiker/biker camps, showers, and drinking water. It
also passes near a number of Forest Service, county, and private
campgrounds that provide tent sites.

Drinking water can be scarce on some stretches, so long-distance
hikers and backpackers should carry water filters and extra water
bottles. Other useful items to pack along include binoculars,
cameras, rainwear, and a good field guide or two for identifying
plants and animals along the way.

The Oregon Parks and Recreation Department publishes a trail
guide with a map of the entire Oregon Coast Trail, as well as detailed
maps of several areas on the north and south coast. The guide is
available at coastal visitor information centers or directly from the
department. (For information, see Oregon Parks and Recreation
Department on page 30.)

Serious backpackers and long-distance hikers might also want
to pick up a good guide book, such as Bonnie Henderson's *120
Hikes on the Oregon Coast.*

The Oregon Coast Bike Route

Whether a bicycle is your sole mode of transportation or a conveyance you take along as you travel by motor vehicle, bicycling is certainly a terrific way to experience the splendors of the Oregon coast. It's also an activity that thousands of people enjoy every year. To serve all these bicyclists, the Oregon Department of Transportation has developed the Oregon Coast Bike Route and continues to improve it every year. The route extends along the entire coast and mainly follows Highway 101, where shoulders are widened to accommodate bikers and promote safe travel. In some places, the route departs the highway and follows city streets and county roads that are more scenic and sometimes less traveled.

The bike route is 370 miles long, or 380 miles for bikers who opt for the Three Capes Scenic Loop instead of Highway 101 between Tillamook and Pacific City. Green-and-white "Oregon Coast Bike Route" signs appear at regular intervals along the entire route and wherever the bikeway leaves Highway 101.

From May through October, the prevailing winds along the Oregon coast blow onshore from the northwest. Consequently, bikers prefer to travel from north to south then. For this reason, the Oregon Department of Transportation has concentrated its bikeway improvement efforts along the southbound lane of the highway, where shoulders are now three feet or wider for most of the length of Highway 101.

The Oregon Department of Transportation has published two essential guides for bicyclists: "Oregon Coast Bike Route" and "Oregon Bicycling Guide." They're available at visitor information centers throughout the state or directly from the department. Bikers can also order them online by visiting the department's Web site. (For information, see Oregon Department of Transportation on page 30.)

Access points and attractions along the entire bike route are covered in detail in the chapters that follow.

Camping Along the Oregon Coast

Campers traveling the Oregon coast will find no shortage of campgrounds, but campsites fill up fast between May and October, especially on summer weekends and holidays. For that reason, it's best to reserve campsites wherever and whenever possible during the busy season.

Private RV Parks and Campgrounds

Numerous private RV parks and campgrounds serve travelers along the entire Oregon coast. Information about these is readily available at coastal visitor information centers and at chamber of commerce Web sites. Addresses, phone numbers, e-mail addresses, and URLs for all chambers of commerce on the coast appear in the "Information" section at the end of each county chapter.

Port RV Parks and Campgrounds

Many anglers and boaters prefer port RV parks, such as those at Newport and Charleston, for their proximity to launch ramps and marinas. These are full-service facilities with amenities comparable to those of most private RV parks and state campgrounds. They accept reservations and, indeed, reservations are advised, not only during the summer months, but also during popular fishing seasons.

County Parks

Campsites at county parks range from primitive to posh, some rivaling the best state and private parks in features. With the exception of those in Tillamook County, where reservations are accepted, campsites at county parks are available on a first-come, first-served basis.

State Parks

State-park campgrounds are the most popular and the first to fill up. Of the eighteen strung along the coast, ten have full-hookup RV service, and sixteen are open all year; Oswald West (Tillamook County) and Beachside (Lincoln County) are closed in the winter.

Reservations are accepted at thirteen of these state-park campgrounds. Parks that don't accept reservations are Oswald West (Tillamook County), Carl G. Washburn (Lane County), Cape Blanco (Curry County), Humbug Mountain (Curry County), and Alfred A. Loeb (Curry County). Yurts and cabins must be reserved, even at those campgrounds that do not accept campsite reservations— namely, Cape Blanco and Alfred A. Loeb State Parks.

Campers must make reservations from two days to eleven months in advance of their first night's stay. Reserve campsites, yurts, and cabins by phone or online at the Oregon Parks and Recreation Department Web site. (For information, see Oregon Parks and Recreation Department on page 30.)

Forest Service Campgrounds

U.S. Forest Service campgrounds generally have primitive tent and RV sites, with tables and fireplaces, but no hookups. Consequently, they don't tend to fill up as fast as state campgrounds. In fact, it's not uncommon for those along Highway 101 to display "Vacancy" signs, even in the middle of the summer busy season.

Forest Service campgrounds are concentrated mainly on the central and south coast and scattered throughout the mountains in the Siuslaw and Siskiyou National Forests. They're situated near creeks, rivers, lakes, sand dunes, and ocean beaches, and they offer campers a variety of outdoor adventure.

Most Forest Service campgrounds do not accept reservations. A few campsites may be reserved through the National Recreation Reservations Service for up to 240 days in advance. (For information, see Siuslaw National Forest and Siskiyou National Forest on page 30.)

Bureau of Land Management Campgrounds

BLM campgrounds range from no-frills, open-camping areas to fine parks in prime locations. Although they don't have RV hookups, most have the rest of the usual amenities. They're mainly situated in the Coast Range and Siskiyou Mountains, usually on creeks, rivers, and lakes. Reservations are not available. (For information, see U.S. Bureau of Land Management on page 30.)

Lodging Along the Oregon Coast

Overnight accommodations along the Oregon coast run the gamut, from inexpensive, no-frills motels to plush, full-service, oceanfront resorts. In between are vacation rental houses, cabins, condos, bed-and-breakfast inns, and all manner of hotels and motels.

All coastal visitor information centers have lists and brochures describing most or all of the local accommodations. Chamber of commerce Web sites also provide lodging information, often with links to the sites of various hotels, motels, inns, and resorts, where travelers can find more information and make reservations online.

Three useful publications to look for at visitor information centers or to request when you phone are *Where to Stay in Oregon, Oregon Bed & Breakfast Guild Destination Guide,* and *Border to Border Bed & Breakfast Directory*.

Erected mainly during the latter half of the nineteenth century, Oregon's nine historical lighthouses stand along the coast in each of the state's seven coastal counties. The Cape Arago Lighthouse, the only twentieth-century structure, was completed in 1934, but was preceded by two other lights built on the same site in 1866 and 1908. Seven of these coastal sentinels are on the mainland, where they are easily approached for closer inspection and photography. The Cape Arago Light-house stands on a nearshore islet, and Tillamook Rock Lighthouse occupies a basalt islet just over a mile offshore of Tillamook Head, between Seaside and Cannon Beach.

Most of Oregon's light stations were established between 1870 and 1896 by the United States Lighthouse Board. Eventually, the United States Coast Guard took over the operation and maintenance of the lighthouses. In the 1960s, automated beacons were installed, and the Coast Guard began transferring management responsibilities to other federal and state agencies, among them the U. S. Bureau of Land Management and Oregon Parks and Recreation Department. Preservation and restoration efforts aided by local volunteer organizations have established these historical landmarks as coastal treasures that attract thousands of visitors each year.

All seven of the mainland lighthouses are open to the public. Yaquina Head, Yaquina Bay, Heceta Head, Umpqua River, and Cape Blanco lighthouses offer regularly scheduled tours. At Cape Meares and Coquille River lighthouses, tours can be arranged.

Only Tillamook Rock Lighthouse is privately owned. "Terrible Tilly," as the lighthouse keepers came to know this storm-battered structure, stands 133 feet above the tumultuous ocean, where it operated from 1881 to 1957 as a guide to ships bound for the dangerous mouth of the Columbia River. It is now a privately held columbarium—a repository for cineary urns containing the cremated remains of the deceased—but also functions naturally as a nesting site for thousands of seabirds.

Two other privately owned lighthouses aren't among Oregon's historical sentinels; they are modern

Oregon's Historical Lighthouses

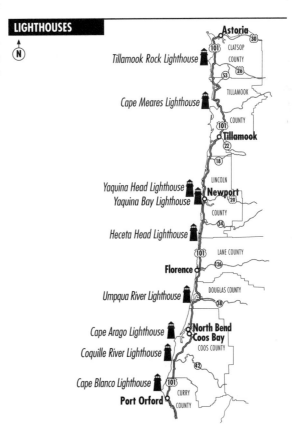

LIGHTHOUSES

N

Astoria

CLATSOP COUNTY

Tillamook Rock Lighthouse

TILLAMOOK

Cape Meares Lighthouse

COUNTY

Tillamook

LINCOLN

Yaquina Head Lighthouse   Newport
Yaquina Bay Lighthouse

COUNTY

Heceta Head Lighthouse

LANE COUNTY

Florence

DOUGLAS COUNTY

Umpqua River Lighthouse

Cape Arago Lighthouse   North Bend
Coos Bay
Coquille River Lighthouse   COOS COUNTY

Cape Blanco Lighthouse

CURRY
Port Orford   COUNTY

Oregon's Historical Lighthouses

beacons associated with residential dwellings, not open to the public. Cleft-of-the-Rock Lighthouse, just south of Yachats, is the residence of maritime author and former lighthouse keeper James A. Gibbs. The other belongs to a couple in Harbor, Oregon, and stands near the Beachfront Inn, overlooking the ocean and the Port of Brookings Harbor.

Details about all of Oregon's agency-operated lighthouses appear throughout the text, at their respective mileposts, in the various county chapters. (For quick reference, consult the accompanying table, "Oregon's Lighthouses at a Glance," below.)

Further Reading

Lighthouse enthusiasts interested in reading more about Oregon's historic light stations should check out two informative and entertaining books, both by James A. Gibbs: *Sentinels of the North Pacific* and *Tillamook Light*. Also, *The Keeper's Log* is the excellent quarterly publication of the United States Lighthouse Society. Its informative articles and superb illustrations cover lighthouses throughout the United States, including those along the Oregon coast.

Lighthouse Organizations

Friends of Cape Meares
P.O. Box 282
Oceanside, OR 97134
(503) 842-5270

Friends of Yaquina
Lighthouses
P.O. Box 410
Newport, OR 97365
(541) 265-5679

Oregon Chapter
United States Lighthouse
Society
P.O. Box 600
Lakeside, OR 97449
(541) 759-3920

United States Lighthouse
Society
244 Kearny Street
San Francisco, CA 94108
(415) 362-7255

Web Sites

URL: www.aracnet.com/~jkandik/
oregon.shtml
URL: www.lighthousegetaway.com
URL: www.teleport.com/~garski/
litehous.htm

Lighthouse	Access or Viewpoint	County	Route	Mile
Tillamook Rock	Ecola State Park	Clatsop	Hwy 101	28
Cape Meares	Cape Meares State Scenic Viewpoint	Tillamook	Three Capes Loop	8.8
Yaquina Head	Yaquina Head Outstanding Natural Area	Lincoln	Hwy 101	137.6
Yaquina Bay	Yaquina Bay State Recreation Site	Lincoln	Hwy 101	141.3
Heceta Head	Heceta Head State Park	Lane	Hwy 101	178.2
Umpqua River	Umpqua Lighthouse State Park	Douglas	Hwy 101	216.7
Cape Arago	Sunset Bay State Park	Coos	Cape Arago Hwy	12.2
Coquille River	Bullards Beach State Park	Coos	Hwy 101	259.2
Cape Blanco	Cape Blanco State Park	Curry	Hwy101	296.4

Life in the Coastal Zone

If anything characterizes the Oregon coast, it's the tremendous variety of landforms and seascapes that combine to form the coastal zone. They range from broad sweeps of sandy beach and uninterrupted surf that go on for miles to the rocky shores and rugged headlands that endure the ocean's relentless battering. The Oregon coast has cliffs, bluffs, rocky intertidal areas, dunes, pocket beaches, sand spits, and marine terraces. More than fourteen hundred islands, islets, sea stacks, rocks, and reefs stand in Oregon's nearshore ocean.

A coastal plain, varying in width from under a mile to more than 20 miles, runs the length of Oregon's Pacific edge, reaching from the ocean to the foothills of the Coast Rangeand Siskiyous. The mountains, with peaks up to 5,500 feet, run parallel to the coastline for the length of the state. The Nehalem, Siletz, Alsea, Coos, Coquille, Chetco, and more than twenty other rivers rise in these mountains, drain their forested slopes, and form lush floodplain valleys. Where they meet the sea, most create rich estuaries, teeming with life. Dotting the coastal plain are marshes, ponds, and dozens of dune lakes.

Many birds—such as this great egret, a south coast resident—inhabit Oregon's bays and rivers all year.

Four species of Pacific salmon and two species of anadromous trout hatch in the headwater gravel beds of the coastal rivers and creeks, migrate to the ocean, and return to their natal streams as adults to spawn and begin the process again. Other anadromous fishes also use many of these waters, and dozens of species of important marine food and sport fishes reside in the ocean off Oregon's coast.

Marine mammals that frequent Oregon's nearshore ocean include harbor porpoises, orcas or killer whales, and gray whales. Pacific harbor seals, northern elephant seals, California sea lions, and Steller or northern sea lions use Oregon's coastal waters, rocks, reefs, and islands. Seals and sea lions feed on fish and invertebrates and haul out on islands and rocks to rest; some also breed and rear their young here.

The islands, rocks, and headland cliffs attract seabirds by the hundreds of thousands, and many breed and rear their young here in the spring and summer. Waterfowl flock to the coastal zone by the thousands during spring and fall migrations, and many remain to feed and rest throughout the winter. Some are year-round residents that nest in the marshes, along the lake shores, and in the river valleys. The ranks of resident shorebirds and wading birds swell as others join them during semiannual migrations. Numerous birds of prey and a variety of songbirds and game birds crowd species lists for many areas to well over two hundred.

Black-tailed deer and Roosevelt elk roam the meadows, bottom lands, foothills, and forests, as do bobcats, cougars, and black bears. Among the many small mammals inhabiting the coastal zone are possums, raccoons, skunks, rabbits, coyotes, foxes, otters, beavers, muskrats, squirrels, and chipmunks.

Climate and Weather in the Coastal Zone

"Never hot and seldom cold" is the way one chamber-of-commerce brochure explained coastal Oregon weather, and that's not an altogether inaccurate assessment. It rarely gets to 90 degrees or below freezing on the coast, killing frosts are almost unheard of, and snowfall is minimal to nonexistent most years, except in the Coast Range and Siskiyou Mountains.

The rainy season generally runs from mid-October to May, with the greatest rainfall recorded in November, December, and January. Average annual precipitation varies along the coast from 63.48 inches at North Bend to 88.65 inches at Tillamook. The Coast Range gets much more rain than the coastal plain, with up to 200 inches a year falling at some of the higher elevations.

Summers are typically cool and dry, with daytime highs normally in the middle to upper 60s and overnight lows in the lower to middle 50s. The spread between summer and winter temperatures is smaller on the coast than anywhere else in the state, amounting to about 15 degrees. Typically, January daytime highs are in the high 40s and low 50s, while overnight lows are in the upper 30s to lower 40s for much of the coast. Of course, cold snaps and unseasonable warm spells are the exceptions that prove the rule.

Dressing for Coastal Weather

On the coast, fashion is mainly a matter of what fits well and feels comfortable. Dressing for the coast equates with dressing for the outdoors. Many coastal residents and visitors enjoy indoor activities, of course, but the reason most folks live here or visit is for the outdoor recreational opportunities.

Oregon's main tourist attraction is the ocean, and while it may be possible to enjoy the ocean from a motel balcony or to view it through the windows of an oceanfront restaurant or lounge, most people want to get outdoors to see it, hear it, feel it, smell it. They hike the beaches and coast trails, fly kites, watch birds and other wildlife, build sand castles, and explore tide pools. They go crabbing, clam digging, fishing, hunting, camping, boating, and sailing. They photograph nature, lighthouses, bridges, sunrises, sunsets, and one another. For maximum enjoyment of these activities, they dress accordingly.

The moderate coastal climate keeps people in similar clothing the year around. The mild winters don't require the heavily insulated attire more appropriate inland and in the mountains, and the cool summer temperatures dictate that people wear or carry togs that ward off chills. Dressing in layers is a good idea any time of the year, because it's easy to add a layer for warmth when it's chilly and remove a layer when it warms up—and either can happen on any

Essential gear for coastal Oregon birders, wildlife watchers, and photographers includes binoculars, cameras, field guides, and notebooks.

day on the coast. Even when the sun is shining, the wind can be cold. Chamois-cloth or heavy flannel shirts, wool sweaters or overshirts, and fleece vests are all excellent choices for layering up in the winter. It's also smart to be prepared for rain with a waterproof outer layer. Good rainwear is essential in the winter, and it's a good idea to keep it handy the rest of the year to prevent an unexpected downpour from ruining an outing.

Among the best outer garments for year-round use on the Oregon coast is a roomy, uninsulated, water-repellent mountain parka. In the summer, it functions as a windbreaker; during the winter, there's enough room to add a layer of wool or fleece and remain toasty warm. The big and numerous pockets, including large bellows pockets, are great for toting sunglasses, tide tables, compact binoculars, photography gear, fishing tackle, gloves, and trail snacks.

In dry places, during dry weather, everyday athletic shoes or outdoor boots do well on the coast. Long hikes on steep trails may call for good boots with adequate ankle support, but by and large, what works elsewhere works well here. In the rain and mud, on spongy trails and wet tidelands, and even in dew-laden grass on an otherwise dry summer morning, waterproof footwear is in order. There's an ever-growing variety of good, comfortable, waterproof shoes and boots available now, including lightweight, lug-soled overshoes that fit snugly over any shoes or boots and can be tucked into a daypack until they're needed.

Although not strictly an item of clothing, a pack of some sort is a useful accessory. A daypack or fanny pack is handy for many outdoor activities. Aside from all the things that can be stuffed into a pack for any outing, consider that as the day wears on, temperatures will probably rise, and a pack is useful for storing those peeled-off layers of clothing. When an afternoon wind rises or as the chill of evening approaches, those extra layers will be welcome once again.

Half the fun of any great trip is carefully planning for it—well, maybe not half the fun, but planning is essential for a successful trip, and it need not be the drudgery some people make of it. Once you have decided where you want to go and what you want to do while you're there, the rest is easy.

Visitor bureaus and chambers of commerce in the coastal cities can furnish you with a wealth of information about all local attractions, shopping, dining, accommodations, and the like. These are also the places to check for city and county maps. Most have excellent Web sites where you can get all or most of your pre-trip planning materials. Contact information for all the visitor bureaus and chambers of commerce for any county appears at the end of the chapter on that county.

Other information sources also appear at the end of each county chapter. For example, county, state, and federal agencies with offices in the county are listed. Some of these agencies also have Web sites worth visiting.

At the end of this chapter are the addresses, phone numbers, and other contact information for state and federal agencies that can supply information and help you with your trip planning.

Maps of the Coast

The Official State Map of Oregon and Oregon Highway Atlas are available free at visitor centers throughout the state and are adequate for traveling to and along the Oregon coast, but most travelers will want something more detailed for negotiating city streets and county back roads. All the city visitor centers have city and county maps, some of which are excellent, while others leave something to be desired. Some are combination maps, with the county printed on one side and city or cities on the other.

The Siuslaw National Forest extends south from the vicinity of Hebo in Tillamook County to the southern boundary of the Oregon Dunes National Recreation Area on the north shore of Coos Bay in Coos County. The Siskiyou National Forest covers most of Curry County, from the Sixes River south to the California border. The Forest Service publishes excellent maps of these forests, which are available at ranger stations along the coast and at the Oregon Dunes National Recreation Area Headquarters in Reedsport.

A good regional map to carry on trips to the south coast is the Southwestern Oregon Recreation Map, which covers an area from Sea Lion Caves, north of Florence, south to Crescent City, California. Copies of this map are available free at visitor information centers, Bureau of Land Management offices, and Forest Service Ranger District stations throughout southwestern Oregon.

Those needing topographical maps can order them from the U.S. Geological Survey. USGS topo maps are also available online and can be downloaded free at *www.topozone.com*. DeLorme Mapping prints topo maps in its series of state atlases. DeLorme's *Oregon Atlas and Gazetteer* contains a full set of topo maps for the entire state and is available through bookstores.

Getting to the Oregon Coast

Travelers heading south from Washington or north from California on Highway 101 enjoy the quickest and easiest route to the Oregon coast—they need only cross the Astoria-Megler Bridge over the Columbia River or the Oregon-California line. Those traveling to the coast from the I-5 corridor have a number of options.

People driving I-5 south through Washington can take State Route 4 west from Kelso along the north bank of the Columbia River to State Route 401 near Naselle, turn south, and drive to the Astoria-Megler Bridge. Another option is to head west from Kelso or Longview to Ranier, cross the bridge south over the Columbia River, turn west on U.S. Route 30, and take that highway along the south bank of the river to Astoria.

Those heading for Astoria from Portland can enjoy the same pleasant and scenic drives along the Columbia River. For access to Washington Route 4 and the north bank, take I-5/I-205 north to Kelso, then Washington Route 4 west to Washington 401 and the Astoria-Megler Bridge. For the south-bank trip, take U.S. 30 west from I-5 in midtown Portland, and follow it all the way to Astoria.

For an alternative route to the Astoria-Warrenton area and the most direct access to Cannon Beach and Seaside-Gearhart, take U.S. Route 26, the Sunset Highway, west from I-5. Use the same highway to reach Tillamook from Portland, but west of Portland, exit southwest on State Route 6, and drive through the Tillamook State Forest and along the Wilson River for a scenic trip to the Tillamook coast.

Those traveling from the greater Portland area to Lincoln City can exit west on State Route 99W at Tigard, pick up State Route 18 near Dayton, and continue on to the coast. Salem travelers should take State Route 22 west to State Route 18, then go west to Lincoln City.

From the Albany-Corvallis area, the straightest shot to the coast is U.S. Route 20 to Newport. Those destined for Waldport, Yachats, or the Cape Perpetua Scenic Area should take the same highway, but can head southwest on State Route 34 at the west end of Philomath.

State Route 126 is one of the shortest and quickest connections between I-5 and the Oregon coast. This is the best route to take west from the Eugene-Springfield area to Florence and the north end of the Oregon Dunes National Recreation Area.

One of the shortest and prettiest coastal links with I-5 takes travelers through the lovely Umpqua River Valley to Reedsport, the Oregon Dunes, and the south coast. Take the State Route 99 exit west off I-5 for Drain, and State Route 38 from there all the way to the coast.

Those traveling from Roseburg to the south coast have two options. The most used and most direct route is State Route 42 west off I-5, over the Coast Range, and to U.S. Highway 101, south of Coos Bay. From there, turn south to reach Bandon, Curry County, and the southernmost coastal attractions, or go north to Coos Bay and the rest of the Oregon coast. For a scenic trip from Roseburg to Reedsport and coastal destinations to the north, head north on I-5 to Sutherlin, take State Route 138 along the Umpqua River to Elkton, turn west on State Route 38, and follow the river to Reedsport.

South from here to California, there's no quick, direct, or easy route to the Oregon coast. County and Forest Service Roads cross the Siskiyou Mountains and eventually reach the coast, but some of these are not maintained in winter and may become snowbound. One exception is U.S. Route 199 out of Grants Pass, which drops south over the mountains, into California, and connects with Highway 101 northeast of Crescent City. This seems a roundabout way to get to the Oregon coast, but it's a delightful route through some great Oregon mountain scenery, and it ends in the California redwood country.

Travelers heading north on I-5 in California and bound for the Oregon coast would do well to consider heading west before reaching Oregon. Take State Route 299 west out of Redding and over the mountains to U.S. Highway 101 between Arcata and McKinleyville. From there, head north on Highway 101 through the wonderful redwood country and on to the southern Oregon coast.

Planning a Coast Trip

Mileposts

Roadside mileposts appear along U.S. Highway 101, the state routes, and most county roads in the form of small green markers with white numbers. Forest Service milepost markers are brown with white numbers. On Highway 101, mileposts run in ascending order from north to south, beginning on the Astoria-Megler Bridge and ending at the California border.

Among Oregon's coastal bridges are some of the most beautiful and interesting structures in the state. Look for details in the Highway 101 text.

The mileages referenced in the following pages for attractions and access points along Highway 101 and other routes are keyed to the roadside signs, but are based on actual measured miles taken from odometer readings on numerous research trips. These mileage measurements indicated a number of minor discrepancies (of 0.1 mile or less) between mileposts on Highway 101 and some of the side-trip routes. Adjustments for those were made en route, mile by mile. Some major discrepancies between mileages shown on mileposts and actual measured mileages are mainly the result of highway construction and realignment. Some of these differences amount to several miles and are noted in the text. In fact, any discrepancy of 0.3 mile or more has been called to the reader's attention.

Many of the mileages have been double-checked or even triple-checked. Every effort was expended to make this mile-by-mile guide as accurate as possible. Keep in mind though, that automobile odometers might differ slightly. Should any reader find a major mileage mistake or a discrepancy of 0.3 mile or more, please notify the author, care of Oregon State University Press. Also, please let us know if we have left out an important access point or a popular attraction we should have included.

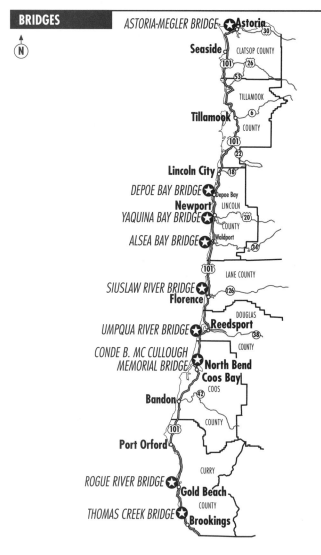

Pacific Standard, Daylight Saving, and Oregon Coast Time

First-time visitors to the Oregon coast should know that people, businesses, and agencies here operate according to Pacific Standard Time from late October to early April, and Daylight Saving Time the rest of the year. During the winter months, however, and sometimes from late fall to early spring, some shops, galleries, museums, interpretive centers, and even visitor information centers operate on Oregon Coast Time. That is, they may or may not be open when you expect them to be, or even when they expect to be.

This book lists days and hours of operation for various attractions along the coast, including off-season days and hours, which are subject to change, perhaps on short notice. Museums and visitor information centers are often staffed by volunteers, many of whom are retired people who travel in the winter, and it might not always be possible to find replacements for them. Sometimes the result is fewer days, shorter hours, or both. A facility in need of repair or remodeling is more likely to be closed for such purposes during the slack winter months than the busy tourist season.

Some art galleries and antique shops might have different operating days and hours from those posted. You might find them closed earlier than expected or on a day when they normally would be open. Or you might find a sign in the window saying the establishment is closed for the month or for the winter.

The point is, if you're planning a winter visit and know of a particular shop, gallery, museum, or other establishment you want to check out, it might be a good idea to phone ahead to make sure it will be open. Things are a little looser here in the winter, which you just might find to be a refreshing change of pace.

Beachcombers discover a variety of treasures along Oregon's beaches, especially after storms.

For as long as ships have navigated along Oregon's rocky shoreline and plied its coastal rivers and bays, countless sailing ships, steamers, freighters, barges, and other vessels have come and gone, none the worse for wear or worry. Not all, however, have fared so fortunately. Facing mean seas, wind, fog, protruding headlands, and perilous bar crossings, as well as more than 1,400 offshore rocks, reefs, sea stacks, islets, islands, and other obstacles, thousands of vessels have met untimely endings in Oregon's territorial sea. Some have even gone down or aground on flat seas, during sunny days, with no wind and unlimited visibility. They have struck reefs, run aground on beaches, foundered on rocks, wrecked on river bars, caught fire, capsized in rough water, collided with other vessels, or simply sunk out of sight for no apparent reason. The losses have amounted to thousands of lives and billions of dollars' worth of cargo and vessels.

In one of his books, maritime author James Gibbs lists more than 1,800 ships of 50 tons or more that sank along the Pacific Coast between 1500 and 1962, many of these in Oregon's coastal waters. In another book, he accounts for more than two hundred ships that have been lost in the waters near the mouth of the Columbia River, known as the "Graveyard of the Pacific." He further concludes that if the tally were to include not only deep-sea vessels, but also harbor craft and fishing boats, the number damaged or destroyed "would likely exceed two thousand, with more than fifteen hundred lives lost."

During four centuries of maritime exploration, travel, and commerce along Oregon's hazardous coastline, early sailing ships, of course, were most vulnerable. In the nineteenth century, the invention of steam power improved the safety of ocean travel and transport, as did the introduction of lighthouses, more accurate charts, and other aids to navigation. In the twentieth century, jetties did much to tame treacherous river-bar crossings. Dredging deepened channels. And the development of radar, Loran, and satellite Global Positioning System (GPS) greatly improved ocean navigation, even in foggy weather and under the cloak of darkness.

Nevertheless, fishing boats, tugs and barges, and even the biggest and best-equipped ships continue to run aground, wreck on jetties, sideswipe bridges, collide with other vessels, and sink in Oregon's coastal waters. What's more, they probably always will.

Among the more modern of Oregon's shipwrecks was the *Blue Magpie*. On November 19, 1963, the 321-foot Japanese-owned cargo vessel struck the north jetty of Yaquina Bay. Although the Coast Guard was able to rescue the nineteen-member crew, the ship broke apart within days, spilling more than 100 tons of bunker fuel. The ship eventually became part of the jetty and another entry in the history of Oregon shipwrecks.

As recently as February 4, 1999, the 594-foot cargo ship *New Carissa* ran aground near Horsfall Beach, north of the Coos Bay entrance. Within days, the relentless Pacific surf cracked the hull, breached fuel compartments, and eventually broke the ship in two. A major oil spill swept up the coast and into the Coos Bay estuary. The ship's bow section was towed out to sea, where a United States Navy submarine eventually sank it with a torpedo. A month after the wreck, cleanup and salvage costs had exceeded $10 million, and the stern section was still stuck in the sand near Coos Bay.

As tragic and costly as all these shipwrecks are, they are part of Oregon's maritime history and make for fascinating, often hair-raising, reading and further study. Several historical museums along the Oregon coast display artifacts from a number of wrecks. The Columbia River Maritime Museum, in Astoria, has a number of shipwreck exhibits, including a superb collection of articles recovered from the wreck of the *Peter Iredale*, which ran aground in 1906 on the Clatsop Spit, where its skeletal remains are still visible.

Further Reading

Two books to get readers started on a study of coastal shipwrecks are *Pacific Graveyard* and *Shipwrecks of the Pacific Coast*, both by James A. Gibbs.

Shipwrecks Along the Oregon Coast

Traveling along the Oregon coast and enjoying its scenic wonders and recreational opportunities are not without potential dangers. Exercising common sense and heeding simple suggestions will go a long way toward making every trip safe and fun. Newcomers, however, and even some seasoned residents, might need a few reminders about safe travel, possible hazards, and the unforgiving nature of the coastal environment.

Personal Flotation Devices

Personal flotation device (PFD) is the unfortunately low-key term the Coast Guard has adopted to describe any throwable or wearable object designed to keep a person afloat in water. The best of these bear more appropriately descriptive designations: *life* vests and *life* jackets. They're meant to be worn, and they *save lives.*

The stories are all too common and far too frequent. A family heads out on a sunny spring day to enjoy a little fishing on the bank of a nearby river. While dad, mom, and the boys are busy casting for trout, little sister steps too near the muddy bank. She slips and falls into the rushing river, where she's swept beneath a fallen tree, caught in its branches, and drowned. A life vest may have saved her.

Each year, in every season, the reports invariably carry the same grim message—"The victims were not wearing life vests." One can only wonder: why not? Boating regulations demand that vessels carry PFDs for all passengers on board. Common sense and survival instincts ought to suggest that people who venture near or onto the water would want to wear life vests or jackets.

Too many people who should know better—experienced boaters, canoeists, anglers, and grizzled old salts with years on the water—refuse to wear life vests. A frequent excuse is that Oregon's waters are so cold that if you don't drown you'll surely die from hypothermia. "All a life vest is good for," they'll tell you, "is to help the Coast Guard find your body." Poppycock!

In 1983, a young mother and her three-year-old daughter were heading toward Elfin Cove, Alaska, in an open skiff, when the boat struck a partly submerged log and capsized. Both were wearing life vests. The mother frantically swam for the child, grabbed her, and towed her to the log, where she boosted her up as far out of the water as possible. There they remained until a passing commercial-fishing boat came to their rescue—45 minutes later! The two were flown to Juneau, where they were treated for hypothermia and released the following day, with no serious or permanent damage done. They returned to Elfin Cove, where the mother told of their harrowing experience, and listeners gained new faith in life jackets.

The waterway they traveled, between Glacier Bay National Park and the north shore of Chichagof Island, isn't called Icy Strait because of its warm, tropical currents. Rest assured, the water there is a tad chillier than any along the Oregon coast.

Modern life vests come in a great variety of styles and sizes to comfortably fit all torsos. They're designed to not only keep a person afloat in a head-up position, but also to protect vital organs. The same material that provides floatation is also a superb insulator. So a life vest or jacket helps keep the wearer warm and comfortable in chilly, windy weather and wards off or lessens the effects of hypothermia in the event of a mishap.

While aboard any small craft, and even larger vessels when conditions warrant, all passengers should wear life vests or jackets. Even on shore, some instances dictate their use by children and adults who can't swim. Small tykes can too easily slip or trip along river banks. Also, people who crab or fish from boat docks and piers should make sure that children in the party are duly protected.

Hazards of Coastal Travel and Recreation

Winter sunlight slants through the coastal Oregon rain forest.

Hazards of Coastal Travel and Recreation

Coastal Shoreline Hazards

Among the most common of shoreline hazards is stranding. Every year, the Coast Guard and other agencies are dispatched to pluck people from pocket beaches, cliffs, inshore rocks, and other areas, simply because these folks have failed to check tide tables or are oblivious to the concept and character of tides. Anytime people go anywhere along the Oregon shoreline, they should consult the tide tables to make sure they will be able to travel safely and avoid being stranded or worse. (For more information about tides, see "Know the Tides" on page 77.)

Avoid straying from designated trails. In some areas, off-trail hiking can promote erosion or harm nearby vegetation. In rocky intertidal areas, climbing around on slippery rocks can not only lead to personal injury, but may well crush organisms living on those rocks. In other places, it's just dangerous, even life-threatening, to veer off the beaten path.

Coastal cliffs and bluffs are particularly perilous. Nearly every year, people get injured or killed while climbing or hiking in such areas. In some places, the cliffs and rocky shoreline are composed mainly of sandstone that eons of wind and waves have shaped into magnificent formations. As inviting as it may seem to climb around on these natural sculptures for closer examination, resist the temptation. The surface of sandstone is often loosely granular and resistant to firm footing. Sandstone ledges and outcrops can be crumbly and insufficient to the task of bearing a climber's weight.

Beware of edges. In some popular places, state and federal agencies have erected fences along the seaward sides of trails near cliffs and other hazardous areas. The fences are meant to warn against closer approach. Along much of Oregon's rugged coastline, however, there are no fences, so hikers and others must exercise caution and call on their practical judgment.

As a general rule, stay away from the edges. If you decide to risk life and limb for a better view or photographic opportunity, don't do so without first thoroughly examining the spot from another vantage. Cliff and bluff edges often have blind undercuts that may cause them to collapse beneath a person's weight. Before venturing out, find another spot beyond, where you can carefully inspect the seaward edge from another angle to make sure it is adequately supported. Then proceed with due caution.

It should go without saying, but bears mentioning anyway: consider all such places off-limits to children.

Killer Logs

Every winter, Pacific storms batter the coast with high winds and heavy rainfall. The same winds that drive precious glass floats and other beachcomber treasures ashore also carry in logs that tumble in the surf until they eventually end up on the beach.

These same storms may also wreak havoc along the coastal rivers. Storm runoff raises water levels, promoting bank erosion that undermines the root systems of trees. The weakened trees are vulnerable to storm winds. Some fall into the swollen rivers and are swept to sea, where they drift in the currents until high winds drive them ashore.

Drift logs add interesting detail to many beaches and are a photographer's delight. Most are harmless enough—once they've been permanently ensconced, high on the beach—but some are potential killers. Logs long stranded upbeach, and those half-buried in sand don't pose much of a threat, but logs in shallow nearshore water, and even those newly beached above the waterline can kill.

Children are particularly drawn to these seemingly harmless tree trunks. They like to climb and play on them or straddle them like ponies. An incoming tide and big waves on any tide may float these logs, which can weigh hundreds or thousands of pounds.

Once afloat, the log may roll in the shallow water, where it can easily crush a person. Or it might rise and float with an incoming wave, then, as the wave recedes, settle back onto the sand, where it can pin a person to the beach. A person so trapped will surely suffer serious injuries, and may be drowned on an incoming tide before rescue is possible.

So stay away from these potential killers. If you take children to the beach, keep them safe and occupied elsewhere. When you encounter parents and children who are apparently unaware of these dangers, let them know by passing on a friendly warning.

Swimming and Wading

There are two times when most people avoid swimming in Oregon's ocean: nighttime and daytime. If water cold enough to chill beer isn't unenticing enough, the widespread threat of deadly rip currents should be.

A rip current, or undertow, is a subsurface, seaward flow or current that runs in a contrary direction to the surface water. Rip currents are common along Oregon's coast, and they're strong enough to thwart the efforts of the best swimmers.

A swimmer caught in a rip current in cold water is soon overcome by fatigue and hypothermia. The swimmer simply wears out, chills out, and drowns.

A swimmer in the grasp of a strong rip current has little or no chance of swimming against it and making progress. Instead, swim

Hazards of Coastal Travel and Recreation

Hazards of Coastal Travel and Recreation

crosscurrent, parallel to shore, to where the current ends; then turn shoreward, swim hard, and hope.

Children seem less affected than adults by Oregon's cold waters. They often play and wade in the shallows along Oregon's beaches. A cause for alarm is that some of these tiny tots dabble at the water's edge while distracted parents are busy elsewhere, perhaps flying kites, running dogs, or just relaxing up the beach a ways, demonstrating a lack of respect for or knowledge of the ocean's authority and unpredictability. No small child on the beach should ever be out of arm's reach of an adult.

If all this sounds like an attempt to discourage swimming and wading along Oregon's beaches, it is partly that, but it's mainly meant as a warning to people who may be unfamiliar with Oregon's ocean and unaware of its capricious capacities. The Pacific, here, is cold, fickle, unforgiving, and fraught with potential peril. What's more, Oregon's beaches offer a tremendous variety of other recreational opportunities that are far safer.

Many of Oregon's coastal creeks and rivers have swimming holes that are popular during the summer, when stream flows are low and the water isn't so cold. Coastal lakes with designated swimming areas are another option. Even in these places, though, swimmers and parents need to stay alert and exercise caution.

Tsunamis

Tsunami is a Japanese term that the scientific community and others have adopted to identify what was once called a seismic sea wave and, erroneously, a tidal wave. Tsunamis have nothing to do with tides, but do result from seismic activities: namely, earthquakes, seaquakes (marine temblors), and volcanic activity. Seaside landslides also can generate tsunamis.

A tsunami is not a wave, but rather a series of waves, emanating in all possible directions from the epicenter of the seismic or generating activity. Toss a pebble into a pond, and watch how the series of circles or tiny waves moves outward from the point of the pebble's entry. That's the way a tsunami works—wave after wave, until its energy dissipates. Drop a rock at the pond's edge, and the semicircular waves emanating outward from shore will demonstrate the typical path of a landslide-generated tsunami.

Contrary to popular belief—fostered by Hollywood productions that show ocean liners, freighters, and military vessels capsized on the open seas by great walls of water—tsunamis cross the ocean at a height of no more than two feet: scarcely a ripple across the bow of a large seagoing vessel. *Tsunami* translates to "harbor wave," which is far more descriptive of its danger and destructive force. Harmless at sea, a tsunami becomes a great threat to life and property as it rushes toward any coast.

As ordinary waves approach open coastlines, they draw waters from previous waves, build to a height, break, and wash ashore, usually with no harm done. As a tsunami advances on a coastline, carrying the energy of its mighty source, it sucks preceding waters into itself and builds into a series of great waves that can wreak havoc wherever it charges ashore.

The fiercest tsunamis can come crashing onshore with waves exceeding 100 feet in height, engulfing everything and everyone in its path. Tamer versions are more subtly dangerous and destructive, rapidly washing into and flooding low-lying areas with wave after wave destroying coastal property and endangering the lives of the unsuspecting and uninformed.

Among the most alarming aspects of a tsunami is the speed at which it travels on the open ocean: more than 600 miles an hour. So a quake in Japan could send a tsunami rushing onto the Clatsop County shore before a 747 could make the flight from Tokyo to Portland. A quake a few or even a few hundred miles off the Oregon coast could send a tsunami speeding ashore in minutes.

Blue-and-white tsunami-evacuation signs have sprouted along the Oregon coast, warning people about potential danger and directing them to higher ground. These signs serve to alert people to the threat, but they won't help anyone who's unaware of an approaching tsunami.

A global alarm system is in place, but people need to take the warnings seriously, and those out of earshot must watch for signs of potential tsunamis. Earthquakes, seaquakes, and other seismic activity in the Pacific basin trigger alerts to vulnerable areas and lead to emergency broadcasts over the electronic media. People need only heed these warnings, and either avoid low-lying coastal areas, or evacuate to higher ground. People hiking beaches and coastal trails may be unaware of any impending disaster and need to pay attention to the natural warning signs.

Anyone out and about on the coast who senses ground rumblings indicating an earthquake should immediately retreat to high ground. Any unusual, rapid rise or fall of water levels in coastal areas, including estuaries, is another indication of a probable tsunami. Beachgoers who notice the ocean receding exceptionally far from shore should escape to high ground at once.

Although seismologists say the West Coast is overdue for a big quake, and some think it will occur off the Oregon coast, there's no need for undue alarm. Earthquakes and seaquakes are impossible to predict with pinpoint accuracy. So the Big One that's due could happen in two days, two decades, or two centuries from now.

Hazards of Coastal Travel and Recreation

Sneaker Waves

Rogue wave, freak wave, sneaker wave, or an unusual wave by any other name is just as deadly. Such waves occur with some frequency along the Oregon coast and are a genuine threat to the unsuspecting. Although they're commonly associated with the stormy winter months, they can rush ashore anytime and engulf the unaware angler, beachgoer, or hiker.

Every year, big waves sweep people off rocks, jetties, and promontories. The lucky ones manage to swim to shore or get fished out of the chilly waters by our vigilant Coast Guard. The unfortunate ones fall victim to tidal or riverine currents, undertow, hypothermia, or injuries caused by the slamming waves.

On Christmas Day, 1985, a couple drove his gift to her—a shiny new Oldsmobile—to the parking area near the south jetty of the Coquille River. On a lovely December day, in calm weather, they began hiking out the jetty, where several people had preceded them. When the husband noticed the end of the jetty disappearing beneath a rising sea, he grabbed his wife's hand, and ran for safer ground. In seconds, the wave advanced and receded, and the freak occurrence was over.

The couple ran back to the jetty to check on the welfare of the others, who turned out to be drenched, but safe. A deputy sheriff sat stunned in his patrol car, where a big boulder had smashed onto the car's hood. The couple then ran to the parking lot and found it strewn with driftwood, overturned trash cans, and debris. Her new car was covered with the sandy slurry of the huge wave, and a log the diameter of a telephone pole lay diagonally under the once-gleaming Olds. Oddly, the car suffered no damage that couldn't be repaired with a quick car wash. Not all such occurrences, however, have happy endings, and not all happen in the winter.

Some years ago, a young G.I., on leave and traveling the Oregon coast, stopped at Bandon to photograph rock formations along the beach. As he climbed among the rocks, only a few feet from shore, a sneaker wave inundated the beach and its backwash towed him to his death.

During the spring of 2000, two athletic young men died only weeks apart at Sunset Bay. In May, a big wave knocked one of two hikers off the rocks near the bay and swept him out to sea, where he drowned. In June, in a similar event, a young man suffered severe head injuries and drowned.

As any experienced surfer, coastal angler, seascape photographer, or other serious ocean observer knows, not all waves are alike, not even those advancing in successive series. Even in the absence of sneaker waves, some breakers just turn out to be bigger than others. Under normal circumstances, waves larger than all the rest crash ashore periodically, perhaps five to ten minutes or more apart. Before venturing out onto a jetty, rocky shoreline, or other potentially dangerous place, it pays to watch the waves awhile, for fifteen or twenty minutes, to determine the size and force of the biggest ones. Then always heed the common coastal admonition: never turn your back on the ocean.

Hazards of Coastal Travel and Recreation

Although the sand beaches aren't as potentially hazardous as rocky areas, sneaker waves can be dangerous there as well, especially on pocket beaches or those backed by cliffs or bluffs. Small children are particularly vulnerable, because it doesn't take much of a wave to topple a toddler. A sneaker wave can claim an unattended child in seconds. Sadly, that happens all too often along the Oregon coast.

There's nothing in nature as awe-inspiring as the magnificence of the ocean. Remember, though, awe is a combination of wonder, reverence, and *fear*.

Have a Safe Trip

None of the foregoing is meant in any way to discourage anyone from visiting the Oregon coast and enjoying its wonders at every opportunity. It is an attempt to alert people to potential hazards and mishaps they might well encounter on any coast in any state. Here in Oregon, though, people have access to so much splendid public shoreline that some may be distracted by the sheer beauty of it all and lose sight of the potential perils and hidden dangers.

This book guides the reader to hundreds of attractions and public-access points along the entire Oregon coast. It in no way expresses or implies that any of these is without possible risk. Drivers and bikers face the same threats here as elsewhere: traffic, incompetent drivers, road hazards, and the vagaries of weather. Boaters likewise face dangers here as elsewhere, and perhaps some that will be new to them, especially if they're not accustomed to operating on coastal rivers, estuaries, and the open ocean. They should check with the Coast Guard and other local experts before venturing onto unfamiliar waters and should remain attentive to current weather and water conditions. Trail hikers, beachgoers, and others who traipse into the natural world also face the possibility of hazard and hardship and should know what to expect and what to avoid.

This book is meant to be a helpful guide and informative companion, but assumes no responsibility for your welfare. Essentially, it is incumbent upon the reader to bear responsibility, to summon native intelligence, pay attention to potential threats, stay informed, heed warnings, and avoid dangerous situations.

All that said, have a safe and wonderful trip to the Oregon coast, and many happy returns.

Information

National Oceanic and Atmospheric
  Administration
Herbert C. Hoover Building, Room 5128
14th and Constitution Avenue
Washington, DC 20230
(202) 482-3384
URL: www.noaa.gov

Oregon Department of Fish and Wildlife
2501 Southwest 1st Avenue
P.O. Box 59
Portland, OR 97207
(503) 872-5310
URL: www.dfw.state.or.us

Oregon Parks and Recreation Department
1115 Commercial Street Northeast, Suite 1
Salem, OR 97301
(503) 378-6305
(800) 551-6949 Information
(800) 452-5687 Reservations
URL: www.prd.state.or.us

Oregon Department of Transportation
355 Capitol Street Northeast
Salem, OR 97310
(503) 986-3200
(503) 986-3556 Maps and Guides
(888) 275-6368
(800) 977-6368 Road Conditions
URL: www.odot.state.or.us/techserv/bikewalk
URL: www.tripcheck.com Road Conditions

Oregon Sea Grant Communications
Oregon State University
322 Kerr Administration Building
Corvallis, OR 97331
(541) 737-2716
E-mail: sea.grant.communications@orst.edu
URL: www.seagrant.orst.edu

Oregon Tourism Commission
775 Summer Street Northeast
Salem, OR 97301
(503) 986-0000
(800) 547-7842
URL: www.traveloregon.com

Siuslaw National Forest
4077 Southwest Research Way
P.O. Box 1148
Corvallis, OR 97339
(541) 750-7000
(877) 444-6777 Reservations
URL: www.fs.fed.us/r6/siuslaw
URL: www.reserveusa.com Reservations

Siskiyou National Forest
200 Northeast Greenfield Road
P.O. Box 440
Grants Pass, OR 97528
(541) 471-6500
(877) 444-6777 Reservations
URL: www.fs.fed.us/r6/siskiyou
URL: www.reserveusa.com

U.S. Bureau of Land Management
Coos Bay District Office
1300 Airport Lane
North Bend, OR 97459
(541) 756-0100
URL: www.or.blm.gov/coosbay

U.S. Bureau of Land Management
1849 C Street Northwest, LSB-204
Washington, DC 20240
(202) 208-3801
URL: www.blm.gov

U.S. Fish and Wildlife Service
1849 C Street, Room 3012
Washington, DC 20240
URL: www.fws.gov

U.S. Forest Service
P.O. Box 96090
Washington, DC 20090
(202) 205-8333
URL: www.fs.fed.us

U.S. Geological Survey
U.S. National Center
Reston, VA 22092
(703) 648-4000
URL: www.usgs.gov

January
Warrenton Crab Feed, Warrenton (503) 861-1031
Artistry in Wood, Lincoln City (541) 994-8378 or (800) 452-2151

February
Oregon Dixieland Jubilee, Seaside (503) 738-3097 or (888) 306-2326
Antique Week and Lincoln Days, Lincoln City (541) 994-8378 or (800) 452-2151
Newport Seafood & Wine Festival, Newport (541) 265-8801 or (800) 262-7844
Charleston Merchants' Crab Feed, Charleston (541) 269-0215 or (800) 824-8486
Whale of a Wine Festival, Gold Beach (541) 247-7526 or (800) 525-2334

March
Original Yachats Arts & Crafts Fair, Yachats (541) 547-3530
Siletz Spring Competition Pow Wow, Lincoln City (541) 994-8378 or (800) 452-2151
Oregon Dune Mushers' Mail Run, Lane County (541) 997-3128
Oregon Dune Mushers' Mail Run, Winchester Bay (541) 271-3495 or (800) 247-2125
Oregon Dune Mushers' Mail Run, Lakeside (541) 759-3981
Oregon Dune Mushers' Mail Run, North Bend (541) 269-0215 or (800) 824-8486

April
Astoria-Warrenton Crab & Seafood Festival, Warrenton (503) 325-6311 or (800) 875-6807
Lincoln City Community Days, Lincoln City (541) 994-8378 or (800) 452-2151
Classic Wooden Boat Show, Crab Feed, and Ducky Derby, Depoe Bay (541) 765-2889 or (877) 485-3848

May
Blessing of the Fleet, Garibaldi (503) 322-0301
Newport Loyalty Day & Sea Fair Festival, Newport (541) 265-8801 or (800) 262-7844
Spring Kite Festival, Lincoln City (541) 994-8378 or (800) 452-2151
Memorial Day Fleet of Flowers, Depoe Bay (541) 765-2889 or (877) 485-3848
Florence Rhododendron Festival, Florence (541) 997-3128
Blessing of the Fleet, Winchester Bay (541) 271-3495 or (800) 247-2125
Stormwatchers Seafood & Wine Festival, Bandon (541) 347-9616

Best Festivals, Fairs, and Events on the Oregon Coast

Sandcastle Building Contest, Bandon (541) 347-9616

Azalea Festival, Brookings/Harbor (541) 469-3181 or (800) 535-9469

June

Scandinavian Mid-Summer Festival, Astoria (503) 325-6311 or (800) 875-6807

Sandcastle Day, Cannon Beach (503) 436-2623

Tillamook Dairy Festival & Parade, Tillamook (503) 842-7525

Tillamook Rodeo, Tillamook (503) 842-7525

Wheeler Crab Festival, Wheeler (503) 368-5100 or (877) 368-5100

Gem, Mineral, and Agate Society Show, Lincoln City (541) 994-8378 or (800) 452-2151

Cascade Music Festival, Lincoln City (541) 994-8378 or (800) 452-2151

Gem & Mineral Show, Newport (541) 265-8801 or (800) 262-7844

Beachcomber Days, Waldport (541) 563-2133

Festival of Gardens, Lincoln City (541) 994-8378 or (800) 452-2151

Jet Boat Marathon, Gold Beach (541) 247-7526 or (800) 525-2334

July

Seaside Old-Fashioned 4th of July Celebration, Seaside (503) 738-3097 or (888) 306-2326

4th of July Open House, Astoria (503) 325-6311 or (800) 875-6807

Independence Day Fireworks, Waldport (541) 563-2133

Fireworks in Boiler Bay, Depoe Bay (541) 765-2889 or (877) 485-3848

4th of July Fireworks Display, Lincoln City (541) 994-8378 or (800) 452-2151

La De Da Parade & Yamboree, Yachats (541) 547-3530

Newport 4th of July Fireworks Display, Newport (541) 265-8801 or (800) 262-7844

Yachats Music Festival, Yachats (541) 547-3530

Yachats Smelt Fry, Yachats (541) 547-3530

Lincoln County Fair & Rodeo, Newport (541) 265-8801 or (800) 262-7844

Independence Day Celebration, Florence (541) 997-3128

Fireworks and Car Cruise, Winchester Bay (541) 271-3495 or (800) 247-2125

Ocean Festival, Winchester Bay (541) 271-3495 or (800) 247-2125

Fun, Food, Fireworks!, North Bend (800) 953-4800

4th of July Celebration in Mingus Park, Coos Bay (541) 269-0215 or (800) 824-8486

Fish Fry and Fireworks, Bandon (541) 347-9616

Oregon Coast Music Festival, Coos Bay (541) 269-0215 or (800) 824-8486

Fireworks at the Port, Brookings/Harbor (541) 469-3181 or (800) 535-9469

Port Orford Jubilee, Port Orford (541) 332-4106

Southern Oregon Kite Festival, Brookings/Harbor (541) 469-3181 or (800) 535-9469

Curry County Fair, Gold Beach (541) 247-4541

August

Clatsop County Fair, Astoria (503) 325-4600

Astoria Regatta Festival, Astoria (503) 325-6311 or (800) 875-6807

Seaside Beach Volleyball Tournament, Seaside (503) 738-3097 or (888) 306-2326

Nehalem Art Festival, Nehalem (503) 368-5100 or (877) 368-5100

Tillamook County Fair, Tillamook (503) 842-7525

Arts & Crafts Festival, Rockaway Beach (503) 355-8108

Nestucca Valley Artisans Festival, Pacific City (503) 398-5945

Sandcastle Building Contest, Lincoln City (541) 994-8378 or (800) 452-2151

Farwest Gem Craft Show, North Bend (541) 269-5085

Salmon Barbecue, Charleston (541) 269-0215 or (800) 824-8486

Southwest Oregon Street Rods Show & Shine, Coos Bay (541) 888-3778

Sunset Bay Sand Castle Contest, Charleston (541) 888-3778

Charleston Seafood Festival, Charleston (541) 888-4875

Blackberry Arts Festival, Coos Bay (541) 269-0215 or (800) 824-8486

Sand Dune Sashay, North Bend (541) 269-0215 or (800) 824-8486

Festival of the Arts, Brookings/Harbor (541) 469-3181 or (800) 535-9469

September

Lewis & Clark Kite Exposition, Seaside (503) 738-3097 or (888) 306-2326

Hot Rod Happenin!, Seaside (503) 738-3097 or (888) 306-2326

Seaside Sand Sculpture Spectacular, Seaside (503) 738-3097 or (888) 306-2326

Berry-Salmon Festival, Wheeler (503) 368-5100 or (877) 368-5100

Best Festivals, Fairs, and Events on the Oregon Coast

Best Festivals, Fairs, and Events on the Oregon Coast

Autumn Festival, Rockaway Beach (503) 355-8108
Crab Festival, Waldport (541) 563-2133
Indian Salmon Bake, Depoe Bay (541) 765-2889 or (877) 485-3848
Fall Kite Festival, Lincoln City (541) 994-8378 or (800) 452-2151
Fall Festival, Florence (541) 997-3128
Oregon Shorebird Festival, Charleston (541) 267-7208
Southern Oregon Dahlia Show, North Bend, (541) 267-0740
Bandon Cranberry Festival, Bandon (541) 347-9616
Salmon Derby, Coos Bay (541) 267-5500
Bay Area Fun Festival, Coos Bay (541) 269-0215 or (800) 824-8486

October
Glass Festival, Lincoln City (541) 994-8378 or (800) 452-2151

November
Stormy Weather Arts Festival, Cannon Beach (503) 436-2623
Regatta on Devils Lake, Lincoln City (541) 994-8378 or (800) 452-2151
Holiday Lights, Coos Bay (541) 269-0215 or (800) 824-8486

December
Holiday Lighting Ceremony, Depoe Bay (541) 765-2889 or (877) 485-3848
Newport's Festival of Trees, Newport (541) 265-8801 or (800) 262-7844
December Festival of Lights, Bandon (541) 347-9616

Early Inhabitants of the Oregon Coast

Earliest inhabitants of the Oregon coast were largely nomadic people who apparently regularly or seasonally visited coastal areas to hunt, fish, and gather food, and over the millennia settled along the coastal rivers, estuaries, and bays. Radiocarbon dating, a process for determining the age of materials of organic origin, indicates that humans have inhabited or regularly visited coastal Oregon for at least the last ten thousand years. It's likely that people were here long before that, but evidence of their residency may be locked up forever in the sediments of the ocean floor, relegated there by the same rising seas that helped create Oregon's estuaries at the end of the last ice age.

Whether they were descendants of the so-called Paleo-Indians, thought to have migrated from Asia to North America over the Bering Land Bridge, is a matter of conjecture. Nor do we know if the Paleo-Indians were ancestors of modern coastal Indians. It could be that later Indians replaced or displaced the Paleo-Indians. What we do know is that the Oregon coast has been steadily inhabited for thousands of years. Archeologists have uncovered a number of ancient sites, some of which were villages, while others were temporary or seasonal encampments. Most have been on or near estuaries or along the banks of coastal rivers, and some have proved to be three thousand years old or older. One dig on the Rogue River has turned up material dating back to 6575 B.C.

Archeologists made one of the most interesting coastal discoveries in 1984 on the west side of Tahkenitch Lake, just north of Reedsport. Materials found at the site in a refuse heap, called a *midden*, dated back to about 6000 B.C. Surprisingly, bones and shells uncovered were from saltwater species only, indicating that Tahkenitch (pronounced *tack*-uh-nitch) was not always a freshwater lake.

Scientists now believe that Tahkenitch was once a deepwater estuary, where fresh water from feeder streams mingled with salt water from the ocean in a coastal embayment. Gradually, silt-laden freshwater runoff and sand-bearing tides raised the bottom and created flats, transforming Tahkenitch into a shallow-water estuary, perhaps much like Coos Bay or Tillamook Bay. About three thousand years ago, the estuary was almost completely closed off from the sea by encroaching sand dunes. Eventually, the waters freshened, leaving a sprawling lake with only a small outlet to the sea.

The Tahkenitch estuary was a rich fishing and hunting area, its abundant fishes, shellfishes, and marine mammals attracting the early nomadic people who regularly visited and ultimately settled there to remain for as long as three thousand years. We can assume that other estuaries along the Oregon coast were equally attractive to other tribes, loose gatherings, or families of these prehistoric humans. Ancient prehistoric peoples, as well as the modern Indians that followed, were enticed to settle along Oregon's estuaries and coastal rivers by the abundant food sources, transportation corridors, and natural protective boundaries. (Later Euro-American pioneers and settlers were drawn to the same areas for similar reasons.)

Oregon's coastal Indians were hunters and gatherers, taking fish, shellfish, and marine mammals from the bays, estuaries, and nearshore ocean. In the bordering forests, meadows, and marshes, they hunted deer and waterfowl, pit-trapped elk, picked berries, dug roots and bulbs, and harvested edible plants. They gathered reeds and grasses to make mats and baskets. They used logs to fashion their dugout canoes and build their plank houses and huts.

The Chinooks of the Columbia River region and other tribes inhabiting the rest of the Oregon coast lived in relative physical and economic comfort in a moderate climate and a land teeming with fish, game, and edible plants. The Indians' habitation of the Oregon coast developed and lasted over a period of many centuries—thousands of years, in fact—but diminished and all but disappeared in mere decades.

Early Explorers Along the Oregon Coast

Spanish Explorers

Having conquered the Incas of South America and Aztecs of Mexico and plundered their wealth, Spaniards, imagining similar treasure among indigenous peoples elsewhere, set their sights on and their sails for the Pacific Coast of North America in the mid-sixteenth century. They also came in search of a passage between the Atlantic and Pacific oceans, which turned out to be as fabled as the gold, silver, jewels, and other booty they hoped to find.

In 1542, Antonio de Mendoza, the Viceroy of Mexico, dispatched an expedition from Acapulco consisting of two vessels under the command of Juan Rodriguez Cabrillo and his pilot, Bartolome Ferrelo, to search for treasure and the Northwest Passage. Although they never made landfall along what is now the Oregon coast, they sailed as far north as the 42nd parallel, which eventually became the Oregon-California border. It is not clear from their records, but they may have even made it as far north as 44 degrees, which would have put them off the coast near present-day Florence.

The Spaniards lost interest in the Pacific Northwest coast and soon turned their attentions to other parts of the world. Thwarted by foul weather, strong currents, and numerous coastal hazards north of northern California, Spanish captains, outbound from Manila in the Philippines, usually kept their galleons well offshore as they steered for their home port at Acapulco. Nevertheless, during the 250 years between the middle sixteenth and late eighteenth centuries that Spanish galleons, laden with treasure from the Far East, plied the Pacific between Manila and Acapulco, at least three Spanish vessels wrecked on or near the Oregon coast, one on Clatsop Beach and two near Nehalem Spit.

Spanish interest in the Pacific Northwest was rekindled in the late eighteenth century when they feared that Russian fur traders, who had already advanced through the Aleutian Islands and to the mainland of what is now Alaska, would continue down the West Coast of North America and threaten Spanish interests. In 1775, Captain Bruno de Hezeta, in an expedition equipped with three ships, made it as far north as the 58th parallel, on the coast of British Columbia. The same expedition also made landfall along the coast of present-day Washington and claimed land there in the name of Carlos III of Spain.

In August of that year, Hezeta's expedition lay off the coast near the mouth of a mighty river he took for the Strait of Juan de Fuca, but which turned out to be the rumored Great River of the West. He did not enter the unnamed waterway, where he might have sailed inland, named the river, and claimed adjacent lands in the name of his own nation. That claim was left to a young American merchant captain who would sail these same waters seventeen years later.

British Explorers

During the 1570s, British privateer Francis Drake, in his ship, the *Golden Hind*, sailed the Pacific in search of Spanish galleons full of gold, spices, and other treasures. He is believed to have reached a north latitude of 43 degrees 21 minutes in 1579, which would have put him off what is now the southern Oregon coast in the vicinity of Cape Arago and the mouth of Coos Bay. He may have anchored in bad weather at South Cove, in the lee of Cape Arago.

Renowned British explorer Captain James Cook first sighted the Oregon coast at Cape Foulweather, between present-day Newport and Depoe Bay, in March of 1778. During that expedition, Cook's ships, the *Resolution* and *Discovery*, sailed on past the as-yet unnamed Great River of the West. He passed the Strait of Juan de Fuca and anchored at Nootka Sound, Vancouver Island, until April 26. From there, he pushed on to Alaska, where he failed in an attempt to discover the Northwest Passage he believed to be in the Arctic Ocean. When his ships were unable to break through the Arctic ice pack, he left the Pacific Northwest and sailed to Hawaii, where he was killed during a skirmish between Englishmen and islanders. The expedition continued on to China, where its cargo of sea-otter pelts fetched high prices.

History of the Oregon coast

History of the Oregon coast

British Prime Minister William Pitt sent Captain George Vancouver to the Pacific Northwest on a complex mission in 1791. Vancouver was ordered to take possession of certain lands, investigate all European settlements in the Pacific Northwest, and to search for the elusive Northwest Passage, even though its existence had been debunked by at least one earlier explorer. Vancouver's descriptions of the Pacific Northwest did much to interest later explorers, pioneers, and settlers. He wrote eloquently of the beauty of the land and of its economic potential, noting that it would be conducive to the development of villages and farms, which it certainly proved to be.

American Explorers

In the 1780s, America was no longer a colony of the British Empire, enjoying privileges in the world marketplace protected by the forces of that empire; it was an independent country, struggling in the grips of a postwar depression. The riches of the Pacific Northwest and the potential of developing trade with China held the promise of future wealth for the fledgling nation.

In 1787, Boston merchant Joseph Barrell formed a syndicate for the purpose of developing Asian markets for the United States. He sent John Kendrick and Robert Gray to China in command of the *Lady Washington* and *Columbia Rediviva*. Some three years passed before Gray's return to Boston. Although water damage spoiled his ship's cargo of China tea and dashed the profits for the voyage's sponsors, the *Columbia Rediviva* became the first American vessel to circumnavigate the world.

Gray's second voyage, lasting from 1790 to 1793, was a resounding and profitable success that helped establish American merchants in global maritime trade. Moreover, it eventually helped America lay claim to the rich lands of the Pacific Northwest known as the Oregon Country. On May 11, 1792, Captain Gray became the first to guide a ship over the treacherous bar of the Great River of the West, which Gray named the Columbia, in honor of his noble vessel.

Fur Traders

More than a century after the Industrial Revolution, in an era of high-tech industry, fiber optics, the Internet, instantaneous global communication, and the pinpoint accuracy of satellite navigation systems, it's easy to lose sight of the important role the fur trade played in the exploration and eventual settlement of Oregon and the rest of the Pacific Northwest. Mountain men, trappers, and fur traders explored the vast wilderness of the West, discovered the mountain passes, and blazed the trails for the countless thousands of pioneers who would eventually join the great westward migration that stopped at the Pacific Coast. British and American fur traders were probably the first to make regular contacts with the Indians of the Columbia River basin, the Oregon coast, and much of the rest of the Pacific Northwest.

The profitable fur business based primarily on marine mammals that traders and Indians enjoyed from Alaska to Oregon during the last twenty years of the eighteenth century was all but over by the early nineteenth century, by which time the fur seals and sea otters had been hunted nearly to extinction. But the highly profitable worldwide commerce in furs was far from over. Indeed, it was a major impetus for America's westward expansion. It would be among the most important reasons for mounting America's greatest exploration expedition ever. It would lead to the establishment of the first permanent settlement west of the Rocky Mountains near the mouth of the Columbia River. It would also draw the first overland explorers to the Oregon coast.

Lewis and Clark

Thomas Jefferson was President of the United States when, in 1803, the U.S. purchased the vast and uncharted Louisiana Territory from France. The Oregon Country was not part of the Louisiana Territory, but Jefferson was eyeing it and its potential contribution to the nation when he persuaded Congress to finance a scientific, exploratory, and investigative expedition into the great wilderness of the West. President Jefferson was certainly interested in the scientific and exploratory aspects of this expedition, but he was also eager to ascertain the fur-trading potential of the vast West. He directed Lewis and Clark to persuade Indians to trade their furs with Americans instead of the British, and to find the best routes for trappers and traders to get their pelts to market.

The men President Jefferson chose to lead the expedition were Captain Meriwether Lewis and Captain William Clark. The two leaders gathered their famous Corps of Discovery at the mouth of the Missouri River, across the river from St. Louis, where they spent five months preparing for their great adventure. On May 14, 1804, the corps headed up the Missouri.

The Corps of Discovery spent the first winter of the expedition at Fort Mandan in present-day North Dakota. The thity-three-member corps set out once again on April 7, 1805, and by October 16 had reached the confluence of the Snake and Columbia rivers in the Oregon Country.

Lewis and Clark led the expedition down the Columbia to the river's mouth, where they got their first glimpse of the Pacific Ocean. After spending several days camping on the north bank in what is now Washington, the corps crossed the river and built their winter headquarters—which they named Fort Clatsop, after the friendly

History of the Oregon coast

local Indians—near a stream now known as the Lewis and Clark River. They remained on Oregon's north coast until March 23, 1806, when they set out on their return journey.

John Jacob Astor

Wealthy New York businessman and founder, in 1808, of the American Fur Company, John Jacob Astor founded the Pacific Fur Company in 1810. In 1812, he established a trading post near the mouth of the Columbia River called Fort Astoria, where he intended to swap trade goods with Indians for beaver pelts, which he would ship to China. His timing was unfortunate, however, for in early 1813 news reached the fort of the outbreak of the War of 1812. Fearing loss of the fort and business holdings to the British, Astor sold the Pacific Fur Company in October to the North West Company, a Scottish- and Canadian-owned venture that had been organized in the 1780s to compete with the British-owned Hudson's Bay Company. Two months later, the British captured Fort Astoria and occupied it for the duration of the war, returning it to the United States in 1818 as one of the provisions of the Treaty of Ghent. Astor's holdings were returned to him after the war, but he decided to pursue other interests, particularly in real estate, which eventually made him the wealthiest man in America.

Although Astor's entrepreneurial venture into the West Coast fur trade was disappointing, discouraging, and short-lived, it established the first permanent American settlement west of the Rockies, helped to publicize the potential of the Columbia River basin, and furthered the cause of America's claim on lands of the Oregon Country.

Jedediah Strong Smith

The most famous explorer and fur trader on Oregon's south coast in the early nineteenth century was Jedediah Strong Smith. He was already a well-known and widely traveled mountain man and explorer by age twenty-nine, when he led the first overland expedition from northern California to the Oregon coast in the summer of 1828.

On December 30, 1827, Jedediah Smith, leading nineteen men and about three hundred horses, headed up through central and northern California. By mid-April of the following year, the expedition was following the Trinity River toward its confluence with the Klamath River, driving through dense brush in incessant rain and fog.

The expedition reached the coast on June 8, then continued north along the coast and, on June 20, reached the mouth of the river in northern California that now bears Smith's name. Three days later, Smith and his party crossed the 42nd parallel into the

Oregon Country and camped on the north bank of the Winchuck River.

During the next three weeks, the expedition pushed north, crossing coastal creeks and rivers, and camping at places that have become favorites of modern-day travelers. The party tried to stay along the shoreline as much as possible, but the rugged terrain of the south coast, where mountains and foothills push to the ocean's edge and break into cliffs and high bluffs, forced the expedition inland at such places as Cape Ferrelo, Cape Sebastian, Humbug Mountain, Cape Blanco, and Cape Arago.

Along the way, they observed beaver sign in various river valleys, including the Chetco, Rogue, and Sixes. They also noted the Sixes River Valley's suitability for ranching and farming. As many modern-day celebrants of Independence Day do now, they spent July 4 at Cape Arago. After four hard, brush-bucking days on the densely vegetated cape, the party finally broke through the thick brush and reached the mouth of the South Slough of Coos Bay on July 8. They found a large Indian village occupying the site of present-day Charleston, where they stayed overnight as guests of the friendly Coos Indians.

Two days later, they crossed lower Coos Bay at its narrowest spot, near the later town site of Empire City, where the bay is only about 600 yards wide. After camping on the North Spit in the vicinity of Henderson Marsh, they headed north. It was easy going from there, along the beach, all the way to Winchester Bay, which they reached on July 11.

The Smith party found the Kelawatset Indians of the lower Umpqua River to be friendly at first. In fact, about fifty of them accompanied the expedition as it crossed the river and set up camp near present-day Gardiner. Even after an incident when Smith and his men subdued an Indian until he gave up a stolen axe, the party traded peaceably with the Indians for sea-otter, river-otter, and beaver pelts. At another campsite the following day, near the mouth of another river that would come to bear Smith's name, they traded for more beaver pelts, elk meat, tallow, and lampreys.

On the morning of July 14, Smith took two men to scout for a route to the Willamette Valley. Apparently because of the axe incident and several other reported disagreements, the Kelawatsets turned on the men in camp, who were cleaning their rifles at the time. Using knives and axes, the Indians killed at least eleven men. One man escaped to the north and, with the help of Tillamook Indians, made it to Fort Vancouver on the Columbia River. Perhaps several others also escaped, but they were never found or heard of again.

As Jedediah Smith and the other two men returned toward camp, Indians fired on them. When Smith determined that none of his

History of the Oregon coast

men remained at the camp, he and the two men made their way north and on to Fort Vancouver, where they arrived on August 10, with Tillamook Indians as their guides.

Three months later, the Hudson's Bay Company dispatched a party, led by explorer and fur trader Alexander McLeod, to travel to the lower Umpqua and investigate the skirmish site. McLeod found the skeletons of eleven slain men and retrieved most of the furs, horses, journals, maps, and other property of the Jedediah Smith Exploring Expedition of 1828.

Smith met his premature end at the hands of Comanche Indians on May 27, 1831, while on a trade caravan to Santa Fe. He was only thirty-two years old, but, in the span of a mere decade as a fur trader, he had earned a reputation as one of America's great explorers.

The Role of the Fur Trade in Oregon

As the fur-seal and sea-otter trade was flagging and on the brink of collapse, the lucrative fur trade in the Pacific Northwest was significantly shifting from marine mammals to land-dwelling furbearers—mainly beavers. These plentiful mammals, nearly wiped out by overharvest in the nineteenth century, would play an important role in the exploration, commerce, economy, and even the politics of Oregon, which came to be known as "The Beaver State."

Twentieth-century efforts by wildlife managers to rectify nineteenth-century overtrapping have resulted in the restoration of beaver populations in watersheds throughout the state, where they perform essential functions in the state's natural environment. In 1969, recognizing the importance of this industrious rodent, the Oregon Legislature named the beaver as Oregon's state animal.

Pioneers and Settlers

Oregon's pioneer period lasted from about 1840 to 1880. During that time, Britain and the United States signed a treaty that resulted in the 1848 formation of the Oregon Territory, consisting of present-day Washington, Oregon, Idaho, and parts of Montana and Wyoming. The Washington Territory was organized in 1853 from the northern portion of the Oregon Territory. In 1859, on the cusp of the American Civil War, Oregon became the 33rd state in the union.

Settlements sprouted all along the Oregon coast during the 1850s and 1860s, and more followed during the next two decades. Some were boom towns that were destined to diminish or disappear altogether when the bust inevitably came. Many, however, eventually grew into the cities and unincorporated communities that now dot the coast.

Manifest Destiny and the Pioneers

The concept of Manifest Destiny, popular during the middle decades of the nineteenth century, held that it was the destiny of the United States to expand its social, cultural, and economic influences, as well as its territorial possessions, throughout North America. Horses, mules, and oxen may have pulled the Conestogas and prairie schooners across the Great Plains, over the Rockies, through the Great Basin, and on to Oregon, but it was Manifest Destiny that drove the pioneers westward.

They came for a variety of reasons. Some were drawn to the promise of economic prosperity, even wealth. Others came to start a new life on the new frontier. A few escaped to the West, leaving behind debt, the threat of disease, natural disasters, or even the long arm of the law. The vast majority, however, came looking for agricultural land.

By a large margin, most of the pioneers who immigrated to Oregon were farmers. Nearly all of them hailed from the Great Lakes region and the major river valleys of the Midwest. Most came from farms in Arkansas, Indiana, Illinois, Iowa, Michigan, Missouri, Ohio, and Wisconsin. They met up with others and formed groups of people with like interests and destinations at the major jumping-off points of Independence, St. Joseph, and Council Bluffs. There, they organized trains of twenty to twenty-five wagons for the cross-country trip that would last four to six months.

While they shared many of the same principles, ideals, and motives, they also shared the same fears. Fear of the unknown had to be near the top of the list. They also had to worry about food and supplies. Would there be enough for the long journey west? Would there be anything left for starting their new life in Oregon? Above all, though, they worried about disease and hostile Indians.

Disease was a constant threat in the Midwest during the mid-nineteenth century and was certainly no less a killer on the Oregon Trail. What's more, the treatment was often more dangerous than the sickness, as medical care was primitive at best. There were no preventive measures or cures for the diseases that struck and killed on the trail—mainly, cholera, measles, smallpox, and mountain fever.

Indians were potentially a threat, of course, but many turned out to be friendly and helpful, providing directions or guidance through the wilderness, across the rivers, and to the grasslands where draft animals could graze. They also sold food, clothing, and horses to the pioneers. There were Indian attacks on wagon trains and fierce battles between whites and Indians, but not to the extent and inevitability portrayed in American films. It wasn't a matter of circling the wagons every few miles or days to fend off massacres. According to one historian, during all of the 1840s and 1850s, skirmishes between Indians and pioneers along the Oregon Trail

History of the Oregon coast

claimed the lives of more than 425 Indians and just over 360 whites, or an average of about eighteen pioneers a year—hardly a blood bath.

Other obstacles the pioneers faced included the physical difficulty associated with crossing the mountains, deserts, and great rivers of the West. Among the many psychological adversities they dealt with regularly and for days on end was sheer boredom: the monotony of vast spaces, distant landmarks that never seemed to get closer, the plodding progress of the wagons, the same daily routine, the same food, the same sameness.

Most of the pioneers were the salt of the earth before they had set out, and by the time they arrived in Oregon they had been further strengthened by the dangers and drudgeries of the journey. They brought with them their many skills, patriotism, faith in their God and country, law-abiding ways, and, yes, their racial prejudice. In spite of encounters with friendly and helpful Indians, and even fierce warriors deserving of respect, most pioneers still considered Indians inferior.

Gold!

Until 1849, the only markets Oregon farmers and merchants had were local—mainly, the new pioneers who had recently arrived and needed provisions. The discovery of gold near Sutter's Mill in California, however, changed all this. Suddenly, there was great and growing demand in the gold fields and the burgeoning city of San Francisco for lumber, beef, wheat, and flour. Seattle and Portland, respectively, became the main sources for lumber and provisions. Soon, entrepreneurs began looking along the Oregon coast for suitable places to exploit natural resources, establish settlements, and create supply sources for lumber-hungry San Francisco.

The discovery of gold in the Rogue River Valley and along the black-sand beaches of Coos and Curry counties in the early 1850s marked the beginning of Oregon's own gold rush. As miners flocked to the southern Oregon coast, more markets developed, with Portland as the main supplier. Shipping of freight and passengers down the Columbia River and along the coast grew rapidly. Other strikes in eastern Oregon, eastern Washington, Idaho, and Montana had miners scurrying in those directions, creating new demands, new markets. While the forests of Washington were the first to feed the mills and load the ships for the California market, Oregon's forest products were soon in great demand, there and elsewhere.

Gold fever and hostile Indians were ingredients for a volatile mixture. The Rogue Indians were among the fiercest warriors in the West, but the miners weren't about to let them stand in the way of getting the gold out of the Rogue Valley. The inevitable skirmishes between the miners and Indians grew into battles, which soon became war, complete with the occupation of military troops near the mouth of the Rogue. The Rogue Indian Wars of 1853-56 took a heavy toll on the tribes inhabiting the Rogue Valley and the coast north and south of the Rogue River. The end of the war was marked by a treaty that called for the surviving Rogue Indians to be rounded up and sent north to a reservation.

Settlement of the Oregon Coast

Indians along the Oregon Coast—even those who had not participated in conflicts with settlers—were perceived as a threat to white settlement. Once they were expatriated to the reservations by the late 1850s, however, vigorous settlement got underway. Settlers and entrepreneurs headed for Oregon's bays and estuaries: gateways to the world's marketplace. Sawmills sprouted like mushrooms in the woods. Shipyards sprang up on the navigable rivers and bays. As loggers denuded the lands near the mills, they began moving farther into the hills and mountains in their attempts to feed the mills that loaded the ships that hauled the wood to market. Meanwhile, homesteaders cleared land around the bays, up their tributaries, and into the valleys of the coastal rivers. They dug ditches, built dikes, constructed tide gates, and turned marshes into agricultural land.

As the pioneer period drew to an end in the late nineteenth century, the Oregon coast had been transformed from the wilderness that had existed before 1850 into a busy, productive region engaged in a variety of industries and occupations, including farming, logging, shipbuilding, coal mining, and commercial fishing. Settlements grew into cities. Salmon canneries lined the banks of the Columbia River and the mouths of other major rivers. Coastal steamers hauled freight and passengers down the Columbia and along the Pacific Coast from Seattle to San Francisco. By the end of the century, coal steamers were making twenty trips a month over the Coos Bay bar, and they were outnumbered by lumber ships.

Coastal Oregon's pioneer period didn't just come to an abrupt end. Rather, it faded seamlessly into the dawn of the industrial era. The twentieth century would bring more change to the Oregon coast—some good, some not. Doubtless, the most significant improvement to life and commerce along the coast was the completion of the coast bridges in the 1930s and the opening of Highway 101 from the Columbia River to the California border.

History of the Oregon coast

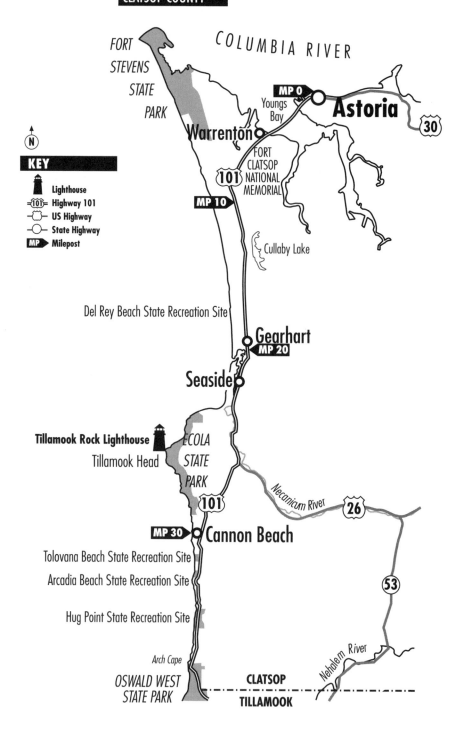

COLUMBIA RIVER

FORT STEVENS STATE PARK

MP 0
Astoria
30

Youngs Bay

Warrenton

FORT CLATSOP NATIONAL MEMORIAL

101

MP 10

Cullaby Lake

KEY

Lighthouse
101 Highway 101
US Highway
State Highway
MP Milepost

N

Del Rey Beach State Recreation Site

Gearhart
MP 20

Seaside

Tillamook Rock Lighthouse
Tillamook Head

ECOLA STATE PARK

Necanicum River

26

101

MP 30 Cannon Beach

Tolovana Beach State Recreation Site

Arcadia Beach State Recreation Site

Hug Point State Recreation Site

53

Nehalem River

Arch Cape

OSWALD WEST STATE PARK

CLATSOP
TILLAMOOK

The Clatsop County Coast

U.S. 101, Mile 0 to Mile 37.1

Clatsop County occupies 843 square miles in Oregon's extreme northwest corner and is home to 34,700 Oregonians. The Columbia River and state of Washington define its northern boundary, and the Pacific Ocean flanks its western edge. The county extends southward to Oswald West State Park.

Established June 22, 1844, Clatsop is Oregon's fourth oldest county. It was named after the Clatsop Indians, one of many tribes among the Chinookan family inhabiting the Pacific Northwest. Astoria, the county's largest community and seat of government, is not only Oregon's first city, but is also the oldest permanent settlement west of the Rocky Mountains.

Lewis and Clark and their Corps of Volunteers for Northwest Discovery spent the winter of 1805-06 here on Oregon's north coast, the terminus of their spectacular expedition. They established their winter headquarters a few miles south of the Columbia River and named the small post Fort Clatsop after the friendly local Indians. Members of the expedition made their way southwest to a beach in the vicinity of present-day Seaside where they built a salt works. Eventually they traveled as far south as the area now known as Cannon Beach.

Five years later, in 1811, wealthy New York businessman John Jacob Astor sent traders aboard his ship *Tonquin* to establish Fort Astoria, a fur-trading post near the mouth of the Columbia River. During the War of 1812, British took over the fort, but by 1818 ownership had reverted to the United States.

By the 1840s, pioneers were settling along Oregon's north coast, cutting timber and clearing land for farms; this period of settlement lasted well into the 1870s. From the 1880s into the early part of the twentieth century, salmon harvesting was the area's principal industry, and canneries lined the banks of the Columbia River. In 1911, the Columbia River salmon catch was a record 49 million pounds, after which salmon stocks declined steadily and dramatically. Although salmon numbers have plummeted to a mere fraction of their historical highs and timber harvesting has dwindled considerably, sport and commercial fishing and the forest-products industry remain crucial components of the Clatsop County economy, as do agriculture, outdoor recreation, and tourism.

Milepost 0 of the Oregon stretch of U.S. Highway 101 is on the Astoria-Megler Bridge over the Columbia River. At the southern foot of the bridge, U.S. 101 turns west, then south over the Youngs

Bay Bridge, leading to Warrenton, Seaside, Cannon Beach, and the rest of the Oregon coast. Also at the southern foot of the bridge is the U.S. Route 30 junction. Turn east here to reach downtown Astoria and the city's many attractions.

In addition to the cities of Astoria, Seaside, and Cannon Beach, and the smaller communities of Warrenton, and Gearhart, Clatsop County has much to offer travelers, sightseers, history buffs, photographers, and outdoor recreation enthusiasts. Among them are a half-dozen worthwhile museums, sprawling Fort Stevens State Park, Fort Clatsop National Memorial, the Astoria Column, four golf courses, fishing and sightseeing charters, miles of broad sand beach, the best razor-clam digging in the state, and the mighty Columbia River.

U.S. 101, mile 0
Astoria-Megler
Bridge

This is one of the newer bridges along Highway 101, built between 1962 and 1966. At 4.1 miles in length, it is Oregon's longest bridge. With a main-span length of 1,232 feet standing 198 feet above the low-water mark, it is also the world's largest continuous-truss bridge, allowing passage of the Navy's largest ships at high tide. The magnificent bridge is an engineering marvel, spanning the one of the world's most voluminous rivers with currents that can reach 9 miles an hour. Each year, about 2.2 million vehicles cross the bridge, and 2,300 large merchant and military ships pass beneath it.

Columbia River

This great river heads in British Columbia, takes a southerly meander through eastern Washington, then turns west to form the Washington-Oregon state line, eventually emptying into the Pacific Ocean near Astoria, 1,243 miles from its source. Along the way, it drains an area of 259,000 square miles and gathers the waters of such notable tributaries as the Pend Orielle, Snake, John Day, Deschutes, Klickitat, Hood, and Willamette rivers. As the mighty river approaches the Pacific, it broadens into Oregon's largest estuary, as wide as 5 miles in places. The average discharge at the mouth of the Columbia is an amazing 262,000 cubic feet of water per second.

French, Spanish, British, and Russian explorers and exploiters searched many years for the fabled Northwest Passage and the legendary Great River of the West. Several got near the mouth of the Columbia, recording in their logs such indications of a major river as discolored water, strong currents, and breaking surf near 46 degrees north latitude. Bostonian Captain Robert W. Gray was the first skipper to take a ship across the river's treacherous bar. Captain Gray sailed his 90-ton sloop *Columbia*

The Astoria-Megler Bridge

Rediviva into the estuary on May 11, 1792, and named the river after his ship.

The Columbia River has always been a major trade and transportation corridor. It was an important source of food for the Chinook people who lived and fished along its banks near the mouth and for the people of many tribes living farther upriver and inland as far as Idaho. In the twenty-first century, the Columbia serves millions of people in the Pacific Northwest, elsewhere in America, and in many far-flung nations, especially in Asia. The river is the major source of hydroelectric power for the northwestern states. It provides irrigation for thousands of square miles of agricultural land, and serves as a barge route for getting wheat, corn, and other products to their markets.

The commerce of the Columbia is evident in the vicinity of Astoria, where, on the average, more than six ships a day pass by. A few are bound for the Port of Astoria, and some anchor in the lower river to take on fuel or await vacant upstream berths. Most, though, head for the busy Port of Portland, or downstream toward the bar, ocean, and some distant port. The city of Astoria, with its accessible waterfront, is ideally situated for watching and photographing the ship traffic. Vessels of every size and sort navigate these waters: tugs with barges in tow, freighters, tankers, auto carriers, container ships, and various military craft. Cargo ranges from inbound ore, oil, and autos to outbound grain, lumber, and wood chips.

Commercial fishing boats, sport-fishing boats, charter boats, sailboats, motor yachts, and other pleasure craft ply the lower Columbia River, the estuary, and nearby ocean, but this is no place for the novice boater. The Columbia bar is always dangerous—the most dangerous on the Oregon coast; it's hazardous in calm weather and treacherous on rough days. There's a reason for its nickname, "Graveyard of the Pacific." In fact, there are more than two hundred reasons—ships that have grounded, foundered, burned, or sunk in or near the gaping jaws of the Columbia.

Only the most experienced boaters in the most seaworthy craft should venture over the Columbia bar, and then only under favorable conditions. Those who are unfamiliar with local waters and conditions should seek advice from the Coast Guard, marina operators, and other local experts before venturing out over the bar.

Even boaters who have no intention of leaving the estuary need to exercise extreme caution and pay close attention to weather and water conditions. The Columbia is a big river with strong currents, changing tides, and enough traffic to demand extra vigilance.

Boaters can find launch ramps, moorage, supplies, and fuel at the Port of Astoria and at the Warrenton and Hammond boat basins. For those without boats, charter craft work out of Astoria, Warrenton, and Hammond, running ocean and river charters. They offer salmon, sturgeon, bottom fish, and crab trips with all gear and bait furnished. Some also specialize in historic river cruises and sightseeing trips.

Columbia River angling opportunities are many and varied. In the estuary, both boat and bank anglers can expect to catch surfperch and seaperch, greenling, and any of a variety bottom fish, including several species of rockfish, lingcod, and the occasional starry flounder. The river gets runs of chinook and coho salmon, beginning with spring chinook as early as February, and lasting into the fall. Steelhead trout enter the river in autumn, as the salmon fishery begins to wane, and are present throughout the winter months. Sturgeon fishing can be outstanding, and anglers concentrate on deep holes from the Astoria-Megler Bridge upstream.

In addition to these popular and traditional fisheries are some often overlooked opportunities. For example, great schools of shad migrate up the river each spring, with legal angling beginning after May 15. In its countless sloughs, backwaters, and intertidal creeks and marshes, the lower Columbia also harbors underutilized populations of warmwater species, including bluegill, crappie, largemouth bass, smallmouth bass, brown bullhead, and channel catfish.

All anglers need to read and heed the *Oregon Sport Fishing Regulations,* available at tackle shops, marinas, and sporting-goods outlets. Angling regulations are complicated everywhere in the state, even more so on the coast, and particularly in the Columbia River and nearby ocean. Moreover, they're subject to change frequently and rapidly.

From the southern foot of the bridge, Astoria (population: 10,100) spreads east and west along the waterfront, and southward into the hills overlooking the city and river. As Oregon's oldest city, it is steeped in the history of the region, its peoples and promises, its disasters and disappointments, its booms and busts. It should come as no surprise, then, that Astoria has four excellent and varied museums, including one of the finest maritime museums in the nation.

U.S. 101, mile 3.6
Astoria
(zip code 97103)

In spite of major fires that destroyed downtown Astoria in 1892 and 1922, the city has more fine old Victorian structures than any other city on the coast. Most are exquisitely preserved or restored private homes, but some serve as bed and breakfast inns. More than twenty are listed on the National Register of Historic Places, as are another nineteen Astoria historical sites.

Astoria's compact downtown area lies primarily along U.S. Route 30, which runs east and west parallel to and one or two blocks south of the waterfront. Many of the city's downtown attractions are within easy walking distance of one another. The named streets—Bond, Commercial, Duane, Exchange, and Franklin—also run parallel to the river and are in alphabetical order from the waterfront south. Numbered streets run north to south and perpendicular to the named streets.

This is the main route through downtown Astoria and along the Columbia River to Portland. Turn east onto Marine Drive here to reach Astoria's city center and attractions in and east of town. (For details, see "Side Trip: U.S. Route 30" on page 71.)

U.S. Route 30
junction

This road exits east off U.S. 101, providing access to the north shore of Youngs Bay and upper Youngs Bay.

U.S. 101, mile 4.2
State Route 202
junction

Although most people reach the Astoria Column via U.S. 30 in downtown Astoria, State Route 202 provides an easy, alternative, more direct and traffic-free route. Drive 1.6 miles east on Route 202, turn north (left) on 7th Street, and follow the signs to the top of Coxcomb Hill. (For information about Astoria Column, see "Side Trip: U.S. Route 30" on page 72.)

Astoria Column

U.S. 101, mile 4
Youngs Bay Bridge
and Causeway

Extending nearly 2 miles across the mouth of Youngs Bay, this structure provides expansive views of Youngs Bay and the Columbia River Estuary.

U.S. 101, mile 5.8
Warrenton
(zip code 97146)

This small community (population: 4,040) is the gateway to Fort Stevens State Park. Its harbor is home port for much of the local commercial fishing fleet and a number of charter operators. The main business district and harbor lie west of U.S. 101, via Harbor Street, with visitor facilities, restaurants, and the largest shopping center in the area right along the west side of Highway 101.

U.S. 101, mile 6.5
Harbor Street/Fort
Stevens Highway

Harbor Street leads west off U.S. 101 and eventually merges with Fort Stevens Highway. Use this route to reach the Warrenton and Hammond harbors and Fort Stevens State Park.

Astoria-Warrenton
Area Chamber of
Commerce Visitors
Center

The center is on the west side of U.S. 101, at Youngs Bay Shopping Center. It is open from 9:00 a.m. to 5:00 p.m. daily, except in the winter; then hours are 9:00 a.m. to 5:00 p.m. Monday through Friday and 1:00 to 5:00 p.m. on weekends.

Warrenton Mooring
Basin and Boat Ramp

To reach the mooring basin, take Harbor Street west of U.S. 101 for 1 mile. Then turn south (left) on Southeast Ensign Avenue at the east end of the Skipanon River Bridge. Facilities include a two-lane paved boat ramp and docks on the river, a large parking area, fuel dock, rest rooms with flush toilets and hot showers, a bait and tackle shop, and trash receptacles. The marina has 385 slips for vessels up to 55 feet on the Skipanon River, a tributary of the Columbia. Transient moorage is available by the day, week, or month. Information: (503) 861-3822.

Hammond Mooring
Basin and Boat Ramp

Take Harbor Street west off U.S. 101 to reach the Fort Stevens Highway and the Lake Drive intersection, 6.1 miles from Highway 101. Turn north (right) on Lake Drive and continue 0.6 mile to reach the mooring basin, which is on the lower Columbia River. Facilities include a four-lane paved boat ramp with courtesy docks, picnic areas with tables, drinking water, and rest rooms with flush toilets. The marina has 175 slips with transient moorage available. Information: (503) 861-3197.

Fort Stevens State
Historical Site and
Military Museum

Exit west off U.S. 101, and drive 6.1 miles to the Lake Drive intersection. Then continue west 0.3 mile past the intersection to reach the historic area and museum. The fort was built during the Civil War and named after Isaac Ingalls Stevens, who served as governor general of the Washington Territory from 1853 to 1857. A major general in the Union Army, he was killed in battle against the Confederates at Chantilly, Virginia, September 1, 1862.

During the late nineteenth and early twentieth centuries, the fort was expanded to include eight artillery gun batteries. Although the big guns are gone now, the concrete batteries remain and are a popular attraction. The fort remained active until just after World War II. When the army abandoned the fort, many of the buildings were demolished, but the museum displays old photographs, exhibits, and a scale model of the fort to give visitors an idea of what the area was like during military occupation. The museum is open daily from 10:00 a.m. to 4:00 p.m., except in winter, when it is closed on Mondays and Tuesdays. The fort is managed by the Oregon Parks and Recreation Department, is part of Fort Stevens State Park, and is a *must stop* for history buffs. During the summer, park personnel offer "living history" programs, museum tours, and truck tours aboard a restored 1954 $2^1/_2$-ton army truck, known among GIs as a deuce-and-a-half.

A self-guided walking tour of the complex is divided into two parts, each taking about an hour, but it's easy to spend a day or more examining the fort, hiking the trails, and taking in the spectacular scenery. Information: (503) 861-2000.

Turn west on Harbor Street and continue 6.1 miles to the Lake Drive intersection in Hammond. Turn south (left) on Lake Drive and go 1 mile to the park entrance, on the west side of the road. At 3,700 acres, this is the largest state park in Oregon, the largest west of the Mississippi River, and one of the biggest campgrounds anywhere. Here campers will find 173 full-hookup sites, 157 sites with water and electricity, 194 tent/RV sites with nearby water, 15 yurts, four group tent-camping areas, and a hiker/biker

Fort Stevens State Park, north access

MUST STOP

One of several Civil War-era cannons on display at Fort Stevens State Historical Site.

The World War I-era boxcar donated to the people of Oregon by the people of France is on display at Fort Stevens State Historical Site.

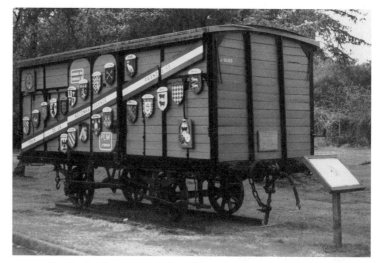

camp. Each site has a paved parking area, picnic table, and fire ring. Other amenities include an RV dump station, hot showers, and rest rooms with flush toilets.

This *must-stop* park has something to offer every traveler: miles of broad ocean beach for hiking, beach combing, kite flying, clam digging, and surf fishing; freshwater lakes for swimming, fishing, and watching wildlife; access to the lower Columbia River and south jetty; wind surfing on the Pacific Ocean or Jetty Lagoon; and sightseeing and photography at every turn. There are 5 miles of hiking trails, 9 miles of bike paths (also open to pedestrians), wildlife viewing platforms overlooking the Columbia River and Swash Lake, and an observation platform near the end of Clatsop Spit. Black-tailed deer roam the park, as do smaller mammals, such as red squirrels, possum, raccoons, porcupine, and beaver. According to Mike Patterson's "Checklist for Birds of Fort Stevens State Park," more than 220 species of birds, from diminutive rufous hummingbirds and tiny chestnut-

Pelicans aplenty flock to the rocks at Fort Stevens State Park.

A viewing platform at Fort Stevens State Park overlooks Clatsop Spit, the Pacific Ocean, and the mouth of the Columbia River.

backed chickadees to regal bald eagles and magnificent trumpeter swans, either regularly occur in or migrate through the area. If all this isn't enough, the park also has a Civil War fort, military museum, and even a historic shipwreck on the beach: the rusted skeletal remains of the 278-foot bark *Peter Iredale*, which ran aground on Clatsop Beach during a storm on October 25, 1906.

With certain restrictions, motor vehicles are allowed on the beach from the south jetty to the Gearhart area. From May 1 to September 15, motor vehicles are prohibited north of the *Peter Iredale* beach access between noon and midnight. Speed limit is 25 m.p.h.

The skeletal remains of the Peter Iredale *fascinate hikers on Clatsop Beach.*

Coffenbury Lake and Boat Ramp

This shallow 56-acre lake in Fort Stevens State Park is popular for swimming, boating, and fishing. Two swimming areas have sand beaches and bathhouses. The paved boat ramp is at the north end of the lake; motors are allowed, but the speed limit is 10 m.p.h. Fishing is for cutthroat and rainbow trout, yellow perch, and brown bullhead. Rest rooms have flush toilets.

U.S. 101, mile 7.1
Fort Clatsop National Memorial, north access

Exit east off U.S. 101, and follow the signs. (For details, see U.S. 101, mile 7.6 below.)

U.S. 101, mile 7.6
Fort Clatsop National Memorial, south access

Take Business Route 101 east off U.S. 101, follow the signs about 2.5 miles to Fort Clatsop Road, and turn south. The visitor center and parking lot lie 0.8 mile beyond. This 125-acre park is the site of the 1805-06 winter headquarters of the Lewis and Clark Expedition. It's managed by the National Park Service and is open to the public all year. In 1955, local citizens built a replica of the original fort. During the summer, park rangers, dressed in period costume, portray life as it was for Lewis and Clark and their Corps of Discovery.

For those who have come to touch all the historical holy places, this is a *must stop*. The fort and its surroundings possess the eerie reverence of a chapel in the wilderness, where the dense forest atmosphere can enshroud you like a fog. If the shafts of light slanting through tree branches and the combined aromas of wood smoke, candle wax, and gunpowder don't set your spine a-tingling and raise the little hairs on the back of your neck, you should turn in your history-buff badge to the nearest park ranger.

The park opens daily at 8:00 a.m. From Labor Day to mid-June, it closes at 5:00 p.m.; from mid-June to Labor Day, it closes at 6:00 p.m. It is closed only on Christmas Day.

U.S. 101, mile 9.4
Fort Stevens State Park, south access

Northbound travelers should exit west off U.S. 101 and follow signs to Ridge Road and Fort Stevens State Park. The campground entrance is 4.5 miles from U.S. 101; the day-use entrance is 0.3 mile beyond. At 5.5 miles from U.S.101, turn west (left) on Pacific Drive to reach the old fort, military museum, and picnic areas. (For details on Fort Stevens State Park, see U.S. 101, mile 6.5, page 52.)

U.S. 101, mile 13.5
Astoria Golf and Country Club

Turn west off U.S. 101, then north at the sign, just off the highway. This is a challenging and beautiful 6,494-yard, 18-hole, par-72 course, laid out in the rolling hills of the Clatsop Plains, punctuated by small ponds and freshwater marshes. Most of the course lies along the west side of Highway 101 and is visible from the road. Amenities include a driving range, putting green,

*Fort Clatsop National
Memorial.*

chipping area, pro shop, bar, restaurant, snack bar, and club
and electric-cart rental. Pull carts are furnished. Although this
is a private course, guests of members are welcome, as are
members of other private clubs. Pro shop: (503) 861-2545.

A half-mile west of U.S. 101 is a small lakefront county park
with picnic tables, stoves, a playground, basketball court,
volleyball court, trash receptacle, and a gravel boat ramp.
Neacoxie Lake, also known as Sunset Lake, is popular for
canoeing, boating, and fishing for stocked rainbow trout early
in the season and warmwater species anytime. The lake holds
populations of bluegill, crappie, brown bullhead, yellow perch,
and largemouth bass.

Sunset Beach Park on
Neacoxie Lake

The road leads west 1 mile to a parking and day-use area with
access to Sunset Beach. Clatsop County maintains a vehicle
access to the broad sand beach. Vehicles must be street legal
and drivers legally licensed. Under normal conditions, there's
no need for four-wheel drive. This is a favorite day-use area for
surf fishing and digging razor clams.

Sunset Beach

This shallow lake lies about a half-mile east of U.S. 101 and is
roughly parallel to the highway. This is the largest of the many
lakes that dot the Clatsop Plains: 188 acres, 2 miles long, and
about a mile wide in places. Several small creeks feed the lake;
its northern drainage forms the headwaters of the Skipanon
River, a tributary of the Columbia River. Swimming, boating,
water skiing, and angling are popular activities on the lake.
Although rainbow and native cutthroat trout are present, the
lake's maximum depth of 12 feet and average depth of 5 feet
primarily support a fishery for warmwater species: bluegill,

U.S. 101, mile 13.8
Cullaby Lake

crappie, yellow perch, brown bullhead, and largemouth bass. Two county parks are situated on the lake's northwest shore.

Carnahan County Park

About a half-mile east of U.S. 101, this attractive small park has picnic areas with tables, horseshoe pits, and a gravel boat ramp providing access to upper Cullaby Lake.

Cullaby Lake County Park

Turn east of U.S. 101, drive 0.2 mile to Hawkins Road, turn south, and continue 0.4 mile to the park entrance. Spread along the lake's northwest shore, this park has large picnic areas with tables and stoves, a swimming area with sand beach, two gravel boat ramps, rest rooms with flush toilets, and trash receptacles.

U.S. 101, mile 17
Del Rey Beach State Recreation Site

Turn west off U.S. 101 on Highlands Road to reach the parking area 0.8 mile from the highway. This no-frills park provides easy access to low dunes, hiking and equestrian trails, and the nearby beach, where people enjoy hiking, picnicking, flying kites, riding horses, fishing, and digging razor clams.

The Highlands at Gearhart

Go west on Highlands Road, 0.5 mile to the clubhouse. Watch for signs for the golf course and Del Rey Beach State Park. This lovely, ocean-view, 1,880-yard, 9-hole, par-32 course, built in 1987, is laid out in the low rolling hills and dunes of the Clatsop Plains. Among its features are a putting green, sand and chipping practice areas, pro shop, resident pro, club and pull-cart rental, snack bar, restaurant, and lounge. Pro shop: (503) 738-5248.

U.S. 101, mile 17.7 to 19.2 Gearhart
(zip code 97138)

A small (population 1,230), mainly residential community, Gearhart lies along the highway and west to the beach and ocean. Centrally located Pacific Way is the main street leading west off U.S. 101 into the town center. Lettered streets to the south and numbered streets to the north run parallel to Pacific Way. Named avenues run parallel to Highway 101.

Several streets terminate at the beach and provide beach access and small parking areas (not suitable for travel trailers or large motorhomes). Ocean Avenue is nearest the beach for much of Gearhart, with Marion Avenue taking its place in northwest Gearhart. Marion Avenue is 0.5 mile west of U.S. 101 and Ocean Avenue is 0.1 mile beyond, via Pacific Way. A small parking area with beach access lies at the foot of Pacific Way.

Turn west on Golf Course Road to reach the clubhouse and parking lot, 0.5 mile from the highway. An alternative route is to turn west on Pacific Way at the traffic light (U.S. 101, mile 18.8), go .05 mile to Marion Avenue, turn north (right), and continue another 0.5 mile to the course. This 6,089-yard, 18-hole, par-72 course, built in 1892, was Oregon's first golf course and is among the oldest in the nation. It has aged gracefully to blend with its splendid natural surroundings. Amenities include a putting green, practice areas, pro shop, resident pro, club rental, pull-cart and gas-cart rental, snack bar, restaurant, and lounge. Pro shop: (503) 738-3538.

U.S. 101, mile 18
Gearhart Golf Links

Intersecting Highway 101 at the only traffic light in Gearhart, this is the community's main east-west street, providing access to the town center and beach.

U.S. 101, mile 18.8
Pacific Way

This compact city of about 6,200 Seasiders lies mainly along U.S. 101 and west about a half-mile or so to the ocean's edge. Centrally situated Broadway is the main east-west street. Numbered avenues run parallel in ascending order from Broadway north; lettered avenues run parallel in ascending order to the south. Named streets run perpendicular to Broadway and parallel to U.S. 101 and the river. For the length of the city, the beach lies only about a half-dozen blocks from the highway, and the Necanicum River runs through the whole town.

U.S. 101, mile 19.2 to mile 22.2 Seaside
(zip code 97138)

Seaside is Oregon's premier oceanfront resort, serving as Portland's beach playground since the middle of the nineteenth century. No other coastal Oregon community is quite like it, and people seem to take to it like kids to cotton candy.

From the mouth of the Necanicum River south to Tillamook Head are about 3.5 miles of broad beach. In town, a concrete promenade runs along the upper edge of the sandy beach for 2 miles. About midway along "the prom," as it's known locally, Broadway terminates at a vehicle turnaround where the flag flies and a bronze statue of Lewis and Clark commemorates their famous expedition. Visitors and locals drive, stroll, jog, pedal, and skate by on their way to somewhere or nowhere in particular. The prom bustles.

Along Broadway and adjacent streets, people move nonstop from café to specialty store to antique shop to art gallery to bistro to boutique to mini-mall and back again. The air is ever-scented with the enticing aromas of fish and chips, steaks, burgers, pizza, tacos, and teriyaki. Half the passersby seem to be warding off starvation, eating hotdogs, ice cream cones, caramel apples, saltwater taffy, and occasionally even something that's good for them. If the sights, sounds, and smells aren't

*Seaside's famous
Turnaround and
Promenade, at the foot
of Broadway.*

reminiscent of a carnival midway, other Broadway and nearby attractions should be enough to convince anyone: bumper cars, shooting galleries, miniature golf, Skee-Ball, video arcades, a carousel, and even a Tilt-a-Whirl. Broadway hustles.

This is a place to park your vehicle and get out among the spring breakers, summer vacationers, and winter weekenders, who move mainly on foot or by such beach-town conveyances as funcycles, surreys, scooters, and skates.

There's no commercial fishing fleet at Seaside, and no harbor full of charter boats. You won't find sawmills or pulp mills along the banks of the Necanicum, or barges plying its waters. Industry, here, is something else entirely. The obvious reason people have been visiting Seaside for a century and a half is that the local economy is based on fun.

U.S. 101, mile 20
Necanicum Estuary
Park

Turn west on 24th Avenue at the south end of the bridge over Neawanna Creek; then veer left onto Holladay Drive. The little park is opposite Seaside High School, near the mouth of the Necanicum River and confluence of Neawanna Creek, about three blocks from Highway 101. The park has an observation platform, boardwalk, and trail to the estuary shore. This is a popular spot for watching and photographing birdlife, which is seasonally abundant.

Seaside's 12th Street Bridge over the Necanicum River Estuary attracts anglers and crabbers.

The Necanicum is a small coastal river with headwaters in the Coast Range, southeast of Seaside, near Saddle Mountain. It flows only about 22 miles before entering the ocean at the southwest end of Gearhart. Although private land borders much of the river's lower reaches, it's a popular steelhead stream with opportunities for fishing from bank and boats.

The Necanicum River and Estuary

The tiny estuary extends from the vicinity of Gearhart Beach, through the entire city of Seaside. The shoreline is heavily developed, but the estuary provides opportunities for fishing, crabbing, boating, canoeing, wildlife watching, and photography right in town.

Although the Necanicum estuary is navigable by small boats, the bar is dangerous and unsuitable for crossing at any time.

About two blocks west of the highway, the 12th Avenue Bridge crosses the lower Necanicum River. The bridge is popular among locals for fishing and crabbing.

U.S. 101, mile 20.6
Necanicum Estuary Walking Trail and 12th Avenue Bridge

At the west end of 12th Avenue, 0.5 mile from the highway, the Necanicum Estuary Walking Trail provides access to the beach and estuary for fishing, birding, photography, and exploring the estuary.

Turn west on 12th Avenue, cross the river, and head south on Necanicum Drive for seven blocks. Or turn west on 1st Avenue, then north on Necanicum Drive for four and a half blocks. The museum is on the west side of the street, between 5th and 6th avenues. Here, visitors can learn about the history of Seaside and the immediate vicinity from a variety of exhibits, including Clatsop Indian artifacts dating back to 230 A.D., collections of early photographs, antique fire-fighting equipment, and more. Also on the property is the expertly restored Victorian-era

Seaside Museum

Butterfield Cottage, which is furnished with period antiques. The museum is open from noon to 3:00 p.m., November through February and daily from 10:30 a.m. to 4:30 p.m. the rest of the year. Information: (503) 738-7065.

U.S. 101, mile 21.1
Quatat Marine Park

Take 1st Avenue west off U.S. 101 to Edgewood Street, and turn left. Go one block, then left on Oceanway. This attractive park lies right in the middle of busy Seaside on the Necanicum River, providing river access or just a pleasant place to relax or enjoy an outdoor breakfast or lunch. There are picnic tables and rest rooms with flush toilets and wheelchair access. The park has an excellent concrete boat ramp, but there's no nearby place to park boat trailers.

Seaside Visitors
Bureau

Situated on the northeast corner of U.S. 101 and Broadway, this may well be the best visitor information center on the entire West Coast and is a *must stop* for all north coast visitors. It's well stocked with literature and maps of Seaside, Clatsop County, and other Oregon coast destinations and attractions. The staff is knowledgeable, helpful, and friendly and is there to help you every day from 8:00 a.m. to 5:00 p.m.

Seaside Turnaround
and Promenade

Turn west on Broadway and drive 0.5 mile to reach Seaside's famous automobile turnaround and promenade, built in the 1920s. Broadway is Seaside's main drag, and "the prom" and turnaround form a central gathering place for locals and visitors alike. Free parking is available on street and at nearby parking lots.

Broadway Park

Turn east on Broadway to reach this city park on Neawanna Creek, two blocks from the highway. The park has picnic tables, stoves, a small playground, drinking water, trash receptacles, and rest rooms with flush toilets. A small paved boat ramp provides access to the creek, but is not usable at low tide.

U.S. 101, mile 21.3
Lewis and Clark Salt
Works

Turn west on Avenue G, drive 0.4 mile and turn south (left) on Beach Drive. Continue for 0.3 mile to Lewis and Clark Way. Parking is limited on Lewis and Clark Way, and there's no trailer turnaround, so park on Beach Drive and walk to the salt cairn. On this site, donated by the Oregon Historical Society in 1979 as an addition to the Fort Clatsop National Memorial and maintained by the Seaside Lion's Club, stands a reproduction of the salt works that members of the Lewis and Clark expedition erected here in the winter of 1805-06.

Captains Lewis and Clark dispatched five men from Fort Clatsop on December 28, 1805, with orders to head for the coast and establish a camp for the purpose of making salt, needed for seasoning and improving the flavor of the foods the Corps of

Lewis and Clark Salt Works at Seaside.

Discovery consumed: mainly fish, game, and dog meat. The salt crew found a suitable spot near present-day Seaside on January 2, 1806, where the sea water was high in salt content. They built a stone furnace, which they used to heat five brass kettles for boiling sea water and rendering salt. With three men working constantly, the crew was able to produce three to four quarts of fine white salt a day. By February 20, when they abandoned the coastal camp, they had boiled approximately 1,400 gallons of sea water and produced $3^1/2$ bushels of salt for their return trip.

Turn west off U.S. 101 on Avenue U, cross the bridge, turn north (right) on Franklin Street, and continue two blocks to the park, on the east side of the street. This small city park has a picnic area, playground, rest rooms with flush toilets, and a paved boat ramp on the Necanicum River with ample parking.

U.S. 101, mile 22.2
Cartwright Park and Boat Ramp

Just west of U.S. 101, on the south side of Avenue G, lies a 2,593-yard, 9-hole, par-35 course in a residential setting, along the Necanicum River. Amenities include a putting green, chipping area, clubhouse, pro shop, resident pro, club rental, pull-cart and gas-cart rental, restaurant, and lounge. Information: (503) 738-5261.

Seaside Golf Course

Turn west off U.S. 101 at Avenue U, then south on Edgewood Drive, which joins Ocean Vista Way, to a parking area 0.7 mile from the highway. A cobble beach extends southward, with miles of sand beach to the north.

Cove Beach

Turn west off U.S. 101 at Avenue U at the south end of Seaside, then left on Edgewood and on to Ocean Vista Way. At road's end is a small parking area and the North Trailhead, which leads

Tillamook Head National Recreation Trail, north trailhead

6 miles south to Indian Beach in Ecola State Park. For hikers who want to make an overnight trek, there's a hiker's camp on Tillamook Head, 4 miles south of here.

U.S. 101, mile 22.9
Sef Johnson Tract
Boat Ramp

The ramp and small parking area are on the west side of the highway, providing access to the Necanicum River. Although the Oregon Marine Board calls this an unimproved ramp, it has been eroded into a steep slide, suitable only for careful launching of drift boats, canoes, and kayaks.

U.S. 101, mile 25
U.S. Highway 26
junction

This major west-to-east road, also known as the Sunset Highway, leads west off U.S. 101 into the Coast Range, on to Portland and beyond. It has long been a favorite route of travelers from Portland and the Willamette Valley for weekend and vacation trips to Seaside, Cannon Beach, and other north-coast destinations.

U.S. 101, mile 27.7
Ecola Historical
Marker and Cannon

A sign on the west side of the highway commemorates the Lewis and Clark Expedition's deepest foray down the coast into what is now southwestern Clatsop County. Captain William Clark and a party of twelve or thirteen hiked down the beach, past the salt works, on to the cobble beach near the base of Tillamook Head, then up and over the headland in search of a dead whale reported beached in the vicinity. Local Indians had butchered the whale for meat, blubber, and oil, and Clark wished to barter with them for oil and blubber to supplement the expedition's diet. The whale had washed ashore near a small creek. On January 8, 1806, Clark named the stream Ecola Creek, or Whale Creek, from the Chinook Indian word for whale, variously spelled *ekkoli, ehkoli,* and *ékoli.* Little was left of the whale by the time the group reached it, but Clark and his men managed to barter for about 300 pounds of blubber and several gallons of oil.

The cannon at this site is one of two reproductions of the original cannon after which Cannon Beach was named. The original is now on display outside the Cannon Beach Historical Society Museum at 1387 Spruce in Cannon Beach. (For more details about the cannon, see U.S. 101, mile 34.4, page 70.)

U.S. 101, mile 28
Cannon Beach and
Beach Loop, north
access

The first of three exits for Cannon Beach and Beach Loop, this is the quickest way to reach Ecola State Park and the Cannon Beach Chamber of Commerce. Follow the signs to reach Beach Loop, the city center, and attractions south of town.

Ecola State Park

Exit west off U.S. 101, and follow the signs to the park entrance, which is 0.5 mile from the highway. Ecola Point is another 1.6 miles, and Indian Beach is 1.5 miles beyond that. Among the most scenic parks on the Oregon coast and one that can rival any of the best stretches of California's Big Sur or Washington's Olympic Peninsula, Ecola State Park extends through mountain forest and along precipitous headlands for 9 miles, from Cannon Beach to Seaside. It's a *must stop* for all travelers.

The Tillamook Head National Recreation Trail, which winds for 6 miles through stands of old-growth Sitka spruce, takes hikers up and over Tillamook Head, through the country that Captain William Clark and other members of the Lewis and Clark Expedition traveled in January of 1806 to trade with local Indians for whale blubber and oil. Several shorter trails lead to other park attractions along Ecola Point and to Indian Beach, the latter popular with surfers.

The headlands of Ecola State Park, consisting mainly of basalt intermixed with sedimentary rock, were sculpted by nature and years of landslides and erosion. Captain William Clark mentioned such slides in the record of his journey to what is now Ecola State Park. He wrote of great slides where "fifty or a hundred acres at a time" gave way and plunged into the ocean.

Ecola State Park also offers visitors opportunities for some of the best views of historic Tillamook Rock Lighthouse, just over 1 mile offshore. The inactive light, now functioning as a columbarium and seabird refuge, stands atop a 100-foot-high basalt sea stack that was once part of the mainland.

In addition to spectacular scenery and miles of hiking trails, the park also has two lovely picnic areas with tables, trash receptacles, and rest rooms with flush toilets and wheelchair access.

MUST STOP

The view south of Cannon Beach and Haystack Rock from Ecola Point, Ecola State Park.

A perfect picnic spot overlooks Indian Beach at Ecola State Park.

Tillamook Head National Recreation Trail, south trailhead

Exit west off U.S. 101, and follow the signs for Ecola State Park. The trailhead is near the Indian Beach parking lot, 3.6 miles from Highway 101. (See Ecola State Park, above, for more details.)

U.S. 101, miles 28, 29.3, and 30.3 Cannon Beach
(zip code 97110)

If the Astoria-Warrenton area is the north coast's historical repository, and Seaside is the state's north shore playground, Cannon Beach is certainly the region's center of cultural activity. A number of artists, writers, and musicians call Cannon Beach home, and legitimate theater is alive and well here. Every year, Portland State University conducts its Haystack Summer Program in the Arts and Sciences, which has attracted thousands of people to Cannon Beach to combine vacation with education. Participants study art, music, writing, and other topics in an assortment of courses, workshops, and lectures that run from mid-July to mid-August. Cannon Beach has an active arts association, and the city conducts a series of outdoor concerts all summer and other cultural events throughout the year.

The city of Cannon Beach is a narrow ribbon, three blocks wide and about 3 miles long, lying between Highway 101 and the ocean. This is a spruced-up little community with a population of 1,425 that swells to several times that number summers and weekends.

Streets are narrow and sidewalks wide in a city center that's often crowded and congested. So this is a place to park and walk to the art galleries, specialty shops, mini-malls, cafés, and restaurants. Many of the resorts, motels, and bed-and-breakfast inns are within walking distance of restaurants and shopping areas, and all are an easy walk to the beach.

Beach Loop is a 3.3-mile route through the city, running parallel to the beach, mostly along Hemlock. Beach-access points are many and are spread throughout the town. The western ends of many of the streets running perpendicular to Beach Loop

terminate in small parking areas and paths to the beach. In the north-central part of town, streets with presidents' names lead to beach-access points: Adams, Jefferson, Madison, Monroe, Jackson, Van Buren, and Harrison. Along the south-central stretch of Beach Loop, streets with Alaskan names lead to the beach: Gulcana [sic], Tanana, Nebesna, Matanuska, Nelchena, Chisana, Susitna, and Delta. At the south end of the loop, look for streets with familiar Oregon names: Umpqua, Coos, and Orford.

Shoppers and browsers stroll the streets of downtown Cannon Beach.

Cannon Beach can lay claim to the most scenic stretch of coastline in Clatsop County, the subject of many an artist's canvas and photographer's film. The rugged brow and rocky shores of Tillamook Head give way to miles of broad sandy beach that sweep south past the city. Every sunset silhouettes the magnificent monolith known as Haystack Rock as well as nearby sea stacks and minor monoliths.

Black-tailed deer and Roosevelt elk roam the forests of Tillamook Head and the nearby Coast Range, as do black bear, cougar, and a bevy of smaller mammals. A tremendous variety of songbirds, shorebirds, wading birds, seabirds, waterfowl, and birds of prey nest here or use the area as a resting and feeding wayside during spring and fall migrations. Among these are the world's largest nesting colony of common murres and one of the world's largest colonies of Brandt's cormorants, found mainly in the vicinity of Chapman Point and Bird Rocks, just offshore at the north end of Cannon Beach. Haystack Rock attracts a variety of birds, including black oystercatchers, tufted puffins, pigeon guillemots, pelagic cormorants, and the ubiquitous western gulls.

Gray whales pass by Cannon Beach during their winter migration to calving grounds in the warm lagoons of Baja

Some of the many shops that line the streets of downtown Cannon Beach.

California, Mexico, and their spring migration to feeding grounds off the coast of Alaska. Ecola State Park offers the best vantage points for watching whales in the Cannon Beach area.

Cannon Beach Chamber of Commerce

At the north end of town, on the northeast corner of 2nd Street and Spruce, stands an attractive, rustic building decked out with lush flower gardens and hanging baskets. Stop here for information about Cannon Beach and the north coast. Public rest rooms with flush toilets and wheelchair access are across 2nd Street from the visitor center. From June 15 through Labor Day, the visitor center is open Monday through Saturday from 10:00 a.m. to 6:00 p.m. and Sunday from 11:00 a.m. to 5:00 p.m.; the rest of the year, it's open Monday through Saturday from 10:00 a.m. to 5:00 p.m. and Sunday from 11:00 a.m. to 4:00 p.m.

U.S. 101, miles 29.3 and 30.3
Cannon Beach and Beach Loop, middle and south access

Exit at mile 29.3 and follow Sunset Boulevard to reach the central part of Cannon Beach in the vicinity of Haystack Rock. Exit at mile 30.3 and follow Warren Way to Beach Loop (Hemlock) and attractions at the southern end of Cannon Beach.

Tolovana Beach State Recreation Site

This park at the west end of Warren Way has a large parking lot and immediate beach access, and Haystack Rock is only a 15- to 20-minute hike north. The park has a picnic area with tables, drinking water, and rest rooms with flush toilets.

U.S. 101, mile 31.7
Viewpoint

Three good-sized parking areas skirt the west side of the highway and afford travelers a grand view of broad beach to the north and south, Haystack Rock, and Tillamook Rock Lighthouse.

U.S. 101, mile 32
Viewpoint

A small parking area on the west side of the highway overlooks the beach and rocks.

Haystack Rock is a familiar landmark at Cannon Beach. This monolith, one of two so-named on Oregon's north coast, stands 235 feet high.

This shady park on the west side of the highway has an easy trail to the sunny beach and is a good place for a rest stop or picnic. Amenities include picnic tables, trash receptacle, and pit toilets with wheelchair access.

U.S. 101, mile 32.2
Arcadia Beach State
Recreation Site

On the west side of the highway is a small wayside with easy beach access and pit toilets with wheelchair access. Before the highway was the beach—the only thoroughfare for wagons and

U.S. 101, mile 33.4
Hug Point State
Recreation Site

Tolovana Beach State Recreation Site.

Shown here are the original cannon and capstan that gave Cannon Beach its name. They were displayed here for years, but were replaced by a replica cannon and moved to the Cannon Beach Historical Society Museum in 1999.

stagecoaches. The original stagecoach trail hugged the point: hence the name, Hug Point. Before hiking the old trail, be sure to check tide tables to avoid being stranded at high tide.

U.S. 101, mile 34.4
Cannon Beach
Historical Marker and
Cannon

On the east side of the highway a historical marker tells of the ill-fated U.S. Navy survey ship *Shark*, which ran aground on the Clatsop Spit while attempting to leave the Columbia River September 10, 1846. In an effort to save the ship, crew chopped down the schooner's three masts and jettisoned her cannons, but the ship broke up and sank anyway. A small cannon and part of her deck washed ashore near Arch Cape, south of Tillamook Head, on a beach that was eventually named after the incident. The ship's cannon and capstan were located at this highway turnout in 1965, but were moved to the Heritage Museum in Astoria in 1989 and then to the Cannon Beach Historical Society Museum in 1999.

U.S. 101,
mile 35.6 to 41.4
Oswald West State
Park

Most of the park and its main features lie within Tillamook County and are covered in the next chapter.

U.S. 101, mile 37.1
Clatsop County/
Tillamook County
Line

Side Trip: U.S. Route 30

From its junction with U.S. 101, U.S. 30 extends about 100 miles to Portland and is the main route through the Astoria city center. Mileposts begin in the greater Portland area and terminate in Astoria at mile 99.2. Instead of relying on highway mileposts, some travelers might prefer to refer to actual mileages from the Astoria-Megler Bridge, or the U.S. 101/U.S. 30 junction.

The mooring basin lies just west of the Astoria-Megler Bridge, but access is via Basin Street, north off U.S. 30, just east of the U.S. 101/U.S. 30 junction. This well-protected basin on the Columbia River is flanked on two sides by the Red Lion Inn and offers a fuel dock, transient moorage, and rest rooms with flush toilets. Restaurants and lodging are within walking distance. Although the basin has no boat ramp, several ramps in the Astoria area can accommodate trailer boats.

U.S. 30, mile 99.2
West Mooring Basin

Port of Astoria, West Mooring Basin

The visitor center on the east side of U.S. 30 is 0.4 mile east of the U.S. 101/U.S. 30 junction. Stop here to pick up a Clatsop County map, *Astoria and Warrenton Information Guide*, and other literature about local attractions. From May through September, the center is open Monday through Saturday from 8:00 a.m. to 6:00 p.m. and Sunday from 9:00 a.m. to 5:00 p.m.; the rest of the year, it's open from 9:00 a.m. to 5:00 p.m. daily. Winter days and hours may vary.

U.S. 30, mile 98.9
Astoria-Warrenton Area Chamber of Commerce Visitor Center

U.S. 30, mile 98.5
River Viewing Tower

On the north side of U.S. 30, 0.8 mile east of the U.S. 101/U.S. 30 junction and at the foot of 6th Street, the tower is the place to stop for stunning river views. Climb the steps of the tower to a viewing and photography platform with views of the lower Columbia, its ship and boat traffic, birdlife, and cruising seals and sea lions.

U.S. 30, mile 98.3
Flavel House

This historic Astoria landmark is 1 mile east of the Astoria-Megler Bridge and U.S. 101/U.S. 30 junction. Now functioning as a Clatsop County Historical Society Museum, the 1885 Queen Anne Victorian house was the home of Captain George Flavel and his family. It features exotic hardwood, Eastlake-style woodwork; imported tile fireplaces; and period furnishings. Trees the Flavels planted during the nineteenth century grace and shade the well-kept grounds—a perfect spot for a picnic lunch or peaceful rest stop. The museum is open daily, except Thanksgiving Day, Christmas Day, and New Year's Day: May through September, 10:00 a.m. to 5:00 p.m.; October through April, 11:00 a.m. to 4:00 p.m. Information: (503) 325-2203.

U.S. 30, mile 98.1
Astoria Column

MUST STOP

About 1.2 miles east of the Astoria-Megler Bridge, turn right on 12th Street, left on Franklin, right on 14th Street, left on Jerome Street, right on 15th Street, then left on Coxcomb Drive, and up the hill to the column parking area for a total of 2.6 miles. Signs along the way mark the route. This is a *must stop*, not only to see the historic column, but also for the best elevated view of the Columbia River Estuary, Youngs Bay, the Coast Range, Saddle

Mountain, Astoria, the Astoria-Megler Bridge, the southwest tip of Washington, the mouth of the Columbia, and Pacific sunsets. Those who have visited before but have not seen the column since its million-dollar restoration was completed in 1995 will surely want to revisit the site.

Fashioned after the Trajan Column built in Rome in 114 A.D., the Astoria Column, completed in 1926, stands 125 feet tall, atop 600-foot Coxcomb Hill, and dominates the Astoria skyline. A pictorial mural, depicting fourteen historical scenes, spirals upward from the column base to the towering cupola, commemorating Pacific Northwest life before and after Euro-American discovery and honoring local Indians, Captain Robert Gray, Lewis and Clark, John Jacob Astor, and pioneer settlers. Inside, a spiral staircase leads 164 steps to the top, providing one of the most stunning panoramic views on the Oregon coast.

The well-kept park is a great place to enjoy a pack-along sunrise breakfast or picnic any time of day. Rest rooms with flush toilets are on the premises.

Located 1.4 miles east of the U.S. 101/U.S. 30 junction, and one block south of U.S. 30, this museum is the showcase of the Clatsop County Historical Society. It is housed in Astoria's old City Hall and has galleries on two floors featuring both permanent and changing exhibits depicting Astoria's rich history, society, industry, and commerce, as well as the people who inhabited, explored, visited, and settled the area. An essential stop for history buffs, the museum has an excellent little bookstore and is open daily, except Thanksgiving Day, Christmas Day, and New Year's Day: May through September, 10:00 a.m. to 5:00 p.m.; October through April, 11:00 a.m. to 4:00 p.m. Information: (503) 325-2203.

U.S. 30, mile 97.9
Heritage Museum

Lightship Columbia, *moored near the Columbia River Maritime Museum.*

U.S. 30, mile 97.8
Columbia River
Maritime Museum

MUST STOP

On the north side of U.S. 30, 1.5 miles east of the U.S. 101/U.S. 30 junction, stands one of the finest museums in the Pacific Northwest, with 24,000 square feet of floor space housing an extensive collection of ship models, maritime artifacts, and fine art. Displays include restored and preserved boats, engines, gear, and superb exhibits pertaining to the early fur trade, whaling, fishing, navigation, naval history, lighthouses, shipwrecks, and Columbia River commerce and navigation. Visitors can take the wheel while standing inside a steamboat pilothouse, stand watch on the bridge of a World War II destroyer, observe Columbia River ship traffic through submarine periscopes, or board and tour the lightship *Columbia*, moored at the museum dock.

Astoria is home port to two U.S. Coast Guard cutters. When in port, they're moored at the Astoria City Pier, adjacent to the maritime museum. Private pleasure craft and river cruise vessels also moor nearby, and river traffic is nearly constant, making the museum and its environs a *must stop* for everyone who enjoys all things nautical.

The museum is open daily, except Thanksgiving Day and Christmas Day, from 9:30 a.m. to 5:00 p.m. Information: (503) 325-2323.

17th Street Transient
Float

This facility on the Columbia River, offering access to the Astoria waterfront and downtown attractions, is available for no-charge temporary moorage on a first-come, first-served basis. Tour-ship operators pay to use the float and have specific dates reserved. Those who wish to moor private pleasure craft here and avoid schedule conflicts with the tour ships should phone ahead, one month if possible, to get an idea about space availability. Information: (503) 325-5821, extension 24.

U.S. 30, mile 97.2
Uppertown
Firefighters Museum

East of downtown Astoria, 2.1 miles from the U.S. 101/U.S. 30 junction, this museum stands at the northwest corner of 30th Street and Marine Drive. The vintage building housing the museum dates to 1896, when it was designed and erected as part of the North Pacific Brewery, which was forced to close during Prohibition. From 1928 to 1961, it functioned as a fire station, and many of the antique apparatuses and much of the fire-fighting equipment from that era are now displayed for close-up inspection, ranging from an 1878 Hayes horse-drawn ladder wagon to a 1912 American LaFrance Chemical Wagon, 1921 Stutz Pumper, and five engines from the first half of the twentieth century.

The museum is open daily, except Thanksgiving Day, Christmas Day, and New Year's Day: May through September, 10:00 a.m. to 5:00 p.m.; October through April, 11:00 a.m. to 4:00 p.m. Information: (503) 325-2203.

On the south side of the highway, 2.4 miles east of the U.S. 101/ U.S. 30 junction, this marker commemorates the U.S. Custom House built here in 1852 as the first federal building west of the Rocky Mountains.

U.S. 30, mile 96.9
Historical Marker

Replica of the U.S. Custom House built here in 1852

On the north side of the highway, 2.6 miles east of the U.S. 101/U.S. 30 junction, this Port of Astoria facility on the Columbia River has a paved boat ramp, dock, large parking lot, and rest rooms with flush toilets and wheelchair access. This is a good place for waterfront photography or hiking and biking along the river.

U.S. 30, mile 96.7
East Mooring Basin

Port of Astoria, East Mooring Basin

Information

Astoria-Warrenton Area Chamber of
  Commerce
111 West marine Drive
P.O. Box 176
Astoria, OR 97103
(503) 325-6311
(800) 875-6807
E-mail: awacc@seasurf.com
URL: www.oldoregon.com

Astoria-Warrenton Area Chamber of
  Commerce
143 Highway 101
Warrenton, OR 97146
(503) 861-1031
URL: www.oldoregon.com

Cannon Beach Chamber of Commerce
2nd and Spruce
P.O. Box 64
Cannon Beach, OR 97110
(503) 436-2623
URL: www.cannonbeach.org

Clatsop County Parks
1100 Olney
Astoria, OR 97103
(503) 325-9306

Ecola State Park
Cannon Beach, OR 97110
(503) 436-2844

Fort Clatsop National Memorial
Route 3, Box 604-FC
Astoria, OR 97103
(503) 861-2471
URL: www.nps.gov/focl

Fort Stevens State Park
Hammond, OR 97121
(503) 861-1671 Campground
(503) 861-2000 Museum
(800) 551-6949 Information
(800) 452-5687 Reservations
URL: www.prd.state.or.us

Haystack Summer Program in the Arts &
  Sciences
School of Extended Studies/Summer Session
Portland State University
P.O. Box 1491
Portland, OR 97207
(503) 725-3276
(800) 547-8887, extension 3276
E-mail: haystack@pdx.edu
URL: www.haystack.pdx.edu

National Weather Service
North Coast and Marine Weather
(503) 861-2722 Recorded Message

Port of Astoria
1 Portway
Astoria, OR 97103
(503) 325-4521

Seaside Visitors Bureau
989 Broadway
Seaside, OR 97138
(503) 738-3097
(888) 306-2326
E-mail: visit@seaside-oregon.com
URL: www.seasideor.com

U.S. Coast Guard Station
Ilwaco, WA 98624
(360) 642-2381 Emergencies
(360) 642-2382 Information
(361) 642-3565 Weather and Bar Conditions

Responding to lunar and solar influences, Pacific waters rise twice daily to inundate rocks and reefs and ocean beaches along the Oregon coast. With force enough to reverse the flow of mighty rivers, the tides sweep past jetties and creek mouths to flood flats and marshes of estuaries and raise levels of sloughs and streams. On extraterrestrial cue, about six hours later, the waters recede whence they came.

If the earth had no moon, and the sun were the only body exerting gravitational pull on the planet, our tides and tidal fluctuations would be much smaller and easier to predict than they are. The tides would also occur at the same time every day. Although the sun's mass is nearly 27 million times that of the moon, it's also about 390 times farther from earth, which accounts for the smaller body's greater gravitational attraction. Nevertheless, the sun does affect our tides. In fact, at a few locations on earth, such as the island of Tahiti, solar tides are dominant.

Elsewhere, the tides roughly coincide with the lunar day—the time it takes the moon to travel its course along any meridian of earth's longitude—which is 24 hours and 50 minutes. Most of us just think of today's tides as running about an hour later than yesterday's.

Phases of the moon also greatly affect the tides. Solar and lunar tides reinforce each other during the new moon and full moon, creating extremely high and extremely low water known as *spring tides*. The smallest tidal ranges occur during the first and last quarters of the moon and are called *neap tides*.

At most places on earth, there are two tide cycles a day: that is, a cycle consisting of a high and low tide, followed by another similar cycle. High tide occurs simultaneously directly beneath the moon and on the opposite side of the earth beneath the sun: the former a *lunar tide*, the latter a *solar tide*.

Along America's Atlantic Coast, two high tides and two low tides occur each day, with relatively little difference between successive high waters and successive low waters. Such tides are classified as *semidiurnal*. Along the north shore of the Gulf of Mexico, the *dirunal* tide moves in and out again only once a day, resulting in one high tide and one low tide each day. Here in the Pacific Northwest, we have semidiurnal tides that are also known as *mixed tides*, characterized by significant disparity between successive high and low tides.

The greatest tides occur at the Bay of Fundy in Nova Scotia, where high and low tide can differ by as much as 50 feet. On the Oregon coast, the range is from about 2.1 feet below to more than 10 feet above average mean tide, for a difference sometimes exceeding 12 feet, which is substantial. In some parts of the world, the difference between high and low tide is measured in inches.

Know the Tides

Tidal currents are most significant and noticeable near shore and wherever water movement is restricted, such as in bays, straits, and the tidewater portions of coastal streams. On the Oregon coast, tidewater extends 20 miles or more up some rivers. On the Columbia River, tidal influences reach all the way to the Bonneville Dam, about 150 miles from the ocean.

An incoming tidal flow is known as a *flood current* or *flood tide;* an outgoing flow is an *ebb current* or *ebb tide.* The period between flood and ebb tides, when there is little or no current, is called *slack water* or *slack tide.*

Those who enjoy hiking, beachcombing, agate hunting, fossil hunting, boating, crabbing, clam digging, fishing, and even watching and photographing wildlife along the coast must pay special attention to the tides. A person's success and safety depend on a knowledge of tides: their times, levels, and relationships with other natural conditions. Everyone venturing onto beaches, rocky shores, and coastal waterways should first check tide tables, which are published in some newspapers, magazines, and coastal phone directories, as well as on the Internet. They are also published in the form of pocket-size booklets, available for under a dollar, and sometimes free, at tackle shops, marinas, sporting-goods outlets, and some coastal visitor centers. These booklets are best, because they provide the most information in the handiest form. The times and depths of the month's high and low tides are usually printed on the same or opposing pages for convenient reference. The booklets also contain correction tables for various places along the coast, as well as tables for sunrise and sunset times—a valuable feature for photographers, hikers, anglers, wildlife watchers, and other outdoor enthusiasts.

Some narrow beaches, especially those backed by cliffs, can be hazardous at high tide and might be passable only at low tide. So those venturing into tidal areas need to pay attention to tides to avoid being stranded or worse. Every year, legions of coastal adventurers sally forth unawares on low tide along Oregon's rocky shoreline, only to be surprised when faced with a long cold and wet wade back to dry land. Some must be plucked from rocks by Coast Guard rescue crews. An unfortunate few meet the most dire circumstances when they're washed from their precarious perches into the chill waters and dangerous currents of the nearshore Pacific.

Big water and bad weather create potentially perilous conditions at the mouths of coastal rivers, where the seas tend to pile up and break. Even in calm weather and good seas, a swift ebb tide can make the shallow bar dangerous. Any boater caught outside the bar then should wait out the tide and cross on the flood. The smart boater uses tide tables and plans ahead.

Exploring tide pools, gathering mussels, and digging clams are low-water activities, and minus tides are best. Most of us like to be on the beach or flats a couple of hours before low tide. Crabbers prefer slow or still waters, so most crabbers set out their gear during the last two hours of a tide and continue crabbing through slack tide.

Anglers who fish in coastal waters also must study tides, which might influence the movement of both forage and predator species. In some places, a flood tide provides superior fishing; in others, the ebb is best. Generally, slack water is seldom as productive as moving water. In some coastal areas, salmon, steelhead, and shad move into coastal streams during the exceptionally high water of spring tides and provide superb angling then. Elsewhere, it might take low water to allow tide gates to open and schooling fish to move into the streams above them. Some predator species, such as striped bass, cruise the flats on the flood tide to feed in water sometimes no more than a foot deep. They head for the deep water of channels and inlets on the ebb tide, where they wait in ambush for forage species to be swept down the current to them.

Many species of shorebirds, wading birds, and waterfowl are most active at low tide, when the dinner table is set. The ebbing tide exposes river and creek banks, estuary shores, mudflats, sandflats, eelgrass beds, the edges of salt marshes, rocky intertidal areas, and broad expanses of ocean beaches, leaving countless organisms vulnerable to predation. That's when birds move in to feed and when those interested in watching and photographing them ought to be nearby.

The Pacific's periodic intrusion on Oregon's estuaries, mudflats, marshes, sloughs, creeks, and rivers provides nutrients to countless organisms, flushes potentially harmful pollutants out to sea, affects outdoor recreation, and generally helps make the coast an exciting place to live and play. For maximum enjoyment and safety, it's essential to know the tides.

Information

Oregon Coast Tide Tables
URL: www.hmsc.ors.edu/gen_info/tides.shtml

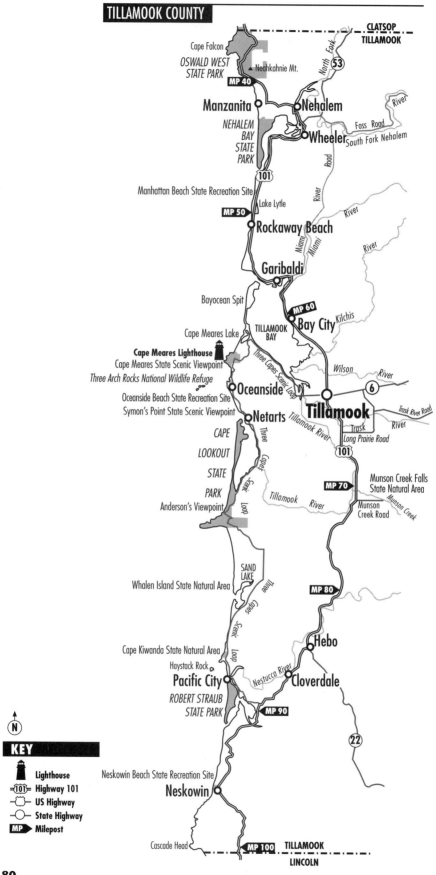

CLATSOP
TILLAMOOK

Cape Falcon

OSWALD WEST STATE PARK

North Fork

53

MP 40

▲ Neahkahnie Mt.

Manzanita

Nehalem

River

Foss Road

Wheeler

South Fork Nehalem

NEHALEM BAY STATE PARK

River

Road

101

Manhattan Beach State Recreation Site

Lake Lytle

River

MP 50

Rockaway Beach

River

Miami

Miami

Garibaldi

River

Bayocean Spit

TILLAMOOK BAY

MP 60

Bay City

Kilchis

Cape Meares Lake

Cape Meares Lighthouse

Cape Meares State Scenic Viewpoint

Three Arch Rocks National Wildlife Refuge

Three Capes Scenic Loop

Wilson

River

6

Oceanside

Oceanside Beach State Recreation Site

Symon's Point State Scenic Viewpoint

Tillamook

Trask River Road

Netarts

Tillamook River

Trask

River

CAPE LOOKOUT STATE PARK

Long Prairie Road

101

Anderson's Viewpoint

Three Capes Scenic Loop

Tillamook River

MP 70

Munson Creek Falls State Natural Area

Munson Creek Road

Munson Creek

SAND LAKE

Whalen Island State Natural Area

MP 80

101

Three Capes Scenic Loop

Cape Kiwanda State Natural Area

Hebo

Haystack Rock

Nestucca River

Cloverdale

Pacific City

ROBERT STRAUB STATE PARK

MP 90

22

N

KEY

Lighthouse

101 **Highway 101**

US Highway

State Highway

MP **Milepost**

Neskowin Beach State Recreation Site

Neskowin

Cascade Head

MP 100

TILLAMOOK

LINCOLN

The Tillamook County Coast

U.S. 101, Mile 37.1 to Mile 102.7

Tillamook County spreads along the coast and inland into the forested Coast Range to occupy 1,125 square miles. About 24,000 people share the county with an estimated 40,000 cows, so it's no wonder that the dairy industry ranks among the most important contributors to the local economy, along with forest products, commercial and sport fishing, recreation, and tourism. Tillamook is the county's largest city and seat of government.

The territorial legislature established the county from parts of Clatsop and Yamhill counties on December 15, 1853, and named it after the Tillamook, or Killamook, tribe of Salish Indians. The people of this large tribe inhabited coastal lands near and south of Tillamook Head and were mentioned in the journals of Lewis and Clark as the Killamuck and Kilamox Indians.

Evidence abounds everywhere of the widespread significance of the dairy business, from the farms filling the verdant valleys to the herds of cattle lazing and grazing in the pastures, from the gleaming tanker trucks hauling the farmers' product to market to the Tillamook County Creamery Association's facilities dominating the Highway 101 landscape at the north end of Tillamook.

Also evident is the county's broad appeal to outdoor enthusiasts and recreationists of every stripe. With 75 miles of coastline—varying in appearance and composition from broad beaches to rocky intertidal areas, miles-long sand spits, and rugged headlands—the Tillamook coast is the county's major attraction. Augmenting the allure of this watery wonderland are Nehalem, Tillamook, Netarts,

Dairy farms dot the Tillamook County landscape.

and Nestucca bays, as well as nine coastal rivers and countless creeks. If all that's not enough, there are the sprawling dunes of Sand Lake, the highest waterfall in the Coast Range, four challenging golf courses, two fine museums, and more than a dozen great state and county parks offering opportunities for every form of recreation from hiking to hang-gliding.

Headlands are the most scenic parts of any coastline, and Tillamook County has been blessed with more than its share. From Cape Falcon and Neahkahnie Mountain in the north to Cascade Head in the south—with Capes Meares, Lookout, and Kiwanda lying in between—Tillamook County has plenty of splendid scenery to please every sightseer and shutterbug.

There are 65.6 miles of U.S. 101 in the county, but only the northernmost 20 miles or so are close to the ocean. In the vicinity of Bay City, on Tillamook Bay, the highway swings inland, and it remains at some distance from the coast all the way to the Lincoln County line (mile 102.7) and beyond to Lincoln City (mile 112.1). To reach the coast from here, take the Three Capes Scenic Loop west out of Tillamook at mile 65.7, for a 35-mile cruise through some of the best country the Oregon coast has to offer. The loop rejoins Highway 101 at mile 90.3, just over 12 miles north of the Lincoln County line.

U.S. 101, mile 37.1
Oswald West State
Park

MUST STOP

The northern park entrance is in Clatsop County, at mile 35.6, but most of the park lies within Tillamook County and extends along U.S. 101 to mile 41.4, for a total of 5.8 miles. Formerly Short Sand Beach State Park, it was renamed and dedicated in 1956 to honor Oregon's youngest governor, elected at age 37, who served from 1911 to 1915 and was responsible for preserving public access to Oregon's beaches. In 1913 Governor West initiated legislation that designated the wet sand beach between high and extreme low tides as part of the state's highway system and unavailable for private ownership. The bill further prevented oceanfront property owners from blocking public access to the beaches.

This *must stop* state park encompasses nearly 2,500 acres of spectacular coastal headlands, rain forest, and beach. The park comprises Cape Falcon, nearly all of Neahkahnie Mountain, a campground, day-use areas, and more than 15 miles of hiking trails, 13 miles of which are part of the Oregon Coast Trail. Many of the old-growth Sitka spruce trees in the park stand 200 feet tall and spread to a trunk diameter of 12 feet. The forest fringes and meadows are home to black-tailed deer, Roosevelt elk, black bear, and numerous small mammals.

Turnouts along Highway 101 allow travelers to pause and take in stunning views of the ocean, headlands, and historic rockwork along the west face of Neahkahnie Mountain. These same turnouts are vantage points for watching gray whales during their winter and spring migrations.

At mile 39 is a small parking area on the west side of the highway for hikers and others wishing to use the park's trails.

On the east side of the highway at mile 39.1, a large parking lot accommodates hikers, anglers, surfers, photographers, and others who want to explore Cape Falcon, Short Sand Beach, and other areas of the park. Features include picnic areas with tables and rest rooms with flush toilets and wheelchair access.

U.S. 101, miles 39 and 39.1
Oswald West State Park Day Use Areas

Just over 0.3 mile from a large parking lot on the west side of the highway is a hike-in campground with 29 primitive campsites. Wheelbarrows are available for hauling in camping gear. Each campsite has a picnic table and fireplace, and firewood is available. Drinking water, trash receptacles, and rest rooms with flush toilets are nearby. Although this lovely campground, flanked by two shallow creeks, lies only a short distance from Highway 101, lush rainforest vegetation buffers highway noises, leaving the rumble of Pacific breakers within earshot. Trails lead from camp and meander along Short Sand Creek and across a footbridge, or along Necarney Creek and over a rustic suspension bridge to connect with the Oregon Coast Trail. A delightful picnic area overlooking Short Sand Beach and Smuggler Cove, a year-round favorite of surfers, is only a brief hike from camp. While the campground closes in winter, trails remain open all year.

U.S. 101, mile 39.3
Oswald West State Park Campground

A small gravel parking area lies on the west side of the highway, adjacent to the trailhead. A good trail, steep in places, leads 1 mile to the beach.

U.S. 101, mile 40.3
Short Sand Beach Trailhead

This trail leads off the east side of the highway, 1.5 miles to the summit of Neahkahnie Mountain.

Neahkahnie Mountain Trail

The turnout on the west side of the highway provides a superb view of the beautiful rockwork, the west face of the Neahkahnie Mountain, and an arching sweep of beach below. This is an excellent spot for photography. A roadside trail leads from here to mile 41.4, providing great views, photo opportunities, and whale watching in season. Traffic is often heavy here, so be careful and alert.

U.S. 101, mile 40.6
Historic Highway Site and Oswald West Commemorative Marker

Two small parking areas on the west side of the highway offer views of the ocean and fine rockwork.

U.S. 101, mile 40.7
Viewpoint

Roadside path and historic rockwork along Highway 101, on the west face of Neahkahnie Mountain.

U.S. 101, mile 40.9
Viewpoint

A very small turnout on the west side of the highway, with room for only one or two vehicles, provides views of Neahkahnie Beach and the historic rockwork.

U.S. 101, mile 41
Viewpoint

A fair-sized parking area on the west side of the highway allows travelers to view and photograph the Neahkahnie coast and highway rockwork.

U.S. 101, mile 41.1
Viewpoint

On the west side of the highway, a tiny pulloff with room for only one car or pickup truck offers views of the ocean, beach, and rockwork.

U.S. 101, mile 41.2
Viewpoint

A good-sized parking area on the west side of the highway provides space for several vehicles, including RVs, and views of the ocean, beach, and roadside rockwork.

U.S. 101, mile 41.4
Viewpoint

A gravel parking area on the west side of the highway allows travelers to pause and take in a sweeping view of Neahkahnie Beach and Manzanita to the south.

U.S. 101, mile 41.6
Neahkahnie
Mountain Trailhead

A good gravel road on the east side of the highway leads 0.1 mile to the trailhead and a small parking area. The trail climbs 1.4 miles to the summit. This spot is worth a stop, even for those who don't intend to hike the trail. Beautiful trees with long, moss-covered, sometimes serpentine branches line the road and pose for photographs.

Turn west off the highway, and drive 0.8 mile to parking areas on both sides of the road and easy access to the broad sand beach. The road continues along the beach into Manzanita.

U.S. 101, mile 42.9
Neahkahnie Beach

Turn west off U.S. 101 at the blinking light onto Laneda Avenue. This small (population: 795), residential beach town, perched on the south slope of Neahkahnie Mountain, serves as a peaceful haven for travelers on vacation or weekend retreats. The community's entire western boundary is broad beach and tumbling surf. Its several inns and motels are within easy walking distance of the beach. Other attractions include Oswald West State Park to the north, Nehalem Bay State Park to the south, and a 9-hole golf course in town.

U.S. 101, mile 43.2
Manzanita
(zip code 97310)

Manzanita Beach spreads southwest from the base of Neahkahnie Mountain and past the city of Manzanita.

At the city center, turn south (left) on Lakeview Drive, and go 0.6 mile to the golf course parking lot. The 2,192-yard, 9-hole, par-32 course with tree-lined fairways lies in a quiet residential area and has been open since 1987. Features include a putting green, driving range, pro shop, pull-cart rental, club rental, snack bar, and bar with beer and wine. Pro shop: (503) 368-5744.

Manzanita Golf
Course

Spread across the 4-mile-long Nehalem Spit, a strip of beach and dunes that separates the ocean from Nehalem Bay, this big park offers a great variety of activities and attractions to campers and outdoor enthusiasts, including several campgrounds, a nearby airstrip, and a paved boat ramp on Nehalem Bay.

U.S. 101, mile 43.8
Nehalem Bay State
Park

The main campground has nine yurts and 284 campsites with electrical and water hook-ups, three of which are wheelchair accessible and located near a utility building with flush toilets, showers, and wheelchair access. Two other utility buildings with flush toilets and showers are available to all campers. Each campsite has a picnic table and fire ring. There's an RV dump station in the parking lot near the registration booth. A hiker/biker camp stands near the park entrance, and a primitive fly-in camp with six sites lies adjacent to the 2,400-foot airstrip. The horse camp has 17 sites, each with a picnic table, fire ring, and one or two corrals.

Bay boaters, beach hikers, and horseback riders will find a remote picnic area with tables and a pit toilet at the end of Nehalem Spit. Other picnic areas lie near the main campground and just west of the boat launch; they have picnic tables, fire rings, and rest rooms with flush toilets.

Both campers and day-users find this park particularly attractive for its variety of activities. It offers hiking, biking, and horse trails. The long, wide ocean beach is a favorite for beach combing and agate hunting. Anglers come for the surf, jetty, and bay fishing. The bay is also a popular waterway for boating, kayaking, crabbing, and clam digging. Abundant year-round birdlife, with numbers swelling dramatically during spring and fall migrations, delights birders and wildlife photographers. Information: (503) 368-5154 or (800) 551-6949. Reservations: (800) 452-5687.

U.S. 101, mile 44.7
Nehalem
(zip code 97131)

This little riverside village (population: 230) is a great place to stop for a meal, snack, or rest break and a stroll along the main drag, lined with galleries and specialty shops. Public rest rooms are near the boat docks.

U.S. 101, mile 45.1
City of Nehalem
Public Docks

On the east side of the highway, at the foot of Tohls Avenue is a tiny park at river's edge with a trash receptacle, benches, and boat docks for temporary moorage. Public rest rooms with flush toilets are at the south end of the adjacent Nehalem Bay Wastewater Agency building. Information: (503) 368-5627.

U.S. 101, mile 45.6
Nehalem River

One of Oregon's longer coastal rivers, the Nehalem courses through the Coast Range for about 100 miles, collecting the waters of the Salmonberry River, North Fork Nehalem, and numerous creeks before discharging into the Pacific. It's a popular river with salmon and steelhead anglers, with runs of spring chinook, fall chinook, and winter steelhead. Here, as elsewhere, fishing seasons may vary year to year and are subject to change. So anglers must consult the current *Oregon Sport Fishing Regulations* before venturing out. Generally, though, the fall chinook season runs on the heels of the spring chinook season, with angling for these fish normally running from late May through December. The lower river, upstream to the Highway 26 bridge at Elsie, is open all year for steelhead fishing. For upper river seasons and closures, consult the regulations. On the entire

The community of Nehalem rests on the north bank of the lower Nehalem River.

mainstem of the Nehalem River, upstream from the Miami River/ Foley Creek Bridge, just east of U.S. 101, anglers are restricted to the use of artificial lures and flies from April 1 to August 31.

In addition to angling, the lower Nehalem offers opportunities for boating, canoeing, kayaking, wildlife observation, and photography. Riverbanks, meadows, and wetlands are good places to watch for black-tailed deer, Roosevelt elk, coyotes, and resident and migratory birds.

U.S. 101, mile 46
Nehalem Boat Launch

This county facility is located at the southwest end of the bridge and includes a paved ramp, dock, large parking area, and pit toilets. From here, boaters have immediate access to the tidewater portion of the river and a short run downstream to Nehalem Bay.

U.S. 101, mile 46.5
State Route 53 junction

Route 53 extends northeast off the east side of the highway for 19 miles through the Coast Range to its junction with U.S. Route 26.

Roy Creek County Park

Take State Route 53 east off U.S. 101 for just over a mile, cross the bridge over the Nehalem River, and turn right onto Miami River Road. Drive 0.9 mile to Foss Road, turn left, and go another 0.3 mile to the park entrance. The park is on the Nehalem River with bank access for angling, a gravel boat ramp, and adequate parking for boat trailers. Campers will find 10 primitive campsites, four with picnic tables and stoves, and limited additional space for parking self-contained RVs. There's a pit toilet with wheelchair access.

U.S. 101, mile 46.9
Wheeler
(zip code 97147)

This small town (population: 385) straddles U.S. 101, with most of its businesses and homes on the east side of the highway. On the west side, along the river, are the water-related businesses, including a canoe and kayak livery and a marina with bait, tackle, fuel, and moorage available. This is a pretty little spot, offering some wildlife-watching and photography opportunities. It's a good place for a picnic on the river or lunch break at one of the local eateries.

U.S. 101, mile 47.3
Wheeler Boat Ramp

On the west side of the highway, this city facility has a paved ramp and transient dock on the lower Nehalem River, with easy access to Nehalem Bay. It has a nice little picnic area with tables and rest room with flush toilets and wheelchair access. There are nearby boat rentals, and crab gear is available for sale or rent.

U.S. 101, mile 47.4
Nehalem Bay Area Chamber of Commerce Visitor Center

On the east side of the highway, this is the place to stop for information about Nehalem, Wheeler, Brighton, and Nehalem Bay. The center is open daily from 10:00 a.m. to 4:00 p.m. from Memorial Day weekend until mid-October. The rest of the year, phone or write for information, or pick up brochures and other literature at the coffee shop next door.

U.S. 101, mile 48
to mile 50
Milepost discrepancies

From the original highway milepost marker 48 to milepost marker 50 is a distance of 6.1 miles, the additional 4.1 miles resulting from highway construction and realignment. Rather than change all the mileposts from here to California, the Oregon Department of Transportation instead added highway milepost markers with Z prefixes, beginning with Z45 after milepost 48.

U.S. 101,
mile Z45.4
Viewpoint

A fair-sized parking area along the west side of the highway invites travelers to stop for a pleasing view of Nehalem Bay. Wildlife that can be observed here includes gulls, shorebirds, wading birds, ducks, geese, and Pacific harbor seals.

Workboat moored at the transient dock, near the Wheeler Boat Ramp.

Nehalem Bay

This scenic, photogenic, and productive bay is among Oregon's larger estuaries and is popular among a variety of outdoor enthusiasts. Shoreline access is good, especially along the west shore in the vicinity of Nehalem Bay State Park, particularly along the east side of the Nehalem Spit. Boat access is excellent, with ramps near Nehalem and at Wheeler, Brighton, the Jetty Fishery, and Nehalem Bay State Park.

Spring and summer fishing is mainly for seaperch, surfperch, sand sole, and the occasional starry flounder. Spring and fall chinook seasons run from early April through December, and fishing for these big salmon can be outstanding. The lower bay is closed to coho fishing, while the upper bay is open for fin-clipped coho from mid-August through October. Although the entire bay is open all year for steelhead trout, the actual fishery is mainly a late-fall proposition in the upper bay. Consult the *Oregon Sport Fishing Regulations* for specifics.

Nehalem Bay is a top pick for crabbing, which can be good all year, but is best from mid-summer through fall. Rental boats, gear, and bait are available at various places along U.S. 101. Although Nehalem Bay doesn't have the variety of clams found in other large bays, it's one of the best places on the coast for digging soft-shell clams. These tasty bivalves often live in dense colonies, making it easy to dig liberal limits.

Other popular activities on the bay include boating, canoeing, kayaking, wildlife watching, and photography. Among the birdlife visitors are likely to encounter are various species of gulls, terns, seabirds, shorebirds, wading birds, ducks, and geese. Pacific harbor seals move into and out of the bay and often haul out on islands and exposed sandbars. Black-tailed deer and smaller mammals live along the bay's edges.

Nehalem Bay, near Wheeler

Although boats do cross the Nehalem Bay bar, the crossing runs from tricky to downright dangerous. The bar breaks on the ebb, and the channel shifts continually. So before venturing across, consult local experts about current conditions, pick the right tide, and proceed with utmost caution.

U.S. 101, mile Z46.6
Brighton Beach Marina

This private marina on the west side of the highway has a paved boat ramp providing quick access to the lower bay. Moorage, fuel, rental boats, crab gear, and bait are available. Information: (503) 368-5745.

U.S. 101, mile Z47.4
Jetty Fishery Marina

This privately owned marina and RV park on the west side of the highway has a paved boat ramp providing immediate access to the mouth of Nehalem Bay. Moorage, fuel, supplies, boat rental, crab gear, and bait are available. Information: (503) 368-5746 or (800) 821-7697.

U.S. 101, mile Z48.7
Manhattan Beach State Recreation Site

Turn west off U.S. 101, cross the railroad tracks, and then turn south (left) into the park. A pretty spot in the shore pines, salal, huckleberries, and blackberries, with picnic areas protected from the wind, this park has drinking water, short trails to the beach, and rest rooms with flush toilets and wheelchair access.

U.S. 101, mile Z49.3
Rockaway Beach
(zip code 97136)

This aptly named small beach town (population: 1,235) straddles Highway 101 for about 2 miles. The highway runs parallel to and about two blocks from a broad sand beach, popular for all beach activities, including kite flying, agate hunting, and surf fishing. Houses, condominiums, and motels obscure the beach to such an extent that some travelers might pass through town without even realizing that it's there and so near. In fact, this beach runs uninterrupted for miles north and south.

U.S. 101, mile Z49.8
Lake Lytle

Turn west on Northeast 12th Avenue, and drive 0.1 mile to the parking area, where there is a good gravel boat ramp and a pit toilet with wheelchair access. The shallow lake is locally popular but doesn't get much fishing pressure, perhaps because of weed problems that develop by mid-summer, particularly in the southern half of the lake. Fishing is best in the spring and early summer for stocked rainbow and cutthroat trout, black crappie, and largemouth bass.

U.S. 101, mile 50
Lake Lytle Dock

Anglers will find roadside parking areas on the east side of the highway and a fishing dock with wheelchair access.

U.S. 101, mile 50.6
Rockaway Beach City Park

Turn east off U.S. 101 on North 3rd Avenue, drive 0.1 mile, turn north (left) on North Coral Street, and drive another 0.1 mile to the park. This attractive park in a residential setting is a good place to enjoy a quiet picnic or turn the kids loose to unwind.

*Rockaway Beach
Visitor Center*

Amenities include a playground, basketball court, horseshoe pits, picnic tables, stoves, drinking water, trash receptacles, and rest rooms with flush toilets and wheelchair access.

You can't miss this center on the west side of the highway in the red caboose. It's open Monday through Friday from 9:00 a.m. to 5:00 p.m. in summer, and 10:00 a.m. to 3:00 p.m. in winter.

U.S. 101, mile 50.8
Rockaway Beach Chamber of Commerce Visitor Center

On the west side of the highway, just beyond the Chamber of Commerce caboose, lies a large parking lot that extends to the edge of the beach, where there are interpretive signs and pay binoculars. The park also has picnic tables, drinking water, trash receptacles, and rest rooms with flush toilets and wheelchair access.

Rockaway Beach City Park

One block west of U.S. 101, at the foot of Washington Street, are a small parking area and a short path to the beach.

U.S. 101, mile 51.7
Beach access

Set at the base of Tillamook Bay's north jetty, this popular park has 60 full-hookup RV sites and 200 primitive sites for tents and RVs with picnic tables and fire rings. Other features include drinking water, showers, trash receptacles, an RV tank dump, and rest rooms with flush toilets. The park offers beach and jetty access. Information: (503) 322-3522.

U.S. 101, mile 53.8
Barview Jetty County Park

Oregon's second-largest bay and third-largest estuary, sprawling Tillamook Bay is fed by five rivers—the Miami, Kilchis, Wilson, Trask, and Tillamook—creating a watershed of 570 square miles. The bay is popular for a variety of outdoor activities, including boating, fishing, crabbing, clam digging, scuba diving, birding, sightseeing, and photography.

Tillamook Bay

Even in the face of declining salmon populations in the Pacific Northwest, Tillamook Bay and its tributaries still get decent runs of fish that attract crowds of anglers who mainly target spring and fall chinook and winter steelhead. Surfperch, rockfish, lingcod, sole, and flounder also provide food and sport much of the year and are seasonally abundant.

Crabbing on the bay is best during the summer and fall, when the salinity is sufficiently high. It can even be outstanding on the lower bay later in the year if there hasn't been much rain, especially in September through December. Heavy winter rains, however, send crabs scurrying for the briny ocean when the tributaries pour their loads of fresh water into the bay. Boaters usually have the greatest success, but those without boats can also do well crabbing off the docks and piers at Garibaldi (see below, page 94).

Although many people consider Coos Bay to be Oregon's best clam-digging area, facts speak for themselves. According to the Tillamook Bay National Estuary Project, Tillamook Bay is the most productive, with commercial and recreational clam harvest amounting to more than 149,000 pounds in a single year. The bay harbors large populations of Oregon's most popular and plentiful bay clams—gapers, quahogs, littlenecks, cockles, and soft-shells—as well as a few razor clams. The bay is virtually rimmed with clam beds, many of which are accessible by foot. Reaching some of the best beds and biggest clams, however, requires a boat.

Many people tow boats to Tillamook Bay and launch them either at Garibaldi for access to the lower bay and ocean or at or near Tillamook for fishing, crabbing, and clam digging in the upper bay. There are also numerous sites on the bay's tributaries for launching drift boats, canoes, and kayaks. For those who don't own a boat, a large charter fleet works out of Garibaldi, offering trips for salmon, halibut, bottom fish, and tuna. Bank-bound anglers fish mainly from the north jetty, the piers at Garibaldi, and the rocky east shore of the bay, south to Bay City.

Tillamook Bay is also one of Oregon's important estuaries for oyster farming. Oyster beds are private property, though, and are off-limits to the public. So anyone who wants to enjoy the famous Tillamook Bay oysters will have to buy them.

Tillamook Bay is a large and diverse estuary with many kinds of habitat supporting a tremendous variety of organisms. The bay's rocky shoreline, long stretches of sandy beach, expansive mudflats, tidal creeks and channels, sandbars, salt marshes, and eelgrass beds are permanent homes, temporary nurseries, seasonal sanctuaries, or periodic feeding areas for hundreds of species of invertebrates, fishes, birds, and mammals. The most visible of these, and the easiest to spot or capture on film, are the numerous birds and a few species of mammals.

Some birds—including gulls, cormorants, and herons—are year-round residents. Others are spring and fall migrants that stop by to feed and rest for a few days or a few weeks. Still others spend the winter feeding and resting, or spring and summer mating and nesting. Some take refuge on the bay to escape fierce winter storms on the ocean. A long and varied list would include most of the puddle ducks and diver ducks in the Pacific Flyway, scoters, mergansers, Canada geese, black brant, brown pelicans, loons, grebes, coots, belted kingfishers, sandpipers, osprey, marsh hawks, peregrine falcons, bald eagles, and dozens upon dozens of seabirds and songbirds.

Wildlife watchers and photographers can also expect to see harbor seals, the most prevalent of marine mammals on the bay, with two to three hundred present in winter and up to seven hundred or more in summer. They often haul out on beaches or sandbars at low tide, where they're easy to spot. The larger sea lions also occasionally move into the bay to feed on seasonally abundant fish. Land mammals most commonly encountered along the bay fringes are black-tailed deer, raccoon, possum, skunk, and Beechey ground squirrel, among others.

Although the Tillamook Bay bar is often a busy place, with commercial and charter fishing boats heading into and out of port, it's deceptively dangerous and unsafe for small craft about 75 percent of the time. The bar breaks on ebbing tides, with strong currents running up to six knots—sufficient to drag a disabled boat into the breakers. The constantly changing channel poses other potential hazards, as do the outer 100 yards of both jetties, which are submerged. Remember that the commercial and charter fleets consist of fairly large craft, with experienced skippers at the helm who know these waters well. Don't even think of following them out before checking with the Coast Guard or other local experts on current bar conditions. Under the best of weather and water conditions, and in the most seaworthy craft, proceed with extreme caution, and carefully study the bar before deciding to cross.

Everyone planning a trip to the Tillamook Bay area—boat owner or not—should write, phone, or stop by the Tillamook Bay National Estuary Project office on the Garibaldi waterfront for a free copy of the "Boater's Guide to Tillamook Bay." This large brochure provides a recreational map of and information about the bay, its wildlife, and popular bay activities.

U.S. 101, mile 54.4
The Three Graces

These three prominent rocks stand just west of the highway in a rocky intertidal area near the mouth of Tillamook Bay. At low tide, tide pools invite exploration. Interpreters are on duty throughout the summer to answer questions and provide information about the area. Photo opportunities abound.

U.S. 101, mile 54.9
Captain Robert Gray
Historical Marker

A parking lot and picnic area with tables overlook the bay and offer a good view somewhat obscured by trees and shrubs. The marker tells of Gray's stay on Tillamook Bay in August of 1788.

U.S. 101, mile 55.1
Garibaldi
(zip code 97118)

Named after the Italian patriot and general Giuseppe Garibaldi (1807-82), this is Tillamook Bay's port city and home to a commercial fishing fleet, charter operators, a U.S. Coast Guard Station, and 970 permanent residents. Port facilities—including marinas, boat launches, crabbing and fishing piers, and RV parks—lie west of U.S. 101 and are the main attractions to travelers.

U.S. 101, mile 55.3
Garibaldi Pier

Turn west off U.S. 101 on South 12th Street. At the bottom of the hill, turn right and go about 100 yards to a large parking area. Steps and a wheelchair ramp lead to the pier, which provides opportunities for fishing and crabbing. Steps to the beach lead to clam-digging flats. The old Coast Guard boathouse on the pier is now a bait-and-tackle shop and a good place to get fishing, crabbing, and clam-digging information and rent crab rings. A hiking trail begins near the parking lot and leads around the shore to the boat basin area, providing photo opportunities along the way.

U.S. 101, mile 55.5
Tillamook Bay
National Estuary
Project office

Turn west off U.S. 101 on South 7th Street, and drive all the way to the end of the boat basin. The TBNEP office is at 613 Commercial Street, which runs parallel to U.S. 101. Several publications, including the "Boater's Guide To Tillamook Bay," are available at the office. Nearby is a small pier with benches, interpretive signs, and pay binoculars. The pier is a good place for fishing, crabbing, sightseeing, or photography and is lighted at night. The office is open Monday through Friday, 8:00 a.m. to 5:00 p.m.

The Garibaldi
waterfront

West off U.S. 101 on 7th Street, just past the Garibaldi sign, adjacent to the Garibaldi Marina, boaters will find an excellent two-lane launch ramp with docks. Facilities include a large parking lot, drinking water, trash receptacles, and rest rooms with flush toilets and wheelchair access. Transient moorage, bait, tackle, and crabbing gear are available at the marina.

Port of Garibaldi
Boat Ramp

West off U.S. 101, via South 3rd Street, stands a small park and playground with a picnic shelter, tables, and rest rooms with flush toilets and wheelchair access. A steam locomotive and train are on display next to an old station house. It's a good spot for a picnic or rest stop.

U.S. 101, mile 55.8
Lumbermen's
Memorial Park

Turn east off U.S. 101 for access to the Miami River. Parking and bank access for anglers are limited on the lower 5 miles of the river, with small roadside parking areas and paths to the river at miles 0.4, 1.3, 3, and 5.

U.S. 101, mile 56.7
Miami River Road

This small river, only 14 miles long, is open briefly for spring chinook fishing from late May to mid-June. The fall chinook season runs from August through December. It is open most of the year for steelhead angling, but the best fishing is from January to early March. The river also gets a good run of jack salmon in the fall. Chum salmon provide catch-and-release sport from mid-September to mid-November.

U.S. 101, mile 56.9
Miami River

A short trail on the west side of the highway leads from a fair-sized parking area to the bay shore.

U.S. 101, mile 58.1
Parking area

During the salmon season, this floating rest room on Tillamook Bay is as busy as any bait shop or boat ramp.

U.S. 101, mile 58.4
Viewpoint

An estuary interpretive sign stands at a fair-sized parking area along the west side of the highway. From here, travelers get a good view of the bay and extensive mud flats exposed at low tide, with opportunities for watching and photographing wildlife.

U.S. 101, mile 59.4
Bay City
(zip code 97107)

Mainly a residential community, Bay City (population: 1,155) offers access to the bay shore for angling, crabbing, clam digging, and watching or photographing wildlife. An oyster operation, right in town on the west side of the highway, easily identifiable by the huge mounds of oyster shells, also provides photo possibilities.

For southbound travelers, Bay City is the last community with bay or ocean frontage for the remainder of U.S. 101 in Tillamook County. Northbound travelers who haven't left the highway on side trips get their first glimpse of Tillamook Bay here.

U.S. 101, mile 61.2
Alderbrook Loop Road and Kilchis River Road, north access

Exiting east off U.S. 101, this 2.7-mile loop road rejoins the highway at mile 63.1. Use this access for the fastest way to Alderbrook Golf Course. Use the south access for the quickest route to Kilchis River Road.

Alderbrook Golf Course

The course entrance lies 0.8 mile east of U.S. 101. Built in 1918, in a rural setting with the Coast Range foothills and mountains as a backdrop, this is one of the oldest courses on the Oregon coast. Alderbrook is a 5,692-yard, 18-hole, par-69 course with tree-lined fairways. Among its other amenities are a putting green, chipping area, pro shop, resident pro, club rental, pull-cart and gas-cart rental, snack bar, restaurant, and bar. Information: (503) 842-6413

Another short coastal river, the Kilchis tumbles out of the Coast Range and wends its way for about 20 miles to Tillamook Bay. It is an attractive river with decent access for anglers, canoeists, kayakers, photographers, and wildlife observers. Upriver from U.S. 101 are three boat launches and a county park and campgrounds.

The spring chinook season runs less than three weeks, from the end of May to mid-June; the river is open for fall chinook from August through December. The Kilchis is open most of the year for steelhead, and it gets both summer and winter runs. From mid-September to mid-November, the chum salmon fishery is catch and release. From the end of May to mid-September, Kilchis anglers are restricted to the use of artificial lures and flies above tidewater.

U.S. 101, mile 62.8
Kilchis River

Use this access for the shortest route to Parks Landing County Boat Ramp and Kilchis River Road. Use the north access for the quickest trip to the Alderbrook Golf Course.

To reach this paved county boat ramp on the Kilchis River, turn east off U.S. 101, proceed 0.1 mile, turn north off Alderbrook Loop Road, and continue another 0.1 mile to the ramp, a good-sized parking area, and chemical toilets. Note: Motorboats are not allowed upriver from this point.

U.S. 101, mile 63.1
Alderbrook Loop Road and Kilchis River Road, south access

Parks Landing

Go east on Alderbrook Loop Road one mile to connect with this road, which provides access to the Kilchis River, boat ramps, and a county park.

Kilchis River Road

At mile 0.7 on Kilchis River Road, turn right, cross the bridge over the river, and turn left into the parking area. There's a good gravel ramp here and some bank access for angling.

Mapes Creek County Boat Ramp

Set in the forested foothills of the Coast Range, this park has good river access. The entrance is on Kilchis River Road, mile 3.6; the campground and earthen boat ramp are at mile 4. The campground includes 40 primitive campsites with tables and fire pits or fire rings, as well as hiking/biking sites. There are picnic areas, trash receptacles, and rest rooms with flush toilets. Information: (503) 842-6694.

Kilchis River County Park

On the east side of U.S. 101, just north of the Tillamook city limits, stands the county's main attraction apart from its natural wonders. Also known as "The Cheese Factory," this cooperative of about one hundred and fifty Tillamook County dairy farmers attracts almost a million people every year who stop to tour the cheese-making facilities, view slide shows and exhibits, visit the museum, and shop for cheese and other products. In addition

U.S. 101, mile 63.7
Tillamook County Creamery Association

MUST STOP

The Tillamook Creamery Association facilities, just north of Tillamook.

to a cheese-sampling counter, where visitors can taste a variety of fine products, the complex includes a gift shop, deli, fudge counter, ice cream counters, and racks full of jerky, smoked meats, and gourmet food items. This is a *must stop* and a good place to stock up on great cheeses and other foods. It's open daily: from mid-June to mid-September, 8:00 a.m. to 8:00 p.m.; from mid-September to mid-June, 8:00 a.m. to 6:00 p.m. Information: (503) 815-1300.

Tillamook County Chamber of Commerce Visitor Center

On the east side of the highway, at the south end of the Tillamook County Creamery Association parking lot, this is the place to stop for maps, brochures, and firsthand information about all of Tillamook County. The center is open Monday through Saturday, 9:00 a.m. to 5:00 p.m., and Sunday, 10:00 a.m. to 4:00 p.m.

U.S. 101, mile 63.8
Bay Breeze Golf

This par-three layout is on the east side of Highway 101, just south of the visitor center. Turn east on Latimer Road to reach the 1,061-yard, nine-hole, par-27 course that includes a driving range, putting green, snack bar, pro shop with resident pro. Rental clubs and both electric and pull carts are available. Pro shop: (503) 842-1166.

U.S. 101, mile 64.1
Wilson River

The Wilson rises in the Coast Range and runs through forested canyons on its way to Tillamook Bay. It's one of the most popular and productive rivers in Tillamook County, perhaps in part because of its accessibility. In its lower 10 miles, it's a good drift-boat stream, with several launch and haul-out sites. In its upper reaches, it offers better bank access than most coastal rivers.

Spring chinook season runs from April to mid-June, with the best angling usually in June. The river is open for the larger fall run of chinook from August through December, with peak fishing in October and November. The Wilson is open all year for steelhead angling, and it gets both summer and winter runs. Although peak periods run from May through August and December through March, anglers can catch Wilson River steelhead any month of the year, water conditions permitting.

This river, however, isn't just for fishing. It's a pretty river, especially in its upper reaches, now that the old Tillamook Burn is a maturing forest. The Wilson invites exploration and demands the photographer's attention.

Tillamook is not only the county's largest city (population: 4,400) and seat of government, but also the gateway to some of the most scenic areas and popular attractions in Tillamook County. The bay is only a short drive from anywhere in town. Side trips from Tillamook take travelers into lush river valleys and forested mountains or along the craggy coast of the Three Capes Loop.

**U.S. 101,
mile 64.1 to 67.2
Tillamook**
(zip code 97141)

U.S. 101 divides in the city center: Main Avenue is the southbound segment and Pacific Avenue is northbound. The primary east-west highway is State Route 6, also known as the Wilson River Highway, which extends 75 miles from Tillamook to Portland.

The downtown shopping area extends south from 1st Street for several blocks along Main and Pacific Avenues and adjacent streets. North of 1st Street, along both sides of Highway 101 for about 2 miles, motels, supermarkets, and stores see to any traveler's needs.

Turn east off U.S. 101 at the traffic light (Shilo Inn on the east side, Fred Meyer on the west), and take this loop 3 miles to connect with State Route 6, east of the city.

U.S. 101, mile 64.5
Wilson River Loop Road

Turn east on Wilson Loop Road, and drive 1.9 miles to reach a paved ramp on the Wilson River. The parking area, ramp, and chemical toilet are on the east side of the road at the south end of the bridge.

Sollie Smith County Boat Ramp

This small city park with picnic tables, a trash receptacle, and a paved boat ramp on Hoquarton Slough is right downtown, on the west side of U.S. 101 at Front Street.

U.S. 101, mile 65.5
Marine Park

The Tillamook Pioneer Museum (on northbound Highway 101 at 2nd Street, one block east of southbound 101) is the biggest and best of its kind on the coast and a *must stop* for history buffs. It occupies the old Tillamook County Courthouse, built in 1905, with three floors of displays to examine. Among the many exhibits are Indian artifacts, a 1902 Holsman Horseless Carriage, a 1909 Buick, a large antique gun collection, and a

U.S. 101, mile 65.6
Tillamook Pioneer Museum

MUST STOP

huge natural history display, as well as fire-fighting, logging, and cheese-making equipment. There are tools and utensils from the pioneer era, relics from the old Tillamook Naval Air Station, and much more. No history buff should miss this fine museum, which is open Monday through Saturday, 8:00 a.m. to 5:00 p.m., and Sunday, 11:00 a.m. to 5:00 p.m. The museum is closed Thanksgiving Day, Christmas Day, and Mondays from October 1 to May 1. Information: (503) 842-4553.

U.S. 101, mile 65.7
State Route 6
junction

The Wilson River Highway, State Route 6, is the main west-to-east road out of Tillamook, extending 75 miles over the Coast Range to Portland. To reach this highway, turn east off Highway 101 onto 3rd Street in downtown Tillamook.

Three Capes Scenic Loop, north access

Turn west on 3rd Street to reach the south and west shores of Tillamook Bay, Bayocean Spit, the ocean and beaches, Cape Meares, Cape Lookout, Cape Kiwanda, and other coastal attractions. (For details and attractions, see "Side Trip: Three Capes Scenic Loop" on page 107.)

U.S. 101, mile 65.8
Carnahan Park

This city park with a paved boat ramp and dock on the Trask River is at the west end of 5th Street, seven blocks from southbound Highway 101. Park amenities include a small playground, picnic area with tables and a grill, drinking water, and rest rooms with flush toilets and wheelchair access.

U.S. 101, mile 66.2
Tillamook River Road
and Tillamook River,
north access

Turn west off southbound U.S. 101 on 12th Street, then immediately south (left) on Tillamook River Road. Stay on Tillamook River Road for 1.3 miles to the bridge over the Tillamook River. At the south end of the bridge, turn west on Fraser Road, which flanks the river for 2.3 miles and terminates at the Netarts Highway. Along the way are several small parking areas on the north side of the road and good bank access for anglers, wildlife watchers, and photographers.

Burton Fraser County Boat Ramp

Just after the turn onto Fraser Road, turn north into the gravel parking area. The large parking area and paved ramp lie at the southwest end of the bridge and provide boater access to the lower Tillamook River and upper Tillamook Bay.

U.S. 101, mile 67.8
Trask River

This beautiful river heads in the Coast Range about 50 miles from Tillamook Bay. The Trask is a fine river, coursing through lovely rural country and forested mountains. Anglers, boaters, canoeists, and kayakers will find several launch sites along the lower reaches. There are plenty of suitable photographic subjects along and near the river, hiking trails, and a lovely county park with campgrounds.

The Trask is a popular river for salmon and steelhead angling and a favorite of fly casters. Spring chinook season runs from April to mid-June, with the best fishing toward the end of the season. The river is open for fall chinook from August through December, but angling for these big fish doesn't really get underway until October. The season for fin-clipped coho is from mid-September through October, upriver from the Highway 101 bridge. The Trask is open all year for steelhead fishing, and anglers catch some fish every month of the year, water conditions permitting. The best fishing, however is during the winter run, from December through March.

U.S. 101, mile 68
Lower Trask County
Boat Ramp

Turn east off Highway 101 onto Long Prairie Road, drive 0.3 mile, and turn north at the boat-ramp sign. Continue 0.2 mile to the gravel parking area and earthen ramp on the lower Trask River, suitable for drift boats, cartoppers, canoes, and kayaks.

Tillamook Air
Museum

Turn east off Highway 101 onto Long Prairie Road, drive 1.6 miles, and follow the signs to this imposing building. The museum is housed in the most dominating landmark in the Tillamook area: a World War II U.S. Navy blimp hangar. One of two such hangars remaining (the other burned to the ground in August 1992), it's the largest wooden building in the world. Built in 1942-43, the hangar is 1,072 feet long, 296 feet wide, and 192 feet high, encompassing an area of more than seven acres. The building would be worth seeing in its own right if it stood empty, but it houses a terrific museum and collection of historic aircraft, which the Experimental Aircraft Association ranked among the top five collections in the nation. Among

It's impossible to miss the turn onto Long Prairie Road for the Tillamook Air Museum. A Navy jet points the way.

the more than three dozen aircraft visitors can view up close are a variety of civilian airplanes and such famous warbirds as the PBY-5A Catalina, F4U Corsair, P-38 Lightning, P-51 Mustang, B-25 Mitchell, F-14 Tomcat, Mk-VIII Spitfire, Bf-109 Messerschmitt, and many more. This is a *must stop* for history and aircraft buffs and any family with kids, especially considering that those under 13 get in free. It's open daily, except Thanksgiving and Christmas: from Memorial Day weekend through Labor Day weekend, 9:00 a.m. to 6:00 p.m.; the rest of the year, from 10:00 a.m. to 5:00 p.m. Information: (503) 842-1130.

U.S. 101, mile 69.2
Tillamook River Road and Tillamook River, south access

Turn west off Highway 101; then veer north (right) onto Tillamook River Road. Drive 2.2 miles and turn west on Fraser Road at the south end of the bridge over the Tillamook River. The road extends along the river for 2.3 miles to the Netarts Highway. Several small parking areas along the north side of the road provide bank access for anglers, birders, and photographers.

Burton Fraser County Boat Ramp, south access

Just after the turn onto Fraser Road, a large gravel parking area and paved boat ramp lie at the southwest end of the bridge, providing access to the lower Tillamook River and upper Tillamook Bay for anglers, boaters, canoeists, kayakers, birders, and photographers.

U.S. 101, mile 70.6
Rest area

A small rest area on the west side of the highway has picnic tables, drinking water, and rest rooms with flush toilets and wheelchair access.

U.S. 101, mile 72.6
Munson Creek Falls State Natural Area

Turn east off U.S. 101, and drive 1.5 miles to the parking area and two short trails leading to the waterfall. Munson Creek tumbles over the mountainside 266 feet to the floor of the canyon, making this the tallest waterfall in the Coast Range. The lower trail follows the creek for a quarter-mile and leads to the base of the falls. The slightly longer and steeper upper trail gradually ascends to an elevation of 250 feet above the creekbed and offers a spectacular view of the falls. The trails are well maintained, and the upper trail certainly offers the better view. At several spots, however, the canyon wall drops away abruptly at the trail's edge, so the upper trail is not a place for small children.

The park, with its magnificent waterfall and creek meandering through stands of ancient Sitka spruce and western red cedar, is a good spot for a picnic or rest break. It has picnic tables, fireplaces, a trash receptacle, and chemical toilets. Parking can be tight, though, and there's no trailer turnaround.

The Three Capes Scenic Loop lies about 6 miles west of the highway, via Sand Lake Road. (For details and attractions, see "Side Trip: Three Capes Scenic Loop" on page 107.)

U.S. 101, mile 76.8
Sand Lake Road,
Three Capes Scenic
Loop access

Turn east on Blaine Road at the sign for the Upper Nestucca Recreation Area. Drive 0.6 mile to Bixby Road, turn right, and continue 1.3 miles to the end of Bixby Road, where there's a small parking area and earthen ramp on the Nestucca River. It's a good spot for launching drift boats, canoes, or kayaks.

U.S. 101, mile 80.3
Bixby County Boat
Ramp

On the east side of the highway is a small parking area and paved ramp on the Nestucca River. Although the *Oregon Boating Facilities Guide* lists this as an improved ramp, erosion has taken its toll on the paved portion of the ramp and the earthen approach, calling for careful launching of small craft. The wayside also has some bank access for angling.

U.S. 101, mile 82.9
Farmer Creek
Wayside and Boat
Ramp

This big river runs 55 miles from its Coast Range headwaters to its mouth near Pacific City. Highway 101 stays near the river from Hebo south to Cloverdale. The river meanders through farmlands, woodlands, and meadows and presents a pretty picture at nearly every bend.

U.S. 101, mile 84.1
Nestucca River

For purposes of regulation, the river is divided into four zones, with the uppermost closed to angling and the lower three having different seasonal restrictions. Although most of the lower river opens to spring chinook fishing from April through mid-June, fish don't generally show up until late in the season. Fall chinook fishing begins in late August on the bay and mid-September on the lower river. The season extends through December, but the best fishing is October and November. Most of the lower river is open all year for steelhead fishing, with fish in the river most of the year. The summer run is from April to August; winter action starts in mid-November and extends into March.

This tiny town, named after nearby Mount Hebo, doesn't amount to much more than a few houses, an intersection, a ranger station, and a sporting goods store that's a favorite stop for anglers. Highway 101 takes a sharp turn due west here, and heads toward the coast, following the Nestucca River.

U.S. 101, mile 84.8
Hebo
(zip code 97122)

This highway heads southeast off U.S. 101, crosses the Coast Range, and makes its way to Salem and beyond.

U.S. 101, mile 84.9
State Route 22
junction
Hebo Ranger District

Turn east on State Route 22, and drive 0.3 mile to the station. Stop here for maps and information about the Siuslaw National Forest—especially trails, campgrounds, and other outdoor attractions in the Hebo District of Tillamook County. The office is open Monday through Friday, 8:00 a.m. to 4:30 p.m.

For as long as the old Hebo Inn building stands, with its whacky backward ens, Highway 101 travelers will know when they've reached this little burg.

U.S. 101, mile 85.4
Three Rivers County
Boat Ramp

Turn west on Hanson Road, drive 0.3 mile to the fork, and bear right. The parking area and gravel ramp on the Nestucca River are another 0.2 mile.

U.S. 101, mile 87.3
Cloverdale
(zip code 97112)

This tiny rural community isn't much more than a bend in the highway on the Nestucca River and perhaps a place to stop for a hamburger and a malt or pie and coffee.

U.S. 101, mile 90.3
Three Capes Scenic
Loop, south junction

Turn west here to reach Nestucca Bay, Pacific City, Cape Kiwanda, Sand Lake Recreation Area, Cape Lookout, Cape Meares, and other attractions along the loop route. (For details and attractions, see "Side Trip: Three Capes Scenic Loop: on page 107.)

U.S. 101, mile 91.3
County Road 130
(Little Nestucca
Road)

This road leads east off Highway 101, follows the course of the Little Nestucca River, and joins State Route 22 near the small community of Dolph.

U.S. 101, mile 91.5
Little Nestucca River

There are two sides…
…to Cloverdale's clever sign.

This pretty little river heads in Yamhill County, flows westward through southwest Tillamook County, and joins with the Nestucca River south of Pacific City to form Nestucca Bay. The lush valley of the Little Nestucca is home to black-tailed deer, Roosevelt elk, and a bevy of smaller mammals. Great blue herons

wade for food in the river's shallows, and Canada geese graze in the meadows and farm fields. In spring and fall the skies and waters are filled with migrating birds. So this is a place to pause, search, watch, and burn a little film.

The river is popular with anglers. Although the fall chinook season is open from August through December, the salmon don't show up until the first rains of autumn, usually in October. The river is closed to steelhead angling from April to late May, but is open the rest of the year. Steelhead angling is at its best during December and January.

Turn east off the highway, go 0.2 mile on Meda Loop, and turn left into an ample parking area. The paved ramp is a good spot for launching any kind of craft for fishing on the Little Nestucca, exploring the peaceful estuary, and observing the area's wildlife. The pit toilets have wheelchair access.

U.S. 101, mile 92
Little Nestucca
County Boat Ramp

At the top of a long grade, a fair-sized parking lot and viewpoint with benches and a wheelchair ramp stand on the west side of the highway. This is a pleasant spot for a rest break with views of the Pacific north and south.

U.S. 101, mile 94.1
Winema Wayfinding
Point

Turn east on Hawk Creek Road to reach the clubhouse at this beautiful creek-valley course with tree-lined fairways. The 2,700-yard, 9-hole, par-34 course includes a putting green and pro shop with clubs, pull carts, and electric carts for rent. Snacks, beer, and other beverages are available; restaurants and lounges are nearby. Pro shop: (503) 392-4120.

U.S. 101, mile 96.9
Hawk Creek Golf
Course

The tiny village of Neskowin (population: 200) nudges the north face of Cascade Head and hides the beach and breakers from passersby onHighway 101. Out of sight, however, doesn't mean out of reach. The beach is just a short walk from the state recreation site parking lot.

U.S. 101, mile 97.1
Neskowin
(zip code 97149)

The village and creek that runs through it were originally called Slab Creek, for an early shipwreck that deposited its cargo of slabwood on the beach. Slab Creek was renamed Neskowin Creek in 1925, and the locality came to be known as Neskowin (pronounced ness-*cow*-in), an Indian word meaning "plenty fish."

With excellent trails nearby at Cascade Head and a quiet stretch of old Highway 101 to explore, hiking and biking are popular area pastimes. These are also the best means for negotiating the narrow streets that wind through Neskowin's beachy residential area west of the highway: big motorhomes and travel trailers are best left at the state recreation site parking lot.

Two distinctly different but equally challenging 9-hole golf courses flank Highway 101: Hawk Creek, with its hills and trees, to the east (at mile 96.9) and Neskowin Beach, laid out in tricky creek bottoms, to the west. A great way to get in 18 holes is to play the first 9 at one course and a second 9 at the other.

Neskowin Beach Golf Course

On Hawk Avenue, west of Highway 101, this 3,012-yard, 9-hole, par-36 course is open from April to November, depending on the timing and length of the rainy season, which floods the lowland creeks in the winter. Amenities include a putting green, pro shop, resident pro, snack bar with beer and wine, and electric-cart rental. Pro shop: (503) 392-3377.

Neskowin Beach State Recreation Site

Just west of U.S. 101 lies a large parking area with picnic tables on Neskowin Creek, trash receptacles, and rest rooms with flush toilets. A paved path leads south along the creek to Proposal Rock and a broad white-sand beach that stretches north for 5 miles to Nestucca Bay. The area is popular for all beach activities, including hiking, beach combing, surf fishing, and photography.

Proposal Rock

This picturesque vegetated hump stands in the surf near the mouth of Neskowin Creek. It was named by Sarah Page, the village's first postmaster, when Charlie Gage proposed to Page's daughter, Della, near the rock. Use the path that follows the creek to the beach. Access to the rock is limited to low tide.

U.S. 101, mile 98.9
Slab Creek Road

East off Highway 101, this is the north access to the Old Highway 101 Scenic Route, also known as the Neskowin Scenic Drive, which loops 10 miles through the Siuslaw National Forest and Cascade Head Experimental Forest, with interpretive signs along the way, and rejoins U.S. 101 at mile 103.8 in Lincoln County.

U.S. 101, mile 99.4
Cascade Head Traverse, north trailhead

On the west side of the highway is a small parking area, not suitable for large RVs, near the trailhead. From here, the trail extends 2.5 miles to Forest Service Road #1861 or 6 miles to the south trailhead at Three Rocks Road. The trails in this system cross creek bottoms, open grasslands, and forests of spruce, hemlock, and red alder, and lead to cliffs overlooking the Pacific Ocean. Hikers might encounter deer, squirrels, hawks, owls, woodpeckers, and other headland denizens. A trail guide is available from the Hebo District Ranger Station (see under "Information" on page 122.)

U.S. 101, mile 102.7
Tillamook County/ Lincoln County Line

Side Trip: Three Capes Scenic Loop

Travelers in a rush to get through Tillamook County should stay on Highway 101, but those who want to enjoy the entire Tillamook coast and visit several *must stop* sites should leisurely drive the 35.3-mile Three Capes Scenic Loop. Southbound travelers can join the loop by turning west on 3rd Street at mile 65.7 in downtown Tillamook. Those heading north from Lincoln County should turn west at mile 90.3. The loop consists of a several connected state and county routes, each with its own roadside milepost markers, which are confusing and useless for people traveling the entire length of the loop. The mileposts and directions that follow do not coincide with the various roadside milepost markers; rather, they are the measured distances from mile 0 at the north end of the loop, the intersection of 3rd Street and U.S. 101 in Tillamook, and ascend from north to south.

The loop crosses the Trask River here. (For details on the river, see U.S. 101, mile 67.8 on page 100.)

Three Capes Loop, mile 0.7
Trask River

The loop crosses the Tillamook River here. Upriver from the bridge, the lower Tillamook offers some photographic possibilities, especially at high tide in calm weather, when the lush riverside vegetation is still and the old marina building reflects in the river's mirror surface. (For details about the Tillamook River, see U.S. 101, mile 66.2 on page 100.)

Three Capes Loop, mile 1.5
Tillamook River

Turn west here to skirt the south end of Tillamook Bay, stay on the loop, and reach the Bayocean Spit, Meares Lake, and Cape Meares, named after eighteenth-century seafaring trader and explorer John Meares. This route appears on some maps as Bayocean Road and others as Three Capes Scenic Loop.

Three Capes Loop, mile 1.7
Bayocean Drive junction

Travelers wanting the fastest, most direct route to Oceanside, Netarts, Netarts Bay, and points south on the Three Capes Loop should go straight here, instead of turning west onto Bayocean Drive. This route, however, bypasses the Cape Meares area.

Netarts Highway

On the east side of the Netarts Highway, 0.2 mile south of the Bayocean Drive turnoff, is a small rest area that provides access to the lower Tillamook River for fishing, wildlife observation, and photography. A wheelchair-accessible boardwalk extends for a short distance from the parking lot to a riverside fishing and wildlife-viewing dock. The facility also has a trash receptacle and vault toilets with wheelchair access.

Tillamook Tidewater Access

Three Capes Loop, mile 3
Memaloose Point County Boat Ramp

This excellent facility on the north side of the loop is popular with anglers, clam diggers, boaters, kayakers, and others looking for access to the lower Tillamook River and upper Tillamook Bay. It features a large parking area, two-lane paved boat ramp with a dock, bank access, trash receptacle, and vault toilets.

Three Capes Loop, mile 6.6
Bayocean Spit

Also known as the Bayocean Peninsula, this broad finger of sand, shrubs, and trees extends north to the mouth of Tillamook Bay and separates the bay from the ocean, but it hasn't always done so successfully. Construction and extension of the north jetty at the mouth of Tillamook Bay in 1917 and 1932, respectively, severely changed local currents, which ate away at the beach, destroying much of the spit and the community of Bay Ocean, a popular resort town of more than one hundred buildings, established in 1906, that was reduced to rubble and driftwood by 1932.

In 1952 the powerful Pacific breached the southern end of the spit with a mile-wide opening, transforming it into an island. Fortunately, the 1965 completion of the south jetty reversed the process and allowed the ocean to rebuild the beach and spit into the splendid natural area it is today. Visitors occasionally come across rusty pipes sticking out of the sand, the only remaining reminders of the resort community that once flourished here.

A gravel road leads north off the loop 0.9 mile along a dike to a fairly large gravel parking area with a trash receptacle and chemical toilets. Hiking and horse trails offer access to Bayocean Spit, Lake Meares, and Tillamook Bay.

The lake attracts good numbers of waterfowl and other birdlife. In fact the entire Bayocean Spit area is a magnet to all

Cape Meares Beach and Bayocean Spit

manner of birdlife, from shore birds and wading birds to gulls, terns, brown pelicans, hawks, eagles, and songbirds. Bring binoculars and keep cameras at the ready.

This pretty lake of about 120 acres is shallow and heavily vegetated by late summer, and most of the shoreline is brushy. The dike road along the east end of the lake provides limited access with a parking area at the end. The best bank access is along Three Capes Loop, where there's also roadside parking, a fishing dock, and a small boat ramp. Watercraft offer the best access of all, and the lake is ideally suited to the use of small cartop and trailer boats, canoes, kayaks, float tubes, and similar craft.

Three Capes Loop, mile 6.6 to 6.9
Cape Meares Lake

The lake attracts anglers who come to fish mainly for rainbow and cutthroat trout that the Oregon Department of Fish and Wildlife stocks from mid-March through early May. The agency also releases excess steelhead hatchery brood stock from time to time, so anglers always have a chance to tie into a lunker. Resident warmwater species include largemouth bass, bluegill, and brown bullhead.

Three Capes Loop turns south here and climbs to Cape Meares.

Three Capes Loop, mile 6.9
Cape Meares Loop Road junction
Cape Meares Lake Boat Ramp

At the west end of the lake and junction with Cape Meares Loop Road, a small earthen ramp provides boat access to the lake. There's limited trailer parking along Three Capes Loop.

Instead of turning south on Cape Meares Loop Road, go straight (west) 0.6 mile to a small parking area with easy access to a cobble and sand beach popular with hikers, beachcombers, and anglers. Another small parking area with beach access is 0.3 mile beyond, at the west end of Pacific Avenue.

Cape Meares Beach Access

Beneath the brow of Cape Meares, broad beach and pounding surf extend for miles along the western edge of Bayocean Spit. This is a great place to slip into the straps of a daypack stocked with lunch, trail mix, beverages, and plenty of film for a day of hiking and photographing unlimited subjects. The spit is also a beachcomber's delight, especially after big winter storms.

Lying along the northwest side of Cape Meares, adjacent to the state park, the national wildlife refuge protects one of the few remaining stands of old-growth forest on the Oregon coast; some of these trees are hundreds of years old and stand more than 200 feet tall. This forest provides important habitat for endangered and threatened birds, such as northern spotted owls, marbled murrelets, and bald eagles. Also to be seen within the

Three Capes Loop, mile 8.8
Cape Meares National Wildlife Refuge

Cape Meares Light, at Cape Meares State Scenic Viewpoint

refuge are pelagic cormorants, common murres, and tufted puffins, present in great numbers during the spring nesting season. The Oregon Coast Trail winds through the refuge and leads into the state park.

Cape Meares State Scenic Viewpoint

This is the northernmost of Tillamook County's famous Three Capes and a *must stop*. The facility that occupies the west end of the cape has more than 3 miles of trails with spectacular views of the coast and interpretive signs along the way. An interpretive kiosk stands adjacent to the parking lot. From there, a short hike west on a paved path leads to the historic Cape Meares Light. An easy hike along a trail in the opposite direction leads to the unique "Octopus Tree."

Although the squat tower of the Cape Meares Light stands only 40 feet tall, its placement on the west face of the 200-foot-high cape gave it a focal plane 217 feet above the ocean and a seaward beam visible to ships more than 21 miles out. The light, completed in 1890, was a reliable sentinel of the Tillamook coast for 73 years. It was decommissioned in 1963 and today serves as a gift shop, historic relic open for tours, and a superb if somewhat tricky subject for photographers.

The unusual "Octopus Tree" is a huge Sitka spruce with no central trunk, but several outstretched, low-lying branches from 3 to 5 feet in diameter. According to legend, Indians shaped the branches when the spruce was young to create a sacred burial tree that could hold the canoes of their deceased chiefs.

The "Octopus Tree," at Cape Meares State Scenic Viewpoint

This park is a great place for a pleasing rest stop or vigorous hike through old-growth spruce forest and along 200-foot cliffs seasonally occupied by nesting seabirds. Its moods change with the seasons and the weather, making it ideal for visits and revisits any time of year. Come in the spring to watch the abundant birdlife, summer and fall for unbeatable weather and photo opportunities, and winter for watching migrating gray whales. Information: (503) 842-2244.

The east trailhead is at road's edge, on the west side, and is marked. A parking area lies less than 100 yards south.

Three Capes Loop, mile 9.2
Cape Meares Lighthouse Trail

With parking areas on both sides of the road, a well-maintained trail with wood steps and gravel landings makes this an easy hike down a steep slope to a terrific stretch of beach and tide pools. Photographers should like this stop.

Three Capes Loop, mile 10.1
Beach access

Go north from here to get to Oceanside, south to reach Netarts.

Three Capes Loop, mile 11.2
Oceanside junction

A tiny residential and beach-getaway village (population: 250), planted on a steep slope overlooking Three Arch Rocks and strung out along a beach as broad as they come, Oceanside is a peaceful place to escape the pace of the twenty-first century. With Cape Meares to the north, Cape Lookout to the south, and Netarts Bay just down the road, Oceanside is in the middle of a sightseer's and photographer's paradise.

Oceanside
(zip code 97134)

Oceanside Beach
State Recreation Site

About 0.3 mile north of the Three Capes Loop, two ample parking areas right in town overlook the broad white-sand beach and Three Arch Rocks. A paved path makes for easy access to a beach that's popular with summer strollers and surfers and winter beachcombers and agate hunters. The park has trash receptacles and rest rooms with flush toilets.

Three Arch Rocks
National Wildlife
Refuge

Lying about a half-mile offshore from Oceanside, this group of rocks and islets is one of the most recognizable landmarks along the Oregon coast. Among the abundant birdlife here are both Brandt's and pelagic cormorants, a huge breeding colony of common murres, and Oregon's largest colony of tufted puffins. Marine mammals using the area are Pacific harbor seals, California sea lions, and the only breeding colony of Steller sea lions on Oregon's north coast.

The refuge is off limits to the public, and from May 1 through September 15 each year, a buffer zone closes all waters within 500 feet of the refuge to prevent disturbance of the wildlife.

Three Capes Loop, mile 11.4
Symon's Point State Scenic Viewpoint

Parking areas on both sides of the road allow travelers to stop for good views and photo opportunities to the north of Oceanside and Three Arch Rocks, to the south of the beach and Cape Lookout. This is also a popular surfing area.

Three Capes Loop, mile 11.5
Viewpoint

On the west side of the road is a small parking area with enough room for only one or two vehicles. Stop here for photo opportunities and a good view of the beach and Netarts Spit.

This small (population: 200) but growing residential and vacation community lies along the east shore of Netarts Bay and serves as headquarters for those who travel to the area for camping, crabbing, clam digging, wildlife watching, sightseeing, photography, and beach activities. The area's main attraction is Netarts Bay.

Three Capes Loop, mile 13.1
Netarts
(zip code 97143)

A narrow, club-shaped stretch of sand known as Netarts Spit pokes north into the Pacific from the vicinity of Cape Lookout State Park (mile 17.4) and nearly touches the coast at Netarts, almost enclosing Netarts Bay. From its marshy south end to its jaws at the north, the shallow bay is about 7 miles long and full of sandbars and tidal flats. Even the main channel is little more than 10 feet deep at high tide. Three Capes Loop flanks the east shore of the bay, providing roadside access for angling, clam digging, wildlife observation, and photography. Those towing boats can launch them at an excellent facility at the northeast end of the bay. Bait, tackle, rental boats, and crabbing gear are readily available.

Three Capes Loop, mile 13.7
Netarts Bay

No major rivers drain the bay's 14-square-mile watershed. Rather, about a dozen creeks deliver a relatively small amount of fresh water to the bay, making it a marine-dominated estuary, saltier than others. Chum salmon enter the bay in the fall and spawn in some of the small creeks. A few coho also move into the bay then, possibly with small numbers of anadromous trout. None of these fish arrive in sufficient numbers to support a fishery, so the bay is closed to salmon, steelhead, and trout angling. The bay fishery mainly centers around perch, greenling, sole, and rockfish in the spring and early summer, with the best catches made at the northern end of the bay, near the mouth. A few skilled boaters cross the bar when conditions are favorable to fish nearby reefs for rockfish, halibut, and various bottom species, but this is no place for the novice. There are no jetties at the bay entrance and no Coast Guard standing by. Even small-boat operators who remain inside the bay with no intention of crossing the bar should stay well upbay from the bar on ebbing tides, when swift currents can tug a small craft into the surf and flip it.

If fishing doesn't rank among the main attractions on Netarts Bay, crabbing and clam digging certainly do. The estuary's relatively high salinity and low freshwater input make for good crabbing all year. The major bay clams—gaper, butter, cockle, littleneck, and soft-shell—inhabit the flats, and diggers even find a few razor clams at the northwest end of Netarts Spit.

Wildlife watchers and photographers find the estuary particularly attractive. Pacific harbor seals cruise and feed in the channels and haul out on sandbars and beaches. Black brandt spend the winter dining on the abundant eelgrass, while brown pelicans show up in summer for the seafood buffet. Spring and fall are good times for watching and photographing waterfowl and other migratory birdlife. Herons, cormorants, gulls, and kingfishers are year-round residents.

Netarts Landing

Follow the signs for Three Capes Loop, and turn northwest into the large parking area. The facility includes an excellent paved ramp with a dock, picnic areas with tables, and rest rooms with flush toilets and wheelchair access. A gravel road at the bay end of the parking lot leads downbay (north) for about 200 yards, providing bayshore access and parking.

Three Capes Loop, mile 14.2
Bayshore RV Park and Marina

This private facility on the east side of the road has a parking area and paved ramp providing easy access to the bay. Rental boats are available.

Roadside parking and bay access

Ample roadside parking on the west side of the loop provides easy access to popular clam-digging flats on the bay.

Three Capes Loop, mile 15.5
Whiskey Creek Fish Hatchery

Tillamook Anglers, a nonprofit organization, operates this hatchery, located on the west side of the road, at the south end of Netarts Bay. Volunteers rear 100,000 spring chinook salmon here every year and release them into Tillamook County streams. Visitors can tour the modern facility, feed the fish, hike a trail with interpretive signs, and enjoy a picnic at one of the tables in the parklike setting.

Three Capes Loop, mile 17.4
Cape Lookout State Park

MUST STOP

This big park lies west of the Three Capes Loop, is a *must stop*, and comprises the rain forest and rugged cliffs of the cape, as well as the sandy beaches north and south of the cape. Within the park are a large campground, a splendid day-use area, more than 8 miles of hiking trails, a quarter-mile nature trail with interpretive signs, and an amphitheater where evening programs are held during the summer.

Three Capes Loop, mile 17.8
Cape Lookout State Park Campground and Day Use Area

Turn west and follow the appropriate signs for the short drive to the campground or day-use area. The campground has 54 full-hookup sites, including two with wheelchair access; one site with water and electricity; 10 yurts; and 185 tent sites with water nearby—all with tables and grills. Other campground amenities include a hiker/biker camp, firewood, tank dump, showers, and rest room with flush toilets and wheelchair access. The day-use area has beautiful picnic sites with tables and grills in wind-protected wooded areas. The park also features hiking and biking trails, a nature trail, a fish habitat project, and easy beach access. A wide bike lane leads south from the entrance along Three Capes Loop, 1.7 miles to the Cape Lookout Trailhead. Information: (503) 842-4981 or (800) 551-6949. Reservations: (800) 452-5687.

Two parking areas on the west side of the road offer one of the grandest views on the Oregon coast. From here, see and photograph sweeping vistas to the north that include Netarts Bay, Netarts Spit, Oceanside, Cape Meares, and Three Arch Rocks National Wildlife Refuge. This is a *must stop* for every sightseer and photographer.

Three Capes Loop, mile 17.9
Anderson's Viewpoint

A fairly large parking lot stands on the west side of the road, near the trailhead and trail-orientation sign. The trail leads 2.5 miles through old-growth forest to the western end of the cape, where there are commanding ocean views and opportunities for whale watching in season.

Three Capes Loop, mile 19.5
Cape Lookout Trailhead

A small turnout off the west side of the road leads to a sign that provides history of and information about the Sand Lake dunes.

Three Capes Loop, mile 21.8
Sand Lake Information Panel

This road leads west about 6 miles to U.S. 101 at mile 76.8. To continue on Three Capes Loop, turn south at the junction.

Three Capes Loop, mile 22.7
Sand Lake Road junction

Turn west at the Sand Lake Store, and drive 2.25 miles on Galloway Road to reach this large recreation area popular with off-road vehicle (ORV) enthusiasts, where there are three campgrounds with a total of 241 campsites. Sandbeach Campground is open from mid-March to October and has 101 tent/RV sites with tables and fireplaces. East Dunes Camp Area has 100 sites and is open all year. West Winds Camp Area, with 40 sites, is also open year around. Campground amenities include picnic areas, drinking water, trash receptacles, vault toilets, and rest rooms with flush toilets.

Three Capes Loop, mile 23.6
Sand Lake Recreation Area

ORV operators have access to sand dunes and a section of beach that's open all year. Horses are also allowed in the recreation area, but not in the campground or camp areas. Equestrians should use the open sand or fishing day-use area to unload and load.

The fishing day-use area has a parking lot and provides access to the ocean and mouth of Sand Lake, which is not a lake at all, but rather the shallow estuary of Sand Creek. The estuary is closed to steelhead fishing from April through the end of May and open the rest of the year, but fishing is mainly a late-winter proposition. Perch and the occasional flounder also show up in the catch in spring and summer. Crabbing and the best angling is from boats, and there's a launch ramp at nearby Whalen Island State Natural Area.

This is a very popular recreation area, and to prevent overuse on major summer weekends, permits are required for Memorial Day, Independence Day, and Labor Day. Some reservation sites are available. For information, write or stop by the Hebo Ranger District office, or phone (503) 392-3161; reservations: (877) 444-6777.

Three Capes Loop, mile 26.1
Whalen Island State Natural Area

Turn west and cross the bridge onto the island. This beautiful park, surrounded by the Sand Lake estuary, has 27 primitive campsites with tables, fireplaces, and water. The park also has a dump station, trash receptacles, rest rooms with flush toilets, and a gravel boat ramp. This is a fine spot for a picnic or rest stop and a good place to watch and photograph birdlife on the estuary. Information: (800) 551-6949.

Three Capes Loop, mile 26.2
Viewpoint

A small parking area on the west side of the road offers a view of the Sand Lake estuary.

Three Capes Loop, mile 27.6
Tierra Del Mar

More than a dozen streets in this residential community run west from the highway and terminate at small parking areas with beach access. The beach is popular with residents and visitors alike for hiking, beach combing, kite flying, and picnicking.

Three Capes Loop, mile 28.3
Parking area and beach access

West off the loop is a parking lot for day users and a beach access for street-legal vehicles.

Three Capes Loop, mile 28.3 to mile 28.6
Roadside parking and beach access

Ample parking areas lie along the west side of the loop and provide easy access to the broad sand beach.

Three Capes Loop, mile 28.8
Viewpoint

A small parking area on the west side of the road offers a view south of Haystack Rock.

Three Capes Loop, mile 31.3 to mile 33.3
Pacific City
(zip code 97135)

The southernmost settlement on the Three Capes Scenic Loop, Pacific City (population: 1,000) is also the largest community between Tillamook and Lincoln City. The village spreads south and east from the base of Cape Kiwanda to the shores of Nestucca Bay. It was once a busy commercial fishing village, but has become a popular retirement and vacation spot, with an increasing number of visitors coming each year for all the recreation possibilities. It is known as "The Home of the Dory Fleet."

Pacific City welcomes visitors with a variety of attractions. Kiwanda, the third cape on the scenic loop, stands at the northwest edge of the village and draws sightseers, photographers, tide-pool explorers, and hang-gliders. The long and wide sand beach stretches south from the base of Cape Kiwanda all the way to the mouth of Nestucca Bay and is popular for all beach activities, including surf fishing and horseback riding. Nestucca Bay and the two rivers feeding it get excellent runs of salmon and steelhead that attract anglers from all over the state. The estuary and adjacent lands and wetlands are home to a variety of wildlife.

Pacific City also offers all the amenities expected of a coastal getaway destination. There are county and state parks for picnics or hikes on the beach or along the estuary, and boat ramps for access to Nestucca waters. Among the local eateries and watering holes are some fine restaurants and a pub and brewery right on the beach. Shoppers can browse and buy at several specialty shops, boutiques, and art galleries. Lodging runs the gamut from inexpensive motels to intimate bed-and-breakfast inns and posh ocean-view resorts; campgrounds and RV parks accommodate those who bring their own digs.

On the west side of the road, opposite the Inn at Cape Kiwanda, lies a *must-stop* beach that's famous for its dory fleet. The park includes a large parking area and access to the beach for street-legal vehicles, many of which tow surf dories for launching and retrieval on the beach. Sightseers and photographers will certainly want to spend time here, enjoying the various beach activities and dory launching and retrieval with the imposing Haystack Rock and beautiful Cape Kiwanda as backdrops. The

Three Capes Loop, mile 31.4
Cape Kiwanda
County Park

Dories at Cape Kiwanda

The Dory Fleet

A dory is a flat-bottomed boat that can be launched in the surf. Dory fishing got its start near Pacific City when gillnetting on Nestucca Bay was banned in the 1920s. Productive fishing grounds lie offshore in the vicinity of Pacific City, but the mouth of Nestucca Bay is full of shoals and shifting sandbars, making the bar a treacherous place, even for seaworthy craft and seasoned skippers. If fishermen could no longer ambush the migrating salmon in Nestucca Bay and couldn't safely cross the bar to reach them, they would have to find another way.

Cape Kiwanda juts into the Pacific far enough to block summer winds and flatten the water in its lee, along the broad sand beach lying east of Haystack Rock. Early dorymen hauled their double-ended craft to the beach by horse-drawn wagons. Once they unloaded the heavy boats and launched them in the surf, they spent the day plying nearby waters with their oar-powered boats, then rowed them through the surf and onto the beach at day's end. For the length of the fishing season, physical exhaustion must have been their constant companion.

Eventually, the dory's design was changed from double-ender to square stern to accommodate swift and powerful outboard engines. The road to Cape Kiwanda, completed in the late 1950s, also played a role in the development of the modern dory fleet. Dory skippers now use four-wheel-drive pickup trucks and sport-utility vehicles to haul their craft to the beach on boat trailers. They can back their trailers right into the edge of the surf for launching and use powerful trailer winches to retrieve their boats. Most of the dory fleet consists of commercial vessels, but some operate as charter boats for fishing trips and sightseeing cruises. All are great sights to see and subjects to photograph, making the beach at Cape Kiwanda essential for every traveler's itinerary.

Haystack Rock, the larger of two such named monoliths along Oregon's north coast, stands 327 feet high, about a mile southwest of the Cape Kiwanda State Natural Area.

park also provides access to the adjacent Cape Kiwanda State Natural Area. Other park amenities include drinking water, trash receptacles, and rest rooms with flush toilets and wheelchair access.

Cape Kiwanda is the smallest, and some argue the most beautiful, of the capes along the Three Capes Scenic Loop. The colorful sandstone cliffs, sculpted by winds and wave action, stand in contrast to the summer blue of sky and water. The natural area is next to the county park and includes the cape and nearby beaches and tide pools. Adjacent beaches and nearby waters attract a variety of recreationists, including tide-pool explorers, surfers, and windsurfers. The cape is popular with hang-gliders and kite flyers in summer, storm watchers and whale watchers in winter, birders and photographers all year.

Cape Kiwanda State Natural Area

MUST STOP

East of the Three Capes Loop, behind the Inn at Cape Kiwanda, this park lies near shops and restaurants and within walking distance of the beach. The campground has seven sites with water and electricity and 30 primitive sites for tents or RVs. All sites have tables and grills. The park also has a dump station, trash receptacles, showers with wheelchair access, and rest rooms with flush toilets and wheelchair access. Information: (503) 965-5001.

Webb County Park

At the west end of Pacific Avenue, just west of Three Capes Loop, is a small parking area for a half-dozen or so vehicles. Hike over the soft sand of the foredune to reach the beach.

Three Capes Loop, mile 32.4
Beach access

Turn west at the west end of the bridge on Pacific Avenue, then immediately south (left) on Sunset Drive, and go 0.4 mile, then left into the large parking lot. An excellent paved ramp provides access to the lower Nestucca River and Nestucca Bay. The south end of the parking lot has access to hiking and horse trails through the dunes and along the Nestucca Spit. This is also a

Pacific City County Boat Ramp

good spot for watching and photographing wildlife, especially birds and waterfowl. The facility includes trash receptacles and rest rooms with flush toilets and wheelchair access.

Robert Straub State Park

Follow the directions for the county boat ramp, but continue 0.1 mile beyond to reach a large parking lot and adjacent picnic areas with tables, trash receptacles, drinking water, and rest rooms with flush toilets and wheelchair access. Bob Straub Park, as it's known locally, provides easy access to the beach, low dunes, Nestucca Spit, and Nestucca Bay for fishing, wildlife watching, photography, hiking, and horseback riding.

Three Capes Loop, mile 32.6
Nestucca Country Sporting Goods Boat Ramp

Turn north at the flashing light, and proceed 0.3 mile on Brooten Road to a small parking area on the east side of the road and west bank of the Nestucca River. This is a private paved ramp, but it's open to the public, and there's no charge to use it. Fuel and supplies are available at the sporting goods store. Next to the ramp is a small county park with picnic tables and rest rooms with flush toilets.

Woods County Park

Turn north at the flashing light, and drive 0.9 mile to the park and campground on the west side of Brooten Road and the east bank of the Nestucca River. Although this is a tiny park and campground, it's off the beaten path and is a good place to check when other campgrounds are full. With five full-hookup sites, a kitchen shelter with fireplaces and grills, trash receptacles, rest rooms with flush toilets, and bank access to the Nestucca River for fishing, this is a fine little park with convenient, if limited, facilities.

Three Capes Loop, mile 33.3
Fisher Tract Boat Ramp

On the west side of the road are chemical toilets, a parking area, and gravel ramp providing access to Nestucca Bay. Although the *Oregon Boating Facilities Guide* lists this as Fisher Tract, locals call it The Guard Rail.

Nestucca Bay

On maps, this relatively small, shallow estuary is shaped like a plump, inverted *V*, with its vertex pointing north. The Nestucca River flows from the northeast and enters the bay at the north end of the west lobe. The Little Nestucca River flows from the southeast and enters the bay at the south end of the east lobe.

Nestucca Bay is famous for its salmon and steelhead fishing and offers fair to good opportunities for various marine species, with some kind of angling available all year. Crabbing and clam digging, while not as important here as on the bigger estuaries, can be good.

The bay gets runs of both spring and fall chinook, with fish reaching 50 pounds or more. Spring chinook season runs from April through mid-June, but fishing is best during the final two

Salmon anglers line the west shore of Nestucca Bay, near the Pacific City County Boat Ramp and Robert Straub State Park.

or three weeks of the season. The bay is open for fall chinook from August through December, and the fish usually start showing up in late August or September. Nestucca Bay is open all year for steelhead fishing, and anglers catch some of these anadromous trout every month of the year. Summer-run fish begin appearing in April and remain available in tidewater through the summer. Winter steelhead enter the bay after the first freshets of fall, as early as October, but the angling doesn't usually pick up until November. Perch fishing in the spring can be good throughout the bay, from the mouth to the upper bay channels. Fishing for rockfish, sole, and the occasional flounder is best in the lower bay.

Crabbing is good in the channels of the lower bay during the summer and fall, before the rains begin. Colonies of soft-shell clams reside in the flats along the east side of the upper bay and are accessible on any minus tide.

With increasing public awareness of the importance of estuaries and their abundant wildlife, more people are visiting them to watch, photograph, and learn. Nestucca Bay is an ideal estuary to explore on foot or by boat, canoe, or kayak. Among the wildlife inhabiting or visiting the estuary and its adjacent lands and wetlands, some of which are part of the Nestucca Bay National Wildlife Refuge, are black-tailed deer and smaller land mammals, Pacific harbor seals, raptors, shorebirds, wading birds, and great numbers of resident and migrating waterfowl. Nestucca Bay is the Oregon coast's largest wintering area for Canada geese, including from 100 to 150 Aleutian Canada geese, a species that was on the brink of extinction in 1962.

Three Capes Scenic Loop joins U.S. 101 here at mile 90.3.

Three Capes Loop, mile 35.3
U.S. 101, south junction

Information

Garibaldi Chamber of Commerce
202 Highway 101
P.O. Box 915
Garibaldi, OR 97141
(503) 322-0301

Hebo Ranger District
Siuslaw National Forest
31525 Highway 22
Hebo, OR 97122
(503) 392-3161
E-mail: hebord@oregoncoast.com
URL: www.oregoncoast.com/hebord

Nehalem Bay Area Chamber of Commerce
495 Nehalem Boulevard
P.O. Box 159
Wheeler, OR 97147
(503) 368-5100
(877) 368-5100
E-mail: nehalembay@pdx.oneworld.com
URL: www.doormat.com

Oregon Department of Fish and Wildlife
Tillamook District Office
4909 3rd Street
Tillamook, OR 97141
(503) 842-2741

Oregon Parks and Recreation Department
Cape Lookout State Park
13000 Whiskey Creek Road West
Tillamook, OR 97141
(503) 842-4981

Pacific City Chamber of Commerce
35215 Brooten Road
P.O. Box 331
Pacific City, OR 97135
(503) 965-6161

Port of Garibaldi
Mooring Basin Road
Garibaldi, OR 97118
(503) 322-3292
(503) 322-3603 Harbor Master

Rockaway Beach Chamber of Commerce
103 South 1st Street
P.O. Box 198
Rockaway Beach, OR 97136
(503) 355-8108

Tillamook Bay National Estuary Project
613 Commercial Street
P.O. Box 493
Garibaldi, OR 97118
(503) 322-2222
URL: www.co.tillamook.or.us/gov/estuary/homepage.htm

Tillamook Chamber of Commerce
3705 Highway 101 North
Tillamook, OR 97141
(503) 842-7525
E-mail: tillchamber@wcn.net
URL: www.tillamookchamber.org

U.S. Coast Guard Lifeboat Station
Garibaldi, OR 97118
(503) 322-3531
(503) 322-3234 Weather and Bar Conditions
(503) 322-3246 Emergencies Only

Fresh crabs are widely available along the entire Oregon coast at restaurants, seafood shops, and supermarkets. They're also available free and for the fun of catching them to those who want to learn how and try their luck. There is no guarded ritual or mystique involved in crabbing, as some might think, and it is an inexpensive sport with seasonally high success rates in most places.

Crabbing gear is sold at tackle shops, marinas, marine chandleries, and sporting-goods outlets all along the coast. Many marinas and shops also rent gear and sell bait. There are no license requirements, and daily catch limits are liberal.

Dungeness Crab

The Dungeness crab is the most popular and widely distributed crab on the West Coast. It's also among the largest of edible crabs, the males attaining a size of 9 inches across the back or carapace when fully grown. The carapace of the Dungeness is brown to reddish or purplish brown, and the legs are long in proportion to the body.

The daily catch limit for Dungeness is 12 male crabs measuring $5^3/4$ inches across the carapace, in front of the points protruding from each side. To determine the sex, turn each crab over and examine the abdomen. The male has a narrow, elongate flap on the abdomen, while the female's flap is rounded and considerably wider.

Red Rock Crab

Another West Coast species, overlapping the range of the Dungeness, is the smaller red rock crab. This crab averages only 5 inches across the carapace, but in quality is just as tasty as the Dungeness. The reddish carapace of the red rock crab is more brightly hued than that of the Dungeness, and the claws and body are heavier in proportion to the legs. The daily limit for red rock crabs is 24 of any size or sex.

Crabbing Tides

Recommendations for the best crabbing tides are as varied as the tides themselves, and crabs are fickle creatures that don't always behave according to experts' advice. Crabs can be taken on high tides, low tides, and slack tides—day or night. They will come to a

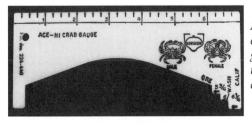

An inexpensive, plastic caliper—called a crab gauge—is ideal for measuring Dungeness crabs.

123

Crabbing on the Oregon Coast

To determine the sex of crabs, turn them over and check the abdominal flaps. The crab at the top, with the narrow flap, is a male; the other, with the wide flap, is a female.

bait on an ebb tide or flood tide. Neap tides, when the range between high and low water is smallest, are generally the most productive. The consensus of experts seems to favor crabbing on high slack or low slack tide, but it's best to allow yourself some leeway. Try to be on the water and setting gear two hours before high or low tide, and plan to continue crabbing through slack tide and an hour or two after the tide changes.

Crabbing Seasons

The Oregon ocean is closed for Dungeness crab from August 15 through November 30, which has little effect on recreational crabbers, who mainly ply the bays, estuaries, and water between the jetties, which are open all year. Sport crabbing seasons are more regulated by nature than by bureaucracies. In Oregon, crabbing is generally good to outstanding throughout the summer months and into the fall, until the autumn rains begin. As the rains bring great amounts of fresh water into the estuaries or bays, the salinity of the bay waters decreases, driving the crabs to saltier waters in the lower reaches of the bays or the open ocean. During midwinter dry spells, the salinity of the bay waters increases, crabs move upbay, and the crabbing can be excellent.

Molting

Although the young crab that has spent perhaps two months developing through several stages following hatching is only about a tenth of an inch wide, it grows rapidly during the summer months, molting about every three to five days and adding to its overall size by one third with each molt. It continues to molt throughout its life to its terminal molt. Females molt from eighteen to twenty times, males twenty-one to twenty-three times, which accounts for the males' larger size.

When a crab starts to molt, its shell cracks between the carapace and abdomen, and the crab simply backs out of its shell. Molting takes about two to three hours, and during the few minutes just before and after the molt, the crab takes up large quantities of water to expand its new shell. During the next twelve hours, the shell will be leathery or papery to the touch, giving rise to the name "paper shell." It takes another twelve to twenty-four hours for the shell to become hard and brittle.

Crabbers should take only hard-shell crabs and release all soft-shell or paper-shell crabs, because the meat of soft-shell crabs is watery and of inferior quality. Also, the yield of usable meat per crab is far lower.

Crabbing Gear

Along the West Coast, most crabbers use some sort of crab trap, pot, or ring. While these differ from one another, they all operate on the same basic principle. The crabber baits them, lowers them into the water, waits for crabs to come to the bait, then raises them to harvest the catch. All of them can be used from bridges, docks, piers, and boats.

Crab traps (also called hand traps) come in several different but similar configurations. They resemble wire cages with collapsible sides that lie flat in the open position, but close and prevent crabs from escaping when the trap is raised. Crab pots are traps with fixed entrances, consisting of a metal frame, either cylindrical or box-shaped, with walls, top, and bottom usually made of galvanized or vinyl-coated wire. Commercial crabbers use large, cylindrical crab pots; smaller pots are sold for recreational crabbing.

Crab rings are another kind of trap, very effective and popular on the West Coast. They're also lighter and cheaper than crab pots, and they collapse for convenient storage and transportation. A crab ring actually consists of two steel rings wrapped with strips of rubber inner tube or waterproof tape. The bottom ring is usually 26 inches in diameter and has a galvanized wire bottom. The top ring is usually 30 inches in diameter and is connected to the bottom ring with side netting that has a stretched-mesh measurement of about 4 inches, to allow undersize crabs to escape. Three ropes of

Crabbing on the Oregon Coast

Crabbing on the Oregon Coast

equal length are secured to the top ring, brought together and tied into a small loop, to which a small float and the pull line are attached. In the water, the float raises the ropes above the baited ring to prevent their interference with the ring, bait, and crabs.

Ideally, the pull rope should be $3/8$-inch-diameter polypropylene rope. Smaller ropes are hard on the hands when hauling in the crab ring and larger ropes create too much drag in tidal currents. The length of the rope depends on how the crab ring will be used. Crabbers working from docks, piers, wharves, and bridges need from 40 to 100 feet, depending on the height of the structure and depth of the water. When crabbing from a boat, the length of the pull rope depends on the water depth. Here, the crabber also needs to attach a marker buoy to the tag end of the pull rope.

Crabbers attach baits to the center of the bottom ring in any of several ways. They tie or wire large fish heads, fish carcasses, and whole fish to the mesh of the wire bottom. Wire bait holders, resembling large safety pins, were popular for years, but they offer little resistance to the marauding, bait-stealing harbor seals that have become so numerous in some waters in recent years. Many crabbers now enclose their baits in heavy-wire bait cages, attached to the bottoms of their crab rings. For baits such as clams and cockles with cracked shells, crabbers use mesh bags.

Of the various types of crab traps available, the crab ring is the most popular for recreational crabbing.

Crab rings should be checked regularly and fairly frequently: about every ten minutes when there are plenty of crabs in the vicinity and every twenty minutes if the crabbing is slow. To keep crabs from escaping over the sides of the top ring, bring the crab ring up fast. Ease any slack out of the pull rope; then give a sharp pull to raise the top ring, entrapping the crabs. Continue pulling up steadily, hand over hand, so the pressure of the water keeps the crabs in the ring. To keep from getting rope burns or blisters on your hands, wear heavy-duty waterproof work gloves, which are also an aid in handling crabs.

In Oregon, each crabber may use up to three baited crab rings, traps, or pots. If you use more than one device, don't put them too near one another. If you're crabbing from a bridge or pier, spread your gear as far apart as possible. When crabbing from a boat, place your gear 30 to 40 yards apart. If any gear isn't producing within an hour, move it to another location, and keep moving it until you find crabs.

Crab Baits

Contrary to popular belief, crabs are not scavengers that eat mainly rotten fish, tainted meat, and soured clams. Quite the opposite— they prefer fresh baits. They are efficient predators with a highly developed sense of smell, so the best baits are those that exude oils and create scent trails. Fatty fish are top choices, and the best bets on the Oregon coast are the heads and carcasses of salmon and albacore. Carcasses of other fish work well, too, and are readily available at coastal marinas and bait shops. Chicken and turkey necks and backs are other excellent crab baits. They're readily available everywhere, relatively inexpensive, and more durable than many other kinds of bait.

Handling Crabs

It's obvious to anyone who has ever seen a crab that these creatures come armed with two claws that can do damage to the unwary crabber. Moreover, with all those legs seeming to move in all directions, the crab appears more dangerous and difficult to handle that it actually is.

Any captured crab will first try to escape. If cornered, it will attempt to defend itself by pivoting to keep its claws in striking position, but its reaction time is slow. So the trick is to work quickly when handling crabs, moving them as fast as possible from the catching device to the holding container.

Although a crab can reach across or under itself with its claws, you can safely pick it up by the two rearmost legs, and your hands will be out of harm's way. You can also safely handle the crab by grasping the rear center of the body, between the two back legs.

Crabbing on the Oregon Coast

Crabbing on the Oregon Coast

Keeping Crabs Alive

Never keep crabs in buckets, tubs, coolers, or other containers of unoxygenated water, because, like fish, they will soon die from lack of oxygen. If you're crabbing from a boat equipped with an aerated livewell, crabs will stay alive there. Most crabbers use large plastic buckets, plastic fish baskets, or plastic laundry baskets to keep their crabs alive and well. For best results, cover crabs with a piece of burlap that has been soaked in salt water. This not only keeps them cool, by evaporation, but also prevents them from crawling out of the container.

Cooking and Cleaning Crabs

Most people prepare crabs by dropping them live into boiling water and cleaning them after they're cooked. For this, all you need is a big stockpot or crab cooker, salt, and water. Clean seawater has always been best for boiling crabs, but you can make a perfect duplicate by dissolving one cup of salt in every gallon of tap water used. Once the water has come to a rolling boil, drop the crabs in, let it return to a boil, cover, and cook for fifteen minutes. Crabs will be ready to clean and eat, chill for later use, or pack in ice for transporting.

To clean the cooked crab, start by pulling off the carapace. Then grasp the crab by the legs with both hands, and break it in half lengthwise. Shake the entrails out of the body cavity, pick away the grayish gill filaments, and rinse each crab half under running water to get rid of anything that's not clean meat and shell.

Some people prefer to kill and clean crabs before cooking them, and there are some good arguments to support that method. First, most of any crab is waste: the maximum meat yield of the meatiest of crabs in prime condition is only about 23 percent. Crabs are bulky creatures, and a good bit of the waste material consists of the back and entrails. By cleaning the crab before cooking it, you eliminate about half the waste, thereby enabling you to cook more crab in any single batch. Another reason for cleaning crabs before cooking them is to increase the salt penetration in the meat, thus improving its keeping qualities. Crabs prepared this way can also be cooled much quicker, which also improves meat quality.

To instantly dispatch the live crab, hold it in place on a cutting board or other working surface, and push the point of a knife blade through the front of the shell, between the eyes. To clean any uncooked crab, grasp it with each hand by the legs and claw on each side. Put an edge of the crab's carapace on the top edge of a table, counter, or similar surface. Now push downward, and the carapace will pop off like a jar lid. Break or cut the crab in half lengthwise, shake out the innards, and pick away the gill filaments. Rinse under cold, running water, and the crab is ready for cooking the same way as whole, live crabs.

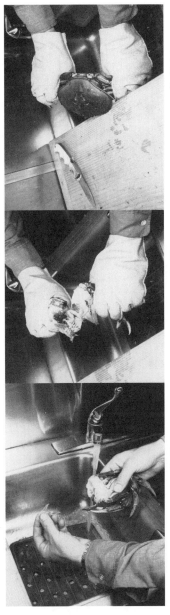

To clean a crab, before or after cooking, start by removing the top shell or carapace.

Break the crab in half, shake out the entrails, and rinse under cold water.

Pick away the gill filaments, rinse under cold water, and the simple cleaning chore is done.

Crabbing on the Oregon Coast

Transporting Crabs

If you must transport crabs for any distance, the best way is in an ice chest. Line the bottom of the chest with a layer of crushed ice, 2 or 3 inches thick. Then add a layer of whole cooked crabs. If you cleaned the crabs before cooking, put the crab halves in one-gallon plastic bags and arrange them in a single layer. Cover the crabs with a 1-inch layer of ice, add another layer of crabs, and continue with alternating layers of crabs and ice. If you must travel more than a day, drain the melt water about every twelve hours, and add ice as needed.

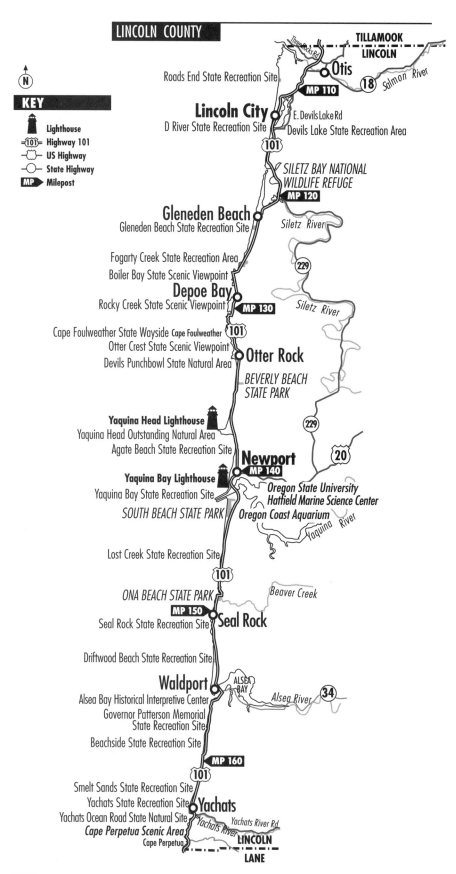

LINCOLN COUNTY

TILLAMOOK
LINCOLN

Three Rocks Rd

Roads End State Recreation Site

Otis

MP 110

18   Salmon River

Lincoln City

E. Devils Lake Rd

D River State Recreation Site

Devils Lake State Recreation Area

101

SILETZ BAY NATIONAL
WILDLIFE REFUGE

MP 120

Gleneden Beach

Glenden Beach State Recreation Site

Siletz River

Fogarty Creek State Recreation Area

Boiler Bay State Scenic Viewpoint

Depoe Bay

Rocky Creek State Scenic Viewpoint

MP 130

229

Siletz River

Cape Foulweather State Wayside   Cape Foulweather   101

Otter Crest State Scenic Viewpoint

Devils Punchbowl State Natural Area

Otter Rock

BEVERLY BEACH
STATE PARK

229

Yaquina Head Lighthouse

Yaquina Head Outstanding Natural Area

Agate Beach State Recreation Site

20

Newport

MP 140

Yaquina Bay Lighthouse

Yaquina Bay State Recreation Site

SOUTH BEACH STATE PARK

Oregon State University
Hatfield Marine Science Center

Oregon Coast Aquarium

Yaquina River

Lost Creek State Recreation Site

101

ONA BEACH STATE PARK

Beaver Creek

MP 150

Seal Rock State Recreation Site

Seal Rock

Driftwood Beach State Recreation Site

Waldport

ALSEA
BAY

Alsea River

34

Alsea Bay Historical Interpretive Center

Governor Patterson Memorial
State Recreation Site

Beachside State Recreation Site

MP 160

101

Smelt Sands State Recreation Site

Yachats State Recreation Site

Yachats Ocean Road State Natural Site

Cape Perpetua Scenic Area

Cape Perpetua

Yachats River   Yachats River Rd

Yachats

LINCOLN

LANE

KEY

- Lighthouse
- Highway 101
- US Highway
- State Highway
- **MP** Milepost

N

The Lincoln County Coast

U.S. 101, Mile 102.7 to Mile 167.6

Lincoln is the youngest of Oregon's coastal counties, established by the Oregon Legislature on February 20, 1893, and named after Abraham Lincoln. Newport is its largest city and county seat. The forest products industry and commercial fishing have long been important contributors to the county's economy, but in the twenty-first century, tourism, recreation, government, and marine science research and education have become economic and cultural mainstays.

Lincoln County welcomes visitors with some of the finest restaurants in the state, more oceanfront accommodations than anywhere else on the coast, five uniquely charming and inviting coastal cities, and a great diversity of natural scenic splendor. The four distinctly different estuaries of the Salmon, Siletz, Yaquina, and Alsea rivers can be explored on foot or by water. Excellent harbors at Depoe and Yaquina bays are home ports for charter fleets running daily fishing, sightseeing, and whale-watching trips, weather permitting. Essential stops on every traveler's itinerary are the Yaquina Head Outstanding Natural Area, Hatfield Marine Science Center, Oregon Coast Aquarium, and the Cape Perpetua Scenic Area. With miles of broad sand beaches alternating with rugged headlands and rocky shorelines, Lincoln County presents sightseers, outdoor enthusiasts, and photographers with a kaleidoscope of changing landscapes and seascapes. Dozens of city, county, and state parks invite picnickers, campers, hikers, bikers, swimmers, anglers, boaters, water skiers, kayakers, surfers, sailboarders, and other recreationists to stay and play. For good measure, toss in four beautiful and challenging golf courses, two historic lighthouses that are open for tours, a factory outlet mall, two microbreweries, a tribal casino, and dozens of art galleries and antique shops, and it's little wonder that Lincoln County is one of Oregon's most popular destinations.

U.S. 101, mile 103.8
Old Highway 101 Scenic Route

Turn east off U.S. 101 on Three Rocks Road, drive 0.6 mile, and turn north on the Old Highway 101 Scenic Route. The old highway carries travelers on a 10-mile loop through the bucolic countryside and the Cascade Head Experimental Forest. Watch for interpretive signs along the way. The scenic route ends about 10 miles north at Highway 101, mile 98.9, in Tillamook County.

Anglers on the Salmon River

Salmon River Estuary

Turn west on Three Rocks Road to reach the Salmon River Estuary, hiking trails, and more. (For details and attractions, see "Side Trip: Three Rocks Road" on page 177.)

**U.S. 101,
mile 104.7**
Salmon River

This little river courses for 24 miles through Lincoln County and forms a small but beautiful estuary west of Highway 101. Not only is the Salmon a popular and highly productive river for salmon and steelhead fishing, it is also one of the most accessible to bank anglers. The river and estuary are open for the taking of chinook and fin-clipped coho salmon from the end of May through December, except for the closure of the estuary west of Highway 101 to salmon angling from July through mid-August. The best salmon angling occurs in September and October, and the fish run big.

The river and estuary are closed to steelhead fishing for the month of April and most of May, but are open the rest of the year. Steelhead follow salmon into the river and provide good angling from December through March.

Anglers and others will find excellent river access and ample roadside parking near the Highway 101 bridge. Farther upriver, access is mainly via State Route 18.

The lower river winds through woods, grassy meadows, and marshes on its way to the Pacific. The estuary and adjacent lands and wetlands attract a variety of wildlife, especially waterfowl, wading birds, and shorebirds. Although several points along Three Rocks Road provide shoreline access for watching and photographing wildlife, the estuary is best explored by small boat, canoe, or kayak. (For details, see "Side Trip: Three Rocks Road" on page 177.)

This busy highway leads east and connects with State Route 22 to Salem and State Route 99W to Portland.

Drive east 1.3 miles on State Route 18 to Otis. Turn north (left) on Old Scenic Highway 101, go 0.3 mile across the river, and turn east (right) on North Bank Road. The hatchery entrance is 0.6 mile beyond, on the south side of the road. Each year, the hatchery produces 200,000 chinook salmon for release into the Salmon River, almost a million coho (300,000 for the Salmon River, 600,000 for Yaquina Bay, and 50,000 for the Siletz River), as well as 80,000 steelhead for release into the Siletz. Visitors will find rearing ponds, a show pond, picnic tables, and a nature trail along the river. Information: (541) 994-8606

Lying along the northeast edge of Lincoln City, this large coastal lake is about 3 miles long and just under a half-mile wide. It covers nearly 700 acres with an average depth of about 10 feet and maximum depth of 22 feet. Visitors can reach the east shore of the lake via East Devils Lake Road at mile 106.1 at the north end of the lake, or mile 115.6 at the south end. To reach the west shore, take West Devils Lake Road east at mile 112.4 at the north end of the lake, or mile 114.4, at Northeast 14th Street, near the south end.

Although the lake is popular for all forms of water recreation, angling has been inconsistent over the years. Increasing human activity around the lake for much of the twentieth century led to water pollution and excessive weed growth—problems that may be in check now. In an effort to control weeds, the lake was stocked in 1986 and 1987 with 27,090 herbivorous fish known as white amur or Chinese grass carp, which grow to 2 feet or more in length and may live longer than 20 years. The planted fish were sterile hybrids, unable to reproduce and overpopulate the lake. Young grass carp can consume their own body weight in vegetation every day, and they seem to be succeeding in their task of reducing the amount of dense shoreline weeds. The lake is closed to the taking of grass carp, but is open all year for warmwater species—largemouth bass, brown bullhead, yellow perch, black crappie, and bluegill—as well as fin-clipped trout.

Boating, water skiing, sailing, sailboarding, canoeing, and kayaking are popular forms of recreation on the lake. State parks at the south end of the lake provide launching and mooring facilities. A private marina at the northwest end of the lake has a launch ramp, fuel, and moorage available and rents canoes, kayaks, paddleboats, motorboats, and personal watercraft. A county boat ramp and three city parks, two with launching facilities, also offer lake access.

Devils Lake attracts a variety of birdlife—including cormorants, grebes, coots, and bald eagles—and is an important wintering area for waterfowl. Large numbers of mallards, widgeons, gadwalls, ring-necked ducks, canvasbacks, and other dabbling and diving ducks gather here to feed and rest, much to the delight of wildlife watchers and photographers.

East Devils Lake Road, north junction

Turn east off the highway to reach this road, which roughly parallels the east shore of Devils Lake for about four miles and provides access to city and state parks as well as county and state boat ramps. It rejoins Highway 101 at mile 115.6.

Sand Point Park

Drive 1.2 miles, turn west on Northeast Loop Drive, and continue 0.4 mile to this tiny gem of a city park in a quiet, wooded, residential area. The facility has a small parking lot not suitable for travel trailers or motorhomes. Amenities include a bench overlooking the lake, two picnic tables, a wood ramp leading to a small beach, a trash receptacle, drinking water, and rest rooms with flush toilets and wheelchair access.

U.S. 101, mile 112
Milepost discrepancy

Because of highway construction and realignment, some highway miles have disappeared here. Between roadside mileposts 105 and 112, the actual distance is only 1.7 miles.

45th Parallel

At mile 112 on Highway 101, travelers are equidistant from or midway between the Equator and the North Pole.

U.S. 101, mile 112.1 to mile 118.5 Lincoln City
(zip code 97367)

On December 8, 1964, the voters of the Lincoln County cities of Oceanlake, Delake, and Taft joined those of the unincorporated communities Cutler City and Nelscott to form a single municipal government with the name Lincoln City. As these districts have grown toward one another, Lincoln City has evolved without a distinct downtown, uptown, or city center. Most of the city's shops, stores, galleries, restaurants, motels, hotels, and resorts stand along U.S. 101 and extend westward to the beach.

Lincoln City is the second-largest city in the county (population: 6,855) and is more than capable of fulfilling any traveler's needs. With more than two thousand rooms and suites available and more oceanfront accommodations than any other city on the Oregon coast, Lincoln City's main industry is obviously tourism. To please the shop-till-you-drop crowd, the city offers several distinctly different shopping areas, a number of fine galleries, more antique shops than anywhere else on the coast, and a large factory-outlet shopping center. The biggest casino on the coast is at the north end of town, and another lies east on State Route 18. The variety, number, and quality of

A winter storm roars ashore near Roads End State Recreation Area and engulfs Cascade Head.

restaurants should satisfy any appetite. Microbrew fans will enjoy the brew pub at the north end of town.

A readily accessible ocean beach flanks the entire western edge of the city and extends beyond its limits. Two golf courses, more than a half-dozen inviting city and state parks, miles of hiking trails, a large coastal lake, estuaries north and south, and a nearby National Wildlife Refuge round out the many attractions of Lincoln City.

U.S. 101, mile 112.4
West Devils Lake Road, north junction

Turn east here, at the traffic light, and follow this road as it meanders for 2.3 miles through a hilly residential area along and above the west shore of the lake, connects with Northeast 14th Street, and rejoins Highway 101 at mile 114.4.

Holmes Road Park

Drive 0.5 mile, and turn east into this city park on the west shore, where there's a paved boat ramp, trailer turnaround, parking lot, courtesy dock, fishing dock, trash receptacle, and rest rooms with flush toilets.

Regatta Grounds Park

Drive 1.7 miles from Highway 101, and turn east into this beautiful park on the lake, characterized by big trees and open grassy areas. Among the park's features are a huge playground, an information kiosk, picnic areas with tables and grills, a sand beach, a 0.5-mile nature trail through old-growth forest, trash receptacles, drinking water, and rest rooms with flush toilets. For boaters, there's a paved launch ramp, docks, and trailer parking. This is an essential stop for travelers with children who could use a good unwinding at the city's best playground.

Lakeside Golf and
Racquet Club

Turn west off U.S. 101 at the traffic light, take Devils Lake Boulevard to Clubhouse Drive, and continue to the parking lot, 0.4 mile from the highway. Set in the rolling green hills along the west side of Highway 101, this beautiful, 4,636-yard, 18-hole, par-65 course straddles the 45th parallel. Amenities include a clubhouse, pro shop, resident pro, club and electric-cart rental, free pull carts, indoor driving range, nine-hole putting green, two pitching greens, spas, sauna, steam room, locker rooms, restaurant, lounge, and beverage cart. Pro shop: (541) 994-8442.

U.S. 101, mile 112.8
Roads End State
Recreation Site

Turn west at the traffic light onto Logan Road, and drive 0.9 mile to the park entrance. The small oceanfront park is a popular beach access with locals and visitors alike. A short paved path leads to the broad sand beach that runs for miles north and south and is a favorite of kite flyers and sailboarders. The park also includes picnic tables, a fire pit, bench, trash receptacles, and rest rooms with flush toilets and wheelchair access.

U.S. 101, mile 112.9
Northwest 40th
Street beach access

Turn west just south of the traffic light at the Shilo Inn sign, and drive the short distance to the Shilo Inn parking lot. A paved ramp with wheelchair access runs between the original Shilo Inn and Shilo Inn Suites buildings and descends to the beach.

U.S. 101, mile 113
Northwest 39th
Street beach access

After turning west off the highway, drive 0.3 mile, turn south (left) on Northwest Jetty Avenue, and go 0.1 mile to reach a public beach access between 3805 and 3755 Northwest Jetty Avenue. Park on the street.

U.S. 101, mile 113.3
Grace Hammond
Beach Access

Head west off Highway 101 on Northwest 34th Street for 0.3 mile, turn north (right) on Northwest Jetty Avenue, then west (left) into the paved parking lot. The small lot has six vehicle spaces, one of which has wheelchair access. A short paved ramp with wheelchair access descends to the beach. The little park also has a trash receptacle and bench overlooking the beach.

U.S. 101, mile 113.4
Holmes Road Park
and Boat Ramp

Take Holmes Road east off U.S. 101 for 0.5 mile to the park, which lies east of West Devils Lake Road. (For details, see U.S. 101, mile 112.4 on page 135.)

U.S. 101, mile 113.7
Northwest 26th
Street beach access

A paved parking lot with nine spaces, including one with wheelchair access, lies 0.4 mile west of Highway 101. A concrete stairway leads to the broad beach.

U.S. 101, mile 114.1
Northwest 21st
Street beach access

Turn west off the highway, and drive 0.2 mile to a small paved parking lot with one wheelchair-access space, three standard vehicle spaces, a trash receptacle, and concrete steps to the beach.

On the west side of Highway 101, at Northwest 17th Street, stands a large public parking lot with trash receptacles and rest rooms with flush toilets and wheelchair access.

U.S. 101, mile 114.2
Public parking and rest rooms

Turn west off Highway 101, and drive 0.3 mile to a steep street that drops to a parking area on the beach, where there is access to a sand beach, rocky intertidal area, and tide pools. Although the nearby rest rooms with flush toilets are wheelchair accessible, they're on a hillside approachable only by way of a steep road.

U.S. 101, mile 114.3
Northwest 15th Street beach access

Turn east off U.S. 101 onto Northeast 14th Street, which becomes West Devils Lake Road three blocks from the highway.

U.S. 101, mile 114.4
West Devils Lake Road, south access

Turn east at the traffic light at Northeast 6th Street; the state park lies just east of the highway, along the southwest shore of Devils Lake. Although the park is in an urban setting, just minutes from all of Lincoln City's attractions, the wooded area and lake form a buffer zone from busy Highway 101. Campground amenities include 31 full-hookup sites, including two with wheelchair access; one site with water and electricity; 55 tent sites with nearby water; and 10 yurts—each of which features paved parking, a picnic table, and fire ring. For those on foot or arriving by pedal power, there's a hiker/biker camp. Showers and rest rooms with flush toilets have wheelchair access. Trash receptacles, a recycle bin, and firewood are available.

U.S. 101, mile 114.7
Devils Lake State Recreation Area

As an added attraction to boaters, this park has a boat dock with 16 mooring slips. A paved boat ramp is a short run across the lake at the day-use area.

Information: (541) 994-2002 or (800) 551-6949. Reservations: (800) 452-5687

On the west side of Highway 101 at Southwest 1st Street, Lincoln City's favorite stretch of beach spreads north and south from the mouth of the D River and invites travelers to turn into the large parking area and step down the short stairway to the sand and surf. Beachgoers enjoy flying kites, tossing Frisbees, building sand castles, dodging waves, or just strolling along the edge of the Pacific. The park also offers picnic areas overlooking the ocean, trash receptacles, and rest rooms with flush toilets and wheelchair access.

U.S. 101, mile 115
D River State Recreation Site

On the west side of the highway is the visitor center and parking lot. Stop here to pick up a city map and literature about the area's attractions. The Bureau is open Monday through Friday from 8:00 a.m. to 5:00 p.m., Saturday from 9:00 a.m. to 5:00 p.m., and Sunday from 10:00 a.m. to 4:00 p.m. In the summer, it stays open until 8:00 p.m. on Fridays.

U.S. 101, mile 115.4
Lincoln City Visitor and Convention Bureau

U.S. 101, mile 115.6
East Devils Lake Road, south junction

Turn east at the traffic light near the factory-outlet mall to reach the east shore of Devils Lake.

Devils Lake State Recreation Area, East Day-Use Area and Boat Ramp

Turn east at the traffic light, drive one mile, and turn west into this state-park facility, where there are picnic tables set in shady woods and open, grassy areas. The park features a paved boat ramp, courtesy and fishing docks, plenty of trailer parking, trash receptacles, and pit toilets.

U.S. 101, mile 116.7
Nelscott public parking and rest rooms

One block west of Highway 101, on Southwest 32nd Street, is a small parking lot with nine standard parking spaces and one with wheelchair access, trash receptacles, and rest rooms with flush toilets and wheelchair access. From here, it's an easy walk to Nelscott shops and restaurants.

U.S. 101, mile 117.9
Lincoln County Historical Museum

The museum stands on the west side of the highway with very limited on-street parking, but there's a large public lot behind the building. Stop at this fine little museum to learn about the history of Lincoln County and its people. Displays include Indian and pioneer artifacts, some great old photographs, and a superb collection of Japanese glass fishing floats. On site is a small gift shop with books available. The museum is open Tuesday through Saturday, except major holidays, from noon to 4:00 p.m. Information: (541) 996-6614.

Public parking and rest rooms

A half-block west of Highway 101 on Southwest 50th Street is a large public parking lot with trash receptacles and rest rooms with flush toilets and wheelchair access.

U.S. 101, mile 118
Bay and beach access and public pier

Turn west on Southwest 51st Street, and drive 0.2 mile to a public parking area with beach access. Continue for another 0.1 mile to reach another parking area, public rest rooms with flush toilets and wheelchair access, a fishing and crabbing pier, and access to the beach near the mouth of Siletz Bay. There are coin-operated binoculars for watching wildlife on the bay, including Pacific harbor seals and a great variety of birds. Fishing and crabbing are seasonally good, and the beach is a favorite for collecting driftwood.

U.S. 101, mile 118.1
Siletz Bay Park

On the west side of the highway, this lovely park offers excellent views of the lower bay and bar with plenty of photo opportunities. Amenities include picnic tables, a grill, information kiosk, easy access to the beach and bay, drinking water, trash receptacles, and rest rooms with flush toilets and wheelchair access.

A shallow estuary spreading along the west side of U.S. 101 for about 3 miles, Siletz Bay is separated from the ocean by a long finger of sand known as the Salishan Spit. Drift Creek, Schooner Creek, and the Siletz River drain directly into the bay, supplying the fresh water that mixes with sea water to create the brackish water of the estuarine environment.

Siletz Bay

Much of the west shore of the bay along both sides of Highway 101 and both banks of the lower Siletz River comprise the Siletz Bay National Wildlife Refuge, established in 1991 to protect the salt marshes, brackish marshes, mudflats, tidal creeks and sloughs, and adjacent forest lands that are essential habitat to a tremendous variety of fish and wildlife. In addition to the various fish and shellfish that reside in or pass through the bay, many species of wading birds, shorebirds, and waterfowl use the bay, and populations of migratory species swell during fall and spring, providing excellent opportunities for wildlife watchers and photographers.

The bay itself is a subject worthy of any shutterbug's lens. Winter floods have strewn the flats, channels, and shoreline with driftwood of all shapes and sizes. Gray ghosts of dead trees stand stark in the lush marshes along the east side of the highway posing for passing photographers. Add an eerie morning fog or the sweet light of late day, and pictures seem to compose themselves.

Siletz Bay has a dangerous, unprotected bar with a shallow channel and almost ever-present surf. Nobody crosses it, and smart boaters steer clear of it, especially during strong ebb tides that rip through the jaws with enough force to carry a disabled boat into the breakers. On the ebb, confine your boating activities to upbay areas and channels.

This metal sculpture of schooling salmon stands near the mouth of Siletz Bay, at the west end of 51st Street.

Mile-by-mile guide continues on page 143

Oregon's Estuaries— The Ocean's Nursery

In their seaward flow from inland headwaters, most coastal rivers eventually meet and mix with the ocean's salty tides to form the dynamic, productive, and mysterious environments known as estuaries. These partly enclosed river mouths contain a variety of freshwater, saltwater, and brackish-water habitats.

Different regions of the estuary encompass a wide range of features, including narrow tidal creeks, deep-water channels, marsh ponds and potholes, broad expanses of mudflats, sandy beaches, and rocky intertidal areas. Salinity levels are generally low in the upper estuary, highest at the mouth, and variable throughout the bay area, though the saltiness of estuarine waters changes markedly with the seasons and the twice-daily flood and ebb of tides. Consequently, freshwater marshes and plants thrive in the upper portions of an estuary, while tidal salt-marsh communities inhabit the lower reaches. Abundant freshwater, saltwater, and uniquely adapted organisms find food and shelter in these diverse habitats.

Oregon's estuaries developed shortly after the last ice age, about ten to twelve thousand years ago. As the glaciers melted into the oceans, sea level rose some 400 feet, inundating the mouths of most coastal rivers and drowning the river valleys. Among Oregon's drowned-river estuaries are the large and economically important Coos, Umpqua, Yaquina, Tillamook, and Columbia tidal systems.

Salt marshes, the croplands and pastures of the estuary, are among the most fertile areas on the planet. An acre of salt marsh, for example, produces six times as much organic matter as the average acre of wheat-producing farmland. It's seven times more fruitful than the waters of the continental shelf and twenty times richer than the deep sea.

Some organisms live out their entire existence within the estuary, while others begin life here and move elsewhere. Still others move to and from estuaries for various reasons, or migrate through them bound for fresh or saltwater.

One of the estuary's most important roles is that of nursery—a vital rearing area for many species of fish and shellfish. It's estimated that at least 65 percent of America's commercial food fish and shellfish species and nearly all inshore and nearshore saltwater sport fish species are vitally linked to the estuarine environment.

A number of important forage, food, and sport fishes—including surf smelt, jacksmelt, and several members of the herring family— spawn in or near the estuaries, where their hatchlings grow to fingerlings or young adults before venturing out to sea. Several of the surfperches regularly visit Oregon's estuaries to feed and bear live young there. A few are permanent estuarine residents. All of the anadromous fish species, those that spend most of their lives in salt water but reproduce in fresh water, use the estuaries. Among the most important in Oregon are Pacific salmon, steelhead trout, white sturgeon, striped bass, and American shad.

Many species that spawn in the open sea produce young that eventually make their way to the estuaries: among them are Dover sole, starry flounder, and cabezon. Estuaries are also rearing grounds for various species of crab and shrimp, some of which are commercially important, while others are critical links in the food chain.

Ambient temperatures and species requirements combine to determine spawning places and times. Eggs and larvae drift shoreward in ocean currents for varied distances, from a few to a few hundred miles. Eventually, they enter the estuary, sometimes in the form of eggs, but usually as larvae or juveniles. Having reached the nutrient-rich waters that have nurtured their kind for untold eons, the young fish and shellfish will find food and become food. A few will eventually mature into adults and begin the cycle anew.

Oregon's Salt Marshes

A distant glance on any summer's day might portray an Oregon salt marsh as no more than a docile field of grass, fringing the sun-dappled waters of an estuary and swaying to the whims of the winds. Belying its simple quiescence, however, are complex assemblages of plant and animal communities that rely upon this intricate wetland, many of which are uniquely adapted to the stresses of life in the salt marsh.

All coastal states contain salt marshes, which flourish near river mouths, in estuaries, and around lagoons in areas protected from battering ocean waves and storms. Along the Atlantic and Gulf coasts, salt marshes are widely dispersed and often sprawl over large areas. On the Pacific coast, however, they are relatively small and sparsely distributed, accounting for only 3 percent of the nation's total acreage—making them all the more valuable for their scarcity. Oregon has only about 7,000 acres of salt marsh, amounting to approximately 17 percent of total estuarine acreage.

Salt marshes develop in coastal areas sheltered from the ocean's surf. In Oregon, they occur in the lower intertidal fringes of coastal rivers. Seaward portions of salt marshes emerge from sandflats, mudflats, or a combination of sandy mud. They rise shoreward and landward, forming a transition zone between estuarine and upland ecosystems, where they support an abundance of aquatic and terrestrial organisms.

Tides are the life blood of these unique habitats. Flood tides sweep sediments and nutrients into the marsh, which drop out and settle during slack-water periods. Ebb tides flush dead plants and other organic material out of the marsh and into the estuary, where they enter the detrital food chain and contribute significantly to estuarine food webs.

Oregon's Estuaries— The Ocean's Nursery

Oregon's Estuaries—The Ocean's Nursery

These natural processes, essential to the survival of many plant and animal species, are also immeasurably valuable to people. As salt marshes maintain or improve water quality and furnish abundant food to countless organisms, they also support coastwide commercial and recreational fisheries and a thriving oyster industry. Moreover, marshes provide opportunities for both passive and active recreation—such as observing and photographing wildlife, hiking, canoeing, fishing, and hunting—as well as education and scientific study.

Fishing is varied and excellent at times, ranging from surfcasting near the jaws of the bay to jigging from the public pier or dunking bait from anchored boats in the upper channels. During spring and summer, the bay gives up good catches of perch, rockfish, and the occasional flounder. Feeder chinook move into and out of the bay during the summer months, but an angling closure from July to mid-August makes them off limits. From mid-August through December the bay is open for chinook salmon, and the fishing can be good through autumn, and superb at times. The bay is open all year for steelhead fishing, and some steelhead come to hook every month of the year, with April and May giving up the fewest fish. The summer run starts in late May, and the winter fishery begins in November.

Crabbing is best on the lower bay near the Taft district. Crabbers sometimes do well hanging their rings and pots from the public pier, but those with boats do better and can cover more water.

Siletz Bay is home to only one of the five popular bay clams, the soft-shell, and its beds aren't the most productive. Nevertheless, there are colonies residing in mud and gravel along the bay's edge and in the flats near the mouth of Drift Creek. Any zero or lower tide exposes digging areas.

A small parking area on the west side of the highway offers excellent views of lower Siletz Bay and good photographic opportunities. There's a trash receptacle and a central-coast historical marker.

U.S. 101, mile 118.2
Viewpoint

This loop road leads southeast off the highway, follows the Siletz River for about 24 miles to the community of Siletz, and eventually joins U.S. Route 20 at Toledo, east of Newport.

U.S. 101, mile 119.9
State Route 229 junction

Movie House Viewpoint

Turn east off Highway 101, and drive 1.2 miles to a parking area on the south side of the road, overlooking the river. This spot offers a good view of and opportunity to photograph the house built for and used in the movie *Sometimes a Great Notion*, based on a novel by Oregon author Ken Kesey. The 1971 film, directed by Paul Newman, starred Newman, Henry Fonda, Lee Remick, Michael Sarrazin, and Richard Jaekel.

One of the longer coastal rivers, the Siletz meanders through the Coast Range and empties into Siletz Bay near the small rural community of Kernville. The main recreational activity on the Siletz is fishing, and the river is most accessible to bank and boat anglers from the town of Siletz downstream to Siletz Bay. It is open to angling for its lower 64.5 miles, but the mainstem is closed from 900 feet below Siletz Falls upstream, as are the North Fork and South Fork.

U.S. 101, mile 120
Siletz River

This house, on the south bank of the Siletz River, was built for the movie Sometimes a Great Notion, *based on Ken Kesey's novel of the same title.*

Filmed on the Oregon Coast

The following films were made, in whole or in part, on the Oregon coast. Most are available as videocassettes. It's fun to rent them and try to pick out all the familiar landmarks.

Title	Year	Location
The Fisherman's Bride	1908	Astoria
Sometimes a Great Notion	1970	Central Coast, Siletz River
One Flew Over the Cuckoo's Nest	1975	Depoe Bay, Salem
Premonitions	1980	Coos Bay
Hysterical	1981	Cannon Beach, Depoe Bay, Newport
California Mix	1981	Astoria
Cry for the Stranger	1982	Florence
Goonies	1984	Astoria
Short Circuit	1985	Astoria, Portland, Columbia Gorge
Benji the Hunted	1986	Statewide
Come See the Paradise	1989	Astoria, Portland, Willamette Valley
Kindergarten Cop	1990	Astoria
Shattered	1990	North Coast
Point Break	1991	Wheeler, Ecola State Park
Claire of the Moon	1991	Coast, Portland
The Bed You Sleep In	1992	Toledo
The Temp	1992	North Coast, Portland
Teenage Mutant Ninja Turtles III	1992	Astoria
Free Willy	1992	Astoria, Portland
Frameup	1992	Newport
Free Willy II	1994	Astoria
The Ox and the Eye	1994	Coos Bay, Portland

Both bank and boat anglers take chinook salmon in good numbers each year, and the river is a top producer of steelhead trout. Although it is open for chinook salmon from April through December, the best fishing doesn't get underway until fall and usually holds up well through November and early December. Steelhead are available all year, with the most productive fishing occurring from December through March. All anglers need to consult the *Oregon Sport Fishing Regulations* for season changes and restrictions on tackle and bait.

Although the Siletz courses through some wild, rugged country, where black-tailed deer, Roosevelt elk, black bear, cougar, and smaller mammals roam and eagles soar, road-bound travelers won't find as many opportunities for sightseeing, wildlife watching, or photography, as they might on most other coastal rivers.

Along this stretch, the refuge spreads east and west from both sides of the highway, offering views of marshes, tidal creeks and sloughs, and seasonally abundant birdlife.

U.S. 101, mile 120.7
Siletz Bay National Wildlife Refuge

Siletz Bay National Wildlife Refuge

The award-winning lodge with its Scottish-style links laid out on both sides of the highway ranks as one of the finest golf resorts in Oregon. The 6,453-yard, 18-hole, par-72 course graces the slopes of wooded hills that offer stunning views of Siletz Bay, Salishan Spit, and the Pacific Ocean. Course amenities include driving range, chipping area, putting green, 350-yard putting course, clubhouse, pro shop, resident pro, club rental and storage, gas-cart rental, coffee shop, and beverage cart. Also on the premises are lodging, two restaurants, a lounge, a wine cellar, a small shopping mall, and hiking trails. Reservations: (800) 452-2300. Pro shop: (541) 764-3632 or (800) 890-0387.

U.S. 101, mile 121.2
The Westin Salishan Lodge and Golf Resort

**U.S. 101,
mile 121.4
Gleneden Beach**
(zip code 97388)
Laurel Street beach
access

This small residential community lies between Highway 101 and the beach, and is accessible via Gleneden Beach Loop, leading west then south off the highway.

Turn west off U.S. 101, veer south on Gleneden Beach Loop and continue for 0.3 mile. Turn west on Laurel Street, and drive another 0.3 mile to a small parking area. Easy beach access is across the street from the parking lot. Hike the beach here, or head north to reach Salishan Spit.

**U.S. 101,
mile 122.3**
Gleneden Beach
State Recreation Site

Turn west off the highway, and drive 0.2 mile to the park entrance. This day-use area has paved paths to the beach, providing access to Salishan Spit. Visitors will also find wind-protected picnic areas with tables and grills, drinking water, trash receptacles, and rest rooms with flush toilets and wheelchair access.

**U.S. 101,
miles 124.8 and
125.3**
Fogarty Creek State
Recreation Area,
north and south
entrances

Turn east off the highway into a lovely park that serves as the site for the famous annual Siletz Indian-style salmon bake. The park features hiking trails through a forest of alder, shore pine, Sitka spruce, and western hemlock and picnic areas with tables set among the trees and shrubs. Wooden bridges cross Fogarty Creek at several places, and a trail leads along the creek and under the highway to a scenic ocean cove with a small sand beach and rocky intertidal area with tide pools to explore. A spouting horn in the rocky rubble south of the beach shoots jets of ocean water skyward during incoming tides. The park has drinking water, trash receptacles, and rest rooms with flush toilets and wheelchair access.

**U.S. 101,
mile 125.7**
Boiler Bay

This small photogenic coastal embayment that might have inspired any of innumerable romantically descriptive names derives its pedestrian designation from a ship's rusty old boiler and shaft mired in the bay's bottom and exposed at low tide. They were parts of the plant that powered the ill-fated *J. Marhoffer*, a small coastal freighter that was steaming north, 3 miles off the central Oregon coast, on the afternoon of May 18, 1910, bound from San Francisco for the Columbia River. When a gasoline torch exploded in the engine room, it instantly set fire to the ship, which had to be abandoned. The captain, his wife, and the ship's crew made for the rocky shore in two lifeboats. All but one, the ship's cook, safely reached land and survived. The disabled, burned-out ship drifted into the picturesque cove, where its shaft and boiler broke free and sank.

Just a swerve west off Highway 101, this gem of a park has more to offer than some many times its size. At low tide, descend a short but rough trail to explore and photograph magnificent tide pools. On the flood tide, watch or photograph wave after incoming wave, crashing into the rocky shoreline and filling the air with salty mist. On sunny days, enjoy a picnic amid the scenic splendor. This is also an excellent vantage point for watching gray whales during their winter and spring migrations or catching glimpses of a variety of seabirds, including albatrosses, black oystercatchers, brown pelicans, jaegers, marbled murrelets, and shearwaters. Those sleek creatures playing in the breakers might be seals or surfers waiting for their next ride. Come here, too, to watch the drama of winter storms unfold. The park has picnic tables, trash receptacles, and rest rooms with flush toilets and wheelchair access.

U.S. 101, mile 126.1
Boiler Bay State
Scenic Viewpoint

Like the diminutive bay that shares its name, the city of Depoe Bay is small (population: 1,100) and its downtown area compact. Most of the town lies north of the bridge. All of its shops, galleries, eateries, and watering holes are within easy walking distance of one another and all stand alongside the coast's primary thoroughfare: Highway 101.

U.S. 101, mile 126.4 to mile 128.5 Depoe Bay
(zip code 97341)

For those who wonder how towns get strange or unusual names, this one seems to be no more than a corrupted spelling. In 1894, the federal government granted the 200 acres comprising the town site and harbor to a Siletz Indian who, according to various sources, was known as Willie, William, Charley, Old Charley, or William Charles Depot. He reportedly worked for an army supply depot and took the name from his employment.

Local historians claim the family name eventually evolved into the more elegant-sounding *De Poe*. The current spelling, *Depoe*, appeared in early records, but the name is pronounced with the first syllable stressed. Curiously, a tidal creek that empties into the nearby Yaquina River above Newport was named after the same person, but it is called Depot Slough.

The main attractions in the Depoe Bay vicinity are the magnificent scenery and sightseeing opportunities, whales and whale watching, and fishing. Although the town has become a popular winter-weekend retreat, with sightseeing and whale-watching excursions departing the harbor hourly, weather permitting, the visitor season traditionally gets underway with the beginning of spring break and lasts well into autumn.

**U.S. 101,
mile 127.2 to
mile 127.5**
Depoe Bay
Promenade

MUST STOP

An attractive stone seawall and sidewalk extend along the west side of the highway south to the bridge and harbor entrance, with adjacent parking spaces for the entire 0.3 mile and interpretive signs along the way. Park here and stroll the promenade or visit the shops and galleries across the highway.

On the seaward side of the promenade, two spouting horns regularly stop traffic when the surf's up. Riled seas on incoming tides shoot fountains of water to heights of 60 feet and spray passing vehicles on the highway. On blue-sky days, they're great photographic subjects, but photographers need to take care to protect cameras and other gear from the salt spray. The best bet is to maintain some distance and shoot with moderate telephoto or zoom lenses.

At the south end of the promenade, next to the bridge, visitors will find public rest rooms with flush toilets and an observation room located at the Oregon Coast Aquarium Store. Picnic tables, a bench, and coin-operated binoculars overlook the harbor entrance.

This *must stop* on the ocean's edge is within easy walking distance of the bay, bridge, harbor entrance, and other Depoe Bay attractions.

**U.S. 101,
mile 127.3**
Depoe Bay Chamber
of Commerce Visitor
Center

This small center stands on the east side of the highway, opposite the promenade. Stop here for information about local attractions, any day from 11:00 a.m. to 4:00 p.m.

**U.S. 101,
mile 127.4**
Depoe Bay and
Harbor

Turn east at the traffic light on Bay Boulevard to reach the bay. A large parking lot flanks the harbor, where visitors can enjoy and photograph the harbor and bridge, or crab and fish from docks during daylight hours. In the vicinity are a fish-cleaning station, trash receptacles, and rest rooms with flush toilets and wheelchair access. A gravel trail at the south end of the harbor leads to Depoe Bay City Park and Boat Ramp; vehicle access to the park is off Highway 101 at mile 127.8.

Bays and estuaries punctuate Oregon's craggy coast, and pairs of parallel jetties flank the entrances to most. At Depoe Bay, however, a mere gash, 50 feet wide and 300 feet long, cuts through basaltic bedrock to connect the sea with a tiny tureen of a harbor nearly surrounded by an amphitheater of hills. The central coastline here indents to form a large outside embayment, at the center of which is the entrance to Depoe Bay. Covering a scant 6 acres, the harbor is 350 feet wide, 750 feet long, and 8 feet deep at mean low tide. Just outside the channel, the bottom drops abruptly to 40 feet, and farther out, the bell buoy is anchored in 60 feet of water. Reefs lie at the north and south ends of the outside bay, creating a bowl that drops to 120 feet in places.

The narrow harbor entrance might intimidate some skippers accustomed to piloting boats between wide-set jetties, but dredging has created fairly sheer rock walls without a lot of underwater surprises. What's more, the bay is not fed by a big river, so there is no menacing bar to cross. In fact, freshwater inflow from the two creeks that feed the bay is minimal, so the silt load is low, and sand transport seems to pose no great problems. The entrance is deceptive: from the outside, it looks worse than it actually is, because just inside, the channel makes a slight dogleg to the north and into the protected harbor. Experienced local skippers consider the Depoe Bay entrance among the easiest to navigate, given a modicum of common sense and boat-handling skills.

About a hundred commercial, charter, and sport boats are moored all year at Depoe Bay. During the summer, as many as two hundred more boats crowd the small harbor, leaving little surface water visible when everybody is in port.

Quick fishing is tantamount to good fishing here. The local brag—"fishing, two minutes from the dock"—is no great exaggeration. While it probably takes that long to negotiate the channel, and few anglers drop gear as soon as they're outside, the fact is, with no long river channel to travel and no bar to cross, it is a quick run to the fishing grounds. When the fish are in close, many anglers catch their limits without even going so far as the bell buoy. Coho and chinook salmon are the main quarry, and Depoe Bay landings are usually among the highest in the state. The salmon begin showing up in good numbers by late June, with angling lasting through the summer or until quotas are filled. Bottom fishing is a year-round activity when weather cooperates. Anglers take at least a dozen species of rockfish from nearshore and offshore reefs and rock piles, along with greenling, cabezon, lingcod, halibut, and the occasional shark or skate.

This is the marine zone, where the Pacific Fishery Management Council sets seasons and restrictions each April. Regulations, which can change on short notice, are published in May and are available at most bait-and-tackle shops. Seasons, restrictions, and closures are also announced through the news media.

A fleet of modern charter boats stands ready to serve anglers, sightseers, and whale watchers. Most fishing trips last five hours, but long-distance and tuna trips are a full day. Sightseeing and whale-watching excursions range in duration from less than an hour to four hours.

Transient moorage for vessels up to 60 feet is available at the north end of the bay and may be reserved or rented by phoning the harbor master: (541) 765-4333. Transient moorage for smaller craft up to 24 feet is available at the south end of the bay, near the city park and boat ramp. Contact City Hall: (541) 765-2361.

U.S. 101, mile 127.5
Depoe Bay Bridge and harbor entrance

The highway crosses the Depoe Bay channel near the mouth of the bay, via a 312-foot concrete bridge, designed by Oregon's greatest bridge builder, Conde B. McCullough. The original structure was built in 1927, and an addition was made on the seaward side in 1940 to increase the bridge's capacity. Characteristic of McCullough's beautiful and functional designs, the Depoe Bay Bridge displays ornate concrete work and other features. A stairwell and walkway at the northeast end provide a passageway beneath the highway and access to the channel-observation area and promenade on the west side of the highway. The bridge is a popular spot with tourists, an ideal place to photograph the bay and boat traffic in the narrow channel, and a good place to begin a walking tour of the town.

U.S. 101, mile 127.8
Depoe Bay City Park and Boat Ramp

The Depoe Bay Bridge and harbor entrance

Turn east off the highway on Southeast Schoolhouse Street, then immediately left on Southeast Shell Avenue. The park and ramp are 0.3 mile from the highway. This is an essential stop for boaters wishing to launch craft on the bay, but it's also a pleasant diversion for others who want to take a rest break, have a picnic, visit a pretty and interesting park, or explore the bayshore on

foot. The city has provided an excellent paved ramp and dock, ample trailer-parking area, and one of the best fish-cleaning stations to be found. The park includes a dam and fish ladder, foot bridge over the creek, interpretive signs about salmon in the watershed, gravel path to the harbor, picnic areas with tables, playground, skateboard ramp, drinking water, and rest rooms with flush toilets and wheelchair access.

This scenic picnic area and ocean overlook on the west side of the highway, with trees, shrubs, and grassy open areas, offers excellent photo opportunities and views of the ocean, rocky intertidal areas, and Whale Cove (to the north). The wave action is spectacular at times, especially during winter storms. There are picnic tables, benches, drinking water, and trash receptacles, but no beach or tide-pool access.

U.S. 101, mile 129.5
Rocky Creek State Scenic Viewpoint

This narrow, winding section of the old coast highway passes through a forested residential area and rejoins U.S. 101 at mile 133. Along the way, it leads to some spectacular ocean vistas and passes near or through Cape Foulweather, Otter Crest, Otter Rock, and Devils Punchbowl, all of which are more directly accessible by way of Highway 101. The scenic loop is a worthwhile drive, but isn't the best route for large motorhomes and travel trailers.

U.S. 101, mile 129.8
Otter Crest Loop, north access

The parking lot and viewpoint for this day-use area stand 0.2 mile west of the highway and 500 feet above the pounding Pacific, commanding a sweeping view south of the sandy beach, Otter Crest, Devils Punchbowl, and Yaquina Head. As with other headlands, the wind usually blows harder here than farther inland, but the weather is no worse. The English explorer Captain James Cook, however, found the weather particularly nasty on March 7, 1778, when he named the cape. When weather belies the name during the winter and spring migrations of gray whales, this is one of the best spots on the coast to watch for them.

U.S. 101, mile 131.2
Cape Foulweather State Wayside

On the west side of the highway is an ample parking lot offering a commanding view to the west of Otter Crest and southward of Beverly and Moolack beaches, as well as Yaquina Head and the lighthouse.

U.S. 101, mile 131.8
Otter Crest State Scenic Viewpoint

Southbound travelers should exit west here to reach Otter Rock and follow the signs to Devils Punchbowl State Natural Area. (See also U.S. 101, mile 133, on page 152.)

U.S. 101, mile 132.4
Otter Rock, north junction

Cape Foulweather (top left), overlooking Otter Crest

Devils Punch Bowl State Natural Area

In Otter Rock, turn west on 1st Street, and go 0.4 mile to the park. Named for a hollow rock formation that, to some eyes, resembles a giant punch bowl, where the surf sometimes churns so violently that it may well be the devil himself stirring it, this is a great place for watching winter storms and migrating whales. In good weather, it's a scenic picnic spot. At low tide, there are tide pools to explore to the north that are rich in marine life, but visitors are asked to leave the various organisms undisturbed. The entire intertidal area extending north from the Devils Punch Bowl to Cape Foulweather is designated a marine garden and is closed to the taking of shellfish and marine invertebrates, except that single mussels may be taken for bait.

The unusual geology and fickle moods of the sea make this park particularly attractive to sightseers and photographers, a neat place for an oceanside hike or picnic, and a *must stop* for all travelers. Among the park's many features are a marine-garden trail, stairway to Beverly Beach south of the Punch Bowl, picnic areas with tables, drinking water, trash receptacles, and rest rooms with flush toilets and wheelchair access.

U.S. 101, mile 133
Otter Rock, south junction

Northbound travelers should exit west here to reach Otter Rock and follow the signs 0.8 mile to Devils Punch Bowl State Natural Area. (See also U.S. 101, mile 132.4, on page 151.)

Otter Crest Loop, south junction

This scenic loop rejoins U.S. 101 at mile 129.8. (See there for details on page 151.)

U.S. 101, mile 134
Beverly Beach State Park

The entrance to this popular park and campground is just east of the highway. Lying midway between Depoe Bay and Newport, this wind-protected campground is the ideal headquarters for folks interested in visiting those cities or exploring all the natural wonders along this stretch of the central coast.

The woodland campground has 53 full-hookup sites, three of which have wheelchair access; 76 sites with water and electricity; 129 tent sites with nearby water; and 21 yurts, six of which have wheelchair access—all with paved parking, picnic tables, and fire rings. More than three dozen RV and tent sites lie alongside Spencer Creek, and 27 RV sites and 15 yurts have even have cable-TV hookups. All sites are near showers and rest rooms with flush toilets, three of which have wheelchair access. Trash receptacles, a recycle bin, dump station, and firewood are available.

The park also features a hiker/biker camp, a day-use area with creekside picnic tables and nearby rest rooms, a nature trail along Spencer Creek, and a trail and tunnel under the highway leading to Beverly Beach, a favorite of beachcombers, fossil hunters, kite flyers, and surfers. Just outside the park entrance are laundry facilities and a grocery store. Information: (541) 265-9278 or (800) 551-6949. Reservations: (800) 452-5687.

U.S. 101, mile 134.8
Emergency beach access road

A parking area and gated road to the beach on the west side of the highway provide easy foot access to the beach. Just be sure to avoid blocking the gate and road access for emergency vehicles.

U.S. 101, mile 134.5 to mile 135.1
Parking areas, viewpoint, and beach accesses

Parking areas on the west side of the highway are near narrow, steep trails to the beach, not recommended for small children or any but the most sure-footed hikers.

A parking area on the west side of the highway at mile 135.1 stands atop a bluff overlooking the ocean with good views of the beaches and tide pools below.

U.S. 101, mile 135.6
Moolack Beach

A parking lot on the west side of the highway provides access to a trail to Moolack Beach, which is popular with kite flyers and good for beach combing and agate hunting after storms.

U.S. 101, mile 136.5 to mile 144.2 Newport
(zip code 97365)

Newport is Lincoln County's largest city (population: 10,240) and seat of government. It's the second-largest city on the Oregon coast and is growing nearly seven times faster than the largest, Coos Bay. It's also billed as the friendliest city on the Oregon coast, and that isn't entirely public-relations hype.

Newport has been welcoming visitors for longer than any other town on the Oregon Coast. That tourism is an integral part of the area's economy is evident everywhere, from the oceanfront motels and resorts overlooking grand expanses of sandy beach to the shops, galleries, restaurants, RV parks, and marinas strung along the busy waterfront. Also on the waterfront at South Beach is a microbrewery and tasting room. Visitors will delight in the abundance of natural and cultural attractions the Newport area has to offer. They will find broad beaches extending north and south from the mouth of Yaquina Bay, rocky intertidal areas rich in marine life, a beautiful bay and sprawling estuary, and miles of scenic coastline to explore and photograph. There are two lighthouses to examine and photograph, a graceful and photogenic bridge over the bay, a little gem of a golf course, two museums, a marine science center, and, topping the list, the Oregon Coast Aquarium.

While homesteading pioneers and early entrepreneurs were claiming land, laying out cities, and building lumber mills along the upper reaches of Yaquina Bay and River to exploit the area's abundant natural resources, Sam Case, a former soldier who had once served in the area, was eyeing the lower bay as a place with special allure to tourists. He laid claim to land along the north shore near the mouth of the bay, and in 1866, he and his partner, Dr. J.R. Bayley, built the Ocean House, named after a resort hotel in Newport, Rhode Island. His original land claim encompassed what is now Newport's Historic Bayfront.

U.S. 101, mile 137.6
Yaquina Head
Outstanding Natural
Area

Turn west off the highway on Lighthouse Drive, and proceed 0.2 mile to the entrance of this Bureau of Land Management (BLM) complex, a *must stop* for all nature lovers, sightseers, wildlife watchers, and photographers.

Since Congress established the 100-acre Yaquina Head Outstanding Natural Area in 1980, BLM has worked to make the history, geology, natural bounty, and scenic splendor of this basaltic headland accessible for all who visit. Rewards awaiting those who take the 1-mile drive off Highway 101 include an entertaining and educational interpretive center, an old rock quarry transformed into a rocky intertidal area, an ancient cobble

At Yaquina Head Outstanding Natural Area, the Bureau of Land Management has transformed an old rock quarry into an intertidal area with interpretive signs and wheelchair access.

Yaquina Head Lighthouse

beach adjacent to tide pools, offshore rocks and islands teeming with wildlife, five distinctly different trails leading to various attractions and providing some of the best views and photo opportunities on the central coast, and a fine old lighthouse at the tip of the promontory.

The interpretive center houses displays depicting the natural and human history of the headland, a rocky island exhibit, audio-visual presentations, and sound stations. There's a ship's wheelhouse to examine and a replica of the Yaquina Head Lighthouse lantern.

The tide pools bristle with life, from seaweeds and green anemones to chitons, whelks, barnacles, starfish, purple sea urchins, hermit crabs, shore crabs, and sculpins. These and other organisms are there for observing and photographing but may not be removed, because the rocky intertidal area bordering Yaquina Head is protected as a marine garden.

Western and glaucous-winged gulls are year-round residents of the area, as are Brandt's and pelagic cormorants and black oystercatchers. From March through the summer, the nearby islands and rocks come alive with nesting seabirds, such as common murres, tufted puffins, pigeon guillemots, and rhinoceros auklets. Watch for marine mammals too. Pacific harbor seals reside here all year and often haul out on Seal Island and nearby rocks lying just off Cobble Beach. Gray whales pass near Yaquina Head in good numbers during their winter and spring migrations, but observers here stand a chance of spotting spouts any time of the year—a few whales hang around this stretch of the coast through the summer months and well into fall.

The road ends at a parking lot and turnaround near the lighthouse, about a mile from Highway 101. Operating since 1873, the Yaquina Head Light is Oregon's second-oldest lighthouse. With a tower height of 93 feet, it's also the tallest lighthouse in Oregon, and some consider it the most beautiful. The light stands 162 feet above the sea and is visible 19 miles out.

The Yaquina Head Outstanding Natural Area is open every day, all year, from dawn to dusk. From October to June, the interpretive center is open daily, 10:00 a.m. to 4:00 p.m.; summer hours are 10:00 a.m. to 5:00 p.m. The lighthouse is open for tours from noon to 4:00 p.m. every day, except during the heaviest rainstorms, when the old structure leaks.

U.S. 101, mile 138.1
Agate Beach Golf Course

On the east side of the highway, this 3,002-yard, 9-hole, par-36 course was built in 1931 and has settled nicely into the rolling, wooded terrain with an ocean view. Features include a pro shop, resident pro, rental clubs and carts, driving range, and restaurant serving beer and wine. Pro shop: (541) 265-7331.

U.S. 101, mile 138.3
Northwest Ocean View Drive

This residential street exits west off U.S. 101 and roughly parallels the highway along the ocean all the way to the Yaquina Bay State Recreation Site and Yaquina Bay Bridge, where it rejoins Highway 101 at mile 141.3. Northwest Ocean View Drive becomes Northwest Spring Street in the Nye Beach area. Follow Spring Street for four blocks, turn west (right) on 8th Street, then south (left) on Northwest Coast Street after one block. Just past 1st Street, turn west (right) on Olive Street, and follow it as it bends south and joins Elizabeth Street, which continues past the oceanfront motels and resorts to Government Street and the entrance to the state park. Turn west (right) and follow the park road to the lighthouse, bridge, and Highway 101, or go under the bridge to reach the Historic Bayfront District.

This route, west off Highway 101 at mile 138.3 in the north or mile 141.3 in the south, is not as complicated as it sounds and is a good way to avoid Highway 101 traffic through the Newport city center. It leads to Agate Beach, Nye Beach, Donald A. Davis City Park, and other attractions along the lower bay and ocean beach.

Agate Beach State Recreation Site

Turn west on Northwest Ocean View Drive; the park entrance is just off U.S. 101 on the east side of the road, where visitors will find a large parking area and tunnel under the street to Agate Beach, a popular place for all beach activities, including beach combing, especially after storms. The park has picnic tables, drinking water, trash receptacles, and rest rooms with flush toilets and wheelchair access.

U.S. 101, mile 140.3
U.S. Route 20 junction

This highway leads east to Toledo, Corvallis, I-5, and beyond. It's the shortest, most direct route between I-5 and Newport.

Nye Beach Historic District

Turn west on Olive Street, and drive 0.5 mile to Northwest Coast Street. Turn north, and drive five blocks to Northwest Beach Drive and the Nye Beach Turnaround. Near the turnaround are ample parking, picnic tables, wheelchair access to the beach, and rest rooms with flush toilets.

Many of the buildings in this historic beach community were erected during the early twentieth century and currently function as restaurants, shops, and galleries. The Yaquina Art Center—originally a public bathhouse, built in 1913—displays the work of more than thirty artists. Nearby oceanfront accommodations range from quaint cottages to deluxe suites. Visitors to the district can park and divide their time between playing on the beach and exploring the historic community. Stop by the Newport Visitor Center to pick up a guide and map.

Donald A. Davis Park

West of the highway 0.5 mile, via Olive Street, lies a pretty little city park on the edge of the ocean with a parking lot, benches, trash receptacles, drinking water, rest rooms with flush toilets and wheelchair access, and a paved path to the beach.

U.S. 101, mile 140.8
Greater Newport Chamber of Commerce Visitor Center

Turn east off Highway 101 at Southwest Fall Street, where the chamber building stands. Stop here to get copies of the excellent city map and guides to Newport's Nye Beach, South Beach, and Bayfront districts. The center is open Monday through Friday from 8:30 a.m. to 5:00 p.m. From May through September, it's also open weekends from 10:00 a.m. to 4:00 p.m.

Log Cabin Museum and the Burrows House

A half-block east of the Visitor Center, the Lincoln County Historical Society's Log Cabin Museum houses interesting displays and photographs of early Newport, the fishing industry, logging and lumber products, farm implements and tools, and Siletz Indian artifacts. Next door, at the Burrows House, see what an 1890s boarding house looked like, complete with period furnishings. They're both open Tuesday through Sunday— summer, 10:00 a.m. to 5:00 p.m.; winter, 11:00 a.m. to 4:00 p.m.—and closed on major holidays. Information: (541) 265-7509.

U.S. 101, mile 141.3
Yaquina Bay State Recreation Site

Turn west off the highway north of the bridge, and follow the road to the large parking lot atop the forested bluff above the mouth of the bay, which offers excellent views of the ocean, jetties, bay, bridge, and lighthouse. There's access to the beach near the north jetty, a favorite among rockhounds, who find agates, jasper, and petrified wood, especially after winter and spring storms. The *must-stop* park includes a playground, picnic areas with tables, trash receptacles, drinking water, and rest rooms with flush toilets and wheelchair access.

Yaquina Bay Lighthouse

The meticulously restored Yaquina Bay Lighthouse stands inside the state park on a hill above the bluff and parking lot and is a *must stop*. The attractive structure, built in 1871, functioned as both lighthouse and keepers' quarters. It was sited at the northwest end of the bay to operate as a harbor-entrance beacon, but it was not visible to ships arriving from the north. When nearby Yaquina Head Lighthouse began operating in 1873, the harbor light was extinguished. The wooden lighthouse, the oldest building in Newport, eventually fell into disrepair and was scheduled for demolition soon after the Oregon State Highway Division acquired the property in 1934. The Lincoln County Historical Society managed to save the lighthouse and used it for some years as a county historical museum. In the 1970s, the state restored the fine old structure and furnished it with period antiques. On December 7, 1996, it once again became an operating lighthouse and stands today as a worthy subject for any photographer's lens. From October 1 to Memorial Day, the lighthouse is open daily from noon to 4:00 p.m.; from

Yaquina Bay Lighthouse

Memorial Day to September 30, daily hours are 11:00 a.m. to 5:00 p.m. Information: (541) 265-5679.

Historic Bayfront District

Southbound travelers should turn west off U.S. 101 near the north end of the bridge, as if heading for the state park, but then turn east under the bridge, and proceed down the hill to Bay Boulevard and the waterfront. Northbound travelers should turn east after crossing the bridge, and continue down the hill to the waterfront. The Bayfront District is Newport's old-town area and the original town site. It's also a busy, working waterfront, chockablock with more than sixty shops, galleries, restaurants, and tourist attractions.

Parking along Bay Boulevard in the westernmost three blocks or so is sometimes tight, at other times impossible. When it's too crowded, head east for the commercial boat basin, where there is additional parking along Bay Boulevard. From there the whole waterfront area is within easy walking distance.

Marine Discovery Tours

The 65-foot excursion boat *Discovery* operates from the Newport waterfront, east of Highway 101, on the south side of Bay Boulevard. The modern vessel, with inside seating for 49, conducts naturalist-narrated, two-hour cruises of Yaquina Bay and the near-shore Pacific, with opportunities for passengers to see oyster farms, the Newport waterfront, gray whales, harbor seals, sea lions, and all manner of birdlife, as well as the spectacular central-coast scenery. Information: (541) 265-6200 or (800) 903-2628.

Embarcadero Marina

This marina/resort complex on the north shore of the bay is about 1.25 miles east of U.S. 101, via Bay Boulevard. Boaters will find transient moorage available for vessels up to 45 feet and end ties up to 60 feet. Shore power and freshwater hookups are available, as are rest rooms with flush toilets and showers. There is a bait-and-tackle shop with crabbing and clam-digging gear for rent. The marina also books fishing, sightseeing, and whale-watching trips. Information: (541) 265-5435.

Sawyer's Landing Marina and RV Park

Located about 5 miles east of Highway 101, via Bay Boulevard and Yaquina Bay Road, this privately owned complex is popular with trailer boaters and upbay anglers and crabbers. The facility offers 40 slips and a hoist for boats up to 24 feet, as well as rest rooms with flush toilets, showers, crab- and fish-cleaning stations, and a crab cooker. Information: (541) 265-3907.

Yaquina Bay Bridge

The 3,223-foot, steel and concrete bridge over lower Yaquina Bay is one of the most gracefully attractive bridges on the West Coast and a fitting tribute to its designer, Conde B. McCullough. It's one of five major bridges completed on the Oregon coast in 1936 to open the entire length of the Coast Highway to vehicular traffic. Among its decorative elements are fluted entrance pylons—a McCullough signature—and a pedestrian plaza at the north end with concrete stairways and observation areas. The bridge is visible throughout the Yaquina Bay area, but the best places for studying and photographing it are the Yaquina Bay State Recreation Site, the south jetty, and the Port of Newport Marina at South Beach. The bridge itself, with sidewalks on both sides of the deck, is a great platform for sightseeing and photography.

U.S. 101, mile 141.3 Yaquina Bay

This 1,700-acre bay is home port to Oregon's largest commercial fleet and one of the state's biggest recreational fleets. It's among Oregon's largest bays and is an important estuary that supports a wide diversity of marine and estuarine life. It's also one of the most beautiful and photogenic bays on the West Coast, offering unlimited sightseeing and photo-taking opportunities.

Yaquina Bay is a busy port and an attractive estuary, with plenty of opportunities for sightseeing, wildlife watching, and photography. The best places to observe boat traffic and wildlife and photograph everything from seabirds to waterfront scenics include the Yaquina Bay State Recreation Site, northwest of the bridge; Bay Boulevard, the Embarcadero Marina, and Yaquina Bay Road, northeast of the bridge; South Jetty Road, southwest of the bridge; the public fishing and crabbing pier and Port of Newport Marina, southeast of the bridge; and the nature trail that begins near the parking lot at the Hatfield Marine Science Center.

Ornamental concrete work and stairway at the northwest end of the Yaquina Bay Bridge.

Settlers were first drawn to this area in the early 1860s by vast beds of tiny, tasty Yaquina Bay oysters, which were harvested in great numbers and shipped by schooner to San Francisco. Overharvest eventually led to depletion of the beds, and today all oyster beds are privately owned and off-limits to the public. Nevertheless, other fish and shellfish that have attracted people to Yaquina Bay and nearby offshore waters for many years are seasonally available.

The bay is blessed with an abundance of clams that reside in the tidal flats that rim parts of the bay and lower tidewater portions of the river. Gaper clams and cockles make up the bulk of the harvest and are the main quarry on the bay flats during minus tides. Butter and littleneck clams are also taken, but in lower numbers. Farther upstream, soft-shell clams inhabit shoreline flats from the Riverbend area nearly all the way to the city of Toledo. They're available for the digging on any low tide.

Yaquina Bay is also one of the top spots in Oregon for recreational crabbing. Most crabbers set their gear in the deeper portions of the lower 3 miles of the bay; check with locals for best recommendations. Crabbing gear is for sale or rent at tackle shops, marinas, and some marine-supply outlets.

Inshore species of fish taken in the bay and lower river include greenling, rockfish, sole, flounder, and several kinds of perch. The biggest residents of the bay and lower river depths are white sturgeon, which are taken from inside the jetties to deep holes upriver as far as Sawyer's Landing and beyond. Offshore reefs give up limits of cabezon, greenling, lingcod, and various species of rockfish, some running to 20 pounds or more. This fishery is year round, ocean conditions permitting. As weather improves and the Pacific begins flattening out in late spring and early summer, more anglers set out in search of these bottom fish. Check at local tackle shops for recommendations, and watch where the charter boats fish.

The hot bite here in May is Pacific halibut. Halibut banks were discovered off Yaquina Bay in 1911, creating a tremendous commercial fishery. The area has remained the top halibut sportfishing spot for years. This is a closely watched and internationally regulated fishery. Seasons and quotas change year to year, so be sure to check with the Oregon Department of Fish and Wildlife or local tackle shops and marinas for the latest information and regulations.

In August and September, warmer nearshore waters attract great schools for forage species that Pacific albacore follow and feed on. Fishing for these fine little tunas, which average about 10 pounds each, is cyclic, but can be phenomenal, especially during El Niño years.

This part of the coast has long been famous for its great coho and chinook salmon fishing. In recent years, however, coho populations have plummeted. Although chinook have generally fared better, the fishery has been regulated to protect both species. Generally, Yaquina Bay is open for chinook angling from the ends of the jetties upstream to the head of tidewater from April through December. The Pacific Fishery Management Council (PFMC) sets seasons and restrictions for the offshore salmon fishery and publishes them each May. So be sure to check the *Oregon Sport Fishing Regulations* and the PFMC announcements before heading out on your own.

A fleet of modern charter boats and the tour boat *Discovery* work out of Yaquina Bay, offering fishing, sightseeing, and wildlife-watching trips. Those interested can book trips at the Newport waterfront, the Embarcadero Marina, and the Port of Newport Marina in South Beach.

Yaquina Bay is boater-friendly, with a jetty-tamed bar and channel dredged to 44 feet to maintain a 40-foot depth. Boaters crossing the bar need to steer clear of the reefs both north and south of the bay entrance and stay on the center ranges. As usual, boaters new to the area and those unsure of bar conditions because of outdated charts or for any other reason should check with the Coast Guard or savvy locals before venturing out.

Scuba diving is another popular area sport, with spearfishing, sightseeing, and underwater photography attracting divers to the jetties, reefs, and several nearshore wrecks. For information and supplies, divers should stop by Newport Water Sports on South Jetty Road, at the southwest end of the bridge, or phone (541) 867-3742.

Southbound travelers should turn west on Abalone Street, and continue under the bridge to Marine Science Drive; northbound travelers should exit east on Pacific Way to connect with Marine Science Drive, which leads to the Port of Newport Marina, Ferry Slip Road and the Oregon Coast Aquarium, and the Hatfield Marine Science Center, all east of the bridge. On the west side of the bridge, Marine Science Drive connects with Abalone Street, 26th Street, and South Jetty Road to reach the South Jetty Recreation Area and beach. The South Beach District also has lodging, restaurants, cafés, a microbrewery, and several shops and galleries.

U.S. 101, mile 142
South Beach District

Follow the directions for the South Beach District. Then, under the bridge, on the west side, take 26th Street west to South Jetty Road, which leads along the lower bay to the jetty, nature trail, beach, and horse access. The road has turnouts for parking and observing or photographing wildlife and boat traffic. This is also a popular area for fishing, scuba diving, surfing, windsurfing, and kite flying. The beach south of the jetty has a small population of razor clams.

South Jetty
Recreation Area

Follow the directions to reach the South Beach District, head for the marina complex just east of the bridge, and park at the west end of the lot. A fine pier extends well into the bay and affords excellent sightseeing and photography opportunities, as well as the intended fishing and crabbing. Fish- and crab-cleaning facilities are adjacent to the parking lot.

Public fishing and
crabbing pier

The public fishing and crabbing pier, breakwater, and South Beach Marina lie across the bay from Newport's Bayfront District.

Port of Newport
Marina and RV Park

Follow the directions for the South Beach District, and turn north off of Marine Science Drive into the large parking lot. The modern facilities of this complex spread along the southeast side of the bridge, directly across the bay from the Coast Guard Station, 1.5 miles from the open ocean. This is one of the largest marinas on the Oregon coast, with 600 slips of 24 to 48 feet and accommodations for larger craft. Freshwater and shore-power hookups are available, as well as a pump-out station, 24-hour fuel dock, store, café, rest rooms with flush toilets and wheelchair access, showers, fish-cleaning stations, and picnic areas. For trailer boats, the marina has a large two-lane, concrete ramp; freshwater boat-wash area; and space for short-term trailer parking.

Recreational vehicle facilities include more than 100 spaces with full hookups and cable TV. There's an RV dump station, and propane is available. Information: (541) 867-3321.

Oregon State
University Hatfield
Marine Science
Center

Follow directions from Highway 101 for the South Beach District. Near the end of Marine Science Drive, turn east into the science-center parking lot. The visitor center of this large research and education complex is a *must stop* for everyone who is interested in the human and natural history of Yaquina Bay and the Oregon coast. This outstanding, 15,000-square-foot museum and aquarium displays ship models, marine artwork, wildlife exhibits, an octopus tank, a touch tank full of intertidal organisms, and aquariums housing local marine life. Lectures, workshops, tours, films, and interactive videos are part of the entertaining educational experience. Also on the premises are rest rooms with wheelchair access and a bookstore specializing in marine-related titles. Admission is free. From October 1 to Memorial Day, the center is open Thursday to Monday, 10:00 a.m. to 4:00 p.m.; from Memorial Day through September, it's open daily from 10:00 a.m. to 5:00 p.m.

Estuary Trail

From the northeast end of the parking lot of the Hatfield Marine Science Center, a paved path extends for 0.5 mile along the shore of Yaquina Bay, past mudflats and salt marsh. The easy, level trail offers excellent bay views and opportunities to observe and photograph resident and migratory birds and waterfowl. The trail connects with a boardwalk over the marsh and ends near the Oregon Coast Aquarium.

Oregon Coast
Aquarium

Follow the directions to the South Beach District, turn south off Marine Drive onto Ferry Slip Road, and watch for signs directing visitors to the parking lot. One of Oregon's major attractions, this exciting and entertaining complex is a *must stop* for all coastal travelers.

Four large galleries full of immaculate aquariums provide visitors with close-up views of all kinds of marine fishes and invertebrates displayed in their natural surroundings. Watch herring and smelt, salmon and steelhead, sharks and skates, flounders and sole, perch and rockfish, lingcod and cabezon, sculpins and wolf eels, and other denizens of the deep cruise in natural surroundings. Stand mesmerized before a large tank full of undulating jellyfish as they dance their graceful water ballet. Check out the touch pool, discovery lab, and video theater.

Outside, walk through the seabird aviary and enjoy the antics of tufted puffins, common murres, black oystercatchers, and other birds, all viewable from above or below the water's surface. Stroll past cliffs and caves with above-water and underwater views of seals, sea lions, and sea otters. Then head for the most exciting exhibit of all: Passages of the Deep, where visitors walk through a clear acrylic tunnel that's suspended under water and traverses three distinct ocean habitats—Orford Reef, the Halibut Flats, and Open Sea—all teeming with marine life. This marvelous exhibit is home to more than sixty species of marine fishes, including salmon, rockfishes, flatfishes, skates, rays, and sharks.

Also on the premises are a covered picnic area, restaurant, gift shop and bookstore, and rest rooms with wheelchair access. Rental strollers and wheelchairs are available.

The aquarium is open every day except Christmas Day. Summer hours are 9:00 a.m. to 6:00 p.m.; winter hours are 10:00 a.m. to 5:00 p.m.

On the east side of the highway is a parking area and trailhead. Stop here to take a 45-minute, self-guided trek through a Sitka spruce forest.

U.S. 101, mile 143.1
Mike Miller County Park Educational Trail

Turn west off the highway to reach the campground, day-use area, and beach. This park, which lies adjacent to the South Jetty Recreation Area, is popular with beachgoers, hikers, anglers, and razor-clam diggers. The campground features 238 sites with electrical and water hookups, 16 yurts, and six primitive tent sites with water nearby. All sites have picnic tables and fire rings, and all but the primitive tent sites have paved parking. Two RV sites and all the yurts have wheelchair access. Other amenities include a hiker/biker camp, trash receptacles, a recycle bin, dump station, horseshoe pits, hot showers, and rest rooms with flush toilets and wheelchair access. There's also firewood available.

U.S. 101, mile 143.3
South Beach State Park

The day-use area has a large parking lot, picnic sites, and rest rooms with flush toilets and wheelchair access. From there, it's an easy walk to the broad sandy beach. Three trails, ranging from 0.25 to 0.5 mile, lead from the campground to the beach.

Another leads 2 miles from the day-use area to the south jetty. The mile-long Cooper Ridge Nature Trail skirts the northern end and eastern edge of the campground.

Information: (541) 867-4715 or (800) 551-6949. Reservations: (800) 452-5687.

U.S. 101, mile 147.2
Lost Creek State Recreation Site

On the west side of the highway is a small oceanfront park with picnic tables, trash receptacles, and pit toilets. Park here and follow the paved path to a beach that's a favorite among beachcombers.

U.S. 101, mile 148.9
Ona Beach State Park

This pretty little park with a large parking area lies along the west side of the highway and is one of the most popular day-use areas along this stretch of the coast. It features frontage along Beaver Creek, wooded picnic sites with tables and fire pits, drinking water, trash receptacles, and rest rooms with flush toilets. A trail leads a short distance to a great stretch of beach that's popular for all beach activities, but especially for beach combing, rockhounding, and fossil hunting.

Beaver Creek Boat Ramp

Turn east on North Beaver Creek Road, then immediately south into the small parking area. A paved ramp provides access to lower beaver creek for fishing, canoeing, kayaking, sightseeing, and photography.

Beaver Creek

Not widely known for its angling opportunities, the placid tidewater section of this creek gives up a few trout and gets a small run of steelhead. It's closed to steelhead angling from April to the end of May, but open the rest of the year. It's also a lovely spot for canoeing and kayaking.

U.S. 101, mile 150.4 to mile 151.2 Seal Rock
(zip code 97376)

This tiny community lies mainly along the east side of the highway and consists of several shops, restaurants, and private residences.

U.S. 101, mile 150.8
Seal Rock State Recreation Site

Turn west off the highway directly into the parking lot of this oceanfront day-use area. The park features a pleasant picnic area with tables set amid spruce and shore pines, paved trails, a viewing deck, and access to the beach and tide pools. Just offshore, formations known as Seal Rocks provide habitat for seals, sea lions, and seabirds. There are trash receptacles and rest rooms with flush toilets.

U.S. 101, mile 153.1
Driftwood Beach State Recreation Site

On the west side of the highway is a large parking lot and picnic area with tables and a fireplace set among the shore pines. A short path leads to a broad sand beach that's a good choice for beach combing and other activities. The park has trash receptacles, drinking water, and rest rooms with flush toilets and wheelchair access.

Turn west off the highway at the north end of the Alsea Bay Bridge, and go 0.2 mile to a small parking lot and turnaround overlooking Alsea Bay and the bridge. Railing and pylons from the original Alsea Bay Bridge, a rustic wood fence, and bent and gnarled shore pines all serve as framing props for photographs of the bay and bridge. A short concrete stairway leads from the wayside to a sidewalk that spans the west side of the bridge, which is also a good spot for views and photographs of the lower bay. The wayside also has benches and a chemical toilet with wheelchair access.

U.S. 101, mile 155
Alsea North Wayside

It was a sad day for Oregon coast bridge lovers—especially for the many fans of the state's greatest bridge designer ever, Conde B. McCullough—when it was announced that the beautiful Alsea Bay Bridge, opened in 1936, was beyond repair and would have to come down. The 3,011-foot concrete structure was typical of McCullough's designs, featuring many decorative touches, such as ornate concrete work, fluted entrance pylons, obelisk spires, graceful arches, and even a pedestrian observation plaza. Many considered this to be the finest concrete bridge in America. How could any boring, modern, uninspiring span ever replace a McCullough masterpiece?

U.S. 101, mile 155.2
Alsea Bay Bridge

Well, while the replacement bridge, opened to traffic in 1991, is not a McCullough design, it's certainly a fitting tribute to

Alsea Bay Bridge

Oregon's premier bridge builder and a handsome structure in its own right. It even expresses some of McCullough's style and incorporates parts of the original bridge in its design. It's a worthy subject for travel photography, and with sidewalks flanking both sides of its deck, it serves as an excellent platform for wildlife watchers, sightseers, and photographers. Stop by the Alsea Bay Historic Interpretive Center at the southwest end of the bridge (mile 155.8) to learn more about the bridge and guided bridge tours.

Alsea Bay and River

The Alsea River flows from the Coast Range toward the ocean for about 50 miles before broadening into the 6-mile-long bay and estuary and emptying into the Pacific at Waldport. U.S. Highway 101 provides access to the bay from the north and south. State Route 34 leads east from Highway 101 at Waldport and flanks the river for the entire length of the mainstem and beyond. The bay, river, valley, and community called Alsea derive their name from the Alsi tribe that once inhabited the land near the mouth of the bay.

The bay isn't heavily fished for marine species, but dedicated anglers catch perch, sole, and a few flounders in the lower bay from spring through summer. There is no spring chinook fishery, but the summer/fall run is generally good, and the fish often run big. The bay and mainstem of the river are open from mid-August through December for chinook salmon, which are usually available in the bay and lower river through the early part of the season and peak in late September and October. Steelhead follow and are in the system through the winter months. Anglers need to check the *Oregon Sport Fishing Regulations* for steelhead closures, but the bay and lower river are generally closed to steelhead angling from April through mid-August.

Crabbing and clam-digging are other popular activities on Alsea Bay. Most crabbers work the lower bay from boats, but some make good catches from the Port of Alsea docks on the Waldport waterfront. Although a few gaper clams reside in the flats west of the bridge, cockles are the main quarry in the sandy shoals of the lower bay. Colonies of soft-shell clams inhabit the muddier flats farther upbay.

Although some anglers and crabbers like to ply the waters near the mouth of the bay, this is a potentially dangerous area, particularly during an ebb tide. There are no jetties, and the sandy channel shifts continually, so this is not a bar to be crossed under any circumstances. Boaters venturing near the mouth of the bay are wise to have auxiliary power onboard or at least a substantial anchor at the ready in case of engine failure.

Alsea Bay is a medium-size estuary that attracts substantial numbers of viewable wildlife. About a hundred Pacific harbor seals reside in the bay and often haul out on sandbars near the bridge, within easy view of binoculars and telephoto lenses. Farther upbay, the salt marshes and mudflats are home to wading birds, shorebirds, ducks, and geese. Migratory birds and waterfowl flock to the bay during spring and fall migrations, and some spend most or all of the winter there, foraging and resting.

The German *wald*, meaning forest, combined with the English "port" gives some indication of what this community was all about when it was settled and named in the early 1880s. The adjacent forested hills and mountains provided the timber that became the mainstay of the Waldport economy for more than a century. Commercial fishing and dairy farming also contributed to the area's development. Although logging still plays a significant role in the area's economy, this small coastal city (population: 1,845) has evolved into a mainly residential community where outdoor recreation and tourism have become increasingly important. In addition to such immediately evident attractions as the ocean, beaches, bay, and estuary, Waldport also stands as the gateway to the Alsea River Recreation Area, extending eastward into the Coast Range.

U.S. 101, mile 155.6 to 156.7 Waldport (zip code 97394)

Clam diggers and rakers on lower Alsea Bay at Waldport.

In town, visitors can browse at a number of shops and galleries and dine at several excellent restaurants and cafés. South of town, oceanside campgrounds, cottages, motels, and resorts provide comfortable overnight accommodations and great scenery.

U.S. 101, mile 155.8
State Route 34 junction

This scenic road leads east off Highway 101, past the Waldport city center, and up the river, through what's known as the Alsea River Recreation Area, then northeast to Corvallis, I-5, and Lebanon. On the lower reaches of the Alsea, a number of private marinas and RV parks provide launching facilities, moorage, and campsites for anglers and other outdoor recreationists. (Use Lincoln County and Siuslaw National Forest maps.)

Port of Alsea

Turn east off Highway 101 on State Route 34, drive 0.4 mile, turn north on Broadway, and proceed 0.3 mile to the port facilities. Amenities include a paved boat ramp, courtesy dock, moorage docks, sidewalk along the waterfront, benches, trash receptacles, and rest rooms with flush toilets and wheelchair access. An adjacent marina rents boats with outboards.

Alsea Bay Historic Interpretive Center

✔

MUST STOP

Turn west at the traffic light just south of the bridge, go one block, and turn north (right) on Maple Street to reach the parking lot. This *must-stop* interpretive center, operated by the Oregon Parks and Recreation Department, is a fine little museum dedicated to the history of Alsea Bay and transportation along the Oregon coast. Interpretive displays focus on the Alsea Bay bridges, with historical photographs, chronological exhibits, and even a 15-foot model of the original bridge. From July 4th to Labor Day, park rangers offer daily narrated bridge tours at 2:00 p.m. Throughout the visitor season, they provide information and demonstrations on Alsea Bay fishing, crabbing, and clam digging. This is also the headquarters for Oregon's coastwide whale-watching program, which coincides with Christmas and spring breaks. The parking lot is an excellent vantage point for views of the lower bay and bridge as well as for wildlife watching and photography. The facility is wheelchair accessible, as are the rest rooms with flush toilets.

From Memorial Day to Labor Day, the center is open daily, 9:00 a.m. to 5:00 p.m. The rest of the year, it is open Tuesday through Saturday, 9:00 a.m. to 4:00 p.m. It's closed on major holidays. Information: (541) 563-2002.

Waldport Chamber of Commerce Visitor Center

See the directions for the Alsea Bay Bridge Interpretive Center. The chamber shares the facilities, provides literature and maps for Waldport and the Alsea Bay area, and has volunteers on duty at the reception desk.

This little city park on the west side of the highway has a small parking area with several picnic areas. Stop here for easy access to the beach, bay, and clam-digging flats. It's also a good spot for photographing the bay.

U.S. 101, mile 156.1
William P. Keady Wayside

Head east off the highway 0.1 mile to the to a U.S. Forest Service office to pick up Siuslaw National Forest maps and literature and brochures on local campgrounds and hiking trails. The office is open Monday through Friday from 7:30 a.m. to 4:00 p.m.

U.S. 101, mile 156.6
Waldport Ranger District

Turn east off the highway, and drive 0.8 mile on Range Drive to the entrance of this pleasant and challenging 3,062-yard, 9-hole, par-36 course. Amenities include a clubhouse, pro shop, resident pro, driving range, putting green, pitching green, rental electric and pull carts, rental clubs, and snack bar. Pro shop: (541) 563-3020.

U.S. 101, mile 156.8
Crestview Hills Golf Course

On the west side of the highway lies a decent-size parking area with easy access to miles of sand beach. You can walk from here to Alsea Bay and Waldport, with good views of the harbor seals. The park has tables for picnics and rest rooms with flush toilets.

U.S. 101, mile 157
Governor Patterson Memorial State Recreation Site

On the west side of the highway is a small park and campground with a descriptive name. Campsites are right next to the beach, so near, in fact, that the park is closed in the winter because of beach erosion and high water in and around the park. From March to November, though, this is a terrific spot for beach lovers to camp, hike, or enjoy a picnic.

U.S. 101, mile 159.3
Beachside State Recreation Site

The campground has 32 sites with water and electrical hookups, 50 tent sites with water nearby, and two yurts. All sites have paved parking, picnic tables, and fire rings, and two have wheelchair access. There's also a hiker/biker camp, trash receptacles, firewood for sale, hot showers, and rest rooms with flush toilets and wheelchair access.

Just north of the entrance lies a day-use parking lot with beach access, picnic tables, and rest rooms with flush toilets and wheelchair access. Information: (541) 563-3220 or (800) 551-6949. Reservations: (800) 452-5687.

This fine U.S. Forest Service campground is set among the shore pines alongside a broad sand beach. It has 59 primitive tent and RV sites to accommodate recreational vehicles of 25 to 40 feet, each with a table and fireplace. The park also has trash receptacles, drinking water, and rest rooms with flush toilets.

U.S. 101, mile 160.5
Tillicum Beach Campground

**U.S. 101,
mile 163.3 to
mile 165.6
Yachats**
(zip code 97498)

Beneath the timbered brow of Cape Perpetua, at the mouth of a small coastal river, is the tiny and tidy village of Yachats (population: 685). Both town and river share the name, pronounced *yah*-hots and said to be a corruption of the Chinook Indian word *yahuts*, which various sources report to mean "at the foot of the mountain" or "dark waters at the foot of the mountain." Yachats hunkers in the hills on the sunset slope of the Coast Range with the Pacific tumbling along its western edge. The coastline in and near town is both rocky and sandy, with a good beach at the mouth of the river and tide pools aplenty in both directions. South of town, from Cape Perpetua to Heceta Head, small pocket beaches occasionally interrupt the rugged and rocky shoreline. North of town, the basaltic rock and rubble of ancient volcanoes and wave-sculpted shelves of sandstone give way to a wide expanse of sandy beach more than 6 miles long.

As the quintessential coastal getaway spot, Yachats in a *must stop*. Attesting to its popularity are more than a dozen seaside resorts and motels, award-winning restaurants, several interesting shops, and some fine galleries. The number-one attraction, of course, is the ocean, which is no more than a short walk, bike ride, or drive from anywhere in town.

**U.S. 101,
mile 163.5**
Smelt Sands State
Recreation Site

Turn west on Lemwick Lane, and proceed 0.2 mile to the parking area and access to a trail, nearby rocky intertidal areas, and sand beach. The Yachats 804 Trail, as it's called, leads north 0.75 mile along the edge of the ocean, following a course that was once destined to be part of County Road 804. Along the way, hikers can explore the little pocket beach, examine tide pools at low tide, and watch spectacular wave action and spouting horns on incoming tides. The gravel trail terminates at the south end of a broad sand beach that leads all the way to Waldport.

The park gets its name from the silvery little fish that arrive annually to spawn along the beaches and which people catch with long-handled, fine-mesh dip nets and A-frame seines made for that purpose. Anglers fish from the rocks for perch, greenling, rockfish, and other marine species. This is also a fine place for photographing the ocean, surf, and birdlife and watching seals, porpoises, and whales. During storms, or any other time the swell is up, however, waves come crashing onshore and are a threat to unsuspecting onlookers and passersby. That's a good time to be extra cautious, maintain some distance, stay off the rocks, and perhaps avoid the trail altogether.

**U.S. 101,
mile 164.3**
Yachats Visitor
Information Center

On the west side of the highway, in a small shopping center, is the place to stop for information on local attractions. It's open from 10:00 a.m. to 4:00 p.m. daily in summer and Friday through Sunday the rest of the year.

The ever-present gulls gather near the mouth of the Yachats River at the Yachats State Recreation Area.

Turn west on 2nd Street or Ocean Drive, and go 0.2 mile to a parking area overlooking the ocean and mouth of the Yachats River. This popular park has picnic tables and benches with great views, drinking water, trash receptacles, and rest rooms with flush toilets and wheelchair access. An ever-present flock of gulls, ready to share picnics and beg bread crumbs, greets all visitors. The park is a favorite with anglers, tide-pool explorers, and whale watchers. Sunsets are sacred events here, with townspeople and visitors alike turning out to enjoy them.

U.S. 101, mile 164.3 and 164.4
Yachats State Recreation Area

On the east side of the highway is a mini-park with a clever sculpture of metal and earth by local artist Jim Adler. Stop and watch; it actually spouts.

U.S. 101, mile 164.4
Spouting Whale Sculpture

This small river, about 15 miles in length, offers fair to good, catch-and-release trout fishing and some opportunities for chinook salmon and steelhead angling. Although the chinook season runs from late May through December, the river west of U.S. 101 is closed for salmon angling from July to mid-August. Except for an April-May closure, the river is open most of the year for steelhead angling, but the fish don't enter the river until fall, with most taken from December through March. Although Yachats River Road follows the river for the length of the mainstem, it doesn't provide much in the way of angler access, because most of the land along the lower river is private.

U.S. 101, mile 164.7
Yachats River

Turn east off the highway to follow the river through a wooded rural valley—a pleasant diversion with some photographic opportunities.

Yachats River Road

This narrow loop extends west off the highway for 1 mile near the mouth of the Yachats River and the rocky ocean shoreline. Turnouts and seaside benches provide places to pause and take

U.S. 101, mile 164.8 and 165.4
Yachats Ocean Road State Natural Site

in the splendor of the rocky intertidal area, crashing waves, and spouting horns. Explore tide pools, watch for whales, observe birds as they search for morsels of food among the rocks and seaweeds, or take the opportunity to put it all on film. The wayside provides easy access to the river, beach, and rocky shore, as well as picnic tables, interpretive signs, and chemical toilets.

U.S. 101, mile 166.2 to mile 167.5
Cape Perpetua Scenic Area

Along this stretch of coast, Highway 101 climbs around the northwestern edge of Cape Perpetua, then descends the south face to meander through one of the most enchanting areas nature has to offer. This *must stop* is a 2,700-acre scenic wonderland and coastal playground with a new view and different opportunity around every bend. Visitors can explore the old-growth rain forest, beaches, and rocky shores, where they will find picturesque picnic areas, ancient middens, tide pools among the volcanic rocks, abundant and varied wildlife, 26 miles of interconnected hiking trails, a 10-mile bike trail, a lofty lookout providing a 65-mile coastal view, and unlimited photographic possibilities.

U.S. 101, mile 166.9
Devils Churn Viewpoint

Pull into the parking lot on the west side of the road, and hike the trail down to the water's edge to see a trench in the basalt where incoming waves funnel landward only to explode into a shower of salt spray. Also at the wayside are a picnic table, trash receptacle, and rest rooms with flush toilets and wheelchair access.

A paved path with switchbacks gentles the slope to the Devils Churn and Cape Cove, providing easy access for people of all ages.

Devils Churn

Turn east off Highway 101; then veer south (right) into the campground. Facilities include 37 sites in a wooded setting for tents and RVs up to 22 feet long, picnic table and fireplace at each site, trash receptacles, drinking water, and rest rooms with flush toilets and wheelchair access.

U.S. 101, mile 167
Cape Perpetua
Campground

Turn east on Klickitat Ridge Road, go 0.8 mile, then north (left) on Forest Service Road 5553, which leads to the overlook parking lot. (You can also hike up to the overlook from the campground.) The overlook stands 803 feet above sea level, commanding a spectacular view of 65 miles of coastline. Contrary to information in some publications, however, this is not the highest point on the Oregon coast. That superlative belongs to Humbug Mountain, on the south coast, which stands at 1,748 feet above the sea.

Cape Perpetua
Overlook

In clear weather, this is one of the best views on the coast and an enticement to all photographers. Even in good weather, the cape can be hazy, partly from drifting ocean mist, partly

West Shelter, at Cape Perpetua Overlook

from the lingering effects of morning fog. Consequently, the best time for photography from the overlook is late afternoon or early evening when any residual fog has burned off, afternoon winds have had a chance to dissipate the haze, and the sun bathes the western slopes in warm light.

A short trail leads west from the overlook to an attractive stone lookout, called the West Shelter, which members of the Civilian Conservation Corps built in the 1930s. This is one of the top picks for whale watching on the Oregon coast.

U.S. 101, mile 167.3
Cape Perpetua
Interpretive Center

Turn east off the highway at the sign, and follow the road up the hill to the parking lot. This enjoyable and educational center is an essential stop for all visitors to the Cape Perpetua Scenic Area. Enjoy the great view from the deck on the west side of the building, or in rainy weather, step inside for a sheltered view through a huge window.

The center is the place to come for all the information you might need to get the most from your visit. Check out all the educational interpretive displays. Watch a 16-minute movie that provides an overview of the area. Pick up maps, guides, and informative brochures about the area and its many attractions. Browse through all the nature titles in the bookstore. If you still have questions, rangers are on duty to answer them.

There are nearby hiking trails through the coastal forest, drinking water, and rest rooms with flush toilets and wheelchair access. The center is open daily from 9:00 a.m. to 6:00 p.m. all summer and from 10:00 a.m. to 4:00 p.m., Saturday and Sunday, the rest of the year. Information: (541) 547-3289.

U.S. 101, mile 167.6
Lincoln County/Lane
County Line

Side Trip: Three Rocks Road

On Highway 101, at mile 103.8, Three Rocks Road leads west for a total length of under 3 miles. Along the way it leads to viewpoints, trailheads, a county park and boat ramp, and the small but beautiful Salmon River Estuary. Opportunities abound for a variety of activities, including boating, canoeing, kayaking, wildlife watching, hiking, biking, and photography.

At the northwest quadrant of the intersection of Highway 101 and Three Rocks Road lies a small parking lot with room for three or four vehicles and a trailhead for a section of the Oregon Coast Trail that roughly parallels Highway 101. From here, the trail leads north 3.5 miles to Forest Service Road 1861 or 6 miles to the north trailhead (on the west side of U.S. 101 at mile 99.4) through spruce, hemlock, and red alder forest.

Three Rocks Road, mile 0
Cascade Head Traverse, south trailhead

On the south side of the road, an interpretive sign tells of early diking and recent rehabilitation efforts on the estuary.

Three Rocks Road, mile 1.4
Estuary interpretive sign and viewpoint

Turn north (right) onto this narrow, winding road, unsuitable for trailers and motorhomes, to drop off hikers at the Cascade Head Trailhead or to reach the lower end of the Salmon River Estuary. The road ends after 0.7 mile at the edge of the estuary, where there is limited parking for two or three vehicles. There are great views of Cascade Head, the estuary, and the mouth of the Salmon River. Access to the beach is short and easy. Among the wildlife visitors are likely to encounter are gulls, ducks, geese, herons, seals, and deer.

Three Rocks Road, mile 2.3
Savage Road junction

On the north side of Savage Road, 0.4 mile from Three Rocks Road, is the jumping-off point for this popular trail that leads for 2 miles along Cascade Head, through open grasslands, creek bottoms, and forests of spruce, hemlock, and red alder. Hikers can expect to encounter a variety of wildlife and discover some splendid ocean scenery. There's no parking at the trailhead, so hikers should arrange to be dropped off or should leave vehicles at Knight Park and make the 0.5-mile trek from there up Savage Road to the trailhead.

Cascade Head Natural Area south trailhead

Situated in a tree-fringed meadow on the north shore of the Salmon River Estuary, this small park provides a paved boat ramp, pit toilets, and a parking area for boaters, anglers, crabbers, clam diggers, and those who come to hike the Cascade Head Trail. There's a sign and map to orient and inform hikers and interpretive signs about the Salmon River Estuary and history of the area.

Three Rocks Road, mile 2.4
Knight County Park

Three Rocks Road, mile 2.7
Central Coast Historical Marker

An interpretive sign at a small turnout on the southwest side of the road tells about an ancient shipwreck at the mouth of the Salmon River.

Three Rocks Road, mile 2.9
End of road

At road's end is a small parking area with a view of the lower estuary. There's no room for trailers or motorhomes.

Information

Cape Perpetua Scenic Area
2400 Highway 101 South
P.O. Box 274
Yachats, OR 97498
(541) 547-3289
URL: www.orcoast.com/capeperpetua

Depoe Bay Chamber of Commerce
70 Northeast Highway 101
P.O. Box 21
Depoe Bay, OR 97341
(541) 765-2889
(877) 485-8348
E-mail: dbchamber@newportnet.com
URL: stateoforegon.com/depoe_bay/chamber

Greater Newport Chamber of Commerce
555 Southwest Coast Highway
Newport, OR 97365
(541) 265-8801
(800) 262-7844
E-mail: chamber@newportnet.com
URL: www.newportnet.com/chamber

Hatfield Marine Science Center
2030 South Marine Science Drive
Newport, OR 97365
(541) 867-0100
URL: www.hmsc.orst.edu

Lincoln City Visitor and Convention Bureau
801 Southwest Highway 101, Suite 1
Lincoln City, OR 97367
(541) 994-8378
(800) 452-2151
E-mail: lcvcb@newportnet.com

Oregon Coast Aquarium
2820 Southeast Ferry Slip Road
Newport, OR 97365
(541) 867-3474
URL: www.aquarium.org

Oregon Department of Fish and Wildlife
2040 Southeast Marine Drive
Newport, OR 97365
(541) 867-4741

Oregon Parks and Recreation Department
South Beach State Park
Business Office
Newport, OR 97365
(541) 867-7451

United States Coast Guard
Yaquina Bay Station
Southwest Naterlin Drive
Newport, OR 97365
(541) 867-4550
(541) 265-5511 Yaquina Bay Weather and Bar Conditions
(541) 765-2123 Depoe Bay Station
(541) 765-2122 Depoe Bay Weather and Bar Conditions

U.S. Fish and Wildlife Service
2127 OSU Drive
Newport, OR 97365
(541) 867-4550

Waldport Chamber of Commerce
Highway 101 and Spring Street
P.O. Box 419
Waldport, OR 97394
(541) 563-2133

Waldport Ranger District
U.S. Forest Service
Siuslaw National Forest
1049 Southwest Pacific Highway
P.O. Box 400
Waldport, OR 97394
(541) 563-3211
URL: www.fs.fed.us/r6/siuslaw

Yachats Chamber of Commerce
241 North Highway 101
P.O. Box 174
Yachats, OR 97498
(541) 547-3530

Yaquina Head Outstanding Natural Area
U.S. Bureau of Land Management
750 Northwest Lighthouse Drive
P.O. Box 936
Newport, OR 97365
(541) 574-3100

Eon upon eon, wave upon wave, the persistent Pacific has tormented Oregon's coastline into a fractured landscape attractive to wildlife and wildlife watchers alike. Wind and water have scoured and sculpted more than fourteen hundred rocks, reefs, sea stacks, islets, and islands that stand in Oregon's nearshore sea as home to a great number and variety of marine birds and mammals.

All but a few of these stony lairs and scenic wonders are protected as part of the National Wildlife Refuge system. Protection, however, extends only to terra firma within the boundaries of the refuge: the area above mean high tide. That renders low-tide areas and surrounding waters susceptible to human encroachment. Consequently, the U.S. Fish and Wildlife Service, in cooperation with other state and federal agencies, and with the help of Oregon's Ocean Policy Advisory Council, has worked to further protect birds and mammals in these sensitive areas.

Oregon's marine-bird population comprises year-round residents, northbound spring migrants, southbound fall migrants, overwintering migrants, inland birds that frequent intertidal areas, and pelagic seabirds that come ashore to nest and rear young. It's the last group that most worries wildlife biologists. Although Oregon's shoreline makes up only one fourth of the contiguous U.S. Pacific Coast, it harbors more than half of the region's breeding seabirds: nearly 1.2 million. In all, thirteen species depend on Oregon's nearshore rocks and islands for breeding, nesting, and resting.

Among the most important and threatened of Oregon's nearshore breeding areas is Three Arch Rocks National Wildlife Refuge, which lies about a half-mile off the coast, near Oceanside. According to the U.S. Fish and Wildlife Service, this is the largest nesting colony in Oregon, with a breeding population exceeding 226,000 birds. The common murre colony, estimated at 220,000 nesting birds, is of national and international importance and is the largest colony south of the Alaska Peninsula. More common murres nest on 1 acre of Three Arch Rocks than in all of Washington and British Columbia combined.

Common murres, which make up about 90 percent of Oregon's nesting seabirds, are particularly vulnerable to disturbance because of the way they nest and rear young. Like other seabirds, murres are long-lived, and a pair produces only one offspring a year. They don't build nests, but rather breed in dense colonies, lay eggs on rocks and cliffs, and incubate them atop their webbed feet, warming them from above with their downy

Marine Birds, Seals, and Sea Lions

A Baker's Dozen Breeders

The following thirteen species of birds use Oregon's nearshore rocks, islands, and coastal cliffs as breeding and nesting sites:

Cassin's auklet (*Ptychoramphus aleuticus*)
rhinoceros auklet (*Cerorhinca monocerata*)
Brandt's cormorant (*Phalacrocorax penicillatus*)
double-crested cormorant (*Phalacrocorax auritus*)
pelagic cormorant (*Phalacrocorax pelagicus*)
pigeon guillemot (*Cepphus columba*)
glaucus-winged gull (*Laurus hyperboreus*)
western gull (*Laurus occidentalis*)
common murre (*Uria aalge*)
black oystercatcher (*Haematopus bachmani*)
tufted puffin (*Lunda cirrhata*)
fork-tailed storm petrel (*Oceanodroma furcata*)
Leach's storm petrel (*Oceanodroma leucorboa*)

Marine Birds, Seals, and Sea Lions

breasts. When startled by nearby boats or low-flying aircraft, the birds flush from their rocky perches en masse, often causing their eggs to tumble and break on the rocks or their young to fall to their deaths. Eggs and hatchlings that don't meet such fates are left unprotected from ever-present predators, such as gulls, crows, and ravens.

Four species of pinnipeds—seals and sea lions—also frequent these rocky refuges for breeding and resting. These mammals are also sensitive to human intrusion, in some cases even more so than the seabirds.

Pacific harbor seals are the smallest; adults weigh from 200 to 400 pounds, pups 20 to 25 pounds at birth. They are permanent coastal residents that breed here and bear young from April through June. Adults are yellowish or brownish gray in color with contrasting spots and are 4 to more than 5 feet long. They use the offshore rocks, reefs, and islands, but also haul out on undisturbed ocean beaches as well as on islands and exposed flats and sandbars in the estuaries.

Northern elephant seals are the largest pinnipeds in the northern hemisphere. Adult males—identifiable by their large, drooping proboscises—can exceed 21 feet in length and weigh up to 5,000 pounds. Adult females can attain weights of more than a ton and lengths of 10 feet. Pups are about 75 pounds at birth. Northern elephant seals spend most of their time at sea, feeding and migrating, but come ashore in winter to breed and in spring to molt. Although their traditional breeding grounds are outside Oregon, three northern elephant seal pups were discovered in January 1993, on Shell Island in the north cove of Cape Arago, near Charleston, representing the first known birth of this species in Oregon.

Both California and Steller sea lions are found along Oregon's coast. California sea lions breed during the summer months along the California coast, where females and their pups spend the entire year. After the breeding season, males, weighing from 500 to 750 pounds each and reaching a length of about 8 feet, migrate up the coast as far north as British Columbia. In the water, they're sleek and dark, almost charcoal in color, but they dry to a chocolate brown. While seals are mostly silent, and the male Steller is the only sea lion that roars, California sea lions are the incessantly noisy barkers.

Steller or northern sea lions are larger. They breed along the Oregon coast during the summer, and use various places as haul-out sites. Males can exceed a ton in weight and 10 feet in length. Females run to about 600 pounds and 7 feet. Pups, born in June and July, weigh about 40 pounds at birth. They dry to a light-brown color.

While the federal Marine Mammal Protection Act of 1972 makes it illegal to kill or even harass pinnipeds, some innocent, even well-meaning, people can harm these creatures unknowingly. The close approach of humans—whether on foot, by boat, or in aircraft—alarms the herds and usually causes them to flee for safety in the water. During such melees, pups are often crushed beneath the tons of stampeding adults. Other young get separated from their parents; those that aren't reunited eventually perish.

Biologists of the U.S. Fish and Wildlife Service have identified 33 particularly sensitive sites along the Oregon coast, from Tillamook Head south to Goat Island (also known as Bird Island), near Brookings. These rocks, reefs, and islands seasonally or permanently harbor a tremendous number and variety of wildlife, including several threatened or endangered species.

Wildlife biologists and managers want to educate the public to potential problems and to establish buffer zones that will further protect these timid birds and mammals from human encroachment—either intentional or accidental. They're also asking pilots to fly farther offshore, or to maintain an altitude of 2,200 feet when over these sensitive areas.

Most of the buffer zones would be seasonal; some would be permanent. A common murre colony might need buffer protection only from April or May through September, whereas such susceptible and important areas as Orford and Rogue reefs, off the south coast, might need permanent buffer zones.

As for the size of the buffer zones, the U.S. Fish and Wildlife Service has asked for 500 feet overall, and 1,000 feet at Orford and Rogue reefs. One biologist explained, "At sea-lion sites, 1,000 feet would be a lot safer, because they're really sensitive. At 500 feet it will work for birds. For mammals, it'll work if people behave themselves."

Currently, only one temporary buffer zone has been established. Waters within 500 feet of Three Arch Rocks National Wildlife Refuge are closed to all watercraft from May 1 through September 15. These and all other rocks and islands are closed to public access all year, and watercraft should stay at least 500 feet away to prevent disturbance to sensitive wildlife.

Whether it's a matter of learning to behave or just learning, those who live on or visit the Oregon coast need to realize that they're sharing this domain with other species. You'll enjoy the coast and its wild birds and mammals more if you learn their habits and needs and, above all, respect their space.

Marine Birds, Seals, and Sea Lions

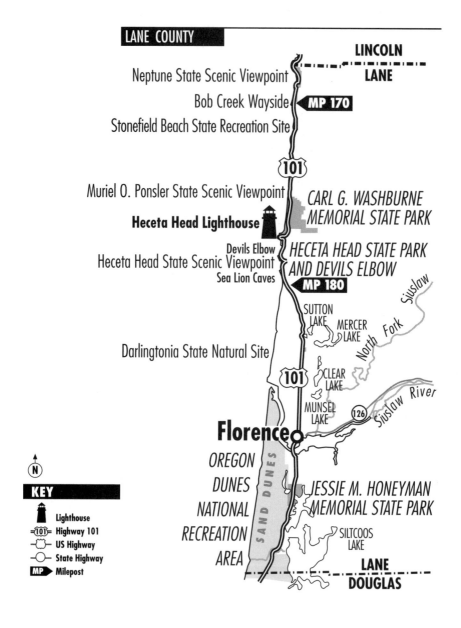

LANE COUNTY

LINCOLN

Neptune State Scenic Viewpoint

LANE

Bob Creek Wayside ◀ **MP 170**

Stonefield Beach State Recreation Site

101

Muriel O. Ponsler State Scenic Viewpoint

CARL G. WASHBURNE MEMORIAL STATE PARK

Heceta Head Lighthouse

Devils Elbow

HECETA HEAD STATE PARK AND DEVILS ELBOW

Heceta Head State Scenic Viewpoint

Sea Lion Caves

MP 180

SUTTON LAKE

MERCER LAKE

North Fork Siuslaw

Darlingtonia State Natural Site

101

CLEAR LAKE

MUNSEL LAKE

Siuslaw River

126

Florence

OREGON DUNES NATIONAL RECREATION AREA

SAND DUNES

JESSIE M. HONEYMAN MEMORIAL STATE PARK

SILTCOOS LAKE

LANE

DOUGLAS

N

KEY

Lighthouse

101 Highway 101

US Highway

State Highway

MP Milepost

The Lane County Coast

U.S. 101, Mile 167.6 to Mile 198.6

Lane County, established by the territorial legislature on January 28, 1851, comprises 4,620 square miles, making it the second oldest and second largest of Oregon's coastal counties, with Clatsop and Douglas counties taking respective first places. It was named after General Joseph Lane, Oregon's first territorial governor.

The county's diverse economy derives from such disparate sources as agriculture, forest products, the high-tech industry, higher education, and recreational vehicle manufacturing—all mainly concentrated along the I-5 corridor, where most of the county's 313,000 residents live. Eugene is its largest city and county seat, and combined with Springfield is the second-largest urban area in the state.

It's quite another story along the coast, however, where Florence, small by most standards, is the only city of any size, and where the major contributors to the economy are tourism and recreation. Lane County spreads eastward from the Oregon coast, past the Willamette Valley, and well into the Cascade Range, with forested land making up 90 percent of its area. The bulk of Lane County lies inland. Only 31 miles of U.S. 101 skirt the county's Pacific edge, but a marvelous 31 miles it is.

Travelers from the north enter the county just south of the Cape Perpetua Scenic Area, as Highway 101 meanders along coastal bluffs, past one viewpoint, wayside, and park after another, where trails, pocket beaches, and rocky shores await exploration. The highway rises and winds over and around Heceta Head, one of the most photographed spots on the coast. Past Sea Lion Caves, it wends its way down the south side of the headland and on toward Oregon's biggest sandbox: great stretches of broad sand beach and towering dunes that extend all the way to Coos Bay, more than 50 miles to the south.

The highway carries travelers on to Florence—a favorite coastal getaway town on the Siuslaw River, offering visitors two fine golf courses, superb restaurants, the best Old Town District on the coast, and an excellent headquarters for recreation in dune country.

U.S. 101, mile 168.1
Beach access

On the west side of the highway is a small parking area with nearby picnic tables. A short trail provides access to a rocky intertidal area with tide pools to examine at low tide.

U.S. 101, mile 168.3
Cummins Creek Trailhead

Forest Service Road 1050 exits east and ends at a parking area near the trailhead, 0.25 mile from the highway. This is a decent but narrow gravel road, not recommended for trailers or large motorhomes. The trail through this old-growth coastal forest is a gem. Pick up a map and guide to the Cummins Creek Wilderness at the Cape Perpetua Interpretive Center, U.S. 101, mile 167.3.

U.S. 101, mile 168.4
Neptune State Scenic Viewpoint

On the west side of the highway is a pleasant little day-use area where travelers can relax on benches overlooking the ocean, enjoy a picnic, hike the beach, hunt for agates, watch seabirds and sea lions, or head south at low tide to check out the tide pools and a cave. The park has picnic tables and pit toilets.

U.S. 101, mile 169
Cummins Ridge Trailhead

Turn east off the highway, and drive 2 miles to road's end and a parking area near the trailhead. This is a decent but narrow, steep, and winding gravel road with few turnouts. It's not recommended for trailers or large motorhomes. Pick up maps and trail guides at the Cape Perpetua Interpretive Center, mile 167.3.

U.S. 101, mile 169.3
Strawberry Hill

On the west side of the highway, a small parking lot and picnic area with benches and tables overlooks the ocean and provides access to pocket beaches and a rocky intertidal area with tide pools to examine at low tide. This is a good place to see seals, basking on the rocks, or swimming; at low tide, it is possible to get close to them, but it is unwise and illegal to disturb them, so keep your distance.

U.S. 101, mile 170
Bob Creek Wayside

A parking lot and picnic area with tables lie at the ocean's edge on the west side of the highway. The little park is next to a gravel beach and rocky intertidal area and is popular with anglers, beachcombers, agate hunters, and tide pool explorers.

U.S. 101, mile 171.5
Stonefield Beach State Recreation Site

Just west of the highway, this small wayside and parking lot provides easy access to a beach that's a short hike south of Tenmile Creek. It's a popular spot for fishing, wildlife watching, beach combing and agate hunting.

U.S. 101, mile 172.5
Parking area

On the west side of the highway, a small parking lot lies adjacent to a steep trail along a creekbed leading to the beach and tide pools.

A pretty picnic site, set on the green hillside west of the highway, overlooks the ocean and provides easy beach access. The little park has picnic tables and vault toilets with wheelchair access.

U.S. 101, mile 173.9
Ocean Beach Wayside

Turn east off the highway, and follow the paved road 0.2 mile to reach a small U.S. Forest Service Campground with 15 primitive campsites, each with a table and grill. The facility also has a trailer turnaround, trash receptacle, drinking water, and rest rooms with flush toilets. Firewood is available, and the campground is closed in winter.

What a delightful surprise awaits lucky campers who find sites at this little jewel of a campground. Beautifully aged and weathered camp spaces lie along Rock Creek, amid ferns, shrubs, and moss-covered trees. It's a quiet and serene spot, kept so by its size and surroundings, where lush vegetation muffles highway noises. Explore the creek. Hike to the beach. Enjoy the peaceful outdoors.

U.S. 101, mile 174.3
Rock Creek Campground

A small parking area just north of the bridge, on the east side of the U.S. 101, lies across the highway from the creek mouth and beach. The creek is closed to angling from April through October, but is open the rest of the year for winter steelhead fishing.

U.S. 101, mile 175
Big Creek

Turn west off the highway into the parking area, where visitors find easy access to a 5-mile stretch of sandy beach and the mouth of China Creek to the south. The area is popular with hikers, wildlife watchers, windsurfers, anglers, and beachcombers, who search for driftwood, agates, jasper, glass floats, and other treasures, especially after winter storms.

U.S. 101, mile 175.3
Muriel O. Ponsler State Scenic Viewpoint

At mile 176, turn west to reach the day-use area, RV dump station, and beach, or east to reach the campground. Camping facilities include 58 full-hookup sites, two primitive sites, two yurts, and six walk-in tent sites with tables and fireplaces. All campsites are first-come, first-served, but yurts may be reserved. The campground also has a hiker/biker camp, firewood, trash receptacles, drinking water, hot showers, and rest rooms with flush toilets. Some facilities have wheelchair access. A creek gurgles through the campground, where spacious campsites lie among native ferns, shrubs, and trees, within earshot of the tumbling surf. The oceanfront day-use area has picnic tables, rest rooms with flush toilets, and easy beach access.

Campers and hikers will be delighted with the several trails of varying length and difficulty. A short, easy trail leads from the campground, under the highway, to a beach that's a favorite with agate hunters and beachcombers. Others hike through second-growth forest, along China Creek, through meadows and bogs, and to Heceta Head and back.

U.S. 101, mile 175.6 to mile 177.2
Carl G. Washburn Memorial State Park

Wildlife inhabiting the upland areas includes black-tailed deer, Roosevelt elk, small mammals, and a variety of song birds and birds of prey. Along the beach and rocky shoreline, watch for whales, sea lions, and the many seabirds that nest and forage nearby. Among the variety of organisms that inhabit the tide pools are starfish, sea anemones, barnacles, crabs, and snails.

Information: (541) 997-3641 (Honeyman State Park) or (800) 551-6949. Yurt reservations: (800) 452-5687.

U.S. 101, mile 177.2
Trailheads

Hikers can park on the east side of the highway and set out on hikes over several trails leading through Washburn State Park: Campground Trail, Valley Trail, Hobbit Trail, and China Creek Trail.

U.S. 101, mile 178.2
Heceta Head State Park and Devils Elbow

✔

MUST STOP

Heceta Head, one of Oregon's most spectacularly scenic headlands, was named after Captain Bruno de Hezeta, an eighteenth-century Spanish explorer. *Heceta* (pronounced huh-*see*-tuh) is the Anglicized spelling of *Hezeta*.

At this *must-stop* state park, more than thirty picnic sites with tables in a wooded park setting overlook a small sand beach and beautiful cove at the mouth of Cape Creek. Near the large parking lot are drinking water, trash receptacles, and rest rooms with flush toilets. A half-mile trail leads from the north parking lot to the lighthouse in a spectacular cliffside location 205 feet above.

Heceta Head Lighthouse

The lighthouse and other buildings of the Heceta Head Light Station were erected in the early 1890s, and light began shining seaward from the 56-foot conical tower in 1894. The old lamp was replaced in 1963 with an automatic beacon, the most powerful on the Oregon coast, visible 21 miles out to sea. The lighthouse and keepers' quarters combine with the stunning surroundings to make this one of the most scenic and frequently photographed locations on the West Coast. Volunteers lead scheduled lighthouse tours in the summer. For schedules and information, phone (541) 997-3641 (Honeyman State Park) or (800) 551-6949.

Heceta Head is also one of the top spots on the coast for watching whales, with the added bonus of a breeding colony of sea lions that inhabit nearby caves and rocks. Cormorants, gulls, pigeon guillemots, tufted puffins, and other seabirds nest on offshore rocks and islands.

U.S. 101, mile 178.3
Cape Creek Bridge and Tunnel

Drivers who just stay on the highway, cross the bridge, and keep on going miss the best view of the Cape Creek Bridge, one of Conde B. McCullough's most attractive and distinctive designs, built in 1932. To fully appreciate the structure, turn west at mile 178.2, and drive to the parking lot at Heceta Head State Park. There, above the small creek, is a 220-foot concrete deck arch, flanked by two tiers of columns and arches, capped by decorative railing that borders the deck of the 619-foot bridge.

U.S. 101, mile 178.8 to mile 179.1
Heceta Head Lighthouse State Scenic Viewpoint

Between the south portal of the Cape Creek Tunnel and the entrance to Sea Lion Caves, three small turnouts and one large enough to accommodate a half-dozen or more vehicles lean west off the highway and invite travelers to tarry and soak in the spectacular view. If this isn't the best viewpoint on the entire West Coast, it certainly ranks among the top five. Countless artists and photographers would consider it number one. Attractive, historic rockwork forms the western borders of the parking areas and warns sightseers and photographers away from the precipitous cliffs that drop vertically to the rocky sea. Sea lions cruise near shore, gulls ride the updrafts, and gray whales pass near Heceta Head during their winter and spring migrations between Alaska and Mexico. Topping off this glorious panorama, the Heceta Head Lighthouse and keepers' quarters gleam in the greenery above Cape Cove.

While this glorious quarter-mile is a *must stop* for all travelers, caution is essential. With the highway twisting along the headland cliffs, northbound traffic crossing the southbound lane to enter and depart parking areas, and pedestrians going every which way, especially near Sea Lion Caves, extra-cautious driving is essential. Congestion is particularly heavy on weekends and all summer.

U.S. 101, mile 179.1
Sea Lion Caves

Parking lots for this popular privately owned attraction occupy both sides of the highway. The entrance and gift shop are on the west side. An elevator descends 208 feet, carrying visitors to a huge tidal cavern that's the largest sea cave in the world and home to hundreds of Steller sea lions. The sea lions crowd into the cave during the fall and winter, but might be seen any time of the year in nearby waters or on offshore rocks and islands. Seabirds are also plentiful, particularly during spring and summer. The facility also has outdoor platforms for viewing and photographing the great scenery and watching whales in season. It's open daily all year, from 9:00 a.m. to 6:30 p.m. Information: (541) 547-3111.

U.S. 101, mile 180.1 to mile 181.4
Viewpoints

Along the west side of the highway, about a dozen roadside parking areas, ranging in size from small (one or two vehicles) to relatively large (big enough for several vehicles, including motorhomes and travel trailers), offer travelers the opportunity to pause and view or photograph coastal scenery.

U.S. 101, mile 182.2
Baker Beach Recreation Area

Turn west off U.S. 101, and proceed 0.4 mile to a U.S. Forest Service facility that includes a parking area with nearby vault toilets and campground with five primitive sites with tables and fire pits. Hiking and horse trails lead to the beach and through the dunes. The snowy plover, listed as a threatened species, nests in dry sand areas here, which are subject to restrictions from mid-March through mid-September to protect breeding birds. Areas to avoid are posted or roped off. Information: (541) 902-8526.

Dry Lake Trailhead and Campground, Coast Horse Trail

Turn east off Highway 101 onto Herman Peak Road, and drive 2.9 miles up Cape Mountain to the trailhead and small campground with two primitive tent/RV sites with tables and fireplaces. This horse camp includes two four-horse corrals, a trailer turnaround, vault toilets, and nearby water for horses, but no drinking water. Miles of interconnected riding and hiking trails course through spruce forests, creek bottoms, and grassy meadows and open onto ocean vistas. Information: (541) 902-8526.

U.S. 101, mile 182.5
C & M Stables

On the east side of the highway, this privately owned operation offers guided horseback trips on the beach, along dune rails, and into the Coast Range. Beach and dune-trail rides are one and a half or two hours, sunset rides are two hours, and Coast Range rides are half-day or all day. Information: (541) 997-7540.

Turn east off the highway, and drive 0.1 mile to the entrance of this pretty and peaceful U.S. Forest Service campground, set in the forested dunes. The campground has 38 primitive tent/RV sites, two of which are pull-throughs. Each site has a table and fire pit. Other campground amenities include drinking water, trash receptacles, and rest rooms with flush toilets.

U.S. 101, mile 183.6
Alder Dune Campground

This fine facility, which rivals many state parks, has two small lakes that are stocked with trout twice a year and are popular not only for fishing, but for canoeing and swimming as well. For hikers and sightseers, 6 miles of trails wind through the dunes, to the beach, around Alder Lake, and near Dune Lake. The campground is closed in winter. Information: (541) 902-8526.

On the east side of the highway is a small parking area with nearby picnic tables, trash receptacle, and rest rooms with flush toilets and wheelchair access. A paved boat ramp and dock provide access to Sutton Lake, which is actually two lakes comprising 107 acres, connected by a narrow, 200-foot-long channel that runs 4 to 5 feet in depth. Maximum depth of the lakes is 33 feet, and average depth about 19 feet.

U.S. 101, mile 184.7
Sutton Lake and Boat Launch

Sutton Lake has some native cutthroat trout and is stocked with rainbow trout every spring. It also offers excellent fishing for largemouth bass, bluegill, and yellow perch growing to 12 inches or more. Mercer Creek enters the lower (southern) basin along the east shore where there is substantial marsh area and important habitat for waterfowl and furbearers. Ospreys nest in the area and use the lake as a source of food. Bank access is poor, so the best way to fish or explore the lake is by boat, canoe, or kayak.

Just east of the highway, on the south side of Mercer Lake Road, is a parking area with nearby picnic tables, drinking water, and rest rooms with flush toilets and wheelchair access. A short trail and boardwalk with interpretive signs lead visitors through a small swampy area where rare California pitcher plants or cobra lilies (*Darlingtonia californica*) flourish. These unusual carnivorous plants use their scent to lure insects, which they trap and consume by means of digestive enzymes. The forested wayside is a fine spot for a picnic or rest stop and a pleasant educational hike along the interesting trail with good photographic opportunities.

U.S. 101, mile 185.1
Darlingtonia State Natural Site

Lying along the north side of Mercer Lake Road, this 359-acre dune lake is popular with anglers, boaters, canoeists, kayakers, and other water recreationists. The shoreline along the road is heavily developed; what's not is brushy and inaccessible.

Mercer Lake

*California pitcher plants (*Darlingtonia californica) *at the Darlingtonia State Natural Site.*

Enjoyment of this lake, for whatever purpose, requires some sort of watercraft. The lake has an average depth of 23 feet and reaches a maximum depth of 38 feet. It is heavily stocked with rainbow trout and harbors populations of native cutthroat trout, and largemouth bass growing to 5 pounds or more. It's one of the best coastal lakes for catching big yellow perch, with fish of 12 to 14 inches taken with some regularity, especially in the fall.

Mercer Lake Landing

Turn east off Highway 101 onto Mercer Lake Road, and drive 3.2 miles to a county facility that includes a paved boat ramp on Mercer Lake, an ample parking area with a trailer turnaround, a trash receptacle, and vault toilets.

U.S. 101, mile 185.3
Sutton Recreation Area

Turn west off the highway, and drive 0.7 mile to reach the campground entrance, or 2 miles to Sutton Beach Day Use Area in this U.S. Forest Service facility.

Sutton Campground has 80 spacious and vegetated camp sites for tents and RVs, including six pull-throughs, each with a picnic table and fireplace and nearby water. Rest rooms have flush toilets and are wheelchair accessible. The day-use area features picnic sites with tables in wooded and grassy open areas, a kitchen shelter, and rest rooms with flush toilets and wheelchair access. A wheelchair-accessible trail and boardwalk lead to Holman Vista, a raised wooden platform overlooking Sutton Creek and the dunes.

The recreation area has miles of interconnected trails traversing lush forest, creek bottoms, bogs, and dunes. Hikers have a chance of viewing any of more than two hundred species of birds that reside in or use the area. About fifty species of mammals inhabit the woods, dunes, and creek banks, among them chipmunks, squirrels, rabbits, possums, raccoons, deer, and black bears. Trailheads are located at Sutton Campground, Sutton Day Use Area, Holman Vista, Sutton Lake Boat Ramp, and Alder Dune Campground. Pick up campground literature and trail guides at the Mapleton Ranger District office in Florence. Information: (541) 902-8526.

Turn west off the highway on Heceta Beach Road, drive two miles to 1st Avenue, turn north (right), and proceed 0.2 mile to the parking area with easy beach access. Nearby are picnic tables, a trash receptacle, and vault toilets with wheelchair access. This is a popular beach, so parking can be troublesome at times.

U.S. 101, mile 187.3
Heceta Beach

Many communities along and near the West Coast developed during the California gold rush of the mid-nineteenth century, either as mining camps or as supply centers for the legions of forty-niners who sluiced and panned rivers and mountain creeks for the precious metal. Florence, a late bloomer that didn't fit the pattern, wasn't settled until the 1880s, when the town burgeoned on the banks of the Siuslaw River and grew with the local timber and commercial-fishing industries. Although the forests and sea are still sources of local income, here as elsewhere along the coast, tourism has become increasingly important. Tourists have at last discovered Florence, or vice versa, but if the town is experiencing a tourism rush, it's a laid-back shuffle of a rush, with no one in much of a hurry. The same comfortable pace that makes Florence easy to enjoy just might let the town grow gradually and flourish without sacrificing its innate charm.

U.S. 101, mile 187.6 to mile 191
Florence
(zip code 97439)

Progress is pushing the city north along a widened stretch of Highway 101, but its the south end of town that attracts most visitors. Florence began here, on the edge of the estuary, the river its reason for being, its connection with the rest of the West and the world. Merchants and innkeepers established businesses on the waterfront along Bay Street. The Siuslaw fed the sawmills and canneries and carried products to market, people to work, and children to school.

Oregon's coastal bridge-building period of the early 1930s finally connected segments of the Coast Highway. The 1936 completion of the Siuslaw River Bridge in Florence marked the beginning of a new era of highway travel. The business community eventually migrated to the U.S. 101 corridor, leaving Bay Street and the waterfront to deteriorate. Florence's Old Town renaissance began in the 1970s and continues today. Most of Bay Street has been refurbished, its buildings now housing a variety of shops, galleries, and restaurants. What started on the waterfront east of the bridge has spread up and down the river and northward along adjacent streets.

Florence has some excellent restaurants and cafés, and there's no shortage of comfortable and reasonably priced accommodations in and near the city. The area also has about two thousand private, state, and U.S. Forest Service campsites, from primitive tent spaces to full-hookup RV spots. The Florence area also offers unlimited opportunities for a great variety of outdoor recreation, from fishing, crabbing, clam digging, and windsurfing on the bay to hiking, beach combing, wildlife watching, and playing in the dunes. Golfers have two 18-hole, links-style courses to play. Beachgoers can enjoy miles of wide, sandy beaches that stretch for miles north and south from the mouth of the Siuslaw. Photographers find no end of suitable subjects in and around town, up the river and down.

Florence (population: 6,715) is either the northernmost city on the south coast or the southernmost city on the central coast—even the Florentines are unsure. No matter its geographical status, it's an ideal place for a day trip, weekend getaway, or extended stay.

U.S. 101, mile 187.8
Munsel Lake

Turn east on Munsel Lake Road, and drive 0.8 mile to reach the lake, on the north side of the road. This 110-acre dune lake is locally popular for swimming, boating, and fishing. With a maximum depth of 71 feet and average depth of 31 feet, it's among the deeper coastal lakes. The upper lake—along the north, east, and south shores—borders foothills and the slope is steep. The west end is shallower and has a gentler grade.

There are summer and year-round dwellings along the west end of the lake and brushy shoreline elsewhere, which restricts shore angling to the vicinity of the public boat ramp. Fishing pressure is relatively light, especially for a lake in a populated residential area, and fishing is considered good for native cutthroat trout, stocked rainbow trout, and brood trout of 5 pounds or more, which the Oregon Department of Fish and Wildlife stocks from time to time. Warmwater species include largemouth bass and yellow perch.

Munsel Landing

Located 0.8 mile east of U.S. 101, this county facility includes a paved boat ramp, large parking area, trailer turnaround, trash receptacle, and chemical toilets.

Ocean Dunes Golf Links

Turn east off Highway 101, and drive 1.6 miles on Munsel Lake Road to the course entrance on the south side of the road. Set in rolling dunes amid the shore pines, beach grass, Scotch broom, rhododendrons, and other natural vegetation, this 6,018-yard, 18-hole, par-71 course is as challenging as it is beautiful. Course amenities include a driving range, putting green, chipping area, pro shop with resident pro, pull-cart and gas-cart rental, club rental, restaurant, snack bar, and bar with beer and wine. Prto shop: (541) 997-3232 or (800) 468-4833.

Oregon Coast Golf Courses at a Glance

Course	Location	Holes	Yards	Par	Phone
Astoria Golf and Country Club	Astoria	18	6,494	72	(503) 861-2545
The Highlands at Gearhart	Gearhart	9	1,880	32	(503) 738-5248
Gearhart Golf Links	Gearhart	18	6,089	72	(503) 738-3538
Seaside Golf Course	Seaside	9	2,593	35	(503) 738-5261
Manzanita Gold Course	Manzanita	9	2,192	32	(503) 368-5744
Alderbrook Golf Course	Tillamook	18	5,692	69	(503) 842-64134
Bay Breeze Golf	Tillamook	9	1,061	27	(503) 842-1166
Hawk Creek Golf Course	Neskowin	9	2,700	34	(503) 392-4120
Neskowin Beach Golf Course	Neskowin	9	3,012	36	(503) 392-3377
Lakeside Golf & Racquet Club	Lincoln City	18	4,636	65	(541) 994-8442
Salishan Golf Links	Gleneden Beach	18	6,453	72	(541) 764-3632
Agate Beach Golf Course	Newport	9	3,002	36	(541) 265-7331
Crestview Hills Golf Course	Waldport	9	3,062	36	(541) 563-3020
Ocean Dunes Golf Links	Florence	18	6,018	71	(541) 997-3232
Sand Pines Golf Links	Florence	18	7,252	72	(541) 997-1940
Forest Hills Country Club	Reedsport	9	3,086	36	(541) 271-2626
Kentuck Golf Course	North Bend	18	5,393	70	(541) 756-4464
Sunset Bay Golf Course	Charleston	9	3,020	36	(541) 888-9301
Coos Country Club	Coos Bay	18	6,032	70	(541) 267-6313
Bandon Dunes Golf Course	Bandon	18	6,732	72	(541) 347-4380
Pacific Dunes Golf Course	Bandon	18	6,557	71	(541) 347-4380
Face Rock Golf Course	Bandon	9	2,100	32	(541) 347-3818
Cedar Bend Golf Course	Gold Beach	9	3,156	36	(541) 247-6911
Salmon Run Golf Course	Brookings	18	6,590	72	(541) 469-4888

U.S. 101, mile 188.1
Mapleton Ranger District

On the east side of the highway, this is the place to stop for a Siuslaw National Forest Map, trail and campground guides, and other helpful literature. The office is open Monday through Friday, from 8:00 a.m. to 4:30 p.m.

U.S. 101, mile 188.7
Sandpines Golf Links

Turn west off the highway on 35th Avenue, drive 0.4 mile to the entrance, turn north, and continue 0.5 mile to the parking lot. *Golf Digest* named this 7,252-yard, 18-hole, par-72 course the best new golf course in America in 1993. In 1996-97, the same magazine ranked it first among the "Top 75 Affordable Courses in America." From tree-lined fairways to rolling dunes, this links-style course has garnered praise and awards from all quarters. The facility includes a driving range, four putting greens, chipping area, clubhouse, pro shop with resident pro, electric-cart and pull-cart rental, club rental, snack bar, and bar with beer service. Pro shop: (541) 997-1940 or (800) 917-4653.

U.S. 101, mile 189.6
Miller Community Park

Take 18th Street west 0.1 mile to the entrance and parking lot. This large city park has big grassy open areas for tossing a Frisbee or football, picnic tables, benches, a playground, basketball court, trash receptacles, and rest rooms with flush toilets and wheelchair access.

U.S. 101, mile 190.2
State Route 126 junction

Heading east out of Florence at the intersection of Highway 101 and 9th Street, State Route 126 runs along the north bank of the Siuslaw River to Mapleton, where it crosses the river and continues inland to I-5 at Eugene/Springfield and beyond. Along the way, it provides access to the estuary and river at many points and leads to several parks, campgrounds, and boat ramps. A number of private RV parks and marinas are situated on the north bank of the river's tidewater reaches. (Use Lane County and Siuslaw National Forest maps.)

North Fork Road

Take State Route 126 east off Highway 101 one mile to the North Fork Siuslaw River, and turn north. Follow this winding road along the North Fork, through rural residential areas and farmlands, into the Siuslaw National Forest and Coast Range. Opportunities abound for sightseeing, wildlife watching, wildlife and scenic photography, hiking, biking, camping, and fishing. (Use Lane County and Siuslaw National Forest maps.)

U.S. 101, mile 190.5
Harbor Vista Park

Turn west at the traffic light on Rhododendron Drive, proceed 3.7 miles, and turn south (left) on North Jetty Road, and go 0.2 mile. Then turn east (left) on Harbor Vista Road to reach the park, which is also accessible off Highway 101 via Heceta Beach Road (mile 187.3) and 35th Street (mile 188.7). The 15-acre county park has 38 campsites with water and electric hookups, set amid native trees and shrubs; one site has wheelchair access. Each site has a picnic table and fireplace. Other park features include picnic areas with tables and fireplaces, drinking water, hiking trails, a playground, trash receptacles, rest rooms with flush toilets and wheelchair access, and an observation deck overlooking the mouth of the Siuslaw River, North Jetty, and ocean. Information and reservations: (541) 997-5987.

North Jetty

Turn west, and follow Rhododendron Drive 3.7 miles to North Jetty Road, turn south (left), and proceed 1.1 miles to the North Jetty parking area. Here visitors will find easy access to the jetty, beach, and dunes, and chemical toilets nearby. This is a popular place for watching and photographing abundant birdlife, harbor seals, and boat traffic, as well as for fishing and hiking in the low dunes or along the beach.

Turn east on Maple Street, and continue 0.2 mile to Bay Street. Park along Maple Street or Bay Street, and stroll the Old Town area on foot. Public rest rooms with flush toilets and wheelchair access are on the south side of Bay Street at Maple Street. With all its shaped-up shops and galleries, cafés and restaurants, and proximity to the photogenic bridge and port facilities, Old Town Florence is a *must stop* for all travelers.

U.S. 101, mile 190.6
Old Town, east access, and public rest rooms

MUST STOP

A short block south of Rhododendron Drive, turn east off Highway 101 on Nopal Street, drive 0.2 mile, turn left on 1st Street, and continue 0.2 mile to the RV Park/Marina complex. The RV park has 59 full-hookup sites and 26 spaces with water and electric hookups; all have cable-TV connections. Some primitive sites are also available.

U.S. 101, mile 190.5
Port of Siuslaw RV Park and Marina

The marina has a two-lane paved boat ramp and courtesy dock on the Siuslaw River and a huge parking lot. Transient moorage is available by the day, week, or month (check at the RV park office). Other amenities include an RV dump station, laundry facilities, car/boat wash, showers, and rest rooms with flush toilets and wheelchair access.

Supermarkets are nearby and Old Town Florence is within easy walking distance. Information and reservations: (541) 997-3040.

Siuslaw River Bridge

**U.S. 101,
mile 190.7**
Florence Visitor
Information Center

On the east side of the highway, just north of the bridge, this is the place to pick up literature on local attractions and a copy of the excellent Florence area map, covering this whole section of the coast from the Sutton Recreation Area south to the Douglas County line. The center is open Monday through Saturday from 9:00 a.m. to 5:00 p.m. and Sunday from 9:00 a.m. to 2:00 p.m.

**U.S. 101,
mile 190.7**
Old Town Loop, west
access

Turn west at the sign on Highway 101, bear left, go down the hill, and turn east (left) on Bay Street. Park on Bay Street or any of the adjacent streets, and enjoy Old Town on foot.

U.S. 101, mile 191
Siuslaw River Bridge

Another example of Conde B. McCullough's engineering genius and artistic flair, this may well be the most decorative of the bridge designer's coastal structures. The bridge at Florence was one of five major projects completed in 1936 to connect the Oregon Coast Highway all the way to California. Concrete girder approach spans lead from each end toward two 154-foot concrete bowstring arch spans with concrete approach pylons. Between them is a 140-foot central drawspan with a pair of obelisk towers at each end. Concrete walkways with ornate concrete railings run along both sides of this 1,568-foot steel and concrete beauty, which may well be the finest-looking drawbridge anywhere.

Photographers and artists should try to capture it in the morning light from the north bank of the river, east of the bridge, along the Old Town waterfront. In late afternoon or early evening sunlight, try the north bank, west of the bridge. The bridge itself is a good platform for photographing the Old Town waterfront in afternoon sunlight.

Siuslaw River and
Estuary

Deep in the Coast Range, west of Cottage Grove, the Siuslaw River rises in the moss-muffled rock and rubble of those ancient mountains and tumbles coastward. On its wobbly way down the sunset slope, it swaps velocity for volume. After 80 miles, it slips beneath the Mapleton Bridge and is navigable for the remaining 20 miles. Just before its inevitable rendezvous with the Pacific Ocean, the river glides green and wide past the city of Florence.

For as long as humans have dwelled along the banks of the Siuslaw (pronounced sigh-*oos*-law), the river has been an important transportation and commerce corridor and source of food and income. While highways have taken over the transport of people and products, and the contribution of the timber and fishing industries to the coastal economy has diminished in recent years, the Siuslaw remains a major attraction to locals and visitors alike. Today, the river, estuary, and adjacent lands provide essential habitat to a variety of plants and animals and offer opportunities for recreation, sightseeing, and photography.

The Siuslaw was once a fishing paradise, where substantial runs of coho, chinook, steelhead, and sea-run cutthroat trout attracted anglers from far and wide. The river and nearby ocean gave up thousands of coho each year, and the river was one of the best cutthroat streams on the entire coast. As recently as the mid-1980s to the early 1990s, boats crowded the river every year between Florence and Mapleton from mid-summer through autumn, trolling for salmon and trout. Drastic declines in the number of coho salmon and sea-run cutthroat have closed those fisheries entirely.

Nevertheless, the Siuslaw system continues to support a viable fishery for other species, some of them in good numbers. Chinook fishing gets underway in mid-August and holds up in the tidewater between Florence and Mapleton into November. Anglers take some big Siuslaw chinook every year. Steelhead follow and provide good fishing opportunities into March in the upper reaches, as well as in the North Fork and Lake Creek.

On the estuary and lower river, anglers also pursue marine species, including surfperch, rockfish, lingcod, and sole. The jetties and the pier near the south jetty are popular places. In February and March, striped bass follow schools of smelt into the estuary to gorge on the easy prey. Patient anglers have a chance then of taking some big fish.

In May and June, schools of American shad—the most underutilized of all coastal Oregon anadromous fishes—arrive and migrate upstream to spawn. The best fishing for them is in the upper tidewater area, near Mapleton.

The lower estuary, from Old Town Florence to the jetties, is good crabbing water from mid-spring until the first heavy rains of autumn. Boaters do best, but those without boats can try their luck by dropping their baited pots or rings from the pier near the south jetty.

Flats on the lower bay, above the north jetty, hold a few gaper clams and cockles, and the ocean beaches give up the occasional razor clam, but the clam digger's main quarry here is the soft-shell. Flats on both sides of the estuary above the Port of Siuslaw Marina are home to large colonies of the succulent bivalves. Flats near the mouth of the North Fork are also a good bet.

The tidal flats, islands, and edges of the estuary are good places to watch and photograph wading birds and shorebirds most of the year. Spring and fall bring migrating birds and waterfowl in greater numbers, some of which overwinter in the area. Up the Siuslaw, in the pastures, meadows, and wetlands between the river and Highway 126, resident Canada geese nest and rear their young. Migrants swell their ranks from fall through spring. Up the North Fork, wildlife watchers and photographers can usually find more ducks, geese, herons, and hawks in and over the marshes and meadows. Keep binoculars and cameras ready for deer and elk, as well.

The Siuslaw River Valley, from Florence to Mapleton, along State Route 126, is a picturesque rural area, well worth the short side trip. There are picture possibilities at every bend of this placid tidewater section of the river. Above Mapleton, along State Route 36, the river changes in character as it tumbles over rocks and shoots between boulders. Here, too, are chances for composing interesting waterscapes.

The Siuslaw River bar has long had a reputation for being tricky in good weather on favorable tides, but downright dangerous when the weather is foul and tide is ebbing. Even a moderate swell can put the bar out of shape and make it unsuitable for small craft. Boaters new to the area should seek the advice of local experts before venturing across the bar in any size vessel, and all boaters should check with the Coast Guard for weather and bar conditions before every trip.

U.S. 101, mile 191.6 to mile 232.6
Oregon Dunes National Recreation Area (NRA)

✔

MUST STOP

Low, rolling dunes; towering, wind-swept dunes; broad sand beaches; mature forests; meadows and marshes; potholes, ponds, and lakes; creeks and rivers; sprawling estuaries; campgrounds and day-use areas; hiking, equestrian, and off-road vehicle (ORV) trails; hundreds of species of amphibians, reptiles, fishes, birds, and mammals—all this and more lies between the Pacific Ocean and Highway 101 and stretches for more than 40 miles between the Siuslaw River and Coos Bay estuaries.

Immediate access to the NRA here is via South Jetty Road at mile 191.8. Over the next 41 miles of U.S. 101 in Lane, Douglas, and Coos counties, many roads lead a short distance off the highway to the NRA and numerous dune-access points, staging areas, trailheads, boat ramps, waysides, parks, and campgrounds. Guides, maps, and other informational literature about this *must*

A dune buggy tops a sand dune at the Oregon Dunes National Recreation Area, south of Florence.

stop are available at the Florence Visitor Information Center, the Mapleton Ranger District office, and the Oregon Dunes National Recreation Area Headquarters in Reedsport. Information: (541) 902-8526 in Florence, (541) 271-3611 in Reedsport.

Turn west off the highway on South Jetty Road to reach the Oregon Dunes National Recreation Area, ocean beach, lower Siuslaw River, and south jetty. Within the recreation area are two ORV staging areas, ORV trails, hiking trails, interpretive viewpoints, parking lots with beach and dune access, drinking water, vault toilets, and rest rooms with flush toilets and wheelchair access.

U.S. 101, mile 191.8
South Jetty

Resident Canada geese breed and nest here and occupy the area all year. When winter rains flood the lowlands, the seasonal lakes attract thousands of ducks, geese, swans, and other birds.

In the vicinity of the south jetty are large parking areas and a pier for fishing, crabbing, and photographing activity on the lower river. This is also a popular spot for sailboarding and scuba diving.

Stop by this excellent little museum on the west side of the highway, and take a trip back to the early days on the Siuslaw River. Study the old photographs and examine Siuslaw Indian and early pioneer artifacts, early logging equipment, and farm implements. From May 1 to Labor Day, it's open Tuesday through Sunday, 10:00 a.m. to 4:00 p.m.; the rest of the year, hours are noon to 4:00 p.m., Saturday and Sunday. Information: (541) 997-7884.

U.S. 101, mile 192
Siuslaw Pioneer Museum

This *must stop* and showcase of the Oregon Parks and Recreation Department lies along both sides of the highway and offers visitors a wide range of activities and amenities. Turn west on Canary Road to reach Cleawox Lake, Lily Lake, the dunes, campground, hiking trails, boat ramp, and day-use areas. Turn east on Canary Road for access to Woahink Lake, group camp, boat ramps, and day-use areas.

U.S. 101, mile 193.1
Jesse M. Honeyman Memorial State Park

The campground has 50 full-hookup sites, 91 sites with water and electric hookups, 237 primitive tent/RV sites, and 10 yurts, each with paved parking, picnic table, and fire ring. Three sites have wheelchair access. Other amenities include a dump station, hiker/biker camp, firewood, drinking water, hot showers, and rest rooms with flush toilets, two of which have wheelchair access.

Mature trees, numerous rhododendron bushes, huge sand dunes, sparkling lakes, and meticulously maintained grounds make this one of Oregon's most beautiful state parks. Hiking

Cleawox Lake, at Jesse M. Honeyman Memorial State Park

trails lead through woods, around lakes, and over dunes. From October 1 to April 30, ORV enthusiasts are permitted direct vehicle access to the dunes from the campground. Information: (541) 997-3641 or (800) 551-6949. Reservations: (800) 452-5687.

Cleawox Lake

Turn west on Canary Road to reach this 87-acre lake, where average depth is 17 feet and maximum depth is 47 feet, deep for such a small body of water. The lake was formed by encroaching dunes, and most of the west shore is flanked by dunes.

Swimming, canoeing, and paddleboating are primary activities on the lake. Facilities include a sand beach, swimming and diving float, bathhouse, food and souvenir concession, and paddleboat rental.

Anglers can launch small craft from a paved boat ramp at the west end of the lake. Although a few largemouth bass and black crappie inhabit the lake, trout are the primary angling targets here. The Oregon Department of Fish and Wildlife annually stocks both rainbows and cutthroats and sometimes plants brood stock of 5 pounds or more.

Woahink Lake

This 820-acre lake lies east of U.S. 101 and is accessible via that highway at the south end and Canary Road in the north. The lake has an average depth of 33 feet and maximum of 68 feet, making it one of the deeper coastal lakes. It's popular for boating, water skiing, canoeing, kayaking, and angling. Stocked rainbow and cutthroat trout, largemouth bass, bluegill, and yellow perch provide the angling action.

Turn east off Highway 101 on Canary Road, go 0.3 mile, and turn south into the park entrance, where there is a nearby group camp, meeting hall, rest rooms with flush toilets, a paved boat ramp, and parking area.

West Woahink Lake Day-Use Area and Boat Ramp

Turn east off U.S. 101 on Canary Road, drive 0.4 mile, and turn south into the park entrance. This lovely spot at the north end of the lake has large open, grassy areas for tossing a Frisbee or setting up a badminton net and a well-trimmed shoreline for easy angling access. For boaters, anglers, and water skiers, there's a two-lane paved boat ramp and courtesy dock. The park also has picnic tables, a picnic shelter, horseshoe pits, a swimming area, trash receptacles, and rest rooms with flush toilets and wheelchair access.

East Woahink Day-Use Area and Boat Ramp

On the east side of the highway at the south end of Woahink Lake is a small parking area and lake access for anglers, canoeists, and kayakers.

U.S. 101, mile 195
Shoreline access and parking

Turn west off the highway on Pacific Avenue, then south (right) into the campground, which lies along the north bank of the Siltcoos River. The campground has 15 primitive tent/RV sites in a wooded setting with tables and fireplaces with grills. There are trash receptacles and vault toilets with wheelchair access. A paved boat ramp on the river provides easy access to Siltcoos Lake, making this a favorite camp spot for anglers.

U.S. 101, mile 196.7
Tyee Campground and Boat Ramp

Also known as the Lane County Boat Ramp on Siltcoos Lake, this fine facility includes a two-lane paved ramp and a long dock for temporary moorage and fishing. Other features include picnic tables, fire pits with grills, trash receptacle, and vault toilets with wheelchair access.

Martin Christensen Memorial Boat Landing

Formerly spelled *Tsiltcoos*, certainly of Indian origin, but of unknown meaning, this big, relatively shallow lake is the largest on the Oregon coast, at 3,164 acres, maximum depth of 22 feet, and average depth of 11 feet. The angling is varied and often good. Coho salmon, steelhead, and sea-run cutthroat migrate up the Siltcoos River and through the lake from late summer to fall. Fishing for native cutthroat and stocked rainbow trout is especially productive in the spring. Spring through fall is the best time for warmwater species—brown bullhead, bluegill, black crappie, yellow perch, and largemouth bass—although anglers

Siltcoos Lake

Sunup at Siltcoos Lake.

take the biggest bass (up to 9 pounds or more) in winter and spring, using bait. Winter and early spring are also good times to prospect for some of the lake's big, wily trout.

Because the lake is large and shallow, weed growth is a problem in the summer. The lake is also wind-whipped most summer days. Consequently, the best fishing is in the morning, before the winds kick up, and in the evening, after they die down. The best summer fishing for bass and catfish is at night, when wind rarely interferes.

The big lake has resident populations of mallards and wood ducks. From fall through spring, it also attracts migrating and overwintering flocks of puddle ducks, diver ducks, and other waterfowl. Great blue herons wade the shallows all year, foraging on fish and frogs. Osprey nest in the spring and spend the summer teaching their young how to catch fish.

This is one of the most popular angling lakes on the Oregon coast. Several privately owned fishing resorts and marinas are located on the Siltcoos shores, in the Westlake area, on the north shore, and on the east side of the lake.

**U.S. 101,
mile 196.9**
Siltcoos River

This short outlet stream runs west from Siltcoos Lake and meanders through the dunes for about 2 miles before emptying into the ocean. Although it is open for steelhead fishing much of the year, angling for these fish is a winter activity. During the summer months, the little river offers angling for warmwater species, especially largemouth bass. Boat anglers can launch at the big county ramp at the west end of the lake or at the Tyee Forest Service Ramp, just off Highway 101. Anglers without boats will find some good bank access in the Siltcoos Recreation Area, west of U.S. 101, at mile 198.

Hiking trails, picnic areas, campgrounds, ORV staging areas, and access to the lake, river, dunes, and ocean beach await visitors to this popular area. Access to all attractions except Siltcoos Lake Trail is via Siltcoos Beach Road, which leads west from Highway 101 for 1.5 miles.

This large Forest Service complex is a *must stop* for hikers, nature lovers, photographers, and ORV enthusiasts. Maps, trail guides, and other literature are available at the Mapleton Ranger District office in Florence and the Oregon Dunes National Recreation Area Headquarters in Reedsport.

U.S. 101, mile 198
Siltcoos Recreation Area

MUST STOP

Turn east off the highway, directly into the parking lot, where there are a nearby trash receptacle and vault toilets with wheelchair access. The trail extends through a forest of second-growth cedar, fir, hemlock, and spruce for 2.25 miles. Roughly midway between the parking lot and the lake, the trail splits and forms a loop. The north leg leads to a lakeside campground with five primitive tent sites, picnic tables, fire rings, and pit toilet. The south leg leads to one campsite with a table, fire ring, and pit toilet.

Siltcoos Lake Trailhead

Turn west off the highway and follow the road 0.5 mile to a pleasant little day-use area on the north side of the road, with picnic sites overlooking the Siltcoos River. Amenities include picnic tables, a picnic shelter, drinking water, trash receptacle, and vault toilets.

Lodgepole Picnic Area

Embraced by a small oxbow lake, this campground lies 0.8 mile west of the highway on the north side of the road. It has 39 tent/RV sites, including 10 pull-throughs, each with a table and fireplace. The campground has trash receptacles, drinking water, and rest rooms with flush toilets and wheelchair access. A 1-mile loop trail encircles the campground along the inside of the oxbow.

Lagoon Campground

A little over 0.8 mile west of the highway, just past Lagoon Campground, on the opposite side of the road, lies a campground with 54 tent/RV sites, including 17 pull-throughs, each with a table and fire pit, and all set amid native vegetation. Other features include trash receptacles, drinking water, and rest rooms with flush toilets and wheelchair access. Access to the Waxmyrtle Trail is near the entrance.

Waxmyrtle Campground

West of the highway 0.9 mile, on the south side of the road, a small parking lot with room for several vehicles lies adjacent to a trailhead that's named for the old stagecoach route that once connected Florence with Coos Bay. From the trailhead, hikers can reach three short hiking trails, each providing distinctly

Stagecoach Trailhead

different experiences. *Chief Tsiltcoos Trail* begins across the road from the Stagecoach Trailhead and courses 1.25 mile through a mixed forest of conifers, evergreen huckleberry, and rhododendron bushes. Mile-long *Lagoon Trail*, which begins 0.25 mile east of the Stagecoach Trailhead, follows the shore of an oxbow lake that was once a bend in the Siltcoos River. This beautiful nature trail offers hikers opportunities to observe and photograph a variety of wildlife, including songbirds, waterfowl, herons, and furbearers. *Waxmyrtle Trail*, accessible from the trailhead, crosses the Siltcoos River and winds 1.5 miles along the river and estuary and terminates at the beach. This trail offers excellent views and photographic opportunities along the way.

Driftwood II Campground

Lying 1.2 miles west of Highway 101, on the north side of the road, is a large campground popular with ORV enthusiasts. The campground has 69 sites 35 to 50 feet in length, trash receptacles, drinking water, and rest rooms with flush toilets and wheelchair access. It also has an ORV loading ramp and sand access.

Siltcoos Beach Day-Use Area

The recreation-area access road ends 1.5 miles west of Highway 101 at a large parking area with easy beach access.

Information: (541) 271-3611. Reservations: (877) 444-6777.

U.S. 101, mile 198.6
Lane County/
Douglas County Line

Information

Florence Area Chamber of Commerce
P.O. Box 26000
Florence, OR 97439
(541) 997-3128
URL: www.florencechamber.com

Mapleton Ranger District
U.S. Forest Service
Siuslaw National Forest
4480 Highway 101 North
Building G
Florence, OR 97439
(541) 902-8526
URL: www.fs.fed.us/r6/siuslaw/mapleton

Merchants of Old Town
P.O. Box 2646
Florence, OR 97439
(541) 997-1646
URL: www.oldtownflorence.com

Oregon Parks and Recreation Department
Jessie M. Honeyman State Park
84505 Highway 101 South
Florence, OR 97439
(541) 997-3851

Port of Siuslaw
1499 Bay Street
Florence, OR 97439
(541) 997-3426

U.S. Coast Guard
Siuslaw River Station
Florence, OR 97439
(541) 997-2486
(541) 997-8303 Weather and Bar Conditions
(541) 997-3631 Emergencies Only

Oregon's plentiful clams attract people to the low-tide flats and beaches as much for the enjoyable outdoor experience as the chance to gather great food. Clam digging requires no licenses or permits, little equipment, and nothing in the way of stylish or trendy attire. It's good exercise, fun for the whole family, and about the cheapest form of recreation you'll find. The bonus, of course, is a harvest of delectable seafood, perfect for steaming or frying, making into fritters, or using in a potful of creamy chowder.

With all its coastal rivers and estuaries, its many bays and coves, and its broad beaches punctuated by rocky outcrops, Oregon has an abundance of clam habitat and a variety of species. So-called bay clams include the gaper, butter, soft-shell, littleneck, and cockle. Sandy ocean beaches are home to the razor clam, and gravelly outcrops often harbor colonies of littlenecks.

A variety of methods and means are effective for harvesting clams. On any outing, you're likely to encounter people who swear by their long-handled garden shovels, while others insist that their short-handled, narrow-bladed spades are the only tools to use on the clam flats. Some use rakes of several kinds, with long or short handles. Still others use fork spades or potato forks in some areas for certain species. On the razor-clam beaches, people use shovels or tools made of polyvinyl chloride (PVC) pipe known as clam tubes or clam guns.

The best clam-digging tides are the morning minus tides that occur from March through September, although some clams are accessible on any low tide. Minus tides uncover beds that are usually underwater, where clams are large and abundant. These favored clamming tides occur in series lasting several days, with the earliest ones often the most productive. During winter, some late-afternoon and early-evening minus tides are good, provided there's sufficient sunlight.

Try to be on the flats or beach an hour before low tide, which will allow you to work near the water's edge with the tide still ebbing. Often, it's possible to collect a limit in that hour, and it seldom takes more than two hours.

While most fish-and-game regulations are complicated and subject to frequent change, often on short notice, clam-harvesting regulations are simple and straightforward, and they rarely change. Generally, clammers must carry their own containers and harvest their own clams, but they may share harvesting tools. No clammer may possess more than one limit while in the clamming area, except under the special regulations pertaining to the Disabled Clam Digging Permit (see *Oregon Sport Fishing Regulations*).

Clam diggers may keep 20 bay clams a day, of which 12 may be gapers. The limit on soft-shells is the first 36 taken, and razor clams, the first 15 taken. Clammers may return unbroken butter, cockle,

Digging Clams on the Oregon Coast

The four most plentiful Oregon bay clams are, clockwise from the top, gaper, cockle, soft-shell, and littleneck.

and littleneck clams to the immediate digging area, but must retain all other clams, regardless of their size or condition.

The razor-clam season in Clatsop County, north of Tillamook Head, is closed from July 15 through September 30. Otherwise, all waters, beaches, and flats are open all year, 24 hours a day.

Mussels are other tasty bivalves that colonize Oregon's rocky ocean shores. The mussel limit is 72 per day.

Gaper Clams

Wherever they reside, gapers are the biggest and most popular of Oregon's bay clams. They're also known as blue, horse, or horseneck clams. On Coos Bay, they're called Empire clams, presumably after the Empire District of Coos Bay, where the clam flourishes in nearby mudflats.

While walking the flats near the water's edge, look for circular holes in the mud an inch or so in diameter, among the many thousands of smaller holes created mostly by worms and other bay-bottom denizens. Poke a finger into the hole, feeling for the tip of the clam's siphon or neck. It feels rubbery and quickly retracts on touch, signaling that this is, indeed, a clam hole. The technique is easily mastered. With a little practice you'll even be able to determine the clam's approximate size by the feel of the siphon, which will ultimately lead you to the largest clams.

The reward for a few minutes of digging is a plump gaper clam.

Digging Clams on the Oregon Coast

When you find a gaper worth digging, use your boot or shovel to make a cross in the mud, with one line parallel to the water's edge, the other perpendicular, and the hole at the intersection. Marking the hole helps you keep sight of it while digging. If the clams are concentrated, find and mark several before digging. Another trick is to carry a 30-inch length of quarter-inch dowel rod and put that into the hole. As the clam retracts its siphon, the dowel rod sinks into the mud and leads to the clam, even if your excavation begins caving in.

Always dig several inches from and on the water side of the clam hole, removing material from one bayside quadrant first, then the other. Dig quickly, and make the hole as narrow as possible to keep seepage and cave-ins at a minimum. When the excavation is about 18 inches deep—more or less, depending on the size and depth of the clam—put the tip of the shovel blade at the top of the clam hole, and carefully push the blade downward to cave the mud and sand away from the clam hole. As soon as you feel or hear the blade touch the clam shell, stop, remove the shovel, and finish digging the clam free by hand, being careful not to break the shell.

Average gapers will be 4 to 5 inches across the shell. The largest will reach or exceed 7 inches and may reside as deep as 2 feet. They're found along the Oregon coast in the lower reaches of bays and estuaries, with the largest concentrations at Coos, Yaquina, Netarts, and Tillamook bays.

Butter Clams

Also known as quahogs, Martha Washington, great Oregon, and beefsteak clams, butter clams aren't particularly abundant in Oregon. Larger specimens, which may exceed 3 inches, are easily distinguished from gaper clams by the much thicker shell, shorter neck, and the absence of a large opening in the shell where the neck protrudes, as in the gaper. These clams reside in sandy mud and gravel, from 6 to 12 inches below the surface. Diggers look for half-inch or larger keyhole-shaped holes and harvest the clams with shovels or rakes. Watch for spouts to see where they've colonized.

Cockles

Cockles also inhabit the downbay flats, are widely distributed along the coast, and are among the easiest to harvest. Although their small double holes are often difficult to detect, cockles are found just beneath the surface or even on the surface, especially in eelgrass beds. You can harvest cockles with a shovel or rake, but avoid digging or raking in the eelgrass, where you could uproot this valuable plant. Instead, walk slowly through the eelgrass and feel with your feet for hard objects, which you can root out with the toe of your boot to make sure they're cockles and not broken bottles or crabs, either of which may cause injury.

Cockle shells are mottled and range in color from nearly white to beige, orange, brown, or charcoal. The shells have prominent ridges emanating from the shell hinges, which make them easy to identify.

Littleneck Clams

The littleneck is a small clam, averaging 1 to 2 inches across the shell and faintly resembling a cockle. Like the cockle, its shell has ridges radiating from the hinge, but it is much smaller. The littleneck's shell is also crosshatched with concentric ridges, which are absent in the cockle. Littlenecks are usually darker in appearance, and gray to charcoal in color.

Known also as steamer, native, cherrystone, and, erroneously, butter clams, littlenecks like gravel and sandy areas on large bays, such as Tillamook and Coos, but are also found in gravel beds on rocky outcrops and coves along the ocean, such as those south of Port Orford and in the vicinity of Brookings. Look for indented holes up to a half-inch long and in the shape of a figure eight, and harvest with a shovel or rake. In eelgrass, feel for them with your feet, as you would for cockles.

Soft-shell Clams

The most widely distributed and abundant of Oregon's bay clams are the soft-shells, commonly called Atlantic soft-shell, eastern, or mud clams. Although large soft-shell clams resemble and are sometimes confused with small gapers, they have thinner and brittler elongate shells and much shorter necks, and they prefer a different habitat. These are upbay clams, often found in gravel only a few inches from the surface. They reside nearer the high-tide line than any other clams and can be dug on any low tide in most areas. They colonize densely and are often found in small estuaries where other bay clams are absent. Where they're concentrated, limits are easy to gather. Sometimes a single shovelful of muddy gravel will unearth more than a dozen clams. Find their beds by stomping on the gravel as you walk and watching for their spouts.

Razor Clams

Razor clams inhabit the sand of open ocean beaches. They're relatively abundant north of Tillamook head, but are also found on the central and south coast on beaches near Florence, Coos Bay, Whisky Run, the Pistol River, and Gold Beach. With their elongate, smooth, light-brown shells that appear varnished, they average 3 to 5 inches in length and are easy to distinguish from bay clams. Their habitat also differs, as does their mobility.

Bay clams, except for cockles, are sedentary, and when threatened can retreat only by retracting their siphons. The razor clam, however, is a digger, able to move vertically through sand at 1 to 2 feet per minute. So when you spot a razor clam, you must act fast.

Along gradually sloping beaches, watch for a *V* in the surface of a receding wave, created by the razor clam's siphon protruding above the sand. Find those beneath the sand by stomping your feet or tapping the sand with the end of a shovel handle and watching for the dimple created by the retreating clam. Some diggers prefer to prospect the surf in about a foot of water, where they tap the sand with their shovel handles and watch for little puffs of sand that result when the clams retract their siphons.

When you spot a clam in the sand above the surf line, position the shovel blade vertically, about 4 to 6 inches seaward of the clam. Push the blade down with your foot; then move the blade upward and forward to remove sand. Continue digging this way, quickly but carefully, until the clam is exposed.

In shallow water or in wet sand after a wave has receded, position the shovel the same way, but once you've forced the blade into the sand, push the handle toward the beach and rock it back and forth several times. Then reach down behind the blade, and work your hand under it. Gradually pull the blade out, and feel for the clam with your hand.

When using a clam gun, face the ocean, position the tube over the dimple in the sand, slightly tilt the top of the gun toward you, and push the tube downward about a foot. Cover the air vent with your thumb, pull the tube out, and uncover the vent to release the

Digging Clams on the Oregon Coast

column of sand. Repeat as often as necessary to capture the clam, checking the sand column for the clam each time. Sometimes it's necessary to reach into the hole and retrieve the clam by hand.

Mussels

Mussels are easily distinguished from clams by their appearance and habitat. Their shells are similar in average size and shape to those of soft-shell clams, but mussels may grow as large as razor clams. Their color is a deep purplish blue or blue-black.

You'll find mussels along the rocky ocean shoreline attached to boulders and ledges, sometimes in great colonies. Harvest them at low tide by pulling them from the rocks, and gather only those nearest the water, which have not been overly exposed to sunlight and air. It's a good practice to collect only those that are exposed on minus tides.

Oregon's Clam-digging Bays

Bay	Soft-shell	Littleneck	Cockle	Butter	Gaper
Nehalem	x				
Tillamook	x	x	x	x	x
Netarts	x	x	x	x	x
Nestucca	x				
Siletz	x				
Yaquina	x	x	x	x	x
Alsea	x		x		
Siuslaw	x		x		x
Umpqua	x				x
Coquille	x				

Shucking and Cleaning Clams

After harvesting clams, rinse them well to remove mud and sand. Transport them to your cleaning area in a burlap bag dampened with clean bay water or in a bucket with wet burlap over the clams, which will keep them cool and alive.

The shucking and cleaning process kills any clam, and this is the method most clammers use for dispatching clams. Anyone who is uneasy about working with live clams can quickly kill them first by blanching them for thirty seconds in boiling water.

Shucking and cleaning clams can be a baffling chore for the person who has never done so before and is unfamiliar with clam anatomy, but it's not difficult. You'll need a small, sharp knife. A paring knife with a 3-inch blade will do fine. Fillet knives or so-called trout-and-bird knives with 4-inch blades are also good.

Use the same technique to shuck gaper, razor, and large soft-shell clams. Holding the clam with the shell hinge in the palm of

To clean a gaper clam (or razor or large soft-shell clam), insert the knife blade at the rear of the shell, and sever the adductor muscles affixing the clam to the shell.

Slit the digger foot, and remove all dark abdominal material.

Digging Clams on the Oregon Coast

your hand and the shell opening toward you, quickly insert the knife blade into the shell near the rear of the clam. Press the knife point against the inside of the shell, between the clam body and one side of the shell, and sever the adductor muscle connecting the clam to the shell near the clam's digger foot. Run the knife along the shell and to the front, and cut the adductor muscle near the neck. Trim the meat from that shell half, and repeat the process on the other side to remove the clam from its shell. Hold the clam under cold running water to rinse away all visible mud and sand. Cut away the black top of the siphon, or neck, on razor and soft-shell clams, split the neck lengthwise, and peel away the neck skin. With gapers, remove the necks from the bodies, split them lengthwise, and cut off the black tips. Rinse them, and refrigerate them while you finish cleaning the clams.

In the clam body, cut away the grayish-colored gills. Then use the knife to split the digger foot lengthwise. Spread the slit digger foot apart, and press the dark abdomen from the opposite side to expose waste material, which you can scrape away with the knife. Also discard the slender, transparent, rodlike structure in the gaper known as the crystalline style. The rubbery meat that runs along the clam's shell opening is the mantle. Peel or scrape away the dark skin on the mantle, and rinse the clam under cold running water. You can leave the clam intact for frying whole or mincing. You can also remove the mantle to use for clam strips.

The skin on gaper necks is thicker and tougher to remove. Bring a pot of water to a boil, and reduce to low or medium heat. Then blanch the necks, two or three at a time, for twenty to thirty seconds.

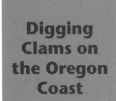

Digging Clams on the Oregon Coast

After blanching a gaper clam neck in hot water, just peel away the dark skin.

Immediately plunge them into cold water to keep them from cooking. Now you can easily peel the skin away.

Use the same techniques to shuck and clean cockles, but you have to be fast to get a knife point into a cockle before it closes tighter than any other clam. If you have trouble, you can steam them or immerse them in boiling water until they open. Then plunge them into cold water to prevent their cooking.

Littlenecks and small soft-shells are the ideal steamer clams, but should be allowed to self-clean first. You can put them in a wire fish basket, nylon mesh bag, or burlap bag and hang them from a dock or boat transom on the bay where they will pump themselves free of sand and grit in about twelve hours. Another way to let clams self-clean is to put them in a bucket of clean, cold sea water, or make your own by dissolving a cup of canning salt in each gallon of cold fresh water. Then, either refrigerate them overnight, or put the bucket in an ice chest, and pack ice around it to keep the clams cool and alive. They should pump themselves clean within twelve hours.

Mussels are among the easiest to clean. They will self-clean in sea water or salted fresh water in about an hour or two. If you plan to steam them, use a brush to thoroughly scrub the shells under cold, running water. The only inedible parts are the shell and byssus, or beard, which is the clump of black, threadlike material with which the mussel attaches itself to rocks and ledges. Remove the byssus before or after cooking.

Freezing Clams

The best way to freeze clams is to shuck them first, then put them into plastic Ziploc freezer bags. Use pint or quart bags only, as the clams will freeze faster and keep better than they might in gallon-size bags. Whether you're freezing whole clams, mantles, gaper necks, or minced clams, after putting them in the bags, pour canned clam juice into the bag to within about an inch of the top, press out the air, and freeze. Clams keep frozen remarkably well this way for up to a year.

Transporting Clams

It's always best to clean clams as soon after harvesting them as possible; then use them immediately, or freeze them for later use. If you must transport them for any distance, shuck and clean them first, and freeze them if you can. If you don't have access to a freezer, put the cleaned clams in plastic bags, and then arrange the bags in a single layer between layers of ice in an ice chest. When you reach home, you can add clam juice to the bags and freeze them.

Digging Clams on the Oregon Coast

So-called red tides, which are actually blooms of microscopic organisms known as dinoflagellates, occur with some frequency in American coastal waters during the warmer months of the year, but Oregon is considered a low-risk area. Nevertheless, the Oregon Department of Agriculture monitors coastal waters and quarantines shellfish populations whenever contaminants exceed acceptable standards. During these rare occurrences, the department notifies print and electronic media, which in turn warn clam diggers.

The term *red tide* is something of a misnomer, inasmuch as the blooms might be red, rust, blue, green, yellow, black, brown, pink, or any of a number of hues, depending on the species of organism and the stage of the bloom. In Oregon, such blooms are usually a shade of brown and are easily mistaken for seaweed.

Mussels, ocean-dwelling colonies of littleneck clams, and razor clams are most prone to this kind of contamination, as dangerous red tides occur mainly on the open ocean, rather than in bays, where other species of clams normally reside. Moreover, the toxin accumulates in the dark digestive glands of shellfish; since mussels and steamer clams are normally consumed whole, the poison is consumed with them. During most red-tide quarantines, only open ocean beaches and coastline are declared off-limits, while estuaries usually remain open to clam digging.

To inquire about red tide and other shellfish quarantines, phone the Recreational Shellfish Hot Line at (503) 986-4728.

Red Tides and Paralytic Shellfish Poisoning

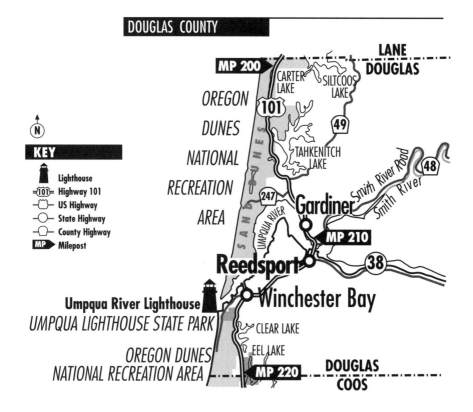

The Douglas County Coast

U.S. 101, Mile 198.6 to Mile 220.6

Although he hailed from Illinois, U.S. Senator Stephen A. Douglas (1813-61)—presidential candidate in 1860, famous for the Lincoln-Douglas debates—was one of Oregon's strongest advocates in Congress. He was known as "The Little Giant," so it's fitting that this giant of a county (5,071 square miles) is named after him. Only a tiny tip of Douglas County emerges at the coast, while its great bulk lies inland, spanning two mountain ranges and containing the entire Umpqua River drainage system as well as the watershed of its largest tributary, the Smith River. The two rivers join near Reedsport, swing north past Gardiner, and then broaden southward through an area known as the Big Bend to form Winchester Bay.

For its 22-mile course through the county, U.S. 101 is separated from the ocean by sand dunes and coastal forest. Except for brief glimpses from several vantages, the ocean remains out of sight. Nevertheless, the highway traverses some extraordinary country as it twists through aging stands of second-growth timber and past dune lakes, coastal marshes, and tidelands.

With a population of about 100,300, Douglas is the second most populous of Oregon's coastal counties, but most of its residents live inland, along or near the I-5 corridor, between the Coast Range and Cascade Mountains. On the coast, the only communities are Gardiner, Reedsport, and Winchester Bay, with a combined population of under 7,000.

U.S. 101, mile 198.8
Carter Lake

This long, narrow dune lake lies west of and parallel to U.S. 101 for its 1-mile length. Its brushy shoreline makes it difficult to fish, except from a boat, canoe, or float tube. Resident species include bluegill, largemouth bass, and native cutthroat trout. The Oregon Department of Fish and Wildlife also stocks the lake each spring with rainbow trout and occasionally releases hatchery brood stock of 5 pounds or more.

Carter Lake Campground

A U.S. Forest Service campground west of the highway at the north end of Carter Lake offers 24 secluded campsites, including three pull-throughs, with tables and fire pits, picnic area, drinking water, rest rooms with flush toilets, and beach and dune access for hikers. Shoreline access is limited, but a small launching area at the south end of the campground accommodates canoes, kayaks, and cartop boats. Campers may use dead and down material for campfires, but are not allowed to cut live trees. The campground is closed in winter.

U.S. Mile 101, mile 199.1
East Carter Boat Ramp

An excellent paved ramp lies 0.1 mile west of U.S. 101, with ample parking and trash receptacle provided.

U.S. 101, mile 200.7
Oregon Dunes Overlook

Part of the Oregon Dunes National Recreation Area, the park, just west of the highway, includes picnic areas with tables, trash receptacles, and drinking water. A covered shelter commands panoramic views of the dunes, beach, and ocean, as well as opportunities for photography and whale watching in season. A hiking trail leads 1 mile through the dunes to the beach. A loop trail, including 1.5 miles of beach, is about 3.5 miles long. The overlook has a self-guided interpretive trail, boardwalks, paved walks, decks, ramps with wheelchair access, RV parking, trailer turnaround, and rest rooms with flush toilets and wheelchair access.

Hikers on the boardwalk at the Oregon Dunes Overlook.

U.S. 101, mile 202.2
Tahkenitch Creek Trailhead

Turn west off the highway into a parking lot adjacent to the trailhead with a nearby trash receptacle and vault toilets with wheelchair access. The system consists of a 1.5-mile loop, a 2.5-mile loop, and a 1-mile-long trail to the beach, with orientation signs and route markers along the way. The longer loop also connects with Tahkenitch Dunes Trail (see Tahkenitch Dunes/ Threemile Lake Trail, mile 203.6, page 218).

Hikers traverse mixed forests, marshes, meadows, deflation plains, and dunes, with chances of observing or photographing a variety of wildlife, including shorebirds, songbirds, birds of prey, deer, black bear, raccoon, river otter, squirrels, rabbits, and other small mammals.

Trail and sand dunes near the Oregon Dunes Overlook.

Tahkenitch (pronounced *tack*-uh-nitch) is a descriptive Indian word meaning "many arms." Lying east of Highway 101 and spreading inland from there, Tahkenitch is one of Oregon's largest coastal lakes and is among the least developed. Only a small part of its 1,674 acres and seven arms is visible from U.S. 101. It's a relatively shallow lake, averaging 11 feet and reaching a maximum depth of 23 feet. Shoreline access is limited to a few spots along the west shore near the highway and the south shore via County Road 49 (see U.S. 101, mile 206.8).

U.S. 101, mile 202.7 to mile 203.4
Tahkenitch Lake

Lack of shoreline development and the aging stands of second-growth timber make this an especially attractive lake. Its many arms and coves provide a superb outdoor experience and many opportunities to watch and photograph wildlife. The best way to enjoy Tahkenitch is by boat, canoe, or kayak, which can take adventurers along the scenic and densely forested shoreline, past islands and marshes for fishing, wildlife watching, photography, sightseeing, or just relaxing.

Native cutthroat trout and stocked rainbow trout provide ample angling opportunities all year. Sea-run cutthroat, coho salmon, and steelhead trout migrate through the lake during fall and winter spawning seasons. Warmwater species include largemouth bass, warmouth, bluegill, crappie, yellow perch, and brown bullhead.

More than eighty-five species of fish, birds, mammals, and amphibians use or inhabit the lake, and another seventy species reside in the bordering forests, meadows and marshes. Songbirds, shorebirds, and waterfowl abound, with populations significantly increasing during spring and fall migrations. Birds of prey include bald eagles, osprey, and several species of hawks and owls. Alert wildlife watchers might also spot beaver, muskrat, nutria, mink, river otter, and raccoon in the marshes and along the shore. Chipmunks, red squirrels, possums, skunks, red foxes, coyotes, and bobcats inhabit the forests and meadows. The largest residents of the lake shore and uplands are black-tailed deer, Roosevelt elk, black bear, and cougar.

U.S. 101, mile 203
Tahkenitch Boat
Ramp

Boaters and anglers will find an excellent paved ramp, trailer parking and turnaround, drinking water, trash receptacles, and vault toilets at this U.S. Forest Service facility on the east side of the highway. The adjacent boat dock is for temporary moorage, not for fishing. Anglers may use the fishing dock at Tahkenitch Landing, just south of the ramp.

**U.S. 101,
mile 203.4**
Tahkenitch Landing

On the east side of U.S. 101, between the highway and lake, lies an attractive Forest Service campground with 22 campsites set among the trees and shrubs along the west shore of the lake, each with a table and fire pit. Facilities include a fishing dock with wheelchair access, paved boat ramp, boat-trailer parking, trash receptacles, and pit toilets. Campers may use dead and down materials for campfires, but may not cut live trees and shrubs. Drinking water is not available.

**U.S. 101,
mile 203.6**
Tahkenitch
Campground

Just west of U.S. 101 is a Forest Service campground with 31 attractive campsites with tables and fire pits. Facilities include trailer turnaround, trash receptacles, and pit toilets. Drinking water and rest rooms with flush toilets are available from May 15 through September 15 only. Hiking trails provide access to lakes, dunes, and ocean beaches (see next entry).

Tahkenitch Dunes/
Threemile Lake Trails

The trailhead is 0.1 mile west of U.S. 101, at Tahkenitch Campground. These well-maintained trails offer easy hiking with some short stretches that are modestly steep. The trail to Elbow and Threemile Lakes forks left 0.25 mile from the trailhead and is 2.75 miles long. The dunes trail reaches the dunes 0.75 mile and the beach 1.5 miles from the trailhead. Although there are no developed campsites, camping is permitted in areas off the trails. Campers may build fires (except during closures) with dead or down material only. With no drinking water or trash receptacles along the trail, campers and hikers should plan to carry in their own water and pack out their trash. The only rest rooms are near the trailhead at the campground. These are good trails for hiking and backpacking. The lakes offer angling for yellow perch, largemouth bass, and native cutthroat trout, but are difficult to fish from shore. (See entries for Elbow Lake at U.S. 101, mile 204.3, and County Road 247, Sparrow Park Road, at U.S. 101, mile 207.5 [page 219].)

Access to this 13-acre lake along the west side of U.S. 101 is by way of a dirt road leading to an unimproved launch area for small boats, canoes, kayaks, and float tubes. Fishing for native cutthroat and stocked rainbow trout, as well as largemouth bass and bluegill, can be good on this small lake. There are no developed campsites or facilities, but camping is permitted.

U.S. 101, mile 204.3
Elbow Lake

A good gravel road leads east off U.S. 101 into the Coast Range, providing access to Mallard Arm at the south end of Tahkenitch Lake. The road also connects with other county and Forest Service roads east of Tahkenitch and Siltcoos Lakes. There are some suitable spots for camping, but no developed sites or facilities. Use the Siuslaw National Forest Map for traveling the backcountry.

U.S. 101, mile 206.8
County Road 49
(Fivemile Road)

A good gravel road leads west off the highway, but it's steep in places, narrow, and not recommended for large travel trailers. The road ends at a turnaround near the beach, 4 miles from the highway. Camping is allowed at various locations off the road, but there are no developed campsites, facilities, or drinking water. The area has hiking trails and access to dunes and beach for off-road vehicles. Beachcombing and surf fishing are productive pastimes on the broad sandy, uncrowded beach.

U.S. 101, mile 207.5
County Road 247
(Sparrow Park Road)

The south trailhead to Threemile Lake is 3.3 miles west of U.S. 101; it leads 0.75 mile to the dunes and 1 mile to the lake. It's a pleasant trail for hiking and outdoor photography. For anglers, it offers easy access to the lake and is especially recommended for anyone who wants to pack in a small inflatable watercraft or float tube.

Once known as the "little white city by the sea," this small community (population 600) is among the oldest remaining settlements on the Oregon coast. When the schooner *Bostonian* wrecked on the Umpqua River bar in 1850, locals salvaged her cargo of trade goods and hauled it 9 miles upstream to the present site of Gardiner. Within a year, a town sprang up and a customs office opened. Lumber milling and exporting, shipbuilding, and salmon canning brought prosperity to the town. In 1881, a fire broke out in the sawmill and quickly spread through the town, engulfing most of its buildings. The mill was rebuilt and free lumber offered to anyone willing to put up new structures. Every building in town was painted white, a custom that prevailed well into the twentieth century. Even today, white is the predominant color of Gardiner's structures.

U.S. 101, mile 209 to mile 209.9 Gardiner
(zip code 97441)

For the first half-century of its existence, Gardiner depended solely on water for transportation, commerce, and mail delivery and functioned as the major town on the lower reaches of the

Umpqua River, a role Reedsport assumed soon after the railroad came to the south coast. International Paper Company built a pulp mill opposite the town proper in the 1960s, which operated as the community's major industry until it was closed in 1999, leaving the future of Gardiner uncertain at best.

The town is important to travelers mainly for its historical significance and for access to the lower Umpqua and Smith rivers. From the city boat ramp, it's a short trip downstream to the Big Bend or upstream to the mouth of the Smith River.

U.S. 101, mile 209.6
Gardiner Landing

On the west side of U.S. 101, just south of the pulp mill, a paved boat ramp provides access to the Umpqua River. Boaters may use the dock for temporary moorage and can park in the narrow area between the highway and the river.

U.S. 101, mile 210.2
Smith River

Named after nineteenth-century explorer Jedediah Smith, the river rises in the Coast Range and courses some 75 miles seaward to its confluence with the Umpqua River near Reedsport. Upriver stretches of placid water are punctuated by rapids and waterfalls and flanked by rocky cliffs and forested hills. About 20 miles above the Umpqua, the Smith broadens into tidewater and slows its pace. From there downstream, it is navigable by powerboat.

The Smith is popular with anglers who fish from boats or bank in its lower reaches. Angling is mainly for steelhead trout and chinook salmon. The river is also one of Oregon's top producers of striped bass. Although the numbers of this fine game and food fish have diminished in recent years, here and elsewhere along the Oregon coast, the Smith's population is still viable, and the fish run large—to 40 pounds or more. Bank access is fair to good along the lower river, near the mouth, and about 5 miles east of U.S. 101. There are also adequate launching facilities for powerboats, as well as drift boats, canoes, and other small craft.

In addition to angling, the Smith offers opportunities for photography, sightseeing, hiking, camping, and wildlife watching, especially in its upper reaches. The river and country it courses through are scenic all year, but particularly during spring, summer, and fall. Fall colors are magnificent along the Smith's forested banks, and that's also a good time to catch glimpses of salmon negotiating rapids and leaping stepped falls.

U.S. 101, mile 210.7
County Road 48
(Smith River Road)

County Road 48 exits east off Highway 101 and flanks the Smith River, providing tidewater access for nearly 20 miles. Beyond, it rises into the Coast Range and connects with various U.S. Forest Service roads, furnishing access to camping and recreation areas. The road provides good bank access, especially in the river's lower reaches, and leads to several boat launches. The region is rich in wildlife and offers countless opportunities for photography, hiking, biking, backpacking, and camping. (Use Douglas County and Siuslaw National Forest maps.)

On the west side of U.S. 101, between the Smith River and Umpqua River Bridges, is a marker commemorating the Jedediah Smith Exploring Expedition of 1828. A 0.63-mile trail leads to a spot overlooking the expedition's campsite, where all but four members of the Smith party were killed when Kelawatset Indians attacked on July 14, 1828.

U.S. 101, mile 210.8
Bolon Island Historical Wayside/ Jedediah Smith Trail

The bridge across the Umpqua River at Reedsport is a historic concrete-and-steel structure, one of five major projects completed in 1936 during a flurry of coastal bridge building. Designed by Conde B. McCullough, Oregon's foremost bridge engineer, it features two 154-foot, reinforced concrete, bowstring-arch spans at each end of the 430-foot central span, making it the largest swing-span bridge in the state. Its walkways provide excellent vantages for viewing and photographing the lower Umpqua River.

U.S. 101, mile 211
Umpqua River Bridge

Heading in the eastern part of the county, deep in the Cascades, the Umpqua tumbles down the western slope of the mountains, then meanders through the Coast Range. On its way to the ocean, it gathers the waters of many tributaries and grows into Oregon's second-largest coastal river. From the mid-nineteenth century until the development of railroads and highways in the early twentieth century, the lower Umpqua was an important transportation corridor, with schooners, steamboats, and tugboats plying the tidewaters from Winchester Bay to Scottsburg, more than 20 miles upstream. This stretch of the river is still an important navigable waterway, but now it mainly carries recreational boaters, sailors, sailboarders, canoeists, kayakers, anglers, crabbers, clam diggers, sightseers, wildlife watchers, and photographers.

Umpqua River

From its headwaters to its estuary, the Umpqua is a river teeming with life. The system gets both summer and winter runs of steelhead trout, spring and fall runs of chinook salmon, and fall runs of coho salmon. Great schools of shad enter the river in April and provide superb angling through June, from tidewater to the middle reaches, well beyond Scottsburg. The same waters also provide outstanding fishing for smallmouth bass, from late spring through autumn. Anglers take striped bass from Winchester Bay to the head of tidewater near Scottsburg. The same stretch offers some of the best sturgeon angling on the coast, especially in the Big Bend area near Gardiner. Huge schools of smelt and herring enter the system in winter and spring, providing food for numerous resident and migratory fishes, as well as for anglers who take the silvery fish with tiny herring jigs.

From Big Bend to Winchester Bay, the influence of salt water increases. Mudflats give up easy limits of soft-shell clams at low tide, with minus tides most productive. Slack tides and the last hour or so of flood and ebb tides offer the best opportunities for taking Dungeness and red rock crabs. Surfperch, seaperch, and starry flounder are included in the catch here.

Bank access is good downstream in the Winchester Bay area and upstream at various places along State Route 38. Launch sites are at Winchester Bay, Reedsport, and several Highway 38 locations.

The Umpqua basin is also a sightseer's, birder's, and wildlife watcher's paradise. Steep, forested bluffs and intermittent meadows flank the river's banks as it wends its way through the Coast Range. Elk and deer roam freely from woods to water's edge, while smaller mammals cruise the coverts, creekbeds, and croplands. Ospreys fish the river and sloughs, and hawks of several varieties forage from fields to fence lines. Canada geese graze on grasses like cattle. Diver ducks, mergansers, coots, and grebes frequent the river's mainstem, while puddle ducks dabble in ponds, backwaters, and wet meadows, often in the company of great blue herons. On the tree-lined benchlands above the river's banks, wild turkeys strut and court in audacious display. The curtain rises on this superb play just a few miles east of Reedsport, along one of Oregon's finest rivers, skirted by one of the state's most scenic highways.

U.S. 101, mile 211.4 to mile 213.4 Reedsport
(zip code 97467)

With a population of about 5,000, Reedsport is the largest community and the only incorporated city on the Douglas County coast. It began as a railroad-construction camp in 1912 and took over as the area's center of commerce and industry when the railroad connecting Coos Bay with the Willamette Valley bypassed Gardiner.

Reedsport's greatest significance to the coastal traveler is as the location of the headquarters for the Oregon Dunes National Recreation Area. This is also the starting point for State Route 38, an important accessway along the lower Umpqua River.

U.S. 101, mile 211.5
Oregon Dunes National Recreation Area Headquarters

This is an important stop for coastal travelers, located on the west side of U.S. 101, at the first intersection south of the Umpqua River Bridge. The NRA headquarters building houses interpretive displays and provides an abundance of books, booklets, brochures, maps, and handouts about the dunes, local flora and fauna, and the kinds of recreation possible in and around the dunes. Excellent maps of the Oregon Dunes N.R.A.

and the Siuslaw National Forest are available, each for a nominal fee. U.S. Forest Service personnel are on duty to answer questions and provide directions. Rest rooms with flush toilets and wheelchair access are on the premises. From June through October, the facility is open daily, from 8:00 a.m. to 4:30 p.m. From November through May, hours are 8:00 to 4:30, Monday through Friday, and 10:00 a.m. to 4:00 p.m. on Saturday.

The chamber of commerce shares space with the Oregon Dunes NRA headquarters. Travelers gathering area information here should be sure to obtain a copy of the "Official Road Map of Douglas County Oregon," one of the better county maps and a handy item to have along while exploring the county's coastal and tidewater areas, as well as the Coast Range and beyond. From May through September, it's open daily, 8:00 a.m. to 4:30 p.m. The rest of the year, the center is open from 10:00 a.m. to 4:00 p.m., and is closed on Sundays from November through February.

Reedsport-Winchester Bay Chamber of Commerce Visitor Center

This highway exits east off U.S. 101, opposite the visitor center and N.R.A. headquarters, and leads through Old Town Reedsport, near the waterfront, then up the Umpqua River. Between Reedsport and Scottsburg, a distance of about 17 miles, this scenic route provides access to the river, several boat ramps, picnic areas, Dean Creek Elk Viewing Area, and Loon Lake Recreation Area. (Use the Douglas County Map.)

State Route 38 junction

To reach Reedsport's original townsite, waterfront, and refurbished Old Town District, turn east off Highway 101, and cross the railroad tracks. Old Town extends eastward along Fir Avenue (Highway 38), from East Railroad Avenue to 3rd Street, with ample parking along Fir and adjacent streets. Visitors will find an assortment of shops, galleries, restaurants, and other attractions here and along the waterfront.

Old Town Reedsport

Take State Route 38 east 0.6 mile, turn north on 3rd Street, then right on Rainbow Plaza 0.2 mile to a paved boat ramp on the Umpqua River, opposite the mouth of the Smith River. Amenities include a boat dock for temporary moorage, parking lot, picnic area with tables, trash receptacles, drinking water, and rest rooms with flush toilets.

Reedsport Landing

Drive east 0.6 mile on Highway 38, turn north on 3rd Street, go a short block, take a right on Water Avenue, and a left on Riverfront Way; then drive 0.1 mile to the parking lot, just west of Reedsport Landing. This waterfront attraction is more than a museum, although it is surely that, and more than an

Umpqua Discovery Center

MUST STOP

View of the lower Umpqua River from the Umpqua Discovery Center observation tower.

interpretive center, which it certainly is. It is, indeed, a discovery center and a *must stop* for all travelers.

Those who take the time will discover a modern facility that examines more than 6,000 years of the cultural and natural history, geology, and inevitable change of the lower Umpqua region. History of the Kuuich tribes that inhabited the area, early explorers and fur traders, pioneer settlers, and all those who followed unfolds in the life-size dioramas, artifact displays, intricate models, and interactive exhibits designed to delight visitors of all ages.

Outside, wheelchair-accessible decks and ramps offer superb views of the river and interpretive signs detailing the nature of the estuary. Steps lead to an observation tower offering a gull's-eye view of the Umpqua. Docks provide temporary moorage for those arriving by boat.

From June 1 to September 30, the center is open daily, 9:00 a.m. to 5:00 p.m.; the rest of the year, hours are 10:00 a.m. to 4:00 p.m. daily. Information: (541) 271-4816.

Dean Creek Elk Viewing Area

MUST STOP

At another *must stop* for all travelers, which lies 2.8 miles east of Highway 101 and extends for three miles along State Route 38, a large herd of about 150 Roosevelt elk frequents the bottom land along the south side of the highway all year. Use the ample pulloffs and roadside parking areas to watch and photograph the elk and other abundant wildlife.

Although elk often feed or bed down near the road, binoculars and telephoto lenses help in spotting and photographing these magnificent creatures. The area is also home to resident populations of waterfowl, shorebirds, wading birds, songbirds, and birds of prey. During fall, winter, and spring, migratory birds and waterfowl flock to the area and adjacent river by the

Roosevelt elk graze near the highway at Dean Creek Elk Viewing Area

thousands, which in turn attract hawks and eagles that prey on birds and waterfowl. On any spring or summer night, after highway traffic has subsided, the chorus of thousands of tree frogs is, if not deafening, certainly impressive.

Most of the refuge is off-limits to humans, but he Bureau of Land Management has provided adequate viewing areas, including widened highway shoulders for much of the area's length, parking lots, viewing platforms, an interpretive kiosk, interpretive signs, picnic tables, trash receptacles, and rest rooms with wheelchair access.

This tributary of the Umpqua River is closed to all angling, except for striped bass. The tidewater section of the creek, from the mouth upstream to the first railroad bridge, is open all year for striper fishing. The creek enters the Umpqua from the south, just downstream from the Umpqua River Bridge. The nearest boat ramp is at Reedsport Landing in Old Town Reedsport, off Highway 38. (See Reedsport Landing on page 223.)

U.S. 101, mile 212
Schofield Creek

Turn west on North 22nd Street, go 0.2 mile, then right on Ridgeway Drive (which becomes Greenbriar Street) for 0.2 mile, right on Country Club Drive, and 0.2 mile to the parking lot. This 3,086-yard, 9-hole, par-36 course lies in a lovely wooded residential area. It has a clubhouse, pro shop with resident pro, driving range, putting green, club rental, pull-cart and electric-cart rental, restaurant, and lounge. Pro shop: (541) 271-2626.

U.S. 101, mile 212.6
Forest Hills Country Club

Both the Umpqua River Estuary and the small community along its eastern shore are called Winchester Bay. The town lies along U.S. 101 and west of the highway, via 8th Street and Salmon Harbor Drive, each of which provides bay access. This is one of coastal Oregon's major recreational centers, offering a variety of activities and attractions. Small shops, galleries, and

U.S. 101, mile 215.6 to 215.8 Winchester Bay
(zip code 97467)

restaurants dot the waterfront area along the east side of Salmon Harbor. Crabbing, clam digging, angling, boating, kayaking, sailing, and sailboarding are popular pastimes on the bay. Hiking, biking, beach combing, surfing, kite flying, and operating off-road vehicles (ORVs) are favorite forms of beach and dune recreation.

The harbor is home port for both commercial and charter boats, recreational power and sailing craft, and U.S. Coast Guard rescue and patrol vessels. Launching facilities are among the best on the coast. Bay, beach, and dune access is plentiful.

Public pier on Winchester Bay

U.S. 101, mile 215.7
Salmon Harbor Recreation Area

Turn west off Highway 101 on Salmon Harbor Drive (County Road 251). This road provides access to the bayside community of Winchester Bay as well as to the estuary and the vicinity's businesses and recreation area. It leads to the harbor, bay, campgrounds and RV parks, public pier, south jetty, sand dunes, trails, and ocean beaches. It also links with Umpqua Lighthouse Road, which leads to the county visitor center and museum, lighthouse, whale-watching station, and state park.

The entire area is a *must stop* for sightseers, photographers, and outdoor recreationists. (See also Umpqua Lighthouse Road, U.S. 101, mile 216.7 and mile 217, on page 227, for information about the state park, lighthouse, and other attractions.)

Salmon Harbor

Douglas County has the oldest park system in the state, and just 0.2 mile west of U.S. 101 lies the crown jewel of the system. The complex includes a campground with 450 sites for self-contained RVs and a 900-slip marina—the largest on the Oregon coast. Facilities include drinking water, hot showers, and rest rooms with flush toilets and wheelchair access, as well as coin-operated laundry, tank dump, pump-out station, paved boat ramps, boat hoist, marine service and repair, and moorage by the day, week, month, or year. Information: (541) 271-3407.

Another in the county-park system, just 0.3 mile west of U.S. 101, Windy Cove has 75 full-hookup sites with tables, rest rooms with flush toilets and showers, drinking water, and playground. The campground is ideally located across the road from the bay, with beaches, dunes, and trails nearby. Information: (541) 271-4138.

Windy Cove Campground

In disrepair for years, this finely refurbished pier provides excellent opportunities and wheelchair access for angling, crabbing, sightseeing, wildlife watching, and photography. It lies 0.9 mile west of U.S. 101.

Public pier

This park is 1.5 miles west of U.S. 101, with Parking Lot #1 at mile 2.2. Trails lead to the beach and south jetty. Although surfers use the area south of the south jetty, these are cold and treacherous waters with dangerous currents—not safe for wading or swimming. The beach is a popular place for kite flying and surf fishing. Anglers also fish from the south jetty, but negotiating the huge, slippery boulders is tricky and potentially dangerous; this is no place for small children. Avoid the jetty when the water is rough, and watch out for sneaker waves.

Ziolkouski Beach County Park

At road's end, 4.1 miles from U.S. 101, Parking Lot #2 provides a large parking and ORV-staging area with a loading ramp, pit toilets, trash receptacles, and access to the dunes and broad sand beach.

Umpqua Beach

Near the top of a long upgrade just south of Winchester Bay, a short loop road exits the west side of U.S. 101 at two locations, 0.3 miles apart. Turn west off the loop road for access to a *must-stop* state park, charming lighthouse, and other attractions.

U.S. 101, mile 216.7 and mile 217
Umpqua Lighthouse Road

Follow Umpqua Lighthouse Road west to the campground and picnic area, which are about 0.5 and 0.7 mile from U.S. 101, respectively. The campground has 20 full-hookup sites, 42 tent sites, two yurts, and two log cabins; two campsites have wheelchair access. Other amenities include a hiker/biker camp, trailer turnaround, drinking water, hot showers, and rest rooms with flush toilets and wheelchair access. The sheltered picnic area has tables, trash receptacles, and rest rooms with flush toilets and wheelchair access. Hiking trails pass through the park and swimmers will find a small beach on pretty little Lake Marie. Information: (541) 271-4118 or (800) 551-6949. Reservations: (800) 452-5687.

Umpqua Lighthouse State Park

✔

MUST STOP

Umpqua River Light Station

Umpqua River Light Station

The picturesque lighthouse stands 0.8 miles west of U.S. 101 and 0.1 mile beyond the picnic area. The original Umpqua River Lighthouse, completed in 1857, stood near the river mouth. Storms and high water during the winter of 1860-61 undermined the structure and toppled it on February 8, 1861. For more than 30 years, the only aid to navigation at Winchester Bay was a second-class can buoy marking the Umpqua's entrance. The present lighthouse, built on high ground and sound footing, began operating in 1894. Standing 65 feet tall, with a focal plane 165 feet above sea level, the lighthouse continues to guide mariners with a red-and-white beacon visible 19 miles out.

Whale watching station

Atop the bluff across the road from the lighthouse—overlooking the Umpqua River bar, beach, and ocean—is an ideal place for watching boats and bay activities anytime. The peak periods for watching migrating gray whales is December through mid-January and mid-March through mid-June. Some whales do not migrate all the way to summer feeding grounds in Alaska and might appear near the river mouth throughout summer and autumn, when it's not unusual to spot cow-and-calf pairs there.

Located just north of the lighthouse, this attractive building functioned as the U.S. Coast Guard barracks and administration building from 1939 to 1971. It now contains the Lower Umpqua Historical Society's collection of artifacts and old photographs and is open to the public Wednesday through Saturday from 10:00 a.m. to 5:00 p.m. and Sunday from 1:00 p.m. to 5:00 p.m., May 1 through September 30. The road continues past the center, 1 mile to Winchester Bay and Salmon Harbor. Information: (541) 271-4631.

Douglas County
Parks Coastal Visitor
Center and Museum

On the west side of the highway, at the crest of the big hill south of Winchester Bay, a large parking area and interpretive wayside invite travelers to stop and take in the spectacular panoramic view of the Umpqua River bar, jetties, ocean, beach, and lighthouse. Interpretive signs orient travelers, provide information on local and Oregon coast attractions, and impart local and coastal history.

U.S. 101, mile 217.2
Winchester Bay
Wayfinding Point

Forested foothills border this untouched and untouchable lake, which lies along the east side of U.S. 101 at the county's southwestern extreme. As the municipal water source for Reedsport, the lake is off-limits to the public.

U.S. 101, mile 218.1 to mile 219
Clear Lake

U.S. 101, mile 220.6
Douglas County/
Coos County Line

Information

Douglas County Park Department
Lighthouse Way
Winchester Bay, OR 97467
(541) 271-4631 Coastal Visitor Center
(541) 271-4138 Windy Cove

Oregon Department of Fish & Wildlife
Courthouse Annex
680 Fir Avenue
Reedsport, OR 97467
(541) 271-4322

Oregon Dunes National Recreation Area
U.S. Forest Service
Siuslaw National Forest
855 Highway Avenue
Reedsport, OR 97467
(541) 271-3611

Oregon Department of Parks & Recreation
Umpqua Lighthouse State Park
Winchester Bay, OR 97467
(541) 271-4118
(541) 271-4182 Booth (summer)

Reedsport-Winchester Bay Chamber of
Commerce
P.O. Box 11-B
Reedsport, OR 97467
(541) 271-3495
(800) 247-2155
www.coos.or.us/~reewbycc

Salmon Harbor
P.O. Box 7
Winchester Bay, OR 97467

United States Coast Guard
Umpqua River Lifeboat Station
Winchester Bay, OR 97467
(541) 271-2137
(541) 271-4244 Weather and Bar Conditions

Watching Whales on the Oregon Coast

Winter comes early to the Arctic, pushing ice from the polar regions into the Chukchi and northern Bering seas, nudging populations of gray whales southward, through Umiak Pass in the Aleutian Islands into the north Pacific. From their summer feeding grounds the whales move to their winter calving grounds in Baja California, Mexico—a journey of 5,000 to 6,000 miles, one way. As they migrate, the whales hug the continental coastline, allowing coastal residents and visitors to witness a rite of nature that attracts more followers each year.

The various species of whales that make up the order Cetacea are divided into two groups: toothed whales (such as sperm and killer whales) and baleen whales (such as blue, humpback, and gray). Toothed whales prey on squid, fish and, in the case of killer whales, larger animals, including seals, sea lions, and even other whales. Baleen whales feed mainly on tiny fish, crustaceans, plankton, krill, and other minuscule organisms.

Although the baleen plates that line the mouths of these whales are sometimes called whalebone, they're not bone, but rather a material more like fingernails or horns. In the gray whale, the plates are short and usually yellowish in color with yellowish-white bristles.

Some 23 species of whales use the waters off Oregon's coast, ranging from the smaller cetaceans—such as porpoises, dolphins, and killer whales—to the much larger humpback, right, sperm, and the huge blue whale, the largest mammal that has ever lived on earth. Although the offshore traveler might catch occasional glimpses of porpoises, dolphins, or any of the larger whales, and the lucky onshore observer might get to see harbor porpoises and killer whales, the most frequently and consistently observable whale in Oregon's nearshore waters is the gray whale.

Like other whales, great grays graze in the sea's briny pastures, sometimes consuming schooling fish and other abundant organisms. But they're primarily bottom feeders, making them unique among whales. On feeding dives, they suck up huge mouthfuls of bottom sediments, then use their tongues to force out the silt and sand, filtering it through baleen bristles, leaving behind a meal of tiny amphipods and isopods.

Adult grays are from 35 to 50 feet long and weigh from 20 to 40 tons. Females are slightly larger than males. Calves at birth are 15 feet long and weigh about 1,500 pounds. Gray whales cruise at 2 to 4 knots, but can reach 10 knots (over 11 miles per hour). Although they can dive to 500 feet and stay down for fifteen minutes, most dives are to depths of 120 to 300 feet and last from three to five minutes. This is the depth range they seem to prefer and the depth contour they migrate along.

First to leave the Arctic feeding grounds, in October, are the pregnant females, which travel alone or in small pods of two or three, covering up to 100 miles a day. In November and December, the rest follow in pods of four to twelve, reaching the shallow lagoons of Baja in six to eight weeks. After a twelve-month gestation period, most calves are born in the warm Baja waters, but a few are born en route. Rich mother's milk, 55 percent fat, nourishes the calves, which consume about 50 gallons and gain 60 to 70 pounds every day. By spring, they weigh 2 to 3 tons and are 18 to 19 feet long.

A two-phase northward migration begins in February with newly pregnant females, juveniles, and adult males. Females with calves remain in the Baja lagoons for another month and usually reach the summer feeding grounds in July. There, the whales gorge themselves on abundant food, building up a layer of blubber from 6 to 10 inches thick.

The best Oregon vantage points for whale watching are the capes and other headlands—the higher the better. Upper stories of ocean-front motels and resorts are good too. Those interested in a close-up look at whales will find charter-boat operators working out of several Oregon ports, with trips of one to three hours costing about $10 to $20.

Watch for spouts. When a gray whale surfaces, it begins exhaling while its blow holes are still slightly submerged, sending a salty mist skyward. Warm air from its lungs condenses as it meets the colder air, forming a spout 15 feet high and visible for miles on a calm day, the sound audible for a half-mile or more. As the whale spouts, a portion of its back rises above the surface. It makes a series of three to five shallow dives at intervals of thirty to fifty seconds, spouting each time. Just before sounding, the gray whale usually raises its flukes, thus steepening its angle of descent for a dive that will probably last three to five minutes.

Calm days are best for sighting whales, and morning hours are often calmer than afternoons. Some recommend overcast days because of reduced glare, but calm, sunny days are as good if not better for the watcher who wears polarized sunglasses, which reduce glare and increase contrast. On cloudy days, glasses with yellow or amber lenses increase contrast and make spouts more visible.

Good binoculars are a great aid to the whale watcher. Those above 10 power are difficult to hold steady, however, and are troublesome to pan in search of whales. So glasses of 7 to 10 power are most popular. Fogproof and waterproof models are a decided advantage along the Oregon coast during the rainy winter months.

Whales migrating south normally appear along the Oregon coast in mid-December and are present in good numbers through January, with the peak period usually from Christmas into early January. The northbound migrants arrive during March and continue along the Oregon coast through May. As many as four to five hundred gray whales get distracted along the way, perhaps by abundant food,

Watching Whales on the Oregon Coast

Watching Whales on the Oregon Coast

and stay the summer along the Oregon coast, often near the mouths of coastal rivers, making sightings possible any time of the year.

Anyone can join the whale-watching fraternity gathering on the Oregon coast. And it takes no great skill or large outlay of money to enjoy the gentle sport. The Oregon Parks and Recreation Department coordinates a whale-watching program from the Historic Alsea Bay Bridge Interpretive Center in Waldport. Trained volunteers are also stationed at key whale-watching areas along the coast during peak migration periods. Look for signs that say "Whale Watching Spoken Here."

Best Choices for Oregon Whale Watching

Warrenton: Observation platform at the south jetty in Fort Stevens State Park, west of town.

Cannon Beach: Cape Falcon, south of town; Ecola State Park and Tillamook Head, north of town.

Manzanita: Neahkahnie Mountain, north of town.

Garibaldi: Check at the harbor for whale-watching cruises.

Oceanside: Cape Meares State Scenic Viewpoint, north of town; Cape Lookout State Park, south of town.

Pacific City: Cape Kiwanda, at the north end of town, on Three Capes Scenic Loop, west of Highway 101.

Lincoln City: Cascade Head, north of town.

Depoe Bay: Cape Foulweather and Otter Crest Loop, south of town and west of U.S. 101; Boiler Bay State Park, north of town. Also check at the harbor for whale-watching cruises, which are very popular here.

Newport: Yaquina Head Outstanding Natural Area, at the north end of town. Check at the harbor for whale-watching cruises.

Yachats: Cape Perpetua, south of town.

Florence: Sea Lion Caves, Heceta Head Lighthouse State Scenic Viewpoint, and Heceta Head State Park, north of town.

Winchester Bay: Whale-watching station at Umpqua Lighthouse State Park, south of town.

Charleston: Coast Guard lookout, above the south jetty, west of town; Bastendorf County Park, hiking trails from Sunset Bay to Cape Arago, Shore Acres and Cape Arago State Parks, and Simpson Reef and Shell Island Overlook, all south of town. Check at the boat basin for whale-watching cruises.

Bandon: Coquille Point, Face Rock State Scenic Wayside, and cliffs along Beach Loop Road on the western edge of town.

Port Orford: Port Orford Heads Wayside, west of town; Cape Blanco State Park, north of town.

Gold Beach: Cape Sebastian State Park, south of town.

Brookings: Harris Beach and Samuel H. Boardman State Parks, north of town. Check at the harbor for whale-watching cruises.

Information

Mark O. Hatfield Marine Science Center
2030 Marine Science Drive
Newport, OR 97365
(541) 867-0100
URL: www.hmsc.orst.edu

National Marine Mammal Laboratory
URL: www.mmm101.afsc.noaa.gov

Oregon Parks and Recreation Department
"Whale Watching Spoken Here"
P.O. Box 693
Waldport, OR 97394
(541) 563-2002
URL: whalespoken.org

Oregon Sea Grant—Extension Sea Grant
Marine Mammal Web Site
URL: seagrant.orst.edu/extension/marmammal.html

WhaleNet
URL: whale.wheelock.edu

Whale-Watching Web
URL: www.physics.helsinki.fi/whale

**Watching
Whales on
the Oregon
Coast**

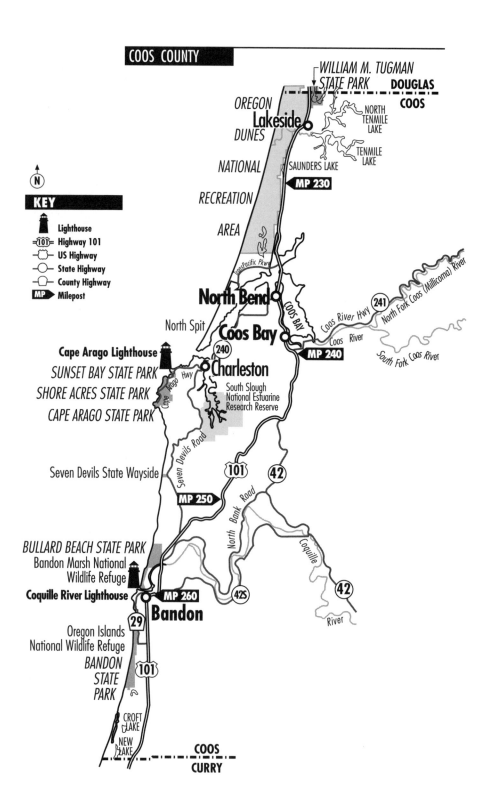

WILLIAM M. TUGMAN
STATE PARK

DOUGLAS

COOS

OREGON

Lakeside

DUNES

NORTH
TENMILE
LAKE

TENMILE
LAKE

NATIONAL

SAUNDERS LAKE

RECREATION

MP 230

AREA

N

KEY

Lighthouse

101 Highway 101

US Highway

State Highway

County Highway

MP Milepost

Trans-Pacific Pkwy

North Bend

Coos Bay

North Fork Coos (Millicoma) River

241

Coos River Hwy

North Spit

COOS BAY

240

Coos River

MP 240

South Fork Coos River

Cape Arago Lighthouse

SUNSET BAY STATE PARK

Charleston

SHORE ACRES STATE PARK

Cape Arago Hwy

South Slough
National Estuarine
Research Reserve

CAPE ARAGO STATE PARK

Seven Devils State Wayside

Seven Devils Road

101

42

MP 250

North Bank Road

Coquille

BULLARD BEACH STATE PARK

Bandon Marsh National
Wildlife Refuge

42

Coquille River Lighthouse

MP 260

42S

29

Bandon

River

Oregon Islands
National Wildlife Refuge

BANDON
STATE
PARK

101

CROFT
LAKE

NEW
LAKE

COOS

CURRY

The Coos County Coast

U.S. 101, Mile 220.6 to Mile 285.8

The territorial legislature took pieces of Jackson County and the short-lived Umpqua County to form Coos County on December 22, 1853. At that time, Coos County extended down the coast to include what is now known as Curry County. Umpqua County, established in 1851, disappeared in just over eleven years as the territorial legislature divided it among other counties.

Coos County residents number 61,400. Coquille is the county seat, and Coos Bay is the largest city. The side-by-side cities of Coos Bay and North Bend rank as the largest and fourth-largest cities on the Oregon coast, with a combined population of just over 25,000.

The county, named after the genial people of the Coos tribe who inhabited the shores of the large estuary that came to be known as Coos Bay, attracted early settlers, developers, and entrepreneurs with its vast and varied natural resources. Logging and lumber production topped the list of contributors to the local economy from early settlement until the end of the twentieth century. A large and diverse commercial-fishing industry has seen boom times and bust from the late nineteenth century to the present and uncertain future, but has always been a significant part of the county's economy. Agriculture, initially essential for providing food to local pioneers and homesteaders, grew to become an important segment of the economy with the export of produce, dairy products, and cranberries. Although the forest-products and commercial-fishing industries remain viable enterprises, mill closures and fleet reductions have diminished their contributions to the area's economy. As Coos County industry has declined in recent years, tourism has gained some economic stature, but is far less a factor here than it is on the north and central coast. Tourism may eventually gain the position it deserves, but for now the county's largest employer with the biggest payroll is government. City, county, state, and federal employees outnumber workers in every other sector of the economy.

For its 65.2-mile course through the county, U.S. Highway 101 lies inland of the coastline, separated from the beaches and rocky shores by dunes, forests, agricultural lands, municipalities, and residential areas, which may account for the number of travelers who pass through Coos County without ever seeing its main attractions. That's a shame, because many roads lead but a short distance from the highway and provide access to some of the best sightseeing and recreational opportunities the Oregon coast has to offer: sparkling lakes, the highest seaside dunes in the world, the biggest bay on the Oregon coast, America's first national estuarine research reserve, one of the finest stretches of state parks on the West Coast, broad ocean beaches, rugged rocky shores, miles of hiking and biking trails, freshwater and saltwater angling, and the best crabbing and clam digging in Oregon. Scenic waterfronts and boat basins at Coos Bay, Charleston, and Bandon delight artists, photographers, and sightseers. Two major coastal river systems, the Coos and Coquille, rise in the nearby Coast Range and form estuaries teeming with life. Coos County also might be considered the golf capital of the Oregon coast, with five distinctly different courses, including the coast's newest golf resort, Bandon Dunes. The county's coastal communities have a number of outstanding restaurants and a wide variety of lodging accommodations to fit every traveler's needs and budget. Campers may choose among county, state, and Forest Service campgrounds, as well as privately owned RV parks.

U.S. 101, mile 221.3
William M. Tugman State Park

This meticulously maintained park stretches east from Highway 101 to the southwest shore of Eel Lake. The campground features five yurts and 115 campsites with water and electric hookups, tables, and fire rings in a pine woods setting. Two campsites, one yurt, and one rest room with showers have wheelchair access. Other amenities include a hiker/biker camp, dump station, trash receptacles, firewood, and rest rooms with flush toilets.

The huge day-use area has wide-open grassy areas, tree-shaded picnic sites, a kitchen shelter, trash receptacles, and rest rooms with flush toilets and wheelchair access. There's a paved boat ramp and large parking area, a swimming beach, fishing dock with wheelchair access, and a hiking trail around the south end of the lake.

Information: (541) 888-4802 or (800) 551-6949. Reservations: (800) 452-5687.

Eel Lake

This large and lovely dune lake lies east of Highway 101, with access via Tugman State Park. Although it is part of the chain that includes Tenmile Lakes to the south, it's much deeper than those two bodies, with an average depth of 34 feet and maximum depth of 65 feet. The 355-acre lake consists of two arms of similar length and width, giving it the shape of a *U*. The west arm lies within Tugman State Park, and the east arm abuts the densely forested foothills of the Coast Range. Unlike nearby Tenmile Lakes, the wooded shoreline of Eel Lake is undeveloped.

Fishing is generally good to outstanding for native cutthroat and stocked rainbow trout, especially in the spring and summer. Largemouth bass, introduced some years ago, have flourished, with some fish growing to 5 pounds or more. There's also a good crappie population. Coho salmon and a few steelhead trout migrate through the lake in the fall, but the lake is closed to coho angling.

There's an excellent paved boat ramp and plenty of trailer parking at the Tugman Park day-use area, where there is also some bank access and a fishing dock with wheelchair access. Supplies, fuel, bait, tackle, licenses, and current fishing information are available in nearby Lakeside.

This small (population: 1,675) residential and resort community lies just east of the highway, at the west end of Tenmile and North Tenmile lakes. Visitors will find several campgrounds, RV parks, and motels here, as well as a supermarket, restaurants, cafés, tackle and hardware store, a fine county park on the northwest shore of Tenmile Lake, and three marinas offering launching facilities, moorage, and boat rentals.

U.S. 101, mile 221.5 to mile 222.8 Lakeside (zip code 97449)

This street exits east off the highway and leads about a mile to the Lakeside city center.

Follow North 8th Street 1.1 mile, turn east (left) on North Lake Avenue, drive 0.2 mile to 11th Street, turn south (right), and drive 0.1 mile to the park entrance. This beautiful and popular park has open grassy areas and picnic sites with tables and grills set among native trees and shrubs. The waters of Tenmile Lake lap at the southern end of the park, where there is a small sand

U.S. 101, mile 221.9 North 8th Street Tenmile Lakes County Park

Swimming area and boat docks at Tenmile Lakes County Park.

beach and swimming area, boat docks, a large fishing dock with wheelchair access, and a four-lane, paved boat ramp. Other amenities include a large parking lot, horseshoe pits, benches, fish-cleaning station, trash receptacles, drinking water, and rest rooms with flush toilets and wheelchair access. The channel connecting Tenmile and North Tenmile lakes is less than a quarter-mile from the boat ramp.

Lakeside Boat Ramp

Turn southeast off Highway 101, and drive 1.3 mile on North 8th Street to the junction of Hilltop Road, where there is a paved ramp on Tenmile Creek, which also provides quick access to lower Tenmile Lake. Park on 8th Street or in the small parking lot nearby.

It's easy to find the fishing dock at Tenmile Lakes County Park.

U.S. 101, mile 221.9 and mile 222.5
Tenmile Lakes

To reach the lakes, turn southeast off U.S. 101 onto North 8th Street (mile 221.9) or east on Airport Way (mile 222.5), and follow directions for Lakeside and Tenmile Lakes County Park. Two large dune lakes, Tenmile and North Tenmile, sprawl north, south, and east into the foothills of the Coast Range, with many arms, inlets, and coves inviting exploration.

The larger of the two, Tenmile Lake, has a surface area of 1,627 acres, an average depth of 10 feet, and maximum depth of 22 feet. North Tenmile Lake, at 1,098 acres, is only slightly deeper, at a 23-foot maximum depth and 11-foot average. A narrow channel joins the northwest end of Tenmile Lake with the southwest end of North Tenmile Lake. Most of the land bordering Tenmile Lakes is private forest, agricultural, and residential property, and some of it is heavily developed. Many houses and cabins dot the shores of both lakes. Nevertheless, with so many arms and fingers poking into the hills, numerous out-of-the-way coves, and 42 miles of shoreline—much of it undeveloped—boaters, anglers, wildlife watchers, and photographers seeking relative seclusion should have little trouble finding it.

Fishing for stocked rainbow trout ranges from fair to good, mainly in the spring, with some good-size holdover fish taken in the winter months. These shallow, weedy lakes are mainly known for superb angling for warmwater species: largemouth bass, bluegill, crappie, yellow perch, and brown bullhead. Largemouth are plentiful and some run to 8 pounds or more.

It's not uncommon for a skilled bass angler to catch and release twenty to thirty or more fish in a day. Bluegills are overpopulated, eager quarry, fun to catch, and good to eat. Crappie and perch are not quite so numerous, but there are plenty of them, and they are fine table fare. Likewise with the brown bullhead, which are good targets for night fishing.

A few hybrid bass, a sterile cross between striped and white bass, remain in the system, holdovers from an experimental stocking program in 1980s. These rod benders top 20 pounds and provide at least an occasional glimpse of the sensational kind of angling Tenmile Lakes could be providing, had the program not been torpedoed by a few opponents.

The lakes' brushy shoreline and numerous shallow marshes provide ideal habitat for resident mallards and wood ducks, which nest and rear young in the spring and summer. During fall and spring migrations, other waterfowl join their ranks. Great blue herons wade the shallows, feeding on abundant fish. Ospreys nest in shoreline trees, and teach their young to catch bluegills. Bald eagles use their shoreline perches for diving and dining mainly on coots and ducks.

Meadows and pastures at the upper ends of several arms of the lakes attract Roosevelt elk. Black-tailed deer browse along the shores and might show up in any small clearing. Families of river otters, sliding into and out of the water, roam secluded coves and pose for patient observers and photographers. Black bears, raccoons, possums, skunks, and muskrats are other common inhabitants of the area.

Tenmile Lakes are among the most popular in Oregon, providing a great variety of recreational opportunities to locals and visitors alike. They're a *must stop* for freshwater recreationists.

U.S. 101, mile 222
Eel Creek
Campground

On the west side of the highway, this Forest Service facility has 53 tent/RV sites with picnic tables and fire pits set amid native trees and shrubs. Other features include trailer turnarounds, drinking water, trash receptacles, rest rooms with flush toilets, and access to the Umpqua Dunes Trail. Information: (541) 271-3611.

U.S. 101, mile 222.3
Umpqua Dunes
Trailhead

A 1-mile interpretive loop trail takes hikers on an easy trek through a mixed forest of fir, spruce, and madrone trees to the active dunes. The beach route, marked with blue-banded posts, is a more ambitious, 5-mile round-trip hike that starts with one leg of the interpretive loop and ends at the beach after about 2 miles of hiking over sand dunes. If all you want to do is go to a beach, there are much easier ways. This tough hike, much of it over soft sand, is for hardy folks who want to enjoy and experience the dunes firsthand and up close. Carry water, and plan a round-trip of three to four hours.

U.S. 101, mile 222.5
Airport Way

This road exits east off the highway and leads to North 8th Street, the Lakeside city center, and Tenmile Lakes. For northbound travelers, this is the shortest route to Lakeside.

U.S. 101, mile 222.9
Tenmile Creek

This is the outlet stream for Tenmile Lakes, and an interesting creek to explore in a small boat or canoe, which can be launched at the Lakeside Boat Ramp (see page 238) or Spinreel Boat Ramp (see below). The creek is closed to steelhead angling from April through October, but open the rest of the year. The winter run usually begins around the end of November and peaks in December; the fish, on their way to the lakes and tributary creeks to spawn, don't linger long. During the summer, largemouth bass and bluegill move into the upper end of the creek from the lake, and angling for them can be good then.

U.S. 101, mile 223.9
Spinreel Campground and Boat Ramp

Turn west on Spinreel Road, travel 0.4 mile, and turn left at the park entrance. This U.S. Forest Service facility, situated on the edge of the dunes and along the south bank of Tenmile Creek is popular with anglers and ORV enthusiasts. The campground has 37 tent/RV sites with picnic tables and nearby drinking water in a wooded setting. Other features include a paved boat ramp on Tenmile Creek, an ATV loading ramp, sand access, trash receptacles, and rest rooms with flush toilets. An ATV rental facility is nearby, just across Wildwood Drive.

U.S. 101, mile 225.6
Clear Lake

On the west side of the highway is a small roadside parking area with room to park a couple of vehicles. The lake is just west of the highway, across the railroad tracks. It's unfortunate that there are bodies of water in Coos, Douglas, Lane, Linn, and Wasco counties all named Clear Lake. Don't confuse this little Clear Lake with the big Clear Lake on the east side of U.S. 101 at mile 218.1, just north of the Coos/Douglas County line; that one is closed to public access, and this one is open to the public. Although there is some bank access for angling alongside the railroad tracks, the lake is better fished from a small canoe or float tube. It's a favorite spot among local anglers for native cutthroat trout.

U.S. 101, mile 226.4 and mile 226.8
Senator Jack Ripper Saunders Lake County Park

Saunders Lake Road, a short loop west off U.S. 101, leads to a fine little county park with good shore access for angling on Saunders Lake and a gravel ramp for boaters. There are also picnic tables, trash receptacles, and vault toilets. This is a good spot for a picnic or a place to take the kids fishing.

One of many dune lakes in the area, Saunders is a 52-acre lake with an average depth of 11 feet and maximum depth of 35 feet. There are many home sites along the south shore and little public shoreline access, except for the county park at the southeast end of the lake. Those with boats, canoes, or float tubes have the best chance of angling success for cutthroat and rainbow trout, largemouth bass, and a good population of yellow perch.

Saunders Lake

This 5.8-mile loop road connects again with U.S. 101 just south of Haynes Inlet at mile 232.9. To reach Haynes Inlet attractions, use the south access.

U.S. 101, mile 229.4
North Bay Road, north junction
North Slough Road

Turn east on North Bay Drive; then take a left onto North Slough Road, 0.2 mile from U.S. 101. The road flanks the slough—just a small creek here—for several miles through some pretty farm and rural residential land. A short side trip can provide good photographic opportunities, especially when fields flood in the winter and attract migrating birds and waterfowl.

Roadside parking areas along the west side of the highway provide views of a large marsh, tidal channels, and the North Slough, which attract wading birds, shorebirds, and waterfowl all year, but in greatest numbers during spring and fall migrations. With bright white sand dunes as a backdrop, this is a good place to get photographs of the marsh and its inhabitants.

U.S. 101, mile 230.3 to mile 231.1
North Slough Salt Marsh

On the west side of the highway, a small parking area offers a sweeping view of the North Slough, Haynes Inlet, and Coos Bay. The gravelly area at water's edge, running parallel to Highway 101 from here to the Trans-Pacific Parkway, holds extensive colonies of soft-shell clams. Clam diggers should be careful to remain on the gravel beach, however, and avoid the adjacent soft mudflats that are as treacherous as quicksand.

U.S. 101, mile 232.2
Viewpoint

The causeway extending west across the bay is the beginning of a short highway that ends 5.4 miles from Highway 101. The newer section of the highway, beginning just over a mile west of Highway 101, was built in the late 1980s as an access route to potential industrial sites along the North Spit, few of which have materialized. The highway does a much better job of leading outdoors enthusiasts to a major bay-area playground that includes the southern boundary of the Oregon Dunes National Recreation Area, several campgrounds and day-use areas, Horsfall Beach, a BLM boat-launch facility, access to the North Spit, and more. (For details and attractions, see "Side Trip: Trans-Pacific Parkway and Oregon Dunes National Recreation Area" on page 266.)

U.S. 101, mile 232.6
Trans-Pacific Parkway

Oregon Dunes National Recreation Area

Turn west off Highway 101 on the Trans-Pacific Parkway to reach the southern-most access and gateway to Oregon's great sandbox and playground. (For details and attractions, see "Side Trip: Trans-Pacific Parkway and Oregon Dunes National Recreation Area" on page 266.)

Horsfall Beach

Turn west on the Trans-Pacific Parkway, and follow the signs for Horsfall Beach, which lies 4.4 miles west of Highway 101. (For details and attractions, see "Side Trip: Trans-Pacific Parkway and Oregon Dunes National Recreation Area" on page 266.)

North Spit

Exit west here to reach the North Spit of Coos Bay, via the shortest highway on the Oregon coast. (For details on recreational opportunities, see "Side Trip: Trans-Pacific Parkway and Oregon Dunes National Recreation Area" on page 266.)

North Spit Boat Launch

Turn west off Highway 101, and take the Trans-Pacific Parkway 4.1 miles to the launch site on the south side of the parkway. (For details, see "Side Trip: Trans-Pacific Parkway and Oregon Dunes National Recreation Area" on page 266.)

U.S. 101, mile 232.8
Haynes Inlet

This northeast arm of Coos Bay extends eastward for more than 3 miles and flanks the east side of Highway 101 for more than a half-mile. Low tide exposes extensive mudflats along the highway that are favorite foraging grounds for great blue herons and great egrets. Egrets often perch in the trees along the north side of the inlet, near the highway. Farther inland, the inlet offers additional birding, photography, and fishing opportunities. Haynes Inlet beneath the Highway 101 bridge is a favorite spot of local anglers for catching surfperch during the spring. Winter steelhead draw anglers to the inlet farther inland.

U.S. 101, mile 232.9
North Bay Road, south junction

Turn east off Highway 101 to reach points along Haynes Inlet for boating, fishing, birding, and photography. Several small roadside parking areas between mile 2 and mile 3 provide shoreline access. The road is only 5.8 miles long and reconnects with U.S. 101 at mile 229.4.

McCullough Wayside and Boat Ramp

Turn east off U.S. 101 onto North Bay Road. The small wayside and parking area with picnic table, paved ramp, and gravel approach are on the north side of the road, one mile from the highway.

U.S. 101, mile 233.2
East Bay Road

This winding road exits east off the highway at the north end of the McCullough Bridge over Coos Bay, extends 7.8 miles along the east shore of Coos Bay, and terminates at mile 3.8 on State Route 241, Coos River Highway. Along the way, it leads to the small rural communities of Glasgow and Cooston, as well as an

18-hole golf course. Several small roadside parking areas offer panoramic views of the bay, McCullough Bridge, tide flats, and marshes, with good opportunities for birding and photography.

To make a complete loop of the bay, follow East Bay Drive to State Route 241. Then turn right, cross the Chandler Bridge, and continue southwest on State Route 241 through the Eastside District of Coos Bay to U.S. 101 at mile 239.1. From there, drive north into Coos Bay or south to Bandon.

Kentuck Golf Course

Turn east off U.S. 101 at the north end of the McCullough Bridge, and follow East Bay Road for 3 miles to the course entrance. This 5,393-yard, 18-hole, par-70 course unfolds in a lush valley on the east shore of Coos Bay, at the head of Kentuck Inlet. Course features include a clubhouse, pro shop, putting green, pull-cart and electric-cart rental, club rental, and snack bar with beer and wine service. Pro shop: (541) 756-4464.

U.S. 101, mile 233.2
Conde B. McCullough Memorial Bridge

Also known as the Coos Bay Bridge and often locally referred to as the North Bend Bridge, this exquisite structure of steel and concrete was posthumously dedicated to its designer in 1947 and is certainly a fitting tribute to the genius of Conde B. McCullough. The 5,305-foot masterpiece was the largest of the five bridges completed in 1936 as part of the Oregon Coast Bridges Project that opened the entire length of the Coast Highway, from the Columbia River to the California border. Typical of the designs of Oregon's premier bridge builder, this graceful span has many eye-pleasing decorative features, including McCullough's signature entrance pylons, 13 rib-type deck arches, and sidewalks on both sides with decorative concrete railings. It's not only a delight to see and photograph, but also an excellent platform to see and photograph from. Park at either end of the bridge, and take cameras and binoculars for a half-mile hike to the center and highest point on the bridge

Conde B. McCullough Memorial Bridge over Coos Bay

for a magnificent view, east or west, of Coos Bay. This is also an interesting place to watch and photograph ship and barge traffic.

Coos Bay

MUST STOP

Seagoing vessels have been regularly crossing the Coos Bay bar since the middle of the nineteenth century, when Oregon's abundant natural resources began attracting people interested in developing them for West Coast and foreign markets. In those early days, though, the bar crossing was more like a finger crossing, for good luck, and an iffy proposition for anyone at the helm. Today's pleasure boaters, anglers, divers, charter operators, and commercial skippers, equipped with modern electronics, confidently point their prows at the broad, well-protected entrance, ease over toward the north jetty, and follow the 45-foot-deep channel into or out of the bay for what is now the safest bar crossing on the Oregon coast. All craft traversing the bar, from small open skiffs and cruisers to huge freighters and tankers, travel under the vigilant watch of Coast Guard personnel who occupy the nearby observation tower from dawn to dusk. When seas are rough, Coast Guard vessels patrol the entrance, ready to offer immediate assistance to anyone who needs it. The Coast Guard Air Station at North Bend also patrols the bay and Oregon's southern coastal waters with search-and-rescue helicopters.

The big, sprawling bay is a top spot for sightseeing, wildlife watching, and photography, with sloughs, inlets, flats, marshes, miles of shoreline, and great expanses of open water to observe or explore. Working waterfronts at North Bend, Coos Bay, Eastside, and Charleston are also great to see and record on film. From colorful sailboards, graceful sailboats, fishing vessels, tugs, barges, and cargo ships, to seabirds, shorebirds, wading birds, waterfowl, and marine mammals, there's always something to watch and photograph on this *must-stop* bay.

Coos Bay is a diverse area, offering a wide variety of crabbing, clam digging, and fishing opportunities. Angling regulations are complicated and subject to change. So it's essential to consult the *Oregon Sport Fishing Regulations* and to ask questions at bay area bait-and-tackle outlets about the latest openings and closures and seek recommendations on the best places, equipment, and techniques for success.

The bay provides protected waters and extensive tidal flats for the best crabbing and clam digging on the Oregon coast. Crabbers set their gear for Dungeness and red rock crabs anywhere from the railroad bridge at North Bend downbay to the Charleston area. Intertidal flats for digging and raking five species of bay clams extend from the South Slough all the way up the bay to Jordan Cove and the North Slough, in the vicinity

The big bay is the best place on the Oregon coast to watch tugs maneuver and dock ships.

of Highway 101. Crabbing is a year-round activity and can be outstanding any time of year, except when torrential rains send crabs scurrying for the salty sea. Normally, crabbing is best on Coos Bay from summer through fall. The best clam-digging tides run from March through September, with May and June the top months.

Fishing opportunities range from nearby offshore rocks and reefs, into the bay, all the way to downtown Coos Bay, and up the navigable stretches of the Coos River and its main forks. Lingcod, cabezon, greenling, and rockfish are the primary rock and reef species and are also taken in the lower bay. Several species of seaperch and surfperch reside in or visit the bay to feed and bear live young. Anglers also take sturgeon and striped bass in the bay and lower reaches of the river system.

Notwithstanding all the dire reports of depleted Pacific salmon stocks along the West Coast, Coos Bay has one of the few runs of fall chinook salmon listed as "healthy," as well as a fishable run of coho salmon. Both begin in late August, extending into September and beyond, with chinook fishing available throughout the Coos system, and fishing for fin-clipped coho allowed in Isthmus Slough. Anglers take a fair number of salmon within sight of downtown Coos Bay and Highway 101.

Another anadromous species that gets relatively little angling pressure here, as elsewhere on the Oregon coast, is the American shad. Big schools of these scrappy and willing gamefish enter the Coos system each spring to spawn in the upper reaches of the rivers. The best angling for them is in May and June in the tidewater sections of the north and south forks of the Coos River.

Striped bass rarely spawn successfully in the Coos system, and the Oregon Department of Fish and Wildlife no longer stocks the bay area with these great gamefish. So, while striper numbers are dwindling, many, if not most, of the fish are big, some reaching 50 pounds or more. Depending on the season, anglers take stripers from the surf along the beaches north and south of the Coos Bay jetties, in the main body of the bay, and up into the north and south forks of the Coos River. The mainstem of the South Fork Coos River and the Millicoma River are closed to striper fishing from April through June.

The biggest denizens of the Coos depths are sturgeon. Both green and white sturgeon use the Coos system, but the larger white is more plentiful. Anglers take them with big baits and heavy tackle from the bay and deep holes in the lower reaches of the rivers. In recent years, a popular and relatively successful winter sturgeon fishery has developed along the edge of the channel, just upbay from the McCullough Bridge. Only sturgeon from 42 to 60 inches in length may be kept, with a limit of one per day and ten per year.

U.S. 101, mile 233.8 to mile 236.5 North Bend (zip code 97459)

As the lower Coos River broadens into the east arm of Coos Bay, it swings north, then bends west and southwest to form the west arm of the bay, and flows on to its inevitable meeting with the Pacific. At the north end of the peninsula formed by the arching bend of the bay, timber tycoon and shipbuilder Asa Meade Simpson built his first sawmill on Coos Bay in 1857. He built a shipyard in 1858, and in the years following developed a waterfront community, known as Old Town, that included a wharf, company offices, company store, workers' quarters, and a school. In 1899, Louis Jerome Simpson, Asa's son, came to the bay area to oversee his father's business operations. With an eye toward creating a great new city on the deep-water port to rival San Francisco, he borrowed $25,000 in 1902 to buy a platted but undeveloped town site called Yarrow. He replatted the site and filed incorporation papers. In December of 1903, the new city of North Bend was established.

Today, North Bend extends south from the McCullough Bridge for 2.7 miles along Highway 101 and spreads westward to encompass the northern tip of the peninsula. It shares its southern and western boundaries with the city of Coos Bay. Within the North Bend city limits are the largest airport, the largest covered shopping mall, and the first casino on the Oregon coast. Its main street is Sherman Avenue, which is also southbound Highway 101, along which are a number of antique and secondhand stores.

The visitor center, which is on the west side of the highway, with parking around back and nearby rest rooms, is the place to stop for a copy of an excellent map of Coos County and the bay area, as well as information and literature about local attractions. The center is open Monday through Friday, from 8:00 a.m. to 5:00 p.m.; Saturday, from 10:00 a.m. to 5:00 p.m.; and Sunday, from 10:00 a.m. to 4:00 p.m. Hours may vary in winter. Information: (541) 756-4613.

U.S. 101, mile 234.5
North Bend Visitor Center

On the west side of the highway, outside the visitor center, this cyclists' rest stop provides picnic tables, drinking water, and bike racks. Adjacent Simpson Park has rest rooms with flush toilets and other amenities.

Timm Slater Rest Area

On the west side of the highway, just behind the visitor center, is a small museum worth a stop to learn about bay area history from a large collection of old photographs and exhibits of Indian and pioneer artifacts, a logging exhibit, homesteaders' tools, and more. An old logging locomotive and tender stand next to the museum. Operating hours are Tuesday through Saturday, 10:00 a.m. to 4:00 p.m.; in summer, the museum is also open Sunday from noon to 4:00 p.m. Information: (541) 756-6320.

Coos County Historical Society Museum

On the west side of the highway, behind the visitor center, is a fine little city park with grand old trees, a grassy lawn, and beautiful rhododendron and azalea bushes. The park offers visitors a convenient spot for a leisurely picnic or quick rest stop. It has picnic tables, grills, a kitchen shelter, playground, trash receptacles, drinking water, and rest rooms with flush toilets and wheelchair access. Hiking and biking trails are nearby.

Simpson Park

Turn east on California and drive two blocks from southbound Highway 101 or one block from the northbound highway to the bay's edge, where there are a paved boat ramp, dock, ample parking area, and chemical toilet. This is the only launch site on the North Bend waterfront. From here it's a short run upbay to Isthmus Slough and the Coos Bay waterfront or downbay to the McCullough Bridge and beyond.

U.S. 101, mile 235
California Boat Ramp

Virginia Avenue is the main east-west route through North Bend, leading to a major shopping mall, supermarkets, the airport, restaurants, and lodging. This is also the beginning of State Route 240, the Cape Arago Highway, signposted for the Charleston harbor and beaches, which leads to various *must-stop* attractions on the cape. Those heading for Charleston, the South Slough, and the state parks on Cape Arago (pronounced *air*-uh-go) should turn west on Virginia Avenue, and drive 0.8 mile to Broadway Avenue. After turning south (left) onto Broadway, ease

U.S. 101, mile 235.1
Virginia Avenue (State Route 240)

The North Bend and Coos Bay waterfronts merge on the upper bay.

into the right lane, which veers right and joins Newmark Avenue 1 mile later. Continue on Newmark Avenue, past the community college, past the Harless Y intersection and traffic light, and to the flashing light at the intersection of Newmark and Empire Boulevard, which is 3.6 miles from U.S. 101. Turn left to reach Charleston and area attractions. (For details and attractions, see "Side Trip: State Route 240, Cape Arago Highway" on page 270.)

Bureau of Land Management

To reach the BLM District Office, turn west on Virginia Avenue, and after passing through the Broadway Avenue intersection, ease into the right lane, follow the signs for the airport, and bear right on Maple Street, 0.9 mile from Highway 101. After 0.3 mile, bear left on Maple Leaf, which becomes Colorado Avenue, continue for another 0.3 mile, turn right on Airport Lane, and drive 0.3 mile to the BLM District Office on the left side of the street. This is the place to go for information, literature, and maps pertaining to lands and trails managed and maintained by BLM, including the Loon Lake Recreation Area, east of Reedsport, and the New River Area of Critical Environmental Concern, south of Bandon. The office is open Monday through Friday from 7:45 a.m. to 4:30 p.m. Information: (541) 756-0100.

U.S. 101, mile 236.2
Newmark Street

Turn west off the highway for the most direct route to Empire Lakes, Empire Boulevard, and the Cape Arago Highway (State Route 240), which leads to Charleston, the state parks, and the

South Slough National Estuarine Research Reserve. At mile 1.8, Hull Street, and 2.2, Ackerman Street are entrances to Middle and Lower Empire Lakes. At mile 2.8, turn left at the flashing light onto Empire Boulevard to reach Charleston and the parks. (For details and attractions, see "Side Trip: State Route 240, Cape Arago Highway" on page 270.)

A settlement that sprouted in 1854 on the shores of upper Coos Bay near the mouth of Wapello Slough, now known as Isthmus Slough, was named Marshfield, after a city by the same name in Massachusetts. It just as well could have been a descriptive name, as the buildings, boardwalks, and docks that eventually spread along the bay shore were erected on filled marshlands. Early Marshfield languished until the growth of lumber and

**U.S. 101,
mile 236.5 to
mile 240
Coos Bay**
(zip code 97420)

The Coos Bay working waterfront lies next to Highway 101.

shipbuilding industries there in the late 1860s. After that, logging, coal mining, and shipbuilding became the driving forces of Marshfield's economy. In 1944, the people of Marshfield voted to change the name of their city to Coos Bay.

From their earliest days, North Bend and Coos Bay grew and prospered as working waterfront communities, and to a great extent they remain so today. North Bend and Coos Bay waterfronts meld along the west shore of the upper bay, where bay waters lap at the edge of Highway 101. In downtown Coos Bay, the southbound highway is Broadway, and the northbound highway is Bayshore Drive. Together, they constitute the main north-south thoroughfare through the city center. Numbered streets run parallel to Highway 101 and in ascending order from east to west, with 1st Street nearest the bay. Named avenues run perpendicular to Highway 101, and from Anderson Avenue south are in alphabetical order: Bennet, Curtis, Donnelly, Elrod, Furgeson, and so on.

Even though Coos Bay is coastal Oregon's largest city, it's still a small town by most standards. It's easy to negotiate and has plenty of free parking on Highway 101 and adjacent streets, as well as in nearby public parking lots, with RV parking at the visitor center parking lot and along northbound Highway 101. Travelers can park anywhere within a couple of blocks of the visitor center and be within easy walking distance of the working waterfront, city docks, boardwalk, hiking/biking path, Coos Bay Mall, art museum, restaurants, theaters, and antique shops.

U.S. 101, mile 237.5
Marshfield Sun Printing Museum

This unique museum in a historic building stands on the east side of northbound Highway 101, Bayshore Drive, with entrance facing Front Street. Northbound travelers can park along Bayshore Drive or nearby side streets. Southbound travelers can turn east on Alder Avenue (mile 237.7) or Market Street (mile 237.8), drive one block to Bayshore Drive, and turn left to reach the museum. There are no traffic lights at these intersections, so if traffic is heavy, Anderson Avenue (mile 238) might be the best choice for reaching Bayshore Drive. This interesting and unusual little museum was once a job-printing shop and home of the *Marshfield Sun* newspaper, published here between 1891 and 1944. The museum's main exhibit is the newspaper office and printing shop preserved in its original condition on the first floor. On the second floor are displays covering the history of printing, newspapers, and the community of Marshfield. Summer hours are Tuesday through Saturday, 1:00 p.m. to 4:00 p.m. The rest of the year, check with the Bay Area Chamber of Commerce Visitor Center for scheduled open-house hours and guided tours. Information: (541) 269-0215.

Signs here direct travelers to Charleston and Sunset Bay. This is the Coos Bay route, one of three in the bay area, to the Cape Arago Highway, Charleston, the South Slough National Estuarine Research Reserve, and the state parks. After turning west on Commercial Avenue, drive six blocks, bear left, go one block, and turn right onto Central Avenue. Continue for seven blocks up the hill, and turn right at the flashing light onto Ocean Boulevard, State Route 243. Stay on Ocean Boulevard for 3.5 miles to what's known as the Harless Y. Bear left at the traffic light onto Newmark Avenue, State Route 240, and ease into the left lane. Continue eight blocks to the flashing light at Newmark and Empire Boulevard, turn left, and continue on to Charleston and the parks beyond. (For details and attractions, see "Side Trip: State Route 240, Cape Arago Highway" on page 270.)

U.S. 101, mile 237.8
Commercial Avenue (State Route 243)

Turn west on Commercial Avenue to reach a small parking lot at the southeast corner of Commercial Avenue and 4th Street. Parking is also available on both sides of Commercial.

Public parking

Turn west on Commercial Avenue, stay in the right lane, and bear right six blocks later to stay on Commercial. Turn right at 10th Street, then right into the lower parking lot. To reach the upper parking lot, pool, and arboretum, continue north on 10th Street for 0.3 mile, and turn left into parking lot.

Mingus Park and Choshi Gardens

Mingus Park—named after John Mingus, one of Coos Bay's founding fathers—is one of the prettiest and most diverse city parks on the Oregon coast. Both conifer and deciduous trees and shrubs dot the grassy landscape surrounding a delightful pond decorated with fountains and a tiny island. A paved path with wheelchair access skirts the pond and leads to other paved paths, a Japanese-style footbridge over the creek at the upper end of the pond, and Japanese gardens, named after Coos Bay's sister city—Choshi, Japan.

From the upper parking lot, visitors can stroll through an arboretum and rhododendron garden, connect with other paved paths and hiking trails, or try the heated, outdoor public swimming pool. From either parking lot, it's a short walk to the pond where people feed the dozens of resident mallards, gulls, and domestic geese. Each fall, flocks of migrating waterfowl that know a good thing when they see it join the permanent population and stay till spring. The park also has benches and picnic tables around the pond, a playground, drinking water, trash receptacles, and rest rooms with flush toilets and wheelchair access.

**U.S. 101,
mile 237.9**
Bay Area Chamber of
Commerce Visitor
Center

The visitor center, located between southbound (Broadway) and north bound (Bayshore Drive) Highway 101, has an adjacent parking lot with limited RV parking and rest rooms with flush toilets and wheelchair access. The center is open Monday through Friday, from 9:00 a.m. to 5:00 p.m., and Saturday, from 10:00 a.m. to 4:00 p.m.

U.S. 101, mile 238
Coos Art Museum

One block west of southbound Highway 101, on the south side of Anderson Avenue, is the only art museum on the Oregon coast, housed in the old Coos Bay Post Office, built in 1934. Anderson is one way, west to east, so visitors should park on or near Broadway and walk, or turn west on Commercial Avenue or Curtis Avenue, then take 4th Street south or north, respectively, to Anderson. Large display galleries feature a permanent collection and changing exhibits of sculptures, paintings, and photographs. Also on the premises are a gift shop, sales gallery, and rest rooms with flush toilets. The museum is open from Tuesday through Friday, 11:00 a.m. to 5:00 p.m., and weekends, noon to 4:00 p.m. Information: (541) 267-3901.

Coos Bay Boardwalk
and Bike Path

East of Highway 101, on the waterfront, is a boardwalk lined with the flags of various nations, which features interpretive displays, including a tugboat that once plied the waters of Coos Bay and a 400-gallon saltwater aquarium containing fish and invertebrates found in the bay. There are benches along the boardwalk and an adjacent paved hiking/biking path that extends for about 0.75 mile along the bay's edge. The boardwalk and path are good places for watching and photographing the waterfront and vessel traffic.

City Docks

Fishing boats, sailboats, and yachts are moored at the docks along the Coos Bay waterfront, near the boardwalk, and are good subjects for photography. Those who bring boats to the bay area may be interested to learn that transient moorage is also available here. Instead of slips, these city-owned docks provide 624 feet of moorage space over 20 feet of water at low tide. Space is available, with 30-amp power hookups, on a first-come, first-served basis. Boaters can pay the modest moorage fees at the Finance Department in the City Building at 500 Central Avenue. Information: (541) 269-1181.

Tour Boat
Rendezvous

A modern, fully equipped, 61-foot tour boat that can accommodate up to 49 passengers operates from the Coos Bay waterfront, offering harbor and river tours for groups of twelve or more and dinner cruises for groups and individuals. Harbor tours, lasting about one and a half hours, take in upper Isthmus Slough to the bridge, cruise the Coos Bay and North Bend

A foggy morning at the Coos Bay City Docks.

waterfront, pass beneath the McCullough Bridge, come about past the railroad bridge, and return to the City Docks. River cruises up the Millicoma to Allegheny or up the South Fork Coos to Dellwood take about three hours. Dinner cruises, offered on weekends all year, take about two hours. The vessel has comfortable indoor and outdoor seating and a bar serving beer, wine, and non-alcoholic beverages. Information: (541) 267-5661.

Turn west on Curtis Avenue to reach a large public parking lot on the north side of Curtis, between 3rd and 4th Streets.

U.S. 101, mile 238.1
Public parking

Watch for signs for Allegheny and Coos River junction, and exit east off southbound Highway 101 at the traffic light. Northbound travelers should turn right one block before the traffic light on Edwards Street, go one block, and turn right again. This is the route to take to reach the Eastside boat ramp on Isthmus Slough, the Millicoma Marsh Trail, and the Coos River system, including the South Fork Coos River, North Fork or

U.S. 101, mile 239.1
State Route 241
(Coos River Route)

Millicoma River, and West Fork Millicoma River. (Use the Oregon's Bay Area and Coos County Map.)

Millicoma Marsh Trail

Turn east off Highway 101 at the traffic light onto State Route 241, Coos River Route, and drive 1.1 mile over the Isthmus Slough Bridge and to the D Street intersection in the Eastside District. Turn left on D Street, drive 0.1 mile to 4th Avenue, turn right, and continue less than 300 feet to a gravel road on the right that descends to a small parking lot behind Millicoma Middle School, adjacent to the athletic field. The parking lot is too small for travel trailers or motorhomes.

There's an orientation map and interpretive sign at the trailhead. The trail is about a half-mile long and runs between a wet meadow and freshwater marsh and pond to a tidal salt marsh and observation deck, with interpretive signs and shelters along the way. It's an easy hike that's wheelchair accessible.

Eastside Boat Ramp

Turn east off Highway 101 onto State Route 241, Coos River Route, and follow this road 1.1 mile to the D Street intersection in the Eastside District. Turn left on D Street, and continue 0.5 mile to the large, paved parking lot and two-lane, paved boat ramp with center dock. This is the best launch for access to lower Isthmus Slough and upper Coos Bay, including the Coos Bay and North Bend waterfronts. There are also a trash receptacle and rest rooms with flush toilets.

U.S. 101, mile 242
Isthmus Slough Boat Ramp

On the west side of Highway 101 and south end of the Shinglehouse Slough Bridge are a paved parking area, paved boat ramp, and dock with a wheelchair ramp on Shinglehouse Slough, providing access to Isthmus Slough. Boaters northbound on Highway 101 should exercise extreme caution when turning into the parking area. The center turn lane is short and ends abruptly at a guard rail. Although the ramp is mainly for fishing access to Isthmus Slough, boaters, canoeists, kayakers, wildlife watchers, and photographers will like it, too, for exploring both Isthmus and Shinglehouse sloughs.

**U.S. 101,
mile 243.5**
Coos Country Club

Turn east off Highway 101 on Coos City-Sumner Road, bear right 0.5 mile from the highway, and turn right after another 0.5 mile. A favorite among local golfers, this 6,032-yard, 18-hole, par-70, semi-private course in the rolling, forested hills is open to the public. Amenities include a putting green, chipping area, driving range, clubhouse, men's and women's locker rooms, pro shop with resident pro, pull-cart and electric-cart rental, club rental, restaurant, and lounge. Pro shop: (541) 267-7257. Clubhouse: (541) 267-6313.

This highway exits east off Highway 101 and leads to the upper end of Isthmus Slough, the cities of Coquille and Myrtle Point, and over the Coast Range to I-5 near Roseburg.

Turn east on State Route 42, proceed 3.2 miles, turn north (left) on Green Acres Road, and continue 0.2 mile to the paved ramp, dock, and picnic table on the west (left) side of the road.

Green Acres Boat Ramp

Drive 10.8 miles east on State Route 42 to the State Route 42S junction, turn west (right), proceed 0.1 mile, and turn north (right) at the park entrance. This large and locally popular city park has an open camping area that accommodates 20 or more recreational vehicles and tents. The park has a playground, softball diamond, soccer field, picnic areas with tables and grills, a picnic shelter, huge charcoal grill appropriate for group barbecues, drinking water, trash receptacles, chemical toilets, and rest rooms with flush toilets and wheelchair access. A two-lane paved boat ramp with a dock provides access to the Coquille River. There's also bank access for fishing and, near the rest rooms, is a fish-cleaning station.

Sturdivant Park

Turn west here, and drive northwest 8 miles to reach the South Slough National Estuarine Research Reserve, 13 miles to Charleston, or 16 miles to the beautiful state parks strung along Cape Arago. (For details and attractions, see "Side Trip: State Route 240, Cape Arago Highway" on page 270.)

Turn west off Highway 101, and proceed northwest on Seven Devils Road 1.7 miles to East Humphreys Road. Turn west, drive 2.4 miles to the intersection of East Humphreys and Randolph roads, and continue straight onto Whiskey Run Road for 1.4 miles to the beach access. A small parking area is near a county beach access for street-legal vehicles.

Whiskey Run Beach

At the intersections of East Humphreys and Randolph roads, turn north (right) on Randolph Road, and continue 1.6 miles to the park entrance on the west side of the road. The park has easy access to miles of broad sand beach stretching in both directions, popular with beachcombers and agate hunters. This secluded little park has picnic tables right next to the beach and rest rooms with flush toilets and wheelchair access.

Seven Devils State Wayside

Turn west off the highway on West Fahy Road, and enjoy the 2.8-mile drive through coastal forest, scrub, meadows, and marsh to the lodge, resort, cottages, nature trails, and two golf courses ranked among the nation's best by *Golfweek* and *Golf Magazine*. Plans for the 2,000-acre oceanfront property call for several more courses, including another 18-hole layout in the dunes and shore pines. First to open, in May of 1999, was Bandon Dunes, a Scottish links-style, 6,732-yard, 18-hole, par-72 course, ranked third (behind Pebble Beach and Pinehurst Number 2) by *Golf Magazine*'s "Top 100." The 6,557, 18-hole, par-71 Pacific Dunes course, rambling among the forested hills and grassy dunes is considered by many to be even more beautiful and challenging than the original course. Other amenities include a 32-acre practice area that includes a driving range and a full acre of putting greens, golf school, pro shop, resident pro, rental clubs, two bars, restaurant, and lodge. Overnight accommodations include lodge rooms, deluxe suites, and cottages. Tee times, reservations, and information: (541) 347-4380 or (888) 345-6008.

U.S. 101, mile 259.2
Bullards Beach State Park

MUST STOP

On the west side of the highway is the entrance to a showcase park that has it all: a paved boat ramp, sheltered campground, beautiful picnic areas, the Coquille River Estuary, a nearby wildlife refuge, historic lighthouse, more than 4 miles of ocean beach, fishing, crabbing, and miles of hiking, biking, and horseback-riding trails. The park road skirts the north bank of the lower Coquille River, leads to picnic areas and beach-access point, and ends 2.8 miles from Highway101 at the Coquille River Lighthouse. It's a *must stop* for all travelers.

The campground, set in a shore-pine forest, features 90 full-hookup sites, 95 sites with water and electricity, and 13 yurts, all with paved parking, picnic tables, and fire rings. Two campsites and three yurts have wheelchair access. The campground also has trash receptacles, recycle bins, a dump station, drinking water, hot showers, and rest rooms with flush toilets, one of which has wheelchair access.

The park also has a hiker/biker camp and a horse camp near the beach with eight primitive campsites with tables and fire rings, four double corrals, four single corrals, a day-use area with tie stalls, drinking water, and access to three equestrian trails and the ocean beach.

The boat launch, picnic areas, and beach access have large parking areas and rest rooms with flush toilets and wheelchair access. A paved path leads just over a mile from the campground, through forest and meadows, over low dunes, and to the beach. There's good bank access along the lower Coquille River for angling, kite flying, wildlife watching, and photography. Boaters, canoeists, and kayakers can launch their craft at the park and explore the estuary and the wildlife refuge directly across the river from the park. Fishing for a variety of species, crabbing, and clam digging are all popular activities on the estuary.

Information: (541) 347-2209 or (800) 551-6949. Reservations: (800) 452-5687.

Coquille River Lighthouse

Turn west off the highway at the Bullards Beach State Park entrance and drive 0.5 mile to the ramp and parking area on the south side of the road. An excellent, two-lane, paved ramp provides access to the lower Coquille River, estuary, and Bandon Marsh National Wildlife Refuge. Also on the premises are drinking water, a fish-cleaning station, and rest rooms with flush toilets and wheelchair access.

Bullards Boat Ramp

Turn west at the entrance to Bullards Beach State park, and drive 2.8 miles to the lighthouse parking lot. This interesting and attractive little lighthouse, at the base of the north jetty, near the mouth of the river, has captured the attention of more artists and photographers than any other lighthouse along the Oregon coast. Completed in 1896, it was the last lighthouse built on the Oregon coast. With a base about 15 feet above the water and a tower standing 47 feet above the base, its light was visible 12 miles out. In 1939, the Coast Guard installed an automated beacon on the south jetty and closed the lighthouse. In the ensuing years, weather, neglect, and vandalism took their toll on the picturesque little lighthouse. The creation of Bullards Beach State Park eventually led to a restoration project that was completed in 1979.

Coquille River Lighthouse

The lighthouse is open daily, except when closed by severe weather or extreme tides. During summer months, volunteers are on hand to offer tours of the tower.

U.S. 101, mile 259.3
North Bank Road

Turn east off the highway, and follow this road along the Coquille River and up the Coquille Valley about 17.5 miles to its junction with State Route 42, a few miles north of Coquille.

Rocky Point County Park and Boat Ramp

Head east on North Bank Road for 2 miles to reach this small park with a paved ramp and dock on the Coquille River, large parking lot, bank access, picnic tables, trash receptacle, and vault toilets with wheelchair access.

U.S. 101, mile 259.5
Coquille River and Estuary

South, Middle, East, and North forks of the Coquille River conjoin in the woolly wolds of southwestern Coos County. The river becomes the sum of its far-flung parts in the approximate vicinity of Myrtle Point, then meanders northwesterly past the city of Coquille and through a verdant valley of the same name. It's a navigable river from here to the sea, gaining volume and strength from the many creeks and sloughs that drain the adjacent farms and forests. As it broadens into a teeming estuary, it flows past the piers of the Highway 101 bridge, sweeps past the seaside town of Bandon, and churns into the Pacific Ocean.

Following early settlement of the Coquille Valley in the 1850s, the Coquille River became the transportation corridor for products and people in what was largely a roadless tract for much of the last half of the nineteenth century. People and cargo traveled between Bandon and other West Coast ports by sailing ships and coastal steamers. Between Bandon and upriver settlements, goods and passengers moved by riverboat. During the twentieth century, railroads and highways assumed the major portion of transportation chores, with people depending less and less on the river for travel and commerce. Eventually, bridges connected all the highways that the coastal rivers fragmented, eliminating the last form of essential river travel, the ferries.

Today, travel on the Coquille River and estuary is mainly recreational, for such purposes as fishing, crabbing, boating, sailing, kayaking, sightseeing, wildlife watching, and photography. Although the river is no longer the life blood of Coquille Valley commerce and transportation, it's certainly an important part of the lifestyle of the thousands who enjoy and value its recreational treasures.

The estuary and lower Coquille River to the confluence of the South Fork are open all year to angling for chinook salmon and steelhead trout. Anglers take a few chinook in the lower reaches during the summer months, but angling for fall chinook gets serious in September. Steelhead move into the system in November and December with the earliest catches made in the tidewater section. Later in the season, the various forks of the Coquille are among the most popular steelhead waters along the south coast. From mid-August to mid-October, the estuary and lower river to river mile 8.5 are open for fin-clipped coho, some of which are caught within sight of Old Town Bandon.

Other species also attract anglers to the estuary and river. In summer months, people crowd onto the pier and docks at the Bandon waterfront to jig for smelt. Anglers also take surfperch, rockfish, and several other marine species in the estuary and from the jetties. Upstream, in the vicinity of Coquille, locals make good catches of brown bullheads. Although the striped bass fishing has declined in recent years in the Coquille system, as elsewhere in Oregon, savvy striper anglers still make good catches in the tidewater section of the river.

The estuary is a favorite crabbing spot and can be outstanding when conditions are right. The best crabbing is from summer through mid-autumn, or until the first heavy rains of the season. Crabbers with boats set their gear along the channel from the lighthouse upstream to the Highway 101 bridge. Those without boats have good luck dropping their baited crab rings and pots from the public pier and docks at the Bandon waterfront.

Clam digging here is for soft-shell clams. The beds lie mainly along the southeast shore of the estuary, north of Bandon, and along the edge of the Bandon Marsh, across the river from Bullards Beach State Park.

Although wildlife watchers and photographers will find plenty of opportunities to catch glimpses of wading birds, shorebirds, seabirds, and waterfowl on the estuary, one of the best birding areas on the West Coast is the Coquille Valley from early fall through mid-spring, once the rich agricultural lands adjacent to the river begin to flood in response to the fall rains. Teal and snipe begin arriving in September to join resident mallards, wood ducks, and Canada geese. The first storms of autumn blow in northern birds and waterfowl, and by December the flooded fields are alive with thousands of puddle ducks, diving ducks, coots, grebes, geese, and even the occasional swan. Herons wade the shallows, and great flocks of shorebirds forage along the edges of the flooded fields. Some of the migrants move through the area, staying a few days or weeks to feed and rest. Many remain for the winter.

A good way to view and photograph this spectacle is to drive along the state and county roads traversing the Coquille Valley. One of the best routes is North Bank Road, which follows the river and passes through the valley for about 17.5 miles from

U.S. 101, mile 259.3 to State Route 42, just north of Coquille. Another choice is State Route 42S, which exits U.S. 101 at mile 261.6 and heads east to Coquille along the south bank of the river.

**U.S. 101,
mile 259.7**
Bandon Marsh
National Wildlife
Refuge

Southbound travelers on Highway 101 get their first glimpse of this 303-acre refuge as they cross the bridge over the Coquille River. The refuge spreads from the southwest end of the bridge and along the gradual southwest bend of the river, encompassing the largest remaining salt marsh on the Coquille River Estuary. The marsh is a popular area for watching and photographing shorebirds, wading birds, waterfowl, and birds of prey. At any tide of 0.5 feet or lower, the exposed mudflats are good places to dig a limit of soft-shell clams.

Access to the refuge is by boat or by way of Riverside Drive (U.S. 101, mile 260.2). The refuge is open to the public from sunrise to sunset. Shoreline Education for Awareness (SEA), Inc.— a Bandon-based environmental-education group—provides interpretive services to people visiting the marsh. SEA will schedule docent-guided tours for groups as small as a family, for which there is no charge. Information: (541) 347-3683.

**U.S. 101,
mile 260.2**
Riverside Drive

This short loop is a back road to Bandon that exits west off U.S. 101 and rejoins the highway near Old Town Bandon, 1.7 miles beyond. Along the way, it reaches the Bandon city limits at mile 0.6, Bandon Marsh National Wildlife Refuge access at mile 0.7, and the intersection of 1st Street Southwest and Fillmore Street Southeast at mile 1.6. Continue straight on Fillmore to connect with Highway 101, or turn west (right) on 1st Street to reach Old Town and the waterfront.

**U.S. 101,
mile 261 to
mile 275**
Milepost discrepancy

Travelers who pay attention only to the roadside milepost signs at mile 261 and mile 275 will get the idea that the little seaside town of Bandon is more than 13 miles long and will wonder why they were able to travel the distance so quickly. The actual measured distance between these mileposts is 2.2 miles, not 14, for a major mileage discrepancy of 11.8 miles, caused by highway construction, which realigned U.S. 101 for a more direct coastal route. The old highway swung inland, through Coquille, then back to the coast, over what are now State Routes 42 and 42S.

**U.S. 101, mile
260.6 to 262.9
Bandon**
(zip code 97411)

This friendly hamlet (population: 2,820) at the end of the Coquille River is the south coast's premier getaway destination. Bandon-by-the-Sea, as locals like to call this delightful oceanside community, is perfect for a weekend escape, but has enough natural and cultural attractions to crowd a weeklong vacation.

Bandon's compact Old Town is ideal for walking, with plenty of free parking available. Browsers and shoppers will find an interesting variety of specialty shops, boutiques, and galleries. In between are several locally favorite restaurants and lounges. More shops and restaurants, as well as the Bandon Historical Society Museum and Bandon Cheese are situated along Highway 101, near Old Town. One of the prettiest little harbors on the coast flanks the north end of Old Town. It's a shaped-up and tidy waterfront that's a pleasure to stroll and is a photographer's delight. When the tide's right, it's also a good spot for crabbing, with rental rings and bait readily available.

A broad expanse of sandy beach extends south for several miles from the south jetty. This is a great beach for hiking and exploring rocky intertidal areas. The numerous nearshore rocks, islets, and sea stacks enhance sunsets and increase the drama of winter storms. The beach is easily accessible via Jetty Road and from Beach Loop Road, which forms Bandon's western edge and leads to several scenic overlooks. Trails and stairways to the beach are well marked. In addition to hiking, beachcombing, and surf fishing, kite flying is a popular pastime here. *Kitelines* magazine, in fact, ranked Bandon among the top ten flying spots in the world.

When they were passing out good eateries and watering holes, Bandon stood in line twice and got more than its fair share. Some even come with dazzling views. The same is true of the overnight accommodations, ranging from motels and bed-and-breakfast inns with terrific river and ocean views to beachfront resorts only a few steps from the tumbling surf.

This stretch of the old Coast Highway leads east off Highway 101 and eventually connects with State Route 42 near Coquille.

U.S. 101, mile 261.6
State Route 42S junction

Bandon Fish Hatchery

Turn east at the traffic light onto State Route 42S, proceed 0.7 mile, turn south (right), and continue 0.3 mile to road's end at the hatchery. The small parking lot is not suitable for travel trailers or large motorhomes. This busy hatchery produces about 70,000 steelhead yearlings for release into the South Fork Coquille River, another 45,000 for the north and east forks, and 525,000 presmolt fall chinook salmon for release into Coos Bay sloughs. The hatchery also incubates more than three million eggs for other hatcheries and the Salmon Trout Enhancement Project (STEP) program. One of the main attractions at the Bandon Hatchery is the trophy rainbow trout program, in which more than two thousand trout grow to about 9 inches at Butte Falls Hatchery before being transferred to the Bandon facility.

Here, they're held for another year and then released in the spring at Bradley Lake, Empire Lakes, and Powers Pond. At time of release they weigh about 5 pounds each.

Also on the premises are a picnic table, trash receptacle, and pit toilets with wheelchair access. The hatchery is open every day, all year, with someone on duty at all times. Fish-feeding times are 7:30 a.m. and 4:15 p.m., but food pellets are always available for visitors to feed the voracious critters. Information: (541) 347-4278.

Riverton County Boat Ramp

Turn east at the traffic light, proceed 10.8 miles to the county park on the north side of the road, where there are a paved ramp on the Coquille River, courtesy dock, and pit toilets.

U.S. 101, mile 262
Bandon Cheese Inc.

On the east side of the highway is one of Bandon's major attractions, where visitors can stop to sample more than a dozen varieties of cheddar and jack cheeses. Hours are 9:00 a.m. to 6:00 p.m. daily. Information: (541) 347-2456 or (800) 548-8961.

U.S. 101, mile 262.1
Coquille River Museum

On the east side of Highway 101 at Fillmore Street, one block south of Bandon Cheese, is a fine little museum that features a large collection of historic photographs depicting life on the Coquille River and in the Bandon area. Exhibits include a collection of Indian artifacts, the natural history of the region, Coast Guard operations, and the great fire that destroyed much of Bandon in 1936. During the summer, the museum is open Monday through Saturday, from 10:00 a.m. to 4:00 p.m., and Sunday, from noon to 3:00 p.m. Winter hours may vary. Information: (541) 347-2164.

Old Town Bandon

✔ MUST STOP

Where Highway 101 curves gently toward the south, southbound travelers should continue straight onto 2nd Street to reach Old Town Bandon; northbound travelers can turn at the visitor center on Chicago Avenue. The compact Old Town lies along 1st and 2nd streets and extends for three blocks to include Chicago, Baltimore, and Alabama avenues. This is a good place to park, walk, and take in all the shops, boutiques, galleries, and restaurants. Free on-street parking is available on all the streets and avenues. There's a public parking lot with RV spaces available at the west end of Old Town and additional parking at the waterfront on 1st Street.

Old Town Bandon lies just across 1st Street from the Port of Bandon waterfront and Coquille River Estuary. It's within easy walking distance of the Bandon Visitor Center, the Coquille River Museum, Bandon Cheese, and a variety of shops along nearby Highway 101, making it a *must stop* for all travelers.

The visitor center, which is located on the west side of the highway, at the edge of Old Town Bandon, is open every day during the summer, from 10:00 a.m. to 5:00 p.m.; daily hours the rest of the year are 10:00 a.m. to 4:00 p.m.

Bandon Visitor Center

Port facilities lie along 1st Street, one block from the visitor center and include a boardwalk overlooking the estuary, public fishing and crabbing pier, public parking lot, trash receptacles, and rest rooms with flush toilets and wheelchair access. Boaters will find

Port of Bandon

Port of Bandon boat basin.

a fine two-lane paved launch ramp and trailer parking lot. Transient moorage is available. The tidy, picturesque waterfront is a great spot to stroll, take in all the boating activity, and watch for harbor seals and seabirds. Photo opportunities abound. Information: (541) 347-3206.

Visitors can reach the south jetty and beach from any of the avenues running between 1st and 2nd streets in Old Town Bandon. From the visitor center, drive north one block to 1st Street, and turn west (left). Follow 1st Street 0.4 mile along the Coquille River Estuary and around the curve to the south. Turn west (right) on Jetty Road, and continue 0.6 mile to the large gravel parking area with easy jetty and beach access, adjacent picnic tables, trash receptacles, and rest rooms with flush toilets and wheelchair access. The jetty is a favorite spot for fishing

South Jetty and beach

South jetty and beach, west of Old Town Bandon. In the background are Bullards Beach and distant Cape Arago.

and an excellent vantage point for wildlife watchers and photographers. The beach is popular for surf fishing, kite flying, hiking, and most other beach activities.

U.S. 101, mile 262.5
Beach Loop Road, north junction

Turn west at the traffic light on 11th Street Southwest, and drive 0.8 mile to Beach Loop Road. Mileposts run from south to north on Beach Loop Road, beginning at the south junction, U.S. 101, mile 277.6. (For details and attractions, see "Side Trip: County Road 29 (Beach Loop Road)" on page 282.)

Bandon City Park

Turn west at the traffic light onto 11th Street Southwest, and drive 0.6 mile to the parking lot of a large city park with much to offer, including a playground, baseball diamond, basketball court, soccer field, benches, and a paved hiking/biking path. Other amenities include tree-shaded picnic areas with tables, a picnic shelter, trash receptacles, drinking water, and rest rooms with flush toilets and wheelchair access. The beach is only an easy 0.3-mile hike away.

Bandon State Natural Area

Turn south on Beach Loop Road 0.8 mile west of U.S. 101, via 11th Street Southwest, to reach several state-park facilities with beach access, picnic areas, and great views. (For details and attractions, see "Side Trip: County Road 29, Beach Loop Road" on page 282.)

U.S. 101, mile 275.6
Beach Loop Road, middle access

Turn west, and proceed 0.8 mile on Seabird Drive to Beach Loop Road for access to various sightseeing and recreation sites. (For details and attractions, see "Side Trip: County Road 29 (Beach Loop Road)" on page 282.)

U.S. 101, mile 277.6
Beach Loop Road, south junction

Turn west onto County Road 29 (Beach Loop Road) to reach various parks, beach accesses, and viewpoints along this scenic route. (For details and attractions, see "Side Trip: County Road 29 (Beach Loop Road)" on page 282.)

Turn west off the highway, follow the gravel road 0.3 mile to the fork, bear left, and continue 0.1 mile to a paved boat ramp, gravel parking area, trash receptacle, and pit toilets.

U.S. 101, mile 278
Bradley Lake Boat Ramp

Private property nearly surrounds this small lake of about 30 acres, so a boat, canoe, or float tube is essential for access. The lake harbors a population of native cutthroat and gets stocked with rainbow trout each year, including trophy trout of about 5 pounds reared at the Bandon Hatchery.

Bradley Lake

Turn west off the highway on Croft Lake Lane. Where the road forks, 1.5 miles beyond, bear right, and continue for 0.4 mile to the parking area and greeting center of this facility, managed by the Bureau of Land Management. Here, visitors will find a lovely picnic area with tables, an information kiosk, trash receptacles, drinking water, and vault toilets with wheelchair access. There's also access to nearly 4 miles of hiking, biking, and horse trails through shore-pine forests, meadows, and sand dunes with views of the Coast Range, New River, and ocean, making this a *must stop* for hikers, bikers, wildlife watchers, and photographers. The road leading from the parking area to a boat ramp, parking lot, and rest rooms on the east bank of New River is closed to motorized vehicles from April through mid-September to protect nesting western snowy plovers, but remains open to hikers, bikers, and equestrians.

U.S. 101, mile 283.1
New River Area of Critical Environmental Concern (ACEC)

✔
MUST STOP

New River was formed during the great flood of 1890 as a new channel of Floras Creek. The area is rich in wildlife, including shorebirds, wading birds, bald eagles, peregrine falcons, black-tailed deer, and a variety of smaller mammals. Pick up a copy of the "New River Trail Guide" at the Coos Bay District Office of the Bureau of Land Management in North Bend. Information: (541) 756-0100.

U.S. 101, mile 285.8
Coos County/Curry County Line

Side Trip: Trans-Pacific Parkway and Oregon Dunes National Recreation Area

MUST STOP

A causeway extending west off Highway 101 at mile 232.6 separates the North Slough from the rest of Coos Bay and is the beginning of a short parkway leading to the Oregon Dunes National Recreation Area, Horsfall Beach, and various attractions along the North Spit. This entire area lying between the highway and the ocean is a *must stop* for anglers, crabbers, clam diggers, boaters, sailboarders, campers, hikers, bikers, equestrians, ORV enthusiasts, wildlife watchers, photographers, and sightseers. It's a grat place for beach coming, kite flying, enjoying a picnic, and watching all bay activities.

Trans-Pacific Parkway, mile 0 to mile 0.7
Causeway

The wide gravel berm on both sides of the causeway provides ample parking for the length of the causeway and access to Coos Bay and the North Slough for birding, photography, fishing, and clam digging. The slough attracts good numbers of great blue herons and great egrets all year, especially when minus tides expose great expanses of tidal flats. Huge colonies of soft-shell clams reside in the gravel along the northeast end of the causeway and east end of North Slough, right next to Highway 101. Diggers can harvest easy limits on any low tide, but should stay on the gravel beach and avoid the adjacent soft mud, which is the consistency of quicksand.

The south side of the causeway offers angler access and superb views of the McCullough Bridge. Fishing is seasonally good for several species of surfperch, sole, flounder, and the occasional steelhead or striped bass.

From fall through early spring, waterfowl pour into the bay, some to rest and feed before continuing their migration, others to remain throughout the winter. Most numerous are mallards, pintails, widgeon, lesser scaup, buffleheads, and ring-necked

The Oregon Dunes National Recreation area is popular with ATV enthusiasts.

ducks. Others that show up throughout the season include green-winged teal, Barrow's goldeneye, common goldeneye, ruddy ducks, shovelers, canvasbacks, and redheads. Both resident and migrant Canada geese also use the area.

At the west end of the causeway, a bridge crosses the narrow channel of north slough. There are parking areas on both sides of the causeway at the east end of the bridge and on the south side at the west end of the bridge. Fishing is good at times, especially during spring and early summer for perch. The bridge itself is popular with crabbers, but heavy traffic, including big trucks, poses potential danger. This is no place for small children or pets.

Trans-Pacific Parkway, mile 0.7
North Slough Bridge

Just past the railroad crossing, the parkway bears right, crosses another set of tracks, then curves to the left. Horsfall Beach Road exits right and leads into the Oregon Dunes NRA. The road ends 2.3 miles beyond at the Horsfall Beach Campground and Day-Use Area.

Trans-Pacific Parkway, mile 1.1
Horsfall Beach Road

This facility, not to be confused with the Horsfall Beach Campground and Day-Use Area, lies east of the road, 0.5 mile from the parkway, and is popular with ORV enthusiasts. The campground has 70 campsites, two ATV loading ramps, drinking water, hot showers, and rest rooms with flush toilets. The day-use area has a parking lot, ATV loading ramp, and pit toilets. Both the campground and day-use area have access to the nearby sand dunes.

Horsfall Campground and Day-Use Area

Left off Horsfall Beach Road 0.9 mile from the parkway is a small picnic area in the scrub pines, adjacent to a large sand dune.

Sandtrack Picnic Area

A surprise to some visitors, but a common occurrence in the Oregon Dunes National Recreation Area, is seeing a dune musher running a team of Siberian huskies along a foredune trail.

Amenities include dune access, picnic tables, grills, and trash receptacles.

Bluebill Lake Trailhead

On the south (left) side of Horsfall Beach Road, 1.5 miles from the parkway, is a parking area adjacent to the trailhead. The trail is an easy, one-mile loop around the lake.

Bluebill Campground

Turn west (left) off Horsfall Beach Road, 1.7 miles from the parkway. This small but lovely campground has 19 protected tent/RV sites with tables and fire pits set among the shore pines and shrubs. There are trash receptacles, drinking water, rest rooms with flush toilets, and access to Bluebill Lake Trail.

Wild Mare Horse Camp

South off Horsfall Beach Road, 1.8 miles from the parkway, is an equestrian campground that features 12 primitive campsites with tables, fire pits, nearby drinking water, trash receptacles, pit toilets, and access to the dunes and beach. Each site has a single or double corral. Reservations: (800) 283-2267.

Horsfall Beach Campground and Day-Use Area

At road's end, 2.3 miles from the parkway, is a large paved parking area and campground, with access to sand dunes and miles of broad sand beach. The campground has 34 primitive RV sites with camping on the pavement. Amenities include an ATV loading ramp, trash receptacles, drinking water, and rest rooms with flush toilets. Horsfall Beach stretches for miles in both directions and is popular for all beach activities. It's also a good spot for surf fishing, mainly for redtail surfperch.

Trans-Pacific Parkway, mile 1.5
Jordan Cove Road

Turn south to reach privately owned land along Jordan Cove and Coos Bay where the Weyerhaeuser Company and Roseburg Forest Products permit public day use to well-behaved people. Large gravel parking areas east of the road and railroad tracks, starting 0.3 mile from the parkway, provide access to several trails leading to Jordan Cove and sweeping views of Coos Bay. Turn south (left) 0.6 mile from the parkway, and cross the railroad tracks for access to the shore of Coos Bay and the Roseburg Forest Products Dock, or go straight to reach the office, where you can get a free permit for fishing and crabbing from the dock.

Anglers fish here in the spring for surfperch and the rest of the year for rockfish, greenling, and other marine species. Crabbing from the dock for Dungeness and red rock crabs is good from summer and into autumn, before the rainy season begins, and improves during winter dry spells.

Wildlife watchers are sure to see great blue herons, great egrets, belted kingfishers, and harbor seals any time of year. Brown pelicans, osprey, and pigeon guillemots are summer visitors. A lucky few might catch a glimpse of a pod of harbor porpoises. This is also a good place for watching and photographing boat and ship traffic on the bay, as well as Coast Guard helicopter exercises at and near the North Bend Air Station, across the bay. Ships inbound for the Roseburg Dock are also fun to watch and photograph, as the tugs turn and maneuver them.

Turn northwest off the parkway to reach this delightful area developed by the Weyerhaeuser Company as part of a mitigation project and opened in the spring of 2001. Drive up the paved road to a small parking lot with spaces for handicapped and RV/bus parking on a hill overlooking the deflation plain, ocean, 24-acre freshwater mitigation pond, and adjacent forest. Enjoy observing nearby wildlife and the commanding view south to Cape Arago. Just south of the overlook road is the entrance to another parking lot, a picnic area with tables set at pond's edge, paved paths, and a chemical toilet—all with wheelchair access. From here, hikers, kite-fliers, wildlife watchers, and other outdoor enthusiasts can reach hiking trails and old, abandoned roads.

Trans-Pacific Parkway, mile 3
North Spit Overlook Viewpoint and Dune Trailhead

Left immediately off the parkway, this excellent BLM facility provides access to lower Coos Bay for boating, fishing, and clam digging. Boaters will find a paved ramp, dock, and large paved parking lot. It's the only boat ramp on the North Spit and is also a good place to park and watch or photograph wildlife or boat and ship traffic. There are interpretive signs, a trash receptacle, drinking water, and rest rooms with flush toilets and wheelchair access.

Trans-Pacific Parkway, mile 4.1
North Spit Boat Launch

On the west (right) side of the road, a four-wheel-drive sand road leads 2.1 miles to the site of the wreck of the M/V *New Carissa*, a 594-foot freighter that ran aground near Horsfall Beach on February 4, 1999, and later broke up in the surf. The road ends at the north jetty, 5.7 miles from the parkway. Nesting sites of the western snowy plover have been fenced off here, and the beach is closed to motorized vehicles from April through mid-September as a further attempt to protect the birds.

Trans-Pacific Parkway, mile 4.4
Coos Bay Shore Lands

The parkway ends at a small turnaround and parking area, beyond which the road is suitable only for four-wheel-drive and off-road vehicles. Those so equipped can reach some of the best clam-digging flats on the bay, where good populations of gaper and other bay clams flourish.

Trans-Pacific Parkway, mile 5.4
End of pavement

Side Trip: State Route 240, Cape Arago Highway

MUST STOP

Although the Highway 101 signs at Virginia Avenue in North Bend, mile 235.1, offer no indication other than to direct travelers west to "Charleston Harbor and Beaches," this is the start of State Route 240, the Cape Arago Highway. This route carries travelers along the bay to Charleston, the South Slough Reserve, Bastendorf Beach, Lighthouse Beach, the stunning parks of Cape Arago, and several points of interest in between. This is the quintessential scenic side trip on Oregon's south coast, and a *must stop* for all travelers.

State Route 240, mile 0.4
Pony Creek

This creek drains an inland freshwater marsh and empties into Pony Slough, an arm of Coos Bay.

State Route 240, mile 0.4 to 0.6
Pony Slough

After the Federal Aviation Administration forced the City of North Bend to close the road that runs between the airport and Pony Slough in 1999, this open, grassy area north of Virginia Avenue became the only vantage point for watching and photographing the abundant birdlife on the slough. For parking and access, turn north at Marion Avenue, mile 0.6.

State Route 240, mile 0.8
Broadway Avenue

Turn south (left) at the traffic light to continue on Route 240, and ease into the right lane within the next mile.

State Route 240, mile 1.7
Newmark Avenue junction

Stay in the right lane as it bears right off Broadway Avenue and merges with Newmark Avenue. Ease into the left lane as traffic permits, because the right lane ends in less than a mile.

State Route 240, mile 2.7
John Topits Park/ Empire Lakes, east entrance

Turn north (right) on Hull Street, 0.4 mile past the traffic light at the entrance to Southwestern Oregon Community College. The parking lot and lakes are 0.3 mile from Newmark Avenue. Although some maps show an upper, middle, and lower lake, the upper lake is actually the upper end of Middle Empire Lake. A fine little city park lies along the southwest shore of the middle lake, where there's good bank access for angling. Other park features include a playground, picnic tables, drinking water, and rest rooms with flush toilets. There's a gravel boat ramp, but motorized watercraft are prohibited. About 4 miles of paved, gravel, and dirt hiking and biking trails wind through the area, along the west shore of the middle lake and around the lower lake.

Both lakes offer good fishing for trout and warmwater species. The Oregon Department of Fish and Wildlife stocks the lakes with rainbow trout, including 5-pound trophy trout reared at the Bandon Hatchery. Each year, the agency also plants big steelhead brood stock, so there's always a chance of hooking a lunker. Both lakes also harbor sustaining populations of largemouth bass, bluegills, and yellow perch.

Turn north (right) on Ackerman Street, 0.4 mile west of the east park entrance, and continue 0.4 mile to the parking area on the west shore of Lower Empire Lake. The gently sloping shoreline near the parking area is suitable for launching trailerboats and other watercraft. Nearby are a small swimming beach and pit toilets. A paved hiking/biking trail encircles the lake and joins other paved, gravel, and dirt trails that traverse the wooded hills around the lakes.

Angling, here, is for the same species found in Middle Empire Lake. On both lakes, small cartop boats, canoes, and float tubes

State Route 240, mile 3.1
John Topits Park/ Empire Lakes, west entrance

An angler tries his luck in the flooded timber of Lower Empire Lake.

are popular craft for angling and exploring. A few wild mallards and a flock of domestic geese are year-round residents, mainly on the middle lake. During the fall and winter, migrating waterfowl join their ranks and offer good opportunities for photography.

State Route 240, mile 3.2
State Route 243 junction

State Route 243, which originates on Commercial Avenue at Highway 101 in Coos Bay, links with Ocean Boulevard and joins State Route 240 from the left here, at what is known locally as the Harless Y. Continue on past the traffic light on Newmark Avenue, but ease into the left lane, as the right lane exits right about 0.2 mile beyond the Harless Y traffic light.

State Route 240, mile 3.7
Empire Boulevard/ Cape Arago Highway

Turn left at the flashing light. From here, it's a 4.7-mile straight shot to Charleston, with the South Slough Reserve, Bastendorf Beach, Cape Arago, and other area attractions lying just a short distance beyond.

Empire Boat Ramp and Pier

Instead of turning left and heading toward Charleston, continue straight on Newmark Avenue, past the flashing light at the Empire Boulevard intersection. At the bottom of the hill, turn left on Mill Street, drive 0.1 mile to Michigan Avenue, and turn right to reach the parking area and two-lane, paved boat ramp with docks. During the winter storm season, the city removes the docks to prevent wave damage. A small public pier adjacent to the parking lot is popular with anglers and crabbers, and there's easy beach access nearby. This is a good spot for watching and photographing boat and ship traffic. Also on the premises are a fish-cleaning station, trash receptacles, and rest rooms with flush toilets.

State Route 240, mile 3.8
Michigan Avenue access

Turn west here to reach the boat ramp parking lot, fishing and crabbing pier, and access to the east shore of Coos Bay.

State Route 240, mile 8.1
Libby Lane

Turn east off Cape Arago Highway, drive 0.4 mile, and turn south on Crown Point Road to cross the bridge over Joe Ney Slough. Park at the south end of the bridge, and walk out onto the bridge for good views of Joe Ney Slough and the private oyster beds there. Continue 2.3 miles to the end of the road, where there are two steep trails to the shore of South Slough and popular clam-digging and cockle-raking flats.

State Route 240, mile 8.3 Charleston
(zip code 97420)

Although the claim Charles Haskell filed on land at the mouth of South Slough dates back to 1853, Charleston didn't flourish until commercial fishing put the little town on the map in the 1920s and '30s. Fishing eventually became one of the bay area's major industries, second only to timber.

Charlie Town, as some of the locals call it, is a compact waterfront village (population: 700) that's now within the Coos Bay city limits. It's situated on both shores of the lower South Slough, with most facilities on the west side. Commercial and sport fishing and seafood processing and sales are Charleston's main economic activities. The downtown area consists of a few shops and stores clustered along Cape Arago Highway at Boat Basin Drive. The village is also the site of a large Coast Guard station, Oregon Department of Fish and Wildlife office, and Oregon Institute of Marine Biology.

MUST STOP

The bay area's charter fleet is berthed at the Charleston Boat Basin, only minutes from the Pacific Ocean.

Situated as it is at the mouth of the South Slough, near the entrance to Coos Bay, across the bay from the North Spit, Charleston lies in a pleasantly photogenic setting. Add to the location its charter-boat, commercial-craft, and large commercial-fishing fleets, and you have the makings for a *must stop*, brimming with sightseeing and photographic opportunities. Seafood fans will certainly want to check out the seafood shops and restaurants, specializing in fresh, local fish and shellfish.

State Route 240, mile 8.5
Boat Basin Drive

Turn north just past the west end of the South Slough Bridge to reach the Charleston Pier, boat basin, RV parks, boat ramp, marina, charter services, and other attractions.

Charleston Public Pier

Turn north on Boat Basin Drive, then immediately east (right), alongside the west approach to the bridge. This popular fishing and crabbing pier stands parallel to and immediately north of the bridge, with access at the northwest end of the bridge.

Charleston Information Center	Turn north on Boat Basin Drive, then immediately east (right), alongside the west approach to the bridge. The center shares a parking area with the public pier and is open from May 1 through September 30. Hours are 10:00 a.m. to 5:00 p.m., Monday through Saturday, and 1:00 p.m. to 5:00 p.m. on Sunday.
Charleston Boat Basin	Turn north on Boat Basin Drive, and go 0.2 mile to Kingfisher Drive or 0.4 mile to Guano Rock Avenue. Turn east on either to reach the boat basin, where visitors can watch the working port, commercial boats, yachts, sport boats, and charter craft. Photographers will find unlimited waterfront photo possibilities.
Charleston Marina RV Park	Turn north on Boat Basin Drive, proceed 0.2 mile to Kingfisher Drive, turn east (right), and continue about 0.1 mile to the RV park entrance on the left side of the street. The park has 110 full-hookup sites with cable TV. Other features include tent sites, a play area, crab-cooking facility, Laundromat, trash receptacles, dump station, drinking water, showers, and rest rooms with flush toilets. Information: (541) 888-9512.
Charleston Boat Ramp	Turn north on Boat Basin Drive, go 0.4 mile to Guano Rock Avenue, and turn right. Then proceed 0.2 mile to Eel Avenue, turn left, and drive 0.1 mile to the launch area. This excellent, six-lane, paved ramp with docks is usable on any tide and is the only minutes from the Coos Bay bar and ocean. The facility includes a large parking area, fish-cleaning station, picnic tables, and rest rooms with flush toilets and wheelchair access. Bait, tackle, ice, dry ice, fuel, and supplies are available nearby.
Charleston Marina Complex	Follow the directions for the boat ramp to reach the marina office. The marina has 560 slips with water and electricity hookups to accommodate vessels up to 120 feet. Transient moorage is available with daily, weekly, and monthly rates. The complex has a pump-out station, Laundromat, showers, and rest rooms with flush toilets. Fish-cleaning facilities are located throughout the marina. Information: (541) 888-2548.
U..S. Coast Guard Lookout Tower	Take Boat Basin Drive north off Cape Arago Highway 0.5 mile to an unnamed road on the left, just past Guano Rock Avenue. Follow the gravel road up the hill 0.4 mile, and bear right at the fork. Continue 0.3 mile to road's end and a small parking area atop Coos Head, not suitable for trailers or large motorhomes. This semisecret but spectacular coign of vantage offers the grandest panoramic views on lower Coos Bay. Watch and photograph ship, barge, and boat traffic passing between the Coos Bay jetties, or pan binoculars seaward for miles, searching for whales, seabirds, fishing boats, and freighters. Turn your gaze northeast to take in the North Spit, North Beach, and lower Coos Bay all the way to North Bend.

Turn south off Cape Arago Highway here to reach the South Slough National Estuarine Research Reserve and Highway 101 12.7 miles south of Coos Bay and 7.9 miles north of Bandon. The road extends 12.2 miles from Charleston to U.S. 101, mile 252.7.

State Route 240, mile 8.7
Seven Devils Road

To get to this *must stop* for hikers, canoeists, and nature lovers, turn south off Cape Arago Highway onto Seven Devils Road. Proceed 4.1 miles to the main entrance, and turn east (left) to reach the interpretive center and nearby trails. To reach the south entrance to the reserve, more trails, and a canoe launching area, continue another 0.9 mile on Seven Devils Road, and turn east (left) at the sign.

South Slough National Estuarine Research Reserve

MUST STOP

The South Slough National Estuarine Research Reserve, established in 1974, was the nation's first in a system that now includes more than twenty reserves located throughout the nation. Although research and education are the main purposes of these reserves, outdoor recreation is a bonus benefit anyone can enjoy. Before launching a canoe or taking to any of the several hiking trails within the reserve, visitors should stop at the interpretive center to learn about the estuary, its surroundings, and its many inhabitants and to pick up trail guides and other helpful literature. Entertaining and educational slide and film presentations are scheduled daily in the auditorium and are free. The reserve also offers guided nature walks along the system's trails, canoe trips, slide lectures, and a variety of educational and recreational programs throughout the year.

Trails of the South Slough are open during daylight hours. From June through August, the interpretive center is open daily from 8:30 a.m. to 4:30 p.m. From September through May, it's open the same hours, Monday through Friday. Information: (541) 888-5558.

Turn west off Cape Arago Highway to reach the U.S. Coast Guard lookout tower at Coos Head, Bastendorf Beach, and the south jetty.

State Route 240, mile 9.4
Coos Head Road

To get to the Coast Guard lookout, stay on Coos Head Road for 0.2 mile; then turn north (right) onto the gravel road. Bear left at the fork 0.4 mile beyond, and continue 0.3 mile to the small parking area at Coos Head.

To reach the north end of Bastendorf Beach and the south jetty, after turning off Cape Arago Highway, stay on Coos Head Road for 0.9 mile. A large parking area beneath Coos Head provides beach and jetty access and has adjacent pit toilets.

State Route 240, mile 10.3
Bastendorf Beach Road

Cape Arago Highway runs roughly east to west here. Turn north off the highway to reach Bastendorf Beach County Park, Bastendorf Beach, and the south jetty.

Bastendorf Beach County Park

Turn north off Cape Arago Highway, and drive 0.2 mile to the park entrance on the east side of the road. This is one of the finest county parks on the coast and one that will rival most state parks for amenities and location. Situated in coastal forest on a high bluff overlooking the ocean, the campground has 56 protected RV sites with water and electricity and 25 tent sites, all with tables and fireplaces. It also has hiking trails, horseshoe pits, tank dump, trash receptacles, firewood, showers, and rest rooms with flush toilets and wheelchair access. There's a super playground and an adjacent picnic area with a spectacular view of Bastendorf Beach, the ocean, and jetties. Information: (541) 888-5353.

Viewpoint

Turn north off Cape Arago Highway, and drive 0.2 mile to a small parking area on the west side of the road, opposite the entrance to Bastendorf Beach County Park. The view takes in the southwest end of Bastendorf Beach and Yoakum Point.

Bastendorf Beach and South Jetty

Turn north off Cape Arago Highway, and drive 0.5 mile to parking areas and access to the beach. The road continues on to join Coos Head Road 0.4 mile beyond. Turn left at the stop sign, and drive 0.2 mile to the south jetty and parking area, or turn right and follow Coos Head Road 0.7 mile back to Cape Arago Highway.

Bastendorf Beach is popular for hiking, kite flying, and other traditional beach activities. It's also a good spot for winter surf fishing for striped bass. The adjacent south jetty is a favorite among anglers who take a variety of marine species from the rocks, including lingcod, cabezon, greenling, and several species of rockfish. The boulders making up the jetty are difficult to negotiate and are often slippery. Also, when the surf is up, huge waves break across the jetty, making it a dangerous place. Sneaker waves can wash over the jetty anytime, so keep a constant watch. This is not a place to take small children.

State Route 240, mile 10.6
Yoakum Point and Lighthouse Beach

Small parking areas flank both sides of the highway, and a trail leads north through the woods to a small but steep bluff overlooking the beach and rocky intertidal area near Yoakum Point. Hike the beach to the south end for close-up views of the Cape Arago Lighthouse. Check tide tables to avoid getting stranded at high tide.

Cape Arago Lighthouse

The beach and picnic-area parking lot are at mile 11.5 and the campground entrance is at mile 11.7. While the summer sun warms the shallow waters, rugged sandstone cliffs protect Sunset Bay, taming the surf and currents and making this a popular beach for wading and playing in the water. Sea kayakers also like the bay for its calm waters and easy ocean access. There's an adjacent picnic area with tables, a picnic shelter, trash receptacles, and rest rooms with flush toilets.

The campground has 29 full-hookup campsites, 36 sites with water and electricity, 66 primitive tent/RV sites, and eight yurts, all with tables and fire rings. Three campsites have wheelchair access. Other amenities include two group tent camps, a hiker/biker camp, firewood, trash receptacles, drinking water, showers, and rest rooms with flush toilets, two of which have wheelchair access.

The scenery at this *must-stop* state park is unsurpassed. Hiking trails lead through the park and along the ocean cliffs, and connect with other parks on the cape. Along the way, hikers can look for a variety of seabirds and marine mammals. Photographers can enjoy unlimited opportunities for framing

State Route 240, mile 11.2
Sunset Bay State Park

MUST STOP

dramatic waterscapes and wave action. Information: (541) 888-4902 or (800) 551-6949. Reservations: (800) 452-5687.

State Route 240, mile 11.5
Sunset Bay Boat Ramp

Turn west off the highway at the beach parking lot; then drive to the north end of the lot. The small paved ramp—suitable for small seaworthy skiffs—is unusable on minus and some low tides. Anglers use this ramp in calm weather to reach the nearshore waters just outside the bay. Even in the calmest weather, it's important to remember that this is the ocean and it can turn nasty anytime. Also, fog can move in quickly and disorient boaters without radar. So use common sense and caution when fishing or boating out of Sunset Bay.

State Route 240, mile 11.7
Sunset Bay Golf Course

Turn east off Cape Arago Highway at the golf-course sign next to the Sunset Bay Campground. This 3,020-yard, 9-hole, par-36 course is laid out in the wooded hills above Sunset Bay, offering golfers a pleasant setting in the fresh salt air. Course amenities include a pro shop, pull-cart and gas-cart rental, club rental, and snacks and non-alcoholic beverages. Pro shop: (541) 888-9301.

State Route 240, mile 12.2
Cape Arago Lighthouse Viewpoint

✔

MUST STOP

Standing just offshore, on a rugged islet near Gregory Point, is a handsome structure with an octagonal tower 44 feet tall, in operation since 1934, and the third lighthouse to occupy this site. The first, a skeletal iron structure, began operating in 1866 and was Oregon's second oldest coastal sentinel. That light was replaced in 1908 with a lighthouse constructed mainly of wood that eventually succumbed to the elements.

The islet where the lighthouse stands is connected to the mainland by a footbridge that is no longer used, now that the light has been automated. The lighthouse is visible from several points along Cape Arago, including the trails of Sunset Bay State Park. The gravel parking area here, on the west side of the highway, is a *must stop* that offers one of the most scenic views and a good photo opportunity for moderate telephoto and zoom lenses.

State Route 240, mile 12.3
Loop Trail

A small gravel parking area on the west side of the highway provides access to two trails that lead to Shore Acres State Park and form a loop of about 2 miles. The westernmost trail carries hikers along ocean cliffs overlooking the rugged, rocky shoreline. The other trail is a straight and level route through the woods. From the cliff trail, hikers can enjoy and photograph some of the most spectacular scenery on the West Coast. This is also an excellent vantage point for whale watching. In the spring, look for the many seabirds that nest along the cliffs.

When the surf's up, there's no more spectacular place to be on the Oregon coast than on the cliff trail between Sunset Beach and Shore Acres State Parks.

Turn west into the entrance of what was once the estate of Louis Simpson, timber tycoon and founder of North Bend. Although the Simpson mansion is long gone, the formal gardens and caretaker's house remain and are kept in perfect order by park staff. The botanical gardens display both exotic and domestic plants and flowers with something in bloom all year. There are two rose gardens, and a lovely pond full of lilies, surrounded by lush foliage and blooming plants. In November and December, the gardens blossom electrically with thousands of lights and artistic holiday displays. This is definitely a *must stop* location at any time of year.

At the south end of the gardens a trail winds down to a perfect pocket beach framed by sandstone cliffs sculpted by winds and waves. The surf shoves its way onto the sand, and when the water ebbs on the tide it leaves pools behind to explore. A trail leads south through the forest, up to the cliffs, and on toward the overlook above Shell Island and Simpson Reef.

State Route 240, mile 12.6
Shore Acres State Park

MUST STOP

The only remaining building of the Simpson estate at Shore Acres is the former caretaker's house in the botanical garden.

Where the Simpson mansion once stood a rock coping remains as a reminder of the bygone days and an indicator of what was doubtless the most spectacular home site on the Oregon coast. In place of the mansion, a fully enclosed observation building displays an interpretive exhibit that shows and tells the history of the Simpson estate.

From here, a paved path meanders along the precipitous edge of the cliffs. During winter and spring migrations, this is an excellent place for watching gray whales. It's also a great spot for observing the sound and fury of winter storms and their aftermath. At storm's end, on an incoming tide, the riled seas crash ashore in a stunning display that rocks the earth and sends waves exploding skyward. Photographers will want to record the drama on film, but should take care to protect their gear from the raining salt spray.

Trails lead north from here along the cliffs and through the forest to Sunset Bay. Nearby are picnic tables, drinking water, and rest rooms with flush toilets and wheelchair access.

Shore Acres is certainly the showcase of the parks of Cape Arago and a pleasant surprise to first-time visitors. With the ever-changing seasons and fickle moods of the sea, it's a different park on every trip, inviting many happy returns.

Turn into the paved parking area on the west side of the road, and enjoy the best nearshore marine mammal viewing on the Oregon coast: a *must stop* for wildlife watchers and photographers. Four species of seals and sea lions haul out on Shell Island and nearby rocks and use the nearshore waters, providing opportunities for observation and photography any month of the year. Pacific harbor seal females give birth in this area, and for that reason, the north cove of Cape Arago is closed to the public from March through June. Most of the northern elephant seals seen on the beach at Shell Island are young, one to four years old. Elephant seals may be present here any time of the year, but are most plentiful in the spring. Only male California sea lions frequent this area, because the females and pups spend the entire year on the California coast. Steller or northern sea lions breed along the coast of Oregon during the summer, but haul out here during the rest of the year.

In addition to the marine mammals, various birds are observable in this vicinity all year, some with seasonal peaks. Great blue herons are year-round foragers, as are the ubiquitous gulls, and the busy black oystercatchers. Pelagic cormorants nest on Shell Island, with chicks in the nest by July.

From Memorial Day to Labor Day, docents from Shoreline Education for Awareness (SEA) set up a spotting scope on a tripod and are on hand to answer questions about Cape Arago. The rest of the year, SEA provides the same services by appointment for groups as small as a family. Information: (541) 347-3683.

State Route 240, mile 13.7
Simpson Reef and Shell Island Overlook

MUST STOP

This park is a *must stop* that lies at the end of the cape and the end of the road as a fitting finale to the Cape Arago experience. It's also a place to visit time and again for the variety of scenery and recreation it offers. No better oceanfront picnic area exists anywhere on the coast. In addition to a picnic shelter and tables set in the woods at the east end of the park, there are individual sites hewn into the west face of the of the headland, with paved paths leading to them. Imagine enjoying a lavish picnic or simple coffee break while sitting at a table above the tumbling surf, watching the foraging seabirds, migrating whales, and passing fishing boats—all of this against a background chorus of barking sea lions.

A trail leads down to the north cove, where there are tide pools to explore, fish to be caught, and treasures to be found along the surf line. Another trail descends to the sandy beach and tide pools of the south cove where people enjoy more of the same.

The park also has open grassy areas for tossing a Frisbee or football, interpretive signs, trash receptacles, and rest rooms with flush toilets and wheelchair access.

State Route 240, mile 13.9
Cape Arago State Park

MUST STOP

Side Trip: County Road 29, Beach Loop Road

MUST STOP

Stretching along the Bandon area's Pacific edge, this delightfully scenic road is a *must stop* that leads to beach accesses, picnic areas, trails, and parks. Although travelers can reach Beach Loop Road from Old Town Bandon and several streets leading west off Highway 101, the county road and milepost markers begin at the south junction with Highway 101 at mile 277.6.

Beach Loop Road, mile 1.2
Bandon State Park
Day Use Area

On the west side of the road are a parking lot and short trails to low dunes and a beach that's uncrowded most of the time and absolutely deserted on other days. This is a good stretch for beach combing, especially after big storms.

Beach Loop Road, mile 1.4
Bandon State Park
Day Use Area

On the west side of the road is a parking lot with nearby picnic tables in a tree-sheltered area, but with no ocean view. A trail leads over a stabilized dune to the beach.

Beach Loop Road, mile 1.9
Bandon State Park
Day Use Area

On the west side of the road is a parking lot with adjacent paved paths leading a short way to the beach. The park also has oceanview picnic sites with tables and rest rooms with flush toilets and wheelchair access.

Beach Loop Road, mile 2
Bandon Beach Riding Stables

A short road on the east side of Beach Loop Road leads to privately owned stables and horse livery offering several options for horseback riding. Beach trips are 3 miles and last an hour. Sunset rides, from May through September, are four miles and last one and a half to two hours. Information: (541) 347-3423.

Beach Loop Road, mile 2.3
Bandon City Limits

A sandsculpture contest draws crowds of artists and onlookers to the Bandon Beach State Park.

Built in 1926, this 2,100-yard, 9-hole, par-32 course is laid out in a quiet, coastal residential area. Amenities include a clubhouse, pro shop, resident pro, putting green, chipping area, pull-cart and electric-cart rental, club rental, bar, restaurant, and adjacent lodging. Pro shop: (541) 347-3818.

Beach Loop Road, mile 2.7
Bandon Face Rock Golf Course

Turn east here, and drive 0.8 mile to reach Highway 101.

Beach Loop Road, mile 2.9
Seabird Drive

Turn west into the parking lot, where picnic tables overlook Face Rock and the ocean. The little park has drinking water, rest rooms with flush toilets, and a paved trail and steps to the beach. Those who want to photograph Face Rock may wish to wait for afternoon sun when the rock can be silhouetted against bright sky or sparkling sea.

Beach Loop Road, mile 3.4
Face Rock State Wayside

A small gravel parking area on the west side of the road provides a view of Face Rock.

Beach Loop Road, mile 3.8
Viewpoint

Turn east, and drive 0.8 mile to reach Highway 101.

Beach Loop Road, mile 4
11th Street Southwest

Coquille Point/ Oregon Islands National Wildlife Refuge

At the west end of 11th Street Southwest, 0.1 mile from Beach Loop Road, lie a small parking lot and an outstanding overlook with interpretive signs, a stairway to the beach, a paved path with interpretive signs, and superb views north and south from the trails. This is definitely a place to park and walk, pausing along the way to take in the scenic wonders of the refuge.

Oregon Islands National Wildlife Refuge, along Bandon's Beach Loop Road.

Beach Loop Road, mile 4.1
Table Rock Beach Access

Just west of Beach Loop Road is a gravel parking area overlooking Table Rock, the beach, and the mouth of the Coquille River. There are steps to the beach and access to the paved path and interpretive signs of the wildlife refuge.

To South Jetty and Old Town

Although this is the last of the attractions along Beach Loop Road, travelers can continue north to reach the south jetty and Old Town Bandon. At mile 4.5 Beach Loop Road becomes Ocean Drive, and at mile 4.7, the road curves sharply to the right into 4th Street Southwest. Continue 0.1 mile to the Edison Avenue intersection, turn left, drive down the hill 0.1 mile, and turn left on Jetty Road, or continue straight and around the curve to the right to reach Old Town.

Information

Bandon Chamber of Commerce
300 Southeast 2nd Street
P.O. Box 1515
Bandon, OR 97411
(541) 347-9616
URL: www.bandon.com

Bay Area Chamber of Commerce
50 East Central Avenue
P.O. Box 210
Coos Bay, OR 97420
(541) 269-0215
(800) 824-8486
E-mail: bacc@ucinet.com
URL: www.ucinet.com/~bacc

Bureau of Land Management
Coos Bay District Office
1300 Airport Lane
North Bend, OR 97459
(541) 756-0100
URL: www.or.blm.gov/coosbay

Coos County Parks Department
250 North Baxter Street
Coquille, OR 97423
(541) 396-3121 Extension 354

Lakeside Chamber of Commerce
P.O. Box 333
Lakeside, OR 97449
(541) 759-3981

Oregon Department of Fish and Wildlife
Charleston Office
4475 Boat Basin Drive
Charleston, OR 97420
(541) 888-5515

Oregon Parks and Recreation Department
Area 4 Office—Southwestern Oregon
10965 Cape Arago Highway
Coos Bay, OR 97420
(541) 888-8867

Port of Bandon
1st Street Southwest
Bandon, OR 97411
(541) 347-3206

Port of Coos Bay
125 Central Avenue, Suite 300
P.O. Box 1215
Coos Bay, OR 97420
(541) 267-7678

South Slough National Estuarine Research Reserve
P.O. Box 5417
Charleston, OR 97420
(541) 888-5558
URL: www.southsloughestuary.com

U.S. Coast Guard
Charleston Lifeboat Station
Charleston, OR 97420
(541) 888-3266
(541) 888-3102 Weather and Bar Conditions

Autumn celebrates its infancy along the southern Oregon coast with sharp and sunny days and longer, cooler nights. The moon sneaks up big and orange, bright enough to sparkle the surf and cast stilt-legged shadows across the beach. Weathered webs, once summer-taut, sag dew-laden in morning meadows, where salt air is as tangy as the cranberries growing crimson in their bogs.

Wild cranberries, a native American species and close kin to the blueberry, were growing on the Clatsop Plains when Lewis and Clark wintered on the north coast in 1805-06. Men of the expedition, in fact, supplemented their diet of fish and game with cranberries they bought from the Clatsop Indians. Berries have been cultivated on the south coast for more than a century.

Charles McFarlin, who hailed from the Cape Cod area of Massachusetts, came to the West Coast in the 1870s, seeking his fortune in the placer-gold rivers of California. Dust and nuggets eluded his pan, however, forcing him to look elsewhere for wealth. He ultimately made his way to Oregon's south coast, and in 1879 had his brother ship cranberry vines to him, by sailing ship around Cape Horn. While he searched for the ideal spot to grow cranberries, McFarlin kept the vines healthy in the mud of Beaver Slough, a tributary of the Coquille River between Bandon and the city of Coquille. He built the first bog and planted his vines in 1885 near Hauser, between Lakeside and North Bend, about 5 miles north of Coos Bay. He then developed several more bogs in the area and hired Coos Indians as pickers. The strain of cranberry he developed, now called the McFarlin, is well suited to local conditions and is the principal variety grown on the Pacific Coast, although others introduced in recent years are flourishing.

Since those early days, southern Oregon's cranberry industry has grown slowly but steadily, with bogs scattered from Hauser south to the Sixes River and concentrated in the vicinity of Bandon. By 1925, about 120 acres of bogs were producing berries, and it took growers another twenty years to add 60 more acres. Cranberry cultivation does not require vast acreage. Today, fewer than a hundred growers work about 2,400 acres of bogs on the south coast, but greatly improved per-acre yields have led to dramatically increased harvests. From 1958 to 1983, the annual harvest grew from 3.1 million to 7.3 million pounds. In 1995, 1,700 acres of bogs produced about 10,000 pounds per acre, or a total of 17 million pounds. By 1997, the per-acre yield for 2,000 acres was a record 17,500 pounds per acre, for a total of 35 million pounds worth more than $21 million.

Although cranberries grow on tough, woody vines and are among the hardiest of fruits, cultivating them is not a simple matter of planting vines, then sitting back and watching the money roll in.

Crimson Berries of the Bogs

Crimson Berries of the Bogs

Like any crop, they require care and hard work. On new bogs, the wait between planting and harvesting can be long.

Bogs are built on peat or on ash-gray and acidic soil known as upland peat. Early growers had to clear land and dig bogs with hand tools. Although such chores are now left to backhoes and bulldozers, preparation and planting remain much the same. After clearing the land of trees, shrubs, and brush, then digging out roots, workers "scalp" the land, removing the surface material to the peat layer. They then divide and ditch the area, build dikes for water control, and install the essential irrigation system. Growers then spread a layer of sand over the peat and try to make sure there are no low spots that will hold water and that the bog is slightly crowned to promote runoff. Finally, they set vine cuttings in the sand about 6 inches apart. The vines take root in the peat and, with sufficient care, spread into a dense mat that will begin producing berries in three to five years.

Cranberries might not be the easiest crop to grow, but they're certainly among the prettiest. If the tiny-leaved and delicate-looking vines remind you of heather, that's because both are in the heath family. During their winter dormancy, cranberry bogs mellow to a light shade of burgundy. In May, they burst into bloom, with tiny flowers the color of blush wine and shaped like the heads of cranes, which is why the Pilgrims named them crane berries. Summer vines are lush green and heavy with berries by Labor Day. It takes the cool of autumn to turn the buoyant berries bright crimson, with the spectacle of harvest dazzling coastal residents and visitors from September to November.

Harvest is a busy time for cranberry growers, but many allow visitors and onlookers to observe and photograph the colorful operation; some even offer farm tours. The bogs spread from both sides of U.S. 101 and along nearby county roads north, south, and east of Bandon. Wherever the roadway shoulders are broad enough, be sure to pull off, park, and take in the fascinating activities. Be careful to avoid getting in the way of workers and farm machinery, and always ask permission before venturing onto anyone's property.

Although most growers in the Bandon area use the wet-pick method of harvesting, about 10 percent of the berries are dry-picked with gasoline-powered machines that are pushed through the dry bogs like lawnmowers. The tines on the picker run through the thicket, lifting the berries from the vines. The machine also prunes the vines as it harvests the berries, feeding berries and cuttings into burlap bags that are collected and hauled to separators and conveyors that load waiting trucks.

For wet picking, the grower floods the bog, then rides a machine called a water reel or beater over the bog, creating a commotion that dislodges the berries. The light and buoyant berries then float to the surface and drift toward the downwind side of the bog, where workers corral them with wood booms, while others, equipped with wooden rakes, gather in any stray berries. Wet-picked berries are loaded into trucks either by conveyor or by the faster and more efficient pump, which can handle a ton of berries in under six minutes.

Most growers belong to the Ocean Spray cooperative and truck their berries to the Bandon plant, where they're cleaned and shipped for processing, mainly into juice products. During the peak of the season, Ocean Spray workers handle from 300,000 to 400,000 pounds of berries a day.

Many of the berries also end up in locally made products, such as the delicious jams, jellies, and syrups sold at roadside stands along Highway 101 and at area gift and specialty shops. Cranberry candies, sauces, relishes, and other treats are also locally available.

The city of Bandon hosts the annual Cranberry Festival, held on a weekend in September. In addition to a parade and numerous events and displays, the festival offers opportunities to sample various cranberry products. It also provides a great excuse for a getaway trip to Bandon—the ruby jewel of the south coast.

Information

Bandon Chamber of Commerce
300 Southeast Second Street
P.O. Box 1515
Bandon, OR 97411
(541) 347-9616
URL: www.bandon.com

Siskiyou Coast Express
URL: www.harborside.com/home/c/cbfrmr/index.html

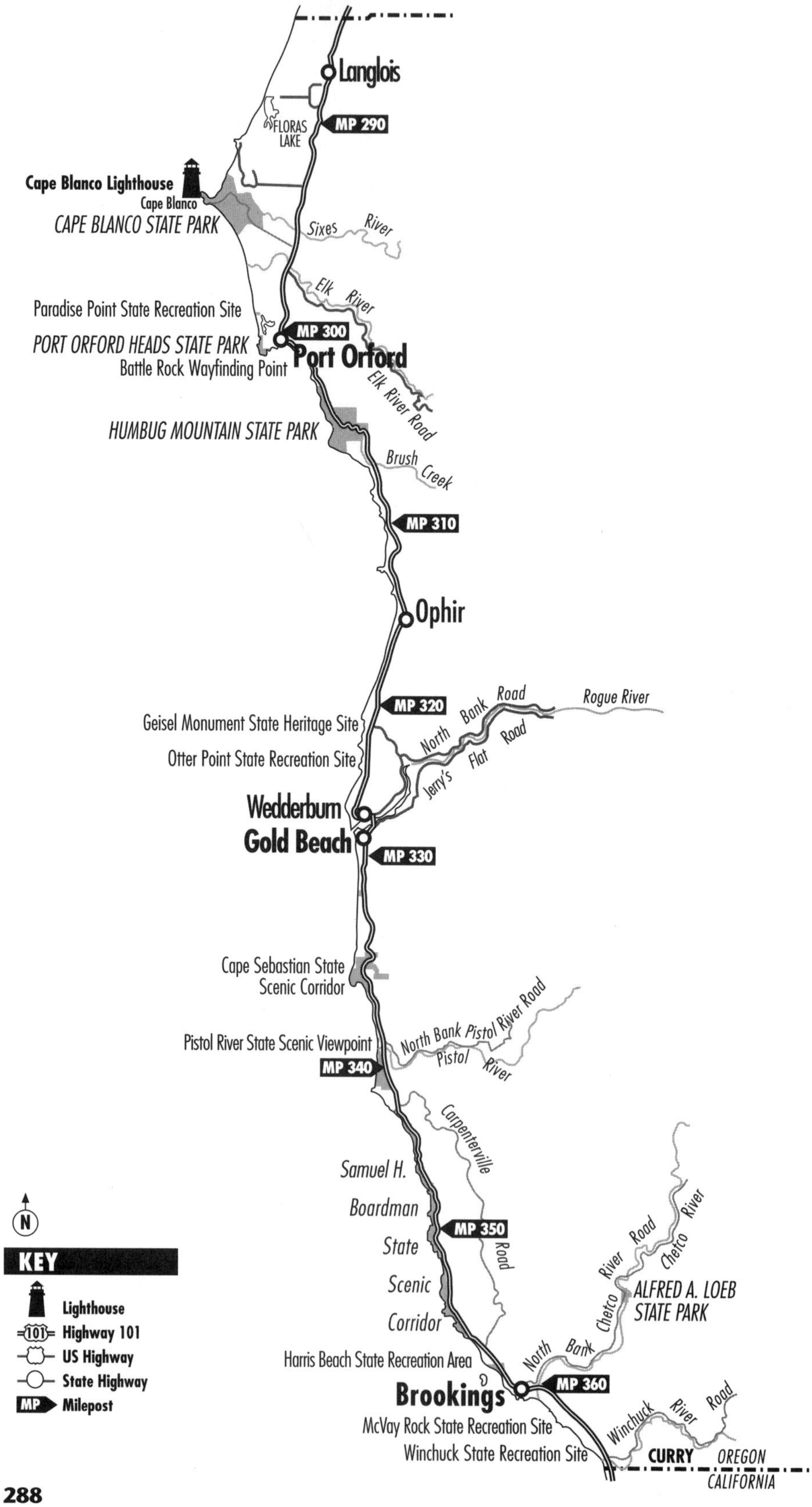

Langlois
MP 290
FLORAS LAKE

Cape Blanco Lighthouse
Cape Blanco
CAPE BLANCO STATE PARK

Sixes River

Elk River

Paradise Point State Recreation Site
PORT ORFORD HEADS STATE PARK
MP 300
Port Orford
Battle Rock Wayfinding Point

Elk River Road

HUMBUG MOUNTAIN STATE PARK

Brush Creek

MP 310

Ophir

MP 320

Rogue River

North Bank Road

Geisel Monument State Heritage Site

Otter Point State Recreation Site
Flat Road

Jerry's

Wedderburn
Gold Beach
MP 330

Cape Sebastian State
Scenic Corridor

North Bank Pistol River Road

Pistol River State Scenic Viewpoint
Pistol River
MP 340

Carpenterville

Samuel H.
Boardman
State
Scenic
Corridor

MP 350

Road

Chetco River Road

Chetco River

ALFRED A. LOEB STATE PARK

North Bank

Harris Beach State Recreation Area

MP 360
Brookings
McVay Rock State Recreation Site
Winchuck State Recreation Site

Winchuck River Road

CURRY OREGON
CALIFORNIA

N

KEY
- Lighthouse
- Highway 101
- US Highway
- State Highway
- **MP** Milepost

The Curry County Coast

U.S. 101, Mile 285.8 to Mile 363.1

Editor and publisher George Law Curry (1820-78) was Oregon's territorial governor when the territorial legislature established Curry County on December 18, 1855, and named it after the popular governor. The 1,648-square-mile county was formed with land taken from the southern half of Coos County. The seat of government was originally at Port Orford, but in 1859 was moved to Ellensburg, now known as Gold Beach. Brookings is the county's largest city, which, combined with the unincorporated community of Harbor, contains more than half the county's 22,000 residents.

From the county's earliest days, timber and wood products have been major contributors to the local economy. In the 1850s, a brief gold rush followed the discovery of the precious metal along the county's black-sand beaches near the mouth of the Rogue River. Commercial fishing began in earnest in the 1870s on the lower Rogue River, where fish plants and canneries lined the banks until the early 1900s when the great salmon runs had all but disappeared. Today, the commercial fishery is offshore, with a large fleet working out of the Port of Brookings Harbor and a small fleet, mainly urchin divers, headquartered at Port Orford. Agriculture is another important part of the county economy, with ranches producing sheep and cattle in the foothills of the Siskiyou Mountains and horticulturists growing Easter lilies and other nursery stock in the rich alluvial soil and mild climate of southern Curry County. In fact, a small group of farmers along a strip of coastal plain extending from Harbor south to the northwest tip of California produces more than 90 percent of all the Easter lilies sold in the United States.

Most of Curry County—all but the northeast tip, northwest tip, and a narrow strip along the coast—lies within the Siskiyou National Forest. The county not only contains the longest stretch of Highway 101 of any Oregon county (77.8 miles), but the highway here also traverses more miles of oceanside scenery than any other county, with a tremendous variety of landforms and a new vista around every bend in the road. Highways, back roads, and trails pass through or near seaside prairies, undulating foothills, lush meadows and wetlands, old-growth forests, groves of myrtlewood trees, and the only ancient redwoods in Oregon. It's no wonder, then, that tourism and outdoor recreation are important aspects of both the economy and culture of this stretch of the south coast.

**U.S. 101,
mile 287.5 to
mile 288.2
Langlois**

Oregon has lumberyards larger than Langlois, but the tiny community and its surroundings deserve more than the cursory glimpse they usually get from travelers on Highway 101. Langlois has a couple of cafés and several antique shops and art galleries that deserve a stop. On any clear day, a short side trip up Langlois Mountain Road is worthwhile.

**U.S. 101,
mile 287.6**
County Road 118
(Langlois Mountain
Road)

Heading east off the highway, this road climbs quickly into ranch country, offering great views and photographic opportunities within the first three miles. On clear days, the ocean to Bandon and beyond is visible, and the rolling hills provide interesting foreground for photographs. Gravel berm wide enough for parking is at miles 0.9, 1, 1.4, 1.6, and 2. A gravel parking area on the north side of the road is at mile 2.6. All these spots offer superb views and photo opportunities.

The rolling ranch land along Langlois Mountain Road.

**U.S. 101,
mile 288.8**
County Road 130
(Floras Lake Loop),
north junction

Southbound travelers heading for Floras Lake should watch for the sign to Floras Lake and Boice Cope County Park. Turn west on Floras Lake Loop, drive 1 mile to Floras Lake Road (County Road 136), turn right, continue 1.5 mile to Boice Cope Road, turn right, and drive 0.2 mile to the park entrance.

Boice Cope County
Park

This popular park has day-use parking and picnic areas and a campground with 17 primitive tent/RV sites, each with a table, fire ring with a grate, and nearby drinking water and firewood. Other amenities include a tent camp, horseshoe pits, tank dump, trash receptacle, hot showers, and rest rooms with flush toilets and wheelchair access. The park is situated on Floras Lake and Floras Creek, also known as New River, providing visitors easy access to both, as well as to the beach, low dunes, and hiking trails. There's a paved boat ramp on the lake and an earthen ramp on the creek.

This 236-acre lake with a maximum depth of 35 feet and average depth of 18 feet was once a small bay that was eventually enclosed by migrating sand dunes. These active dunes lie along the west shore of the lake, beyond which is a sand beach on the ocean, which is good spot for surfperch fishing.

Lake angling is mainly for stocked rainbow and cutthroat trout, as well as largemouth bass, some of which run to 6 pounds or more. The lake is also open all year for chinook salmon and steelhead trout, which migrate through on their way to tributary streams, but the angling is mainly a fall and winter game. Chinook usually begin showing up in late October, with steelhead following in December and available through March.

Strong and persistent winds that are a nuisance to anglers and canoeists delight the sailboarding and paraboarding enthusiasts who flock to the lake, especially during the summer.

Northbound travelers heading for Floras Lake should watch for the sign for Floras Lake and Boice Cope County Park. Turn west on Floras Lake Loop, drive 1 mile to Floras Lake Road (County Road 136), turn left, continue 1.5 mile to Boice Cope Road, turn right, and drive 0.2 mile to the park entrance.

Turn west off the highway, and drive 0.1 mile past the store to a gravel ramp and parking area and a gravel bar providing angler access to the Sixes River. Folks at the store also provide shuttle service for Sixes River anglers. Information: (541) 332-6666.

Turn east off Highway 101 to reach the Sixes River, boat ramp, and campgrounds.

Floras Lake

U.S. 101, mile 289.9
County Road 130 (Floras Lake Loop), south junction

U.S. 101, mile 295.4
Sixes River Store Boat Ramp

Sixes River Road

Windy Floras Lake is popular with sailors and sailboarders.

Edson Creek Recreation Area

Drive east on Sixes River Road 4.2 miles to reach this Bureau of Land Management facility on both sides of the road. On the north side of the road, in a wooded setting, is a campground with 30 primitive tent/RV sites with tables and fireplaces. There's drinking water available, a trash receptacle, and vault toilets. On the south side of the road are chemical toilets and an earthen boat ramp on the river.

Sixes River Campground

This Bureau of Land Management facility lies 11.1 miles east of Highway 101 in the forested mountains along the north bank of the Sixes River, near the confluence of the South Fork. It includes a day-use picnic area on the river and a campground with 19 primitive tent/RV sites with tables and fireplaces. There's drinking water available and vault toilets. This is a popular spot for gold panning.

U.S. 101, mile 295.6
Sixes River

The Sixes heads in the Coast Range and flows seaward for about 36 miles before emptying into the ocean near Cape Blanco. It's a decent chinook-salmon and steelhead river that's open to angling most of the year, up to the South Fork. Low water is a summer certainty, so the best angling begins in late autumn and continues through March. Fall chinook arrive late here, usually in November, and are legal quarry through December. Steelhead angling begins about the same time and holds up until the season closes at the end of March. The river is also open for fin-clipped rainbow trout (half-pounders) from November through March. East of Highway 101, the Sixes River has a good bit of private property along its banks. West of the highway, Cape Blanco State Park provides excellent bank access on the lower river. Because of limited bank access upriver, the Sixes is popular with drift-boat anglers. A favorite drift is to put in at Edson Creek Recreation area and take out at the Sixes River Store.

U.S. 101, mile 296.4
Cape Blanco

MUST STOP

Cape Blanco juts west into the Pacific farther than any other point on the Oregon coast. Much of the cape lies within the boundaries of Cape Blanco State Park and is a *must stop*. At the end of the windblown headland, just over 5 miles from Highway 101, stands Oregon's first lighthouse. Oddly, the mileposts along the road to the end of the cape run in ascending order from the lighthouse to Highway 101, so the first roadside marker travelers encounter after leaving the highway is for milepost 5.

The Hughes House

Turn west off Highway 101, drive 3.9 miles, and turn north (right) to reach the parking area. Built in 1898, this 3,000-square-foot, eleven-room Eastlake Victorian was the home of the pioneer Hughes family who occupied and worked a ranch along the lower Sixes River for 111 years. The sturdy, handsome structure

The Hughes House at Cape Blanco State Park.

was framed with 2x8 old-growth Port Orford cedar. The finished house cost Patrick and Jane Hughes $3,800. The house is furnished with period antiques and is now part of Cape Blanco State Park. It is open to the public from May through September, Thursday through Monday, from 10:00 a.m. to 3:30 p.m. It's also open during the Christmas season and decorated for the holidays, when tours are free and visitors are greeted with cookies and hot cider. For dates and hours of the Christmas opening, check with Cape Blanco State Park personnel as the season nears.

Cape Blanco State Park Boat Ramp

Travel west from Highway 101, take the turnoff for the Hughes House, and drive past the house to the parking lot and day-use area on the south bank of the Sixes River. There's a gravel ramp, good bank access for anglers, picnic tables, and chemical toilets with wheelchair access. This is a beautiful valley and fine place for a picnic or rest stop.

Cape Blanco Pioneer Cemetery

On the south side of the road, 4.3 miles west of Highway 101, is a small parking area and a path leading to the old cemetery where members of the Hughes family and other area settlers lie buried.

Cape Blanco State Park Horse Camp

Drive west from Highway 101 out the cape 4.7 miles, turn south on the gravel road, and watch for the entrance to the horse camp on the west side of the road. The camp has eight primitive campsites with tables and fireplaces, five corrals, chemical toilets, and access to equestrian trails.

Cape Blanco State Park Campground

Turn west off Highway 101, drive 4.9 miles, and turn south to reach the campgrounds featuring 54 wind-protected sites with water and electrical hookups, paved parking, tables, and fire rings. One site has wheelchair access. The park also has four log cabins, a hiker/biker camp, group camp, firewood, dump station, trash receptacles, hot showers, and rest rooms with flush toilets.

MUST STOP

At this *must-stop* park, campers and day-users have access to more than 8 miles of hiking and equestrian trails leading to the lighthouse, cliffs, ocean beach, and a number of outstanding viewpoints. A road descends from the campground to the beach, where there is a parking area. Street-legal vehicles can access the beach here; it's easy to get stuck on this beach, so four-wheel-drive is recommended. Information: (541) 332-6774 or (800) 551-6949.

Cape Blanco
Lighthouse

Just over 5 miles west of Highway 101 lies the parking lot adjacent to Oregon's oldest, highest, and most westerly lighthouse, now managed and maintained by the Bureau of Land Management. The structure, completed in 1870, was built of bricks made on site with local clay. From its lofty perch, the light is 245 feet above the sea, visible 22 miles out. The lighthouse—a *must stop* for sightseers, photographers, and all lighthouse enthusiasts—is open for tours that last about twenty minutes and include ascending the 64 stairs to the lantern room. Lighthouse grounds are open Thursday to Monday, 10:00 a.m. to 3:30 p.m. Information: (541) 756-0100.

*Cape Blanco
Lighthouse*

This small river tumbles out of the Coast Range and wends its way coastward for about 30 miles before emptying into the Pacific south of Cape Blanco. The river is open for chinook-salmon and steelhead angling for most of the year, but the fishery here, as on the Sixes River, is pretty much a late-fall and winter proposition. Fall chinook usually move into the river in November, after there has been sufficient rainfall, where they remain available to anglers until the close of the season after December 31. Steelhead also enter the river after the first good rains of the fall, usually in November, and can be taken through the end of the season on March 31. The river is also open from November though March for fin-clipped rainbow trout (half-pounders).

The best fishing on the Elk is in the lower reaches of the river, where private property prevents access. So most anglers fish from drift boats—their own, or those of hired fishing guides.

U.S. 101, mile 297.3
Elk River

This road leads east along the river to a hatchery operated by the Oregon Department of Fish and Wildlife where there are also two boat launches. The road continues beyond the hatchery, but is reduced to one lane with turnouts through steep terrain.

U.S. 101, mile 297.7
Elk River Road

Take Elk River road 7.5 miles east, and turn north at the sign for the hatchery. Each year, the hatchery produces 325,000 fall-chinook smolts for the Elk River, 230,000 for the Chetco River, and smaller amounts for a number of other south-coast streams. The hatchery also produces 50,000 winter steelhead smolts a year for the Chetco River. There's a picnic table on the premises and chemical toilets with wheelchair access. Information: (541) 332-7025.

Elk River Hatchery

At the Elk River Fish Hatchery, 7.5 miles east of U.S. 101 are two gravel boat ramps with nearby parking. The upper ramp is just east of the hatchery entrance. The lower ramp is near the rearing ponds.

Fish Hatchery Boat Ramps

Described by nineteenth-century historian Hubert Howe Bancroft as "a little hamlet on the wrong side of the mountain," Port Orford is situated on a marine terrace that embraces one of the most beautiful natural harbors on the West Coast. Presumably, the mountain Bancroft referred to is Humbug Mountain, which stands at the ocean's edge, south of town. The nearby headland we know as Cape Blanco was called Cape Orford in June 1851 when Captain William Tichenor landed nine men south of the cape to help him build the town of Port Orford, the first settlement on what is now the Curry County coast. Tichenor then sailed south to San Francisco for more men

U.S. 101, mile 299.8 to mile 301.8 Port Orford
(zip code 97465)

and provisions, leaving the hapless landing party to fend off Indian attacks at Battle Rock, a tiny near-shore islet. After two weeks of intermittent fighting, the landing party ran low on ammunition and escaped to the north.

It took Tichenor a month to return from San Francisco, but this time he brought 67 men who set to work at once building the new settlement and a house for Tichenor and his family. Fortifications erected on a hillside overlooking Battle Rock and the harbor came to be known as Fort Orford. During the Rogue River Indian Wars of 1853-56, 244 soldiers were stationed there.

In the 1850s, the black-sand beaches of Curry County held rich gold deposits that attracted placer miners by the hundreds. Tiny Port Orford boomed with a population of about one thousand. When the gold played out, though, the population dwindled, and the town was left to grow gradually, supported eventually by the timber industry, commercial fishing, sheep ranching, and dairy farming. Today, the town's population is about the same as it was during the gold rush.

U.S. 101, mile 299.8
Paradise Point State Recreation Site

Turn west on Paradise Point Road, and drive 1 mile to the gravel parking lot and overlook. A trail at the north end of the parking lot leads to the beach, which is popular for beachcombing and agate hunting, especially after winter storms.

U.S. 101, mile 300.5
Buffington Memorial Park

Turn west on 14th Street, and drive 0.2 mile to this city park with a picnic shelter, picnic tables, trash receptacles, and rest rooms with flush toilets. The park also has a nature trail, baseball diamond, tennis courts, basketball court, horse arena, horseshoe pits, playground, and 9-hole miniature golf course.

U.S. 101, mile 300.6
Garrison Lake

Lying west of Highway 101 is a 90-acre dune lake that consists of two basins joined by a narrow channel. The maximum depth is 26 feet and average depth is 8 feet. Private dwellings occupy more than 85 percent of the shoreline, which severely restricts public access to the lake. The shallow lake also has a long history of water-quality and weed problems. Nevertheless, the lake is popular for angling, and it offers opportunities for wildlife observation.

The lake holds some native cutthroat trout and the Oregon Department of Fish and Wildlife stocks it with rainbow and cutthroat trout. Warmwater species include largemouth bass and yellow perch. Garrison Lake attracts a variety of waterfowl and other birds, including puddle ducks, diving ducks, coots, grebes, loons, herons, and more. Mammals that roam the lakeshore include deer, possum, raccoon, beaver, otter, and muskrat.

Lying 0.5 mile west of Highway 101, via 12th Street, is a paved boat ramp and boat dock on Garrison Lake, a picnic shelter with a table and grill, a fishing dock with wheelchair access, and chemical toilets.

12th Street Boat Launch

Turn west on 9th Street, drive two blocks, turn left on Coast Guard Road, and continue to the park's entrance, 0.7 mile from Highway 101. Protected picnic sites with tables set amid tall trees, old Coast Guard buildings, and grassy open areas make this a top choice for a picnic. A short, easy trail to an overlook commanding a superb view of Port Orford's natural harbor, rocky shoreline to the south, and Humbug Mountain make it a *must stop* for sightseers and photographers. Several spots along the trail also provide outstanding ocean views and opportunities for bird watching and whale watching in season. Black-tailed deer, squirrels, and other mammals roam the grounds. There's no trailer turnaround at the park.

U.S. 101, mile 300.7
Port Orford Heads State Park

Sunset at Port Orford Heads State Park.

Where the highway curves east, stay on Oregon Street, up the hill 0.2 mile to a parking area and small shelter overlooking the Port Orford Harbor.

U.S. 101, mile 300.8
Port Orford viewpoint

Turn west on Harbor Drive to reach viewpoints overlooking the harbor, beach access, and port facilities that lie 0.3 mile from Highway 101. Port Orford's waterfront area is one of the most interesting and unusual anywhere. Instead of bobbing in boat slips with mooring lines fast to dockside cleats, the Port Orford

U.S. 101, mile 301.2
Port of Port Orford

Boats are launched by hoist at the Port of Port Orford.

fleet is cradled on rubber-tired dollies, high and dry atop a large wharf. When it's time to set to sea, a large hoist lifts each boat, swings it over the wharf's edge, and gently lowers it to the water. This is also where local commercial divers unload their catches of sea urchins, which are processed here for the Japanese market. Visitors are allowed to watch and photograph the boat launching, unloading, and retrieval at their own risk.

The wharf has day-use boat-trailer and vehicle parking areas with adjacent access to the breakwater and nearby rocky shoreline, popular with anglers and scuba divers. Those towing boats can have them launched for a fee for a quick run to nearby fishing and diving grounds. There's no river bar to cross here, and the natural harbor provides a safe haven to boaters during storms or when northwest winds kick up.

Other facilities include showers and rest rooms with flush toilets and wheelchair access.

U.S. 101, mile 301.4
Battle Rock
Wayfinding Point

On the west side of the highway, at the south end of town, are a large parking area and city park with interpretive signs. Short, easy paths lead to the beach and historic Battle Rock. The little park also has oceanview picnic sites with tables, trash receptacles, drinking water, and rest rooms with flush toilets and wheelchair access.

Port Orford Visitor
Center

A small visitor center at the south end of the parking lot is staffed by volunteers and provides information about some of the local

Battle Rock, at Port Orford

attractions. The center is open daily from 10:00 a.m. to 3:00 p.m., but winter hours may vary.

A large gravel parking area on the east side of the highway, at the south end of the bridge, provides access to an easy trail leading to Hubbard Creek and the beach. The trail extends from the north end of the parking area, under the bridge, and on to the mouth of the creek.

U.S. 101, mile 302.3
Hubbard Creek Beach Access

A narrow, rough, paved road on the west side of the highway leads about 0.1 mile down the hillside to a small gravel parking area not recommended for trailers or large motorhomes. From here, a moderately easy trail leads a short distance to the beach.

U.S. 101, mile 304.3
Beach access

This exquisite park at the base of Humbug Mountain is situated in a forested canyon that's well protected from ocean winds and is often warmer than other coastal parks. Visitors can enjoy a fine campground, wooded picnic area, a beautiful little creek, hiking trails, and beach access.

U.S. 101, mile 304.6 to 307.7
Humbug Mountain State Park

Highway 101 swings east, here, along the north side of the mountain. When southbound travelers turn right or left along this stretch, they will be turning south or north, respectively, not west or east, as is usually the case along Highway 101.

A gravel parking area on the south side of the highway provides access to a 3-mile hiking trail that starts at the base of Humbug Mountain and leads through forest and ferns to the 1,748-foot summit.

U.S. 101, mile 306.6
Humbug Mountain Trailhead and Parking Area

The dominating landform of the southern Oregon coast, even more impressive for its oceanside location, was known among local Indians as *Me-tus*. Others called it Mount Franklin or

Humbug Mountain

This crescent of sandy beach sweeps southeasterly from Port Orford (top center) and is virtually deserted, even in mid-summer.

Sugarloaf. In 1851, Captain William Tichenor, founder of Port Orford, dispatched a party of men to establish a pack trail to the Jacksonville mining area, which, according to Tichenor, was only 20 miles to the east. The men became hopelessly lost, and when they finally made their way back to Port Orford more than two weeks later, they renamed the mountain Tichenor's Humbug. It later came to be known as Humbug Mountain.

U.S. 101, mile 307
Humbug Mountain
State Park
Campground

The entrance, on the north side of the highway, leads to a lovely campground that has 30 sites with water and electrical hookups and 78 primitive tent/RV sites with paved parking, picnic tables, and fire rings; two sites have wheelchair access. Other amenities include a hiker/biker camp, hiking trails, dump station, firewood, showers, and rest rooms with flush toilets. Information: (541) 332-6774 or (800) 551-6949.

U.S. 101, mile 307.7
Humbug Mountain
State Park Day-Use
Area

Turn south off the highway to reach a parking lot along the rushing waters of Brush Creek. Cross the foot bridge over the creek to hike the paved paths or enjoy a picnic in a mixed forest of cedar, fir, maple, and myrtlewood trees. Amenities include picnic tables, trash receptacles, benches, drinking water, and rest rooms with flush toilets. There's also a group area with picnic tables and a kitchen shelter.

U.S. 101, mile 316.9 Ophir
(zip code 97464)

This small rural residential area east of the highway, along Euchre Creek, is said to be named for a country mentioned in the Bible (I Kings 10:11) that was known for its gold, as this part of Curry County once was.

Cedar Bend Golf
Course

This lovely course, lying in the forested, rolling hills east of the highway and normally beyond coastal wind and fog, is 2.3 miles from U.S. 101. Head east off the highway, drive 0.1 mile to Coy

Northbound travelers on Highway 101 glimpse the heavily forested spine of Humbug Mountain.

Creek Road, turn south (right), and proceed 0.3 mile to Squaw Valley Road. Turn east (left), and drive 1.9 miles to this 3,156-yard, 9-hole, par-36 course with a driving range, chipping area, putting green, pro shop, electric-cart and pull-cart rental, club rental, snack bar, and bar. Pro shop: (541) 247-6911.

On the west side of the highway stands a parking area with nearby picnic tables in grassy areas just steps from a broad sand beach that stretches for miles in both directions and is popular with beachcombers, birders, and hikers. Drinking water, trash receptacles, and rest rooms with flush toilets and wheelchair access round out the wayside's offerings.

U.S. 101, mile 318.9
Rest area and beach access

Turn west, then immediately north on a short section of the old Coast Highway, 0.4 mile to an easy trail leading to the beach. Park along the side of the road.

U.S. 101, mile 320.8
Nesika Beach

Just west of the highway is a small park with picnic tables, burial sites of the Geisel family, and a monument commemorating the skirmish during which most of the family died. On February 22, 1856, during the Rogue Indian Wars, John Geisel, 45; son John, 9; son Henry, 7; and son Andrew, 5, died in a battle with local Indians. John's wife, Christina, died September 20, 1899, at age 75, and is also buried here.

U.S. 101, mile 322.4
Geisel Monument State Heritage Site

A narrow, winding section of the old coast route loops west off Highway 101, leads to several trails and beach accesses, and rejoins the highway 2.6 miles beyond. It makes for an interesting side trip, but is not recommended for trailers and large motorhomes.

U.S. 101, mile 324.1
Old Coast Road, north access

Otter Point State Recreation Site

Turn west off Highway 101, drive 0.2 mile on the Old Coast Road, turn right on the gravel road, and continue another 0.2 mile to a gravel parking area with no trailer turnaround. The parking lot overlooks the beach and ocean. Hiking trails lead to the little-used beach and interesting sandstone formations. The elevated parking area is a good spot to watch for whales during their winter and spring migrations.

Old Coast Road, middle access

At 0.8 mile south of the north access, the middle access joins from the east side of the road. Turn east here to return to Highway 101.

Beach access

At 1.5 miles from the start of the Old Coast Road loop is a small parking area on the east side of the road and an easy trail to the beach leading from the west side. The beach is popular with razor-clam diggers.

County Road 575

At 1.8 miles south of the start of this loop, the Old Coast Road joins this two-lane county road. Continue another 0.8 mile to rejoin Highway 101 or 1.3 miles to reach the north jetty and mouth of the Rogue River. (See details at U.S. 101, mile 326.3, below.)

U.S. 101, mile 324.9
Old Coast Road, middle access

Turn west here to join the old coast route, which roughly parallels the highway. (For details about the Old Coast Road, see U.S. 101, mile 324.1, on page 301.)

U.S. 101, mile 326.3
Old Coast Road, south access

Turn west, go 0.1 mile to County Road 575, and turn north to reach the Old Coast Road. (For details about the Old Coast Road, see U.S. 101, mile 324.1, on page 301.)

Mouth of the Rogue River and North Jetty

Turn west off Highway 101, go 0.1 mile to County Road 575, turn south, and continue 0.5 mile to the large gravel area along the base of the north jetty. This is not only a favorite fishing spot, but also a great place to get a look at the lower Rogue River, the port, and Gold Beach. Wildlife watchers can catch glimpses of pelicans, cormorants, seals, sea lions, and more. Beechy ground squirrels live among the jetty rocks and boulders and freely pose for photos.

U.S. 101, mile 326.8
Rogue River viewpoint

The highway curves east here to run parallel with the river for just under a mile. On the south side is a gravel parking area with a good, elevated view of the mouth of the river, jetties, port facilities, and lower river activities.

U.S. 101, mile 327.3
Wedderburn

R. D. Hume, known as the "salmon king" of the Rogue, was one of the most prosperous and enterprising business tycoons to have lived and worked on the lower Rogue River. With fish-

Salmon anglers ply the waters near the mouth of the Rogue River, while the community of Wedderburn hunkers on the north bank.

plant and cannery interests along the coast, from San Francisco to Astoria, Hume built a cannery in 1876 at Ellensburg (now Gold Beach) on the south bank of the lower Rogue. Within a few years, he owned most of the property along both banks of the lower river—15,000 acres in all. When the Ellensburg cannery burned in 1893, he rebuilt on the north bank, where he established a company town he named Wedderburn, after ancestral property in Scotland. Today, a few houses and businesses clustered along the lower north bank, west of the bridge, occupy the site of the old town.

U.S. 101, mile 327.5
North Bank Road

Turn east at the north end of the bridge to reach the road that flanks the north bank of the Rogue River for just over 11 miles and leads to a number of attractions along the way, including the headquarters for the Rogue River Mail Boat Trips. North Bank Road ends near a one-lane bridge that crosses the river and joins County Road 595, where travelers can turn east and go on to Agness or west and return to Gold Beach. For a pleasant, scenic loop trip of less than an hour, drive up the river along North Bank Road, cross the river, and return along the south bank via County Road 595. Make a day of it by stopping along the way to take in or photograph the great scenery, enjoy a picnic, or do a little fishing.

Rogue River Mail Boat Trips

Head east off Highway 101 on North Bank Road 0.4 mile to the jet-boat facilities on the south side of the road. From May through October, jet-boat trips are among the Gold Beach area's greatest attractions, with round-trip excursions of 64 to 104 miles. Rogue River Mail Boat Trips—in operation since 1895, when boats were poled, rowed, and sailed up the river—

continues to carry mail and passengers upriver and offers morning, afternoon, and dinner cruises, with accommodations for disabled people. Flagship of the fleet is the *Rogue Queen*: a covered, 43-foot, 70-passenger, three-engine hydrojet capable of slipping through water only 10 inches deep. Information: (541) 247-7033 or (800) 458-3511.

Public boat launch

Located 4.6 miles east of Highway 101, on the south side of the road, is a small parking area and paved ramp on the Rogue River.

North bank access

At 5.1 miles east of Highway 101, turn south down a rough gravel road to reach a large gravel bank area providing access to the Rogue River.

Bridge

After flanking the river for 11 miles, North Bank Road joins a Forest Service road and crosses the river at mile 11.2. This one-lane bridge doesn't get a tremendous amount of traffic, so is an excellent place for great views and photography upstream and down. It's an ideal spot for photographing jet boats from an elevated position.

U.S. 101, mile 327.6
Rogue River Bridge

Also known as the Gold Beach Bridge and locally as the Patterson Bridge, this engineering marvel and work of art is another of Conde B. McCullough's great designs and one that, in 1982, was designated as a National Historic Civil Engineering Landmark. The bridge was completed in 1931 and the following year was dedicated to Isaac Lee Patterson, who served as governor of Oregon from 1927 to 1929. McCullough's signature is everywhere to be found on this ornate but graceful concrete structure, from the fluted entrance pylons and spandrel columns to the ornate sidewalk railings and graceful deck arch spans. The bridge reaches 1,898 feet across the river and consists of eighteen concrete approach spans and seven 230-foot reinforced-concrete deck arch spans.

Rogue River

The Rogue heads in the Cascade Mountains near Crater Lake and roars through the Coast Range, gathering the waters of many tributaries before emptying into the Pacific. Besides the Columbia, the only other Oregon river that cuts through both mountain ranges is the Umpqua.

The Rogue and other high-gradient rivers of the south coast don't form estuaries the way rivers from the Coquille north do. Consequently, there are no productive clam-digging flats here, although there are a few spots on the ocean beaches for digging razor and littleneck clams. Crabs do move in and out of the lower Rogue, and recreational crabbing can be good, especially from summer through fall, before seasonal rains begin. Crabbers with boats set their gear in the lower river, downstream from the bridge. Those without boats can drop their baited rings and pots from the docks at the Port of Gold Beach.

The Rogue has been famous as an angling destination for the better part of a century. Probably no other Oregon river has attracted more celebrities to its banks, including authors, movie stars, professional athletes, and political dignitaries. Salmon continue to lure anglers to the Rogue's rich emerald waters and to nearby offshore grounds. The legendary runs of chinook salmon are augmented by angling for summer and winter steelhead, as well as sturgeon, perch, smelt, and an assortment of bottom fish in the lower river. The Rogue offers year-round angling opportunities, with winter steelhead fishing from January through March, spring chinook from April through June, fall chinook and summer steelhead from July through September, fin-clipped coho salmon from September through November, and early winter steelhead in December.

Boaters crossing the Rogue River bar should stay near the north jetty in the 300-foot-wide channel, which is maintained to a depth of 13 feet. Gravel bars and shoal water extend from inside the south jetty toward the channel and can create breakers up to 6 feet high, posing a threat to boaters and anglers. During salmon runs, many small boats crowd into the lower river between the jetties, where anglers like to troll in the channel. An engine can fail anytime, but with fishing lines out it's easy to foul a prop, increasing the likelihood of becoming disabled. Consequently, anyone joining the fleet should have auxiliary power or a stout anchor on board to avoid being swept into dangerous areas.

Year-round angling is not the only attraction the Rogue River holds. Several outfitters offer whitewater raft, kayak, and drift-boat trips down the Rogue with overnight camping on the riverbank or accommodations at various river lodges. Those interested in such trips are advised to plan ahead and book early, as access to the wild section of this designated Wild and Scenic River is strictly regulated and limited.

This road flanks the south bank of the Rogue River, eventually connects with various Forest Service roads, and leads to the town of Agness and beyond. Several campgrounds on the river attract large numbers of campers and anglers every year.

U.S. 101, mile 327.8
County Road 595 (Jerry's Flat Road)

About 7 miles east of Highway 101, on the north side of the road is a Port of Gold Beach facility that includes 60 primitive tent/RV sites with tables and fire rings set in a beautiful mixed forest of conifers, madrone, and myrtlewood trees. There's plenty

Huntley Park and Campground

Little Lobster Creek trickles into the mighty Rogue River, opposite the boat ramp and huge gravel bar at Lobster Creek Campground.

of riverbank access, and boats can be launched and retrieved from the gravel bar. Park amenities include picnic areas, a hiking trail, trash receptacles, showers, and rest rooms with flush toilets. Information: (541) 670-7691.

Lobster Creek Campground

At 9.6 miles east of Highway 101, on the south side of the road, this U.S. Forest Service campground has seven primitive tent/ RV sites with tables and fire pits set in a mixed coniferous/ deciduous forest and a grove of myrtlewood trees. There is also unlimited overflow camping on a huge gravel bar. Other amenities include excellent river access, a paved boat ramp, trash receptacles, recycle bin, and rest rooms with flush toilets and wheelchair access.

Quosatana Forest Service Campground

Lying 14 miles east of Highway 101, along the Rogue River, is one of the finest and best-maintained Forest Service campgrounds to be found. Here, visitors will find 43 primitive tent/RV sites with tables and fire rings scattered throughout a huge grove of myrtlewood trees rimmed by a forest of mixed conifers and hardwoods. There's also overflow camping on a large adjacent gravel bar. Among the park's many features are a nature trail, excellent river access, paved boat ramp, plenty of trailer parking, fish-cleaning station, trash receptacles, recycle bin, and rest rooms with flush toilets and wheelchair access.

U.S. 101, mile 327.8 to mile 330 Gold Beach (zip code 97444)

Gold in the black-sand beaches of Curry County is responsible for attracting fortune seekers to the coast near the mouth of the Rogue River in the mid-nineteenth century, but it's the river that drew settlers and enticed them to stay. And it's the river that continues to attract visitors by the droves to the town of Gold Beach.

The placer miners showed up a quarter of a century after the Jedediah Smith Exploring Expedition made its fateful trek up the coast from California in 1828. By 1853, hordes of miners were sluicing and panning untold tons of beach sand in search of the glittering precious metal. Within a decade, however, the gold rush was already a bygone era, and salmon fishing began to take over as the area's principal industry. According to one source, Rogue River salmon runs were so dense in the 1850s that early settlers had difficulty keeping their horses from spooking when crossing the river. The commercial fishery flourished from the 1870s until the early 1900s—a period when R.D. Hume earned his title of "salmon king" of the Rogue. During the last twenty years of the nineteenth century, Hume's cannery packed an average of sixteen thousand cases of salmon a year. In a single year, he also salted 107,000 pounds of salmon in barrels. Ultimately, the great salmon runs dwindled to a trickle, and in order to salvage and restore them, the state closed the river to commercial fishing in 1935.

Today, the commercial fishery is beyond the breakers, but the Rogue remains the main attraction at Gold Beach, followed closely by broad beaches that extend north and south from the mouth of the river. Upriver lodges and wilderness trails are other attractions that keep people coming to this part of the south coast.

Gold Beach is a small community (population: 2,150), but more than fifteen motels, a number of wilderness resorts, riverside campgrounds and RV parks, and plenty of restaurants to fit every appetite attest to its popularity among travelers. The area easily satisfies a variety of tastes and desires, with facilities ranging from full-service resorts near ocean beaches to Spartan campsites in the upriver benchlands, from burger joints and pizza parlors to restaurants serving some of the best steaks and seafood on the Oregon coast. Add to all this the miles of ocean beaches and nearby state parks, subtract heavy traffic and dense crowds, and Gold Beach shakes out as a good choice for an enjoyable day trip, a relaxing weekend, or an exciting vacation.

Just south of the bridge, turn south on Harbor Way to reach the port, waterfront, restaurants, gift shops, charter operations, funcycle and kayak rentals, and more. At the east end of the port, on the south bank of the river, stop at the interpretive display to learn about the Rogue River Bridge. Information: (541) 247-6269.

U.S. 101, mile 328.1
Port of Gold Beach

In the water near the bridge interpretive display is the rotting hulk of a once-proud ship, built by R. D. Hume and named after his wife. The boat was built in Gold Beach in 1880 and served

Mary D. Hume

Once-proud Mary—the Mary D. Hume at her final resting place on the lower Rogue River, at Gold Beach.

until 1978 in various capacities, including cannery tender, tugboat, and coastal steamer. After a long absence, she was returned to Gold Beach to be renovated as a tourist attraction, but was irreparably damaged and sank at her moorage, where she remains, partly submerged and listing to starboard.

Jerry's Rogue Jets

Go west on Harbor way 0.1 mile to the booking office for this jet-boat tour operation. In business since 1958, Jerry's runs 64-mile, 80-mile, and 104-mile round-trip excursions through the Rogue River canyon. Boats leave the docks daily between 8:00 and 8:30 a.m. from May through October and twice a day from July through Labor Day, with lunch or dinner at the turnaroud. Overnight packages are available, with lodging at Half Moon Bar Lodge or Paradise Bar Lodge. Information: (541) 247-4571 or (800) 451-3645.

Jerry's River Museum and Gift Shop

✔
MUST STOP

Go west on harbor Way 0.1 mile to reach this small but surprisingly superb free museum that features professionally prepared and displayed historical photographs and artifacts from the Indian and pioneer days on the Rogue River. Learn about the cultural and natural history of the Rogue, including transportation and the salmon industry, with a short but entertaining and educational *must stop*. The museum is open daily: from April through October, 7:00 a.m. to 9:00 p.m., and 8:00 a.m. to 6:00 p.m. the rest of the year. Winter hours may vary. Information: (541) 247-4571.

Port of Gold Beach Marina

Drive west 0.2 mile on Harbor Way, and watch for signs to the marina, where boaters will find temporary moorage, transient-moorage slips, an excellent fish-cleaning station, picnic tables, and rest rooms with flush toilets and wheelchair access. This is a good spot to enjoy a picnic, watch the waterfront activities, and record it all on film.

Turn west off the highway, and take Harbor Way 0.3 mile, turn right, and follow the signs to a two-lane paved ramp with dock and nearby rest rooms with flush toilets.

Port of Gold Beach Boat Ramp

Drive west 0.4 mile on Harbor Way, go right on Moore Street 0.1 mile, right on Airport Way 0.1 mile, then left and 0.3 mile to the south jetty parking area. There's easy access to the jetty for fishing, sightseeing, and wildlife watching, as well as to the driftwood-strewn beach for hiking, beach combing, and other activities.

South Jetty and beach

The museum is on the west side of the highway at the north end of the fairgrounds parking lot; the annex is on the east side. The main museum features cultural and natural-history displays that portray the early days of Curry County and what is now Gold Beach, including Indian history and craft work. Exhibits in the annex depict the gold-mining, timber, and fishing eras with historic photographs and artifacts. The museum and annex are open Tuesday through Saturday, from 10:00 a.m. to 4:00 p.m. Information: (541) 247-6113.

U.S. 101, mile 329.4
Curry County Historical Museum and annex

Turn west off the highway at the south end of the fairgrounds parking lot, and follow the paved road west to the beach parking area with adjacent foot and equestrian trails to the low dunes and beach. This small park also has benches, picnic tables, and a trash receptacle.

Beach and equestrian access

The center, on the east side of the highway, has a foyer with racks of maps, guides, and brochures that's open 24 hours a day. For answers to questions about Curry County and the Gold Beach area, stop by during business hours: Monday through Friday, 8:00 a.m. to 5:00 p.m.

U.S. 101, mile 329.6
Gold Beach Chamber of Commerce Visitor Center

The U.S. Forest Service shares quarters with the Gold Beach Chamber of Commerce. Stop here for information about and maps of the Siskiyou National Forest, trails, and wilderness areas. The Curry County Map handed out free at various visitor centers leaves a lot to be desired, so those planning to drive the back roads in and near the Coast Range should pick up a copy of the Siskiyou National Forest Map, which is far superior and available for a nominal fee. The office is open Monday through Friday, from 8:00 a.m. to 5:00 p.m.

Gold Beach Ranger District

**U.S. 101,
mile 329.8**
South Beach Park

Turn west off the highway at the south end of town into a large paved parking lot suitable for all recreational vehicles. Paved and gravel paths with wheelchair access lead a short distance to the beach.

**U.S. 101,
mile 330.2**
Hunter Creek

The lower reaches of this small stream are open for chinook-salmon fishing from October through December and steelhead angling from January through March. Despite its diminutive size, Hunter Creek gives up some decent fish every year. Access east of Highway 101 is via Hunter Creek Road.

**U.S. 101,
mile 330.6**
Parking and beach access

A large paved parking area on the west side of the highway is adjacent to easy trails leading to the sand beach, tide pools, and mouth of Hunter Creek.

**U.S. 101,
mile 331.1**
County Road 635
(Hunter Creek Road)

This road leads east off the highway, follows Hunter Creek, and provides some bank access for several miles.

**U.S. 101,
mile 334.8**
Cape Sebastian State
Scenic Corridor

Turn west to reach two parking lots and viewpoints that are more than 200 feet above the ocean. The north viewpoint offers a good view seaward and is an excellent spot for observing gray whales during their winter and spring migrations. The southern viewpoint offers spectacular views and excellent photographic opportunities, making this a *must stop*. From here on a clear day the view north extends 43 miles to include Humbug Mountain;

The view south from Cape Sebastian.

the 50-mile south view takes in northern California and Point Saint George Lighthouse. Hike the 1.5-mile trail to the cape for more great views and photo possibilities. Keep watch along the edges of the dense Sitka spruce forest for the abundant brush rabbits, especially early and late in the day. There's access to the Oregon Coast Trail from the south parking area. A chemical toilet is located roadside between the two parking areas.

MUST STOP

A large paved parking area stands on the west side of the highway and provides access to several trails to the beach, the easiest of which is at the south end of the parking area. The trails lead to Myers Beach, a wide strand of sand and tide pools with many nearshore rocks and sea stacks providing a background for seascape photography. From here to Pistol River the nearshore ocean is a popular area for windsurfing and a good place to photograph the colorful sailboards as they race with the wind.

U.S. 101, mile 336.4
Viewpoint and beach access

A large gravel parking area with easy access to Myers Beach and tide pools is at the southwest end of the bridge. With nearshore rocks and sea stacks providing interesting details, the views north and south include photo possibilities.

U.S. 101, mile 336.8
Myers Creek

On the west side of the highway is a large paved parking area that's part of Pistol River State Park, where there's access to the beach and superb views and photo opportunities to the north, south, and west.

U.S. 101, mile 337.3
Myers Beach viewpoint and access

A large gravel parking area on the west side of the highway provides easy access to low dunes and the beach.

U.S. 101, mile 337.6
Parking and beach access

On the west side of the highway is a small gravel parking area and chemical toilet. A nearby trail through the dunes leads to the beach and tide pools.

U.S. 101, mile 338
Parking and beach access

A small gravel parking area on the west side of the highway offers an excellent view of low dunes and small lagoons that attract a variety of waterfowl and other birds, especially during the winter.

U.S. 101, mile 338.2
Viewpoint

The story couldn't be any simpler: a militia soldier named James Mace lost his pistol in the river in 1853, and the small stream has been known as Pistol River ever since. The river is bar bound during the summer months, so fish migrations can't commence until after fall rains sufficient to raise stream levels enough to break through the sandbar. The river is open for chinook fishing from October through December, with most fish taken in November. Although the river is open for steelhead much of

U.S. 101, mile 339
Pistol River

Myers Creek Beach at Pistol River State Park.

the year, most of the action takes place from December through February. The season for fin-clipped rainbow trout (half-pounders) runs from November through March. County Road 690 runs east off Highway 101 along the north bank of the river for several miles before linking up with Forest Service roads and provides some bank access. Bank access near the mouth, in the vicinity of Highway 101, is also good.

Viewpoint and river mouth access

At the northwest end of the Pistol River Bridge is a large gravel parking area with an excellent view and access to the mouth of the river. A historical marker on site tells about local skirmishes during the Rogue Indian Wars of 1853-56.

U.S. 101, mile 339.2
Pistol River State Scenic Viewpoint

South of the Pistol River Bridge, turn west into a large paved parking lot with easy access to low dunes, deflation-plain wetlands, and sand beach. This is a superb birding area with resident wading birds and shorebirds joined by flocks of migratory waterfowl from fall through spring. Opportunities for scenic and wildlife photography abound.

U.S. 101, mile 339.6
Pistol River/ Carpenterville Road, north access

This stretch of the Old Coast Highway loops east off the highway, climbs into the forested foothills, and rejoins Highway 101 at mile 354.8 at the north end of Brookings. Along the way, it offers travelers several stunning ocean views, particularly at sunset. Roadside parking is limited along the narrow, winding road, so it's not the best choice for travel trailers or large motorhomes.

A small gravel parking area on the west side of the highway provides a view to the south of the rocky Curry County coastline and ocean. Growth of young trees along the edge of the parking area has obscured the view somewhat. There are still good photo opportunities, but the view could be completely blocked in a few years if the trees and shrubs aren't trimmed.

U.S. 101, mile 343.1
Viewpoint

This long, narrow park, encompassing a strip of steep, forested coastline overlooking pocket beaches, cliffs, and nearshore islands, sea stacks, and rocks was named after Oregon's first parks superintendent. Nowhere on the West Coast is there a more scenic 9-mile stretch of Highway 101, with one *must-stop* viewpoint after another.

A small gravel parking area on the west side of the highway at the north entrance to the park commands a spectacular view north of the rocky shoreline and ocean and offers superb photographic opportunities. From this point on, the view changes around every bend, with opportunities for travelers to park and savor the unsurpassed wonders of the south coast, photograph unusual rock formations, hike through forests of 300-year-old Sitka spruce trees, or enjoy a quiet picnic at the precipitous edge of the continent.

U.S. 101, mile 344.1 to 353.3
Samuel H. Boardman State Scenic Corridor

MUST STOP

A large gravel parking area on the west side of the highway offers superb seaward views of the rocky, rugged coastline and a small pocket beach, with trees to enhance photographic composition. Grasses dry up and turn brown here in the summer and fall. They green up again in the spring and early summer when they're dotted with wildflowers. During the early morning on sunny days, ephemeral fog often enhances the scene and changes the mood from moment to moment.

U.S. 101, mile 344.6
Arch Rock Viewpoint

On the west side of the highway, a large paved parking lot lies adjacent to a grassy, wooded picnic area on the edge of cliffs overlooking the rocky coastline. A paved path leads to Arch Rock Point and more views and photo opportunities. There are picnic tables, a trash receptacle, and vault toilets with wheelchair access.

U.S. 101, mile 344.8
Arch Rock Point Picnic Area and Viewpoint

A gravel parking area on the west side of the highway overlooks the unusual nearshore island with its spruce crewcut. From the parking lot, there's access to the Oregon Coast Trail.

U.S. 101, mile 345
Spruce Island Viewpoint

A fair-sized gravel parking area on the west side of the highway overlooks a small scenic cove, provides a good vantage point for watching gray whales during their winter and spring migrations, and connects with the Oregon Coast Trail.

U.S. 101, mile 345.8
Thunder Rock Cove Scenic Viewpoint

**U.S. 101,
mile 345.9**
Natural Bridges Cove
Viewpoint

On the west side of the highway, a short paved and gravel path leads south from the south end of the parking lot less than 100 yards to a wooden viewing platform overlooking the bridges, which are unusual nearshore rock formations. The small viewpoint offers good photo opportunities and access to the Oregon Coast Trail.

**U.S. 101,
mile 346.5**
Viewpoint

One small and one mid-size gravel parking area on the west side of the highway provide a view of the cliffs dropping vertically to the ocean.

**U.S. 101,
mile 347.8**
Thomas Creek Bridge

From highway level, this modern, unimposing, 956-foot-long structure seems an ordinary bridge over an ordinary ravine. But the ravine turns out to be deep, very deep, and the bridge, supported on steel-frame towers and concrete piers, stands 345 feet above it, making it the highest bridge in Oregon. A gravel parking area with a view of the bridge and trail access is at the southwest end of the bridge.

*The view north from
Indian Sands
Viewpoint, Samuel H.
Boardman State Park.*

Turn west, and drive 0.1 mile to a large gravel parking lot. From here is a terrific view north of the rugged coastline and offshore rocks, with other great views along the nearby stretch of the Oregon Coast Trail.

U.S. 101, mile 348.4
Indian Sands Viewpoint

Turn west off the highway, and drive 0.2 mile to a lovely picnic spot overlooking the sand beach, mouth of a small creek, and Whaleshead Rock. Picnic tables are situated in shaded and open grassy areas. Vault toilets are nearby. There's easy access to the beach and the Oregon Coast Trail.

U.S. 101, mile 349.2
Whaleshead Beach State Park

On the west side of the highway, a gravel parking area provides good seaward views, photo opportunities, and access to the Oregon Coast Trail.

U.S. 101, mile 349.7
Whaleshead Viewpoint

Turn west off the highway, and drive 0.3 mile to the gravel parking area overlooking House Rock and the rocky shoreline and providing access to the Oregon Coast Trail.

U.S. 101, mile 351.2
House Rock Viewpoint

Turn west, and drive 0.1 mile to a small paved parking lot with a good seaward view and access to the Oregon Coast Trail. This is a good spot in winter and spring for watching migrating gray whales.

U.S.101, mile 351.9
Cape Ferrelo Viewpoint

**U.S. 101,
mile 352.6**
Lone Ranch State
Park

Turn west, and drive 0.2 mile down the grassy hill to the parking and picnic areas overlooking a beautiful pocket beach with rocks and sea stacks in and beyond the surf. At low tide there are tide pools to explore. Park amenities include oceanfront picnic tables, fire rings, and vault toilets with wheelchair access.

**U.S. 101,
mile 353.7**
Rainbow Rock
Viewpoint

A large paved parking area on the west side of the highway commands a great seaward view. On clear days, the Point Saint George Lighthouse is visible to the southwest.

**U.S. 101,
mile 354.4 to
mile 357.7
Brookings**
(zip code 97415)

Brookings (population: 5,620) is Curry County's largest city, but Harbor, its unincorporated neighbor, is even larger, with nearly eight thousand residents. More than half the people living here are retirees, drawn to the area's pleasant climate, scenic splendor, and abundant opportunities for outdoor recreation. The same features attract many visitors each year, from inland and up-coast communities as well as from out of state.

Several geological features combine here to create a phenomenon meteorologists refer to as the "Brookings Effect" and what everybody else simply calls nice weather. Brookings is often the hottest spot on the Oregon coast, and during the winter months frequently records the highest temperatures in the state, sometimes in the balmy 70s and 80s, even in January and February. The same mild, frost-free climate that keeps flowers blooming all year and gives Brookings its nickname—"Home of Winter Flowers"—also coaxes people to the beaches, parks, and hiking trails with which Oregon's south coast is so well endowed.

Highway 101, already on a southeasterly tack between Cape Ferrelo and the mouth of the Winchuck River, swings almost due east in downtown Brookings, crosses the Chetco River, then bends back westerly to resume its southeast course. Brookings lies northwest and Harbor southeast of the river, but the two share facilities and for all practical purposes are one metropolitan area. Shops, stores, galleries, restaurants, and overnight accommodations are scattered throughout the area but are mainly concentrated along or near Highway 101. In recent years, a number of new shops, galleries, and restaurants have opened at and near the Port of Brookings Harbor, where there are also several RV parks, ocean beach, an oceanfront motel, and full-service marina.

**U.S. 101,
mile 354.8**
Pistol River/
Carpenterville Road,
south access

Also known as the Old Coast Highway, this road exits east off Highway 101. It wends its way north, parallel to but well above the newer coast route, and rejoins U.S. 101 near the mouth of the Pistol River at mile 339.6. The two routes make a good loop trip that can last from two hours to all day, depending on the number of stops along the way for sightseeing, hiking, picnicking, picture-taking.

Harris Beach is one of the most popular and interesting stretches of shoreline on the Oregon coast, with the sand beach and surf punctuated by rocks and sea stacks, perfect for sunset photography. Bird Island, the largest of Oregon's islands, stands offshore as part of the Oregon Islands National Wildlife Refuge and is a breeding site for seabirds, including tufted puffins. Low tide exposes tide pools to view and photograph, but most are within the Harris Beach Marine Garden, which is closed to the taking of shellfish and marine invertebrates, except for single mussels, which may be taken for bait.

U.S. 101, mile 355.7
Harris Beach State Recreation Area

The day-use area parking lot lies within steps of the beach, and there is easy access to the beach and rocky intertidal areas, some of the most scenic picnic spots to be found anywhere, trash receptacles, and rest rooms with flush toilets and wheelchair access. The campground has 34 full-hookup sites, 52 sites with water and electricity, 63 primitive tent sites with water nearby, and six yurts, each with paved parking, picnic table, and fire ring. One of the sites with water and electricity and one yurt have wheelchair access. Other amenities include a hiker/biker camp, firewood, hiking trails, beach trail, nature trail, bike path, dump station, recycle bin, trash receptacles, showers, and rest rooms with flush toilets.

Information: (541) 469-2021 or (800) 551-6949. Reservations: (800) 452-5687.

East of the highway a large paved parking area and parklike rest area greet visitors with big trees, rhododendrons, azaleas, and open grassy areas with picnic tables set here and there. Other

Oregon State Welcome Center and Rest Area

The Brookings coastline

features include an information kiosk stocked with travel brochures, an RV dump station, trash receptacles, drinking water, and rest rooms with flush toilets and wheelchair access. A staffed visitor center is open during the summer months. This is a good spot for a rest break or a picnic in a park protected from the wind.

U.S. 101, mile 357
Chetco Ranger District

Turn east on 5th Street, go one block, and turn north into the parking lot. Stop here to check on current Forest Service road and trail conditions and to pick up a copy of the Siskiyou National Forest Map and other maps and guides to trails, campgrounds, and various attractions on nearby Forest Service lands. The office is open Monday through Friday, from 8:00 a.m. to 4:30 p.m.

U.S. 101, mile 357.8
North Bank Road

Turn east off Highway 101 to reach Azalea Park, Alfred A. Loeb State Park, boat ramps and access points along the Chetco River, campgrounds, trails, and other attractions in the Siskiyou National Forest and Siskiyou Mountains. (Use the Siskiyou National Forest Map.)

Azalea Park

Turn east off Highway 101, drive 0.1 mile, turn left on Park Road, and follow it around the curve to the right to reach the park entrance. Brookings is well known for its azaleas, some of which were mature shrubs when Lewis and Clark wintered on the north coast in 1805-06. About 1,100 wild azaleas thrive in Azalea Park, which was dedicated as a park in 1939. After years of budget restraints and neglect, the state relinquished the park to the city in 1992. It was obvious that reclaiming the land and restoring the park would take more than city coffers allowed and would have to be left to volunteers—more than 1,500 local residents and businesses who donated time, money, and materials to transform the aging park into a *must-stop* showcase. Now sidewalks meander through the azaleas, rhododendrons, flowering trees, and beds of flowers. The park has lovely picnic spots, a covered stage for concerts, a volunteer-built playground called KidTown that's every child's fantasy kingdom, and rest rooms with flush toilets and wheelchair access. Although the peak bloom period can occur anytime from late April to early June, something is in flower here all year.

Turn east off Highway 101, drive 0.1 mile, turn right, and continue on North Bank Road for 7.4 miles to the park entrance, on the south side of the road. This fine park is nestled in a grove of myrtlewood trees along the north bank of the Chetco River. The campground has 53 campsites with water and electrical hookups, paved parking, picnic tables, and fire rings; one site has wheelchair access. There are three riverfront log cabins with lights, heat, and beds with mattresses. The park also has a dump station, firewood, trash receptacles, recycle bin, showers, and rest rooms with flush toilets. The day-use area has a parking lot, riverfront picnic area with tables, gravel-bar access, and drift-boat launch and haul-out site. A 0.75-mile trail leads along the river to the northernmost redwood grove in the United States. Information: (541) 469-2021 or (800) 551-6949. Reservations: (800) 452-5687.

Alfred A. Loeb State Park

Rising in the Kalmiopsis Wilderness and coursing through more than 40 miles of mountains and foothills, the Chetco River washes great beds of gravel and nurtures the salmon and steelhead spawned there annually. Its unsullied waters gain volume and lose velocity as they spill toward the ocean.

U.S. 101, mile 357.9
Chetco River

Although not as famous as the Rogue River, the Chetco is an excellent salmon and steelhead stream, popular for both bank angling and drift-boat fishing. Fall chinook may move into the lower river in September, but the run normally peaks in October, with some big fish taken every year. Fall rains bring the steelhead in, and fishing for them runs from December through March, when the season ends.

The Chetco may well be the ideal drift-boat river, not only because of the generally good angling, but also because of its ease of navigation and sheer beauty. It passes through old-growth Sitka spruce forests, groves of Oregon myrtle, and the only stand of redwoods in Oregon. Whether the fish cooperate or not, a float trip down the Chetco is an experience to cherish.

Salmon Run Golf and Wilderness Preserve

At the mouth of the river, fishing near or from the south jetty and public fishing dock produces catches of surfperch, rockfish, cabezon, and lingcod. Offshore, the angling is seasonally good for salmon and a variety of bottom fishes. For those who bring their own boats, there's an excellent launch ramp and full-service marina at the Port of Brookings Harbor. Those without boats will find charter craft working out of the port and running trips for salmon, bottom fish, tuna, and whale watching. The harbor is a short run from the ocean over a jetty-protected bar. Locals boast of having one of the safest bar crossings on the coast, and many commercial fishermen and other experienced boaters have validated that claim.

U.S. 101, mile 358.1
Salmon Run Golf and Wilderness Preserve

Turn east on South Bank Chetco River Road, and drive 3.2 miles to the entrance, on the south side of the road. This beautiful, 6,590-yard, 18-hole, par-72 course set in the forested hills along Jack Creek may be unique in all golfdom. Where else might golfers repeatedly cross a stream full of spawning salmon and or share their outdoor experience with Roosevelt elk, black bears, and wild turkeys? This challenging and exciting course, which opened the first nine holes in 1999, is kind to beginners and tough on pros, with yardages ranging from 4,837 to 6,590 and five sets of tees to fit every level of expertise. Amenities include a driving range, putting green, practice green, clubhouse, pro shop, resident pro, electric-cart rental, club rental, bar, and grill. Pro shop: (541) 469-4888.

U.S. 101, mile 358.1
Port of Brookings Harbor

Turn west off Highway 101 to reach shops, restaurants, visitor center, RV parks, the beach, a public fishing dock, rest rooms, charter boats, boat ramp, and a full-service marina. Information: (541) 469-2218 or 469-7962.

Turn west on Lower Harbor Road, drive 0.2 mile, and turn north (right) at the Port of Brookings Harbor sign. In addition to a six-lane paved boat ramp, the facility includes a paved parking lot, fish-cleaning station, drinking water, and rest rooms with flush toilets and wheelchair access.

Port of Brookings Harbor Boat Ramp

Turn west on Lower Harbor Road, and drive 0.3 mile to the chamber parking area on the north side of the road. Some visitor information and literature is available 24 hours a day at a covered information booth. The center is open Monday through Friday, from 8:00 a.m. to 5:00 p.m.

Brookings-Harbor Chamber of Commerce Visitor Center

Turn west on Lower Harbor Road, drive 1 mile to Boat Basin Road, and turn north to reach the park entrance. This port facility, on the beach and Chetco River, has 53 full-hookup sites, 48 of which have cable TV; 36 sites with water and electricity, nine of which have cable TV; 19 primitive RV sites; and 30 primitive tent sites—all with picnic tables. The park also has a tank dump, trash receptacles, Laundromat, restaurant, showers, rest rooms with flush toilets and wheelchair access, and immediate access to the beach, south jetty, and public fishing dock. Information: (541) 469-2021 or (800) 441-0856.

Beachfront RV Park

The Port of Brookings Harbor, near the mouth of the Chetco River.

Beach and South Jetty

Turn west on Lower Harbor Road, drive one mile to Boat Basin Road, turn north (right), bear left at the fork, and continue 0.1 mile to the beach. The jetty lies at the north end of the beach. The beach and jetty are just steps from the parking area, where drinking water and rest rooms with flush toilets and wheelchair access are nearby.

Public fishing dock

Turn west on Lower Harbor Road, drive one mile to Boat Basin Road, turn north (right), bear right at the fork, and continue for 0.4 mile to the parking area adjacent to the fishing dock near the mouth of the Chetco River. There's a chemical toilet with wheelchair access on site.

U.S. 101, mile 360.5
Chetco Valley Historical Society Museum

On the east side of the highway, this little museum, housed in a building that was once the home of a local pioneer family, has displays of pioneer and homestead artifacts, gold-mining equipment, antique furniture, and a collection of historical photographs. Outside the museum stands the world's largest Monterey cypress tree. From Memorial Day through Labor Day, the museum is open Tuesday through Saturday, from 2:00 p.m. to 6:00 p.m., and Sunday, noon to 6:00 p.m. The rest of the year, it's open weekends, from noon to 5:00 p.m. Information: (541) 469-6651.

U.S. 101, mile 362.2
McVay Rock State Recreation Site

Turn west on Oceanview Drive, and proceed 1.3 miles to the park entrance, on the west side of the road. Here, a gravel parking lot and grassy open area stand atop a bluff above a gravel and sand beach. Paths provide easy access to a good spot for beach combing and agate hunting. This is also a popular beach for surf fishing, clam digging, and whale watching.

The public fishing dock, at the base of the south jetty, near the mouth of the Chetco River.

This road exits east off U.S. 101 and follows the north bank of the Winchuck River, leading to some bank access, trails, and several campgrounds.

Winchuck River Road

Turn east on Winchuck River Road, and drive 7.9 miles to the campground entrance, on the south side of the road. This small Forest Service campground has three primitive sites for tents or RVs. Each site has a table, and one has a fire ring with a grate. There's a chemical toilet, trash receptacle, and bank access.

First Camp

Take Winchuck River Road east for 8.4 miles to where the road forks, bear left, and continue another 1.3 miles to the campground entrance. Here, visitors will find seven primitive sites for tents and RVs in a beautiful forest setting. Each site has a table and fire ring with a grate. The Forest Service facility also has a picnic area with tables, drinking water, vault toilets with wheelchair access, and a hiking trail along the river.

Ludlum Campground

Drive east on Winchuck River Road 8.4 miles, bear right at the fork, and continue 0.1 mile to the campground, on the north side of the road, and the day-use area, on the south side. This Forest Service campground has 15 primitive campsites, several of which are pull-throughs, for tents or RVs, each with a table and fire ring with grate. The facility, set in a mixed forest of conifers and hardwoods, also has drinking water, and rest rooms with flush toilets. The day-use area has picnic tables and a trail along the river.

Winchuck Campground

West of the highway, at the north end of the bridge, is a gravel road that leads a short distance to a gravel parking area and turnaround on the north bank of the Winchuck, near the river's mouth. From here, it's an easy walk to the beach, popular for fishing, beach combing, and clam digging.

U.S. 101, mile 362.6 Winchuck State Recreation Site

This little stream gets runs of chinook salmon and steelhead and is a local favorite for trout fishing during the spring and fall. Fall chinook enter the river in October and may be taken through December, when the season ends. Steelhead angling is mainly from December through March and the season closure. Anglers on the Winchuck must fish from the bank or by wading, because fishing from a boat or any device capable of supporting an angler is prohibited.

Winchuck River

Northbound travelers may slow down now and enjoy the pace and spectacular beauty of the Oregon coast. Southbound travelers should take the first opportunity to turn around, and head back north to revisit all their favorite places and check out any of the great attractions they missed.

U.S. 101, mile 363.1 Oregon/California Border

Information

Brookings-Harbor Chamber of Commerce
16330 Lower Harbor Road
P.O. Box 940
Brookings, OR 97415
(541) 469-3181
(800) 535-9469
E-mail: chamber@wave.net
URL: www.brookingsor.com

Chetco Ranger District
555 5th Street
Brookings, OR 97415
(541) 469-2196
URL: www.fs.fed.us/r6/siskiyou

Gold Beach Chamber of Commerce
29279 Ellensburg Avenue #3
Gold Beach, OR 97444
(541) 247-7526
(800) 525-9469
E-mail: goldbeach@harborside.com
URL: www.harborside.com/gb

Gold Beach Ranger District
29279 Ellensburg Avenue
Gold Beach, OR 97444
(541) 247-3600
URL: www.fs.fed.us/r6/siskiyou

Port of Brookings Harbor
16408 Lower Harbor Road
Brookings, OR 97415
(541) 469-2218
(541) 469-7962

Port of Gold Beach
P.O. Box 1126
Gold Beach, OR 97444
(541) 247-6269

Port of Port Orford
P.O. Box 490
Port Orford, OR 97465
(541) 332-7121

Port Orford Chamber of Commerce
P.O. Box 637
Port Orford, OR 97465
(541) 332-8055
(541) 332-4106 Visitor Center

U.S. Coast Guard
Chetco River Lifeboat Station
Brookings, OR 97415
(541) 469-3885
(541) 469-4571 Weather and Bar
    Conditions

Marine mammals that forage in Oregon's coastal waters include members of the order Cetacea and the suborder Pinnipedia. So-called cetaceans include the whales, dolphins, and porpoises. Among Oregon's pinnipeds are several species of seals and sea lions.

Sometimes, marine mammals that may have died for any of a variety of reasons wash up on shore. Occasionally, live animals become stranded on beaches or in shallow intertidal waters. In either case, anyone who encounters a beached carcass or a stranded live animal should immediately notify the proper authorities. Scientists may be interested in performing a necropsy on a dead marine mammal to determine the cause of death or learn more about the animal. A stranded live animal could be rescued and returned to the sea. In some instances, injured or otherwise distressed marine mammals may be rehabilitated, then returned to the wild.

Cetacean Strandings

Whales, dolphins, and porpoises die of old age, disease, injury, and predation and sometimes end up on beaches around the world. Live individuals—and even groups, known as pods or herds—can get disoriented in nearshore waters and become stranded and disabled on shore or in shallow coastal waters.

Some species, including right whales and common porpoises, usually become stranded as individuals. Mass strandings of other species, such as sperm whales and pilot whales, have occurred worldwide. In one such event on the Oregon coast, 41 sperm whales were beached near Florence in July 1979. Reasons for strandings are unclear, but may result from one or several of various factors.

Scientists have found some stranded cetaceans to be suffering from inner-ear infections, others from brain parasites. Such afflictions may disorient the animals or interfere with their ability to navigate by echo location.

In rough seas, an individual may stray too near shore or shallow water, where it could touch bottom and become panicked. If it is traveling in a group or pod, its distress calls may lure others nearby, where the entire pod becomes endangered and may be beached.

The physical makeup of the coastline itself can pose threats. Cetaceans wandering into bays or estuaries with narrow entrances can become disoriented and feel trapped, only to end up beached while searching for an escape route. Along open ocean beaches, the gently sloping bottom can interfere with cetaceans' echo-sounding pulses, disorient the creatures, and ultimately leave them high and dry on the beach.

Marauding pods of killer whales, stalking and chasing small whales and dolphins, may panic their prey, forcing them shoreward and onto the beach. Killer whales themselves are able to run right up onto shore in pursuit of cetaceans and pinnipeds, then use their powerful bodies, fins, and flukes to return safely to the sea.

Stranded Marine Mammals

Cetaceans also can become entangled in crabbing gear, fishing lines, and nets, which can impede their activities or even lead to their death. Injuries, sometimes fatal, can result from gear entanglement, collisions with vessels, and attacks by sharks or killer whales.

Gray whales also occasionally show up in seemingly unlikely places, such as the upper reaches of bays or well up the tidewater stretches of coastal rivers. As recently as the summer of 2000, a gray whale cruised into Catching Slough, off the Coos River, east of Coos Bay. It stayed for a couple of days, amusing locals, before heading back to the ocean. Some years ago, a gray whale cow and calf ascended the Siuslaw River all the way to Mapleton, near the head of tide, where they lingered for several days. Camera crews and crowds of onlookers watched the pair as they swam, rolled, breached, blew, and appeared to brush against the steep river banks. Eventually, they descended the river, crossed the Siuslaw River bar, and returned to sea.

Scientists believe this seemingly unusual behavior may have a practical and beneficial purpose. They surmise that gray whales periodically enter fresh water to kill irritating marine parasites and other organisms infesting their skin. Rubbing against shoreline roots, branches, and other structure may help to dislodge parasites and encrusted barnacles.

Although whales encountered in these freshwater environments may seem to be out of their element, they are usually not endangered. Nevertheless, they could become disoriented or entrapped in shallows at low tide. So it's a good idea to notify authorities who can keep an eye on the creatures and ensure that they eventually make a safe return to the ocean.

Pinniped Strandings

Like whales, dolphins, and porpoises, seals and sea lions forage in Oregon's coastal waters. Unlike cetaceans, however, when pinnipeds aren't hunting for food, they beach themselves, or haul out, on rocks, exposed reefs, jetties, breakwaters, islands, and secluded shores to rest, molt, mate, bear offspring, and suckle their young. The vast majority of pinnipeds on land belong there. They are not stranded.

Like cetaceans, however, pinnipeds also die of old age, disease, and injuries and sometimes wash up on shore. Occasionally, diseased, injured, or otherwise distressed or dying individuals, perhaps too weak to swim or fend for themselves, come ashore or intentionally beach themselves. Such hapless creatures may be at once vulnerable to terrestrial dangers while posing threats to humans and pets. Pinnipeds bite and can carry diseases that may be transmitted to people and other animals.

Any person who finds a dead or obviously stranded seal or sea lion should immediately notify authorities. Many apparently stranded pinnipeds, however, aren't stranded at all, but are on land for good reasons.

Elephant seals, for example, spend weeks on shore during their annual molt. As the animal sheds, it looks terrible, may even appear injured or diseased, and is probably very grumpy. There's nothing anyone can do for it, except to allow it some space and leave it alone, as one might do with any human having a bad hair day.

Anyone who spends much time hiking Oregon's coastline during spring and early summer stands a good chance of coming across a harbor seal pup on the beach. Mother seals often deposit their pups there while they go off to forage in nearby waters. Pups that have been weaned and left to their own devices frequently haul out on beaches to rest.

Perhaps because they aren't as shy or wary of humans as adult seals, or maybe because they're just too weak or tired to escape, seal pups are easy to approach. People should avoid the temptation, though, because it is illegal and could prove harmful to the young seal.

The electronic media along the coast make frequent public-service broadcasts, warning people to leave seal pups alone. Nevertheless, every year, well-meaning but misguided people, assuming the pups have been abandoned, carry them off to police stations, wildlife-agency offices, and animal shelters, only to learn that they have broken the law and may well have caused the pups' eventual death.

What to Do About Stranded Marine Mammals

In the event that you discover a dead marine mammal or a live animal that appears to be stranded, you should notify authorities. Your report should contain all essential information, and you may need to take certain precautions to secure the carcass of a dead animal or protect a live animal from potential dangers.

• Identify the animal. If it's a pinniped, try to determine whether it's a harbor seal, elephant seal, California sea lion, or Steller sea lion. In the case of a cetacean, identify it first as a whale, dolphin, or porpoise, and name it by species if you can. A field guide is handy for such purposes. Note the animal's color, and estimate its size.

• Determine the animal's condition. Is it dead or alive? If dead, does it appear to have died recently, or are there signs of decomposition. If alive, does it appear to be injured? Is it moving freely, perhaps in shallow water? Does its breathing seem normal or labored?

Stranded Marine Mammals

• Determine the animal's location. Be as precise as possible. If the area is one you frequent, pinpoint the animal's location specifically: North Spit of Coos Bay, 50 yards south of the mouth of Henderson Creek. If you're not all that familiar with the area, do your best to name the beach, cove, bay, or general vicinity. Describe any nearby landmarks, and note the animal's distance from them.

• Determine the animal's accessibility. Can authorities, scientists, or rescuers reach it by car, four-wheel-drive vehicle, all-terrain vehicle, or boat? Is it strictly a hike-in site?

• Secure the animal or stranding site. If the animal is dead and in the water, try to prevent it's being washed out by the tide. In the case of a small mammal, such as a harbor seal, try to drag it to a point above the high-tide line. Secure a larger dead mammal with a rope anchored to a boulder, tree, beached log, or other stationary object. If the animal is alive, leave it alone, keep people and dogs away, and wait for authorities to arrive.

Notifying Authorities

Time is of the essence, especially in the case of a stranded live animal, so the sooner you notify authorities the better. Sometimes, this means getting word to the nearest state or federal agency. For example, if you discover a carcass or stranded live marine mammal in a state park, notify park personnel right away. At such places as Cape Perpetua, the Oregon Dunes National Recreation Area, or other facilities managed by the U.S. Forest Service, immediately report your finding to a forest ranger.

In the absence of nearby authorities, phone the nearest office of the Oregon State Police or one of the following toll-free hotlines:

Oregon State Police: (800) 452-7888

NOAA 24-hour hotline: (800) 853-1964

Informative Publications

Two helpful publications produced by Oregon State University Marine Mammal Program and Oregon Sea Grant are available at several places on the Oregon coast. The brochures, written by Dr. Bruce Mate et al. and illustrated by Pieter A. Folkens, are printed on durable plastic stock that's waterproof and won't smudge or tear, making them ideal for carrying in a pack or parka pocket in any weather.

"Marine Mammals of the Eastern North Pacific" covers all fifty species of marine mammals that inhabit this part of the Pacific Ocean, from southern Alaska to the Hawaiian Islands and Sea of Cortez. It provides excellent color illustrations of and information about sea otters, seals, sea lions, dolphins, porpoises, and whales, including their distribution, migrations, behavior, habitat preferences, and identifying characteristics. The brochure also describes the Marine Mammal Program at Oregon State University.

"Marine Mammals on the Beach" informs readers about when and how to respond to apparent strandings of marine mammals. It tells how to determine whether or not mammals are, in fact, stranded and how to act if they are. It provides useful tips on what to do and what not to do in the rare event of an actual stranding.

Both brochures are available for a fee at the following locations on the Oregon coast:

Cape Meares Lighthouse, Oceanside

Inn at Spanish Head, Lincoln City

Oregon Coast Aquarium Store, Depoe Bay

Beverly Beach State Park, Newport

Yaquina Head Outstanding Natural Area, Newport

Yaquina Bay Lighthouse, Newport

Oregon Coast Aquarium, Newport

OSU Hatfield Marine Science Center, Newport

South Beach State Park, Newport

Alsea Bay Bridge Interpretive Center, Waldport

Sea Lion Caves, north of Florence

Shore Acres State Park, south of Charleston

Cape Blanco State Park, north of Port Orford

Harris Beach State Recreation Area, Brookings

Informative Web Sites

A number of organizations and agencies headquartered in various parts of the world provide a wealth of information about marine mammals, including strandings and what to do about them. Those interested in learning more should visit the following sites on the World Wide Web:

Georgia Museum of Natural History
www.museum.nhm.uga.edu/mnhnews/
  marmam3.html

Marine and Coastal Species Information
  System
www.fwie.fw.vt.edu/WWW/macsis/
  mammals.htm

Marine Mammal Stranding Center
www.mmsc.org

National Marine Fisheries Service
www.nmfs.noaa.gov

National Marine Mammal Laboratory
www.nmml01.afsc.noaa.gov

Oregon Department of Fish and Wildlife
www.dfw.state.or.us

Oregon Parks and Recreation Department
www.whalespoken.org/enpmm.html

Oregon State University Marine Mammal
  Program
www.hmsc.orst.edu/groups/
  marinemammal/index.html

Tasmania Parks and Wildlife Service
www.parks.tas.gov.au/wildlife/Care/
  whstrand.html

Texas Marine Mammal Stranding Network
www.tmmc.org/whatyou.htm

WhaleNet Internet Resource List
www.whale.wheelock.edu/whalenet-stuff/
  interwhale.html

Bibliography

Learning about the cultural and natural history of the Oregon coast significantly contributes to the enjoyment of any trip to the coast. Following are some books that are sure to enlighten and entertain any interested reader.

Blair, Csuti, et al. *Atlas of Oregon Wildlife*. Corvallis, Oregon: Oregon State University Press, 1997.

Castle, Darlene, et al. *Yaquina Bay 1778-1978*. Newport, Oregon: The Lincoln County Historical Society, 1979.

Cone, Joseph and Sandy Ridlington, eds. *The Northwest Salmon Crisis: A Documentary History*. Corvallis, Oregon: Oregon State University Press, 1996.

Dicken, Samuel. *Pioneer Trails of the Oregon Coast, 2nd Edition*. Portland, Oregon: Oregon Historical Society, 1978.

Dodge, Orville. *Pioneer History of Coos and Curry Counties*. Bandon, Oregon: Western World Publishers, 1969.

Douthit, Nathan. *A Guide to Oregon South Coast History: Traveling the Jedediah Smith Trail*. Corvallis, Oregon: Oregon State University Press, 1999.

Douthit, Nathan. *The Coos Bay Region 1890-1944: Life on a Coastal Frontier*. Coos Bay, Oregon: River West Books, 1981.

Gibbs, James A. *Pacific Graveyard*. Portland, Oregon: Binfords & Mort, 1973.

Gibbs, James A. *Sentinels of the North Pacific*. Portland, Oregon: Binfords & Mort, Publishers, 1955.

Gibbs, James A. *Shipwrecks of the Pacific Coast*. Portland, Oregon: Binford & Mort, 1957.

Gibbs, James A. *Tillamook Light*. Portland, Oregon: Binford & Mort, 1979.

Guard, Jennifer B. *Wetland Plants of Oregon & Washington*. Redmond, Washington: Lone Pine Publishing, 1995.

Henderson, Bonnie. *120 Hikes on the Oregon Coast, Second Edition*. Seattle: The Mountaineers, 1999.

Johnson, Daniel M., et al. *Atlas of Oregon Lakes*. Corvallis, Oregon: Oregon State University Press, 1985.

Kozloff, Eugene N. *Life of the Northern Pacific Coast: An Illustrated Guide to Northern California, Oregon, Washington, and British Columbia*. Seattle: University of Washington Press, 1983.

Kozloff, Eugene N. *Plants and Animals of the Pacific Northwest: An Illustrated Guide to the Natural History of Western Oregon, Washington, and British Columbia*. Seattle: University of Washington Press, 1976.

Maser, Chris. *Mammals of the Pacific Northwest: From the Coast to the High Cascades*. Corvallis, Oregon: Oregon State University Press, 1998.

Maser, Chris and James R. Sedell. *From the Forest to the Sea: The Ecology of Wood in Streams, Rivers, Estuaries, and Oceans*. Delray Beach, Florida: St. Lucie Press, 1994.

Maser, Chris et al. *Natural History of Oregon Coast Mammals*. U.S. Department of Agriculture, Forest Service, General Technical Report PNW-133, 1981.

McArthur, Lewis A. *Oregon Geographic Names, Fifth Edition*. Portland, Oregon: The Press of the Oregon Historical Society, 1982.

McConnaughey, Bayard H. and Evelyn. *Pacific Coast*. New York: Alfred A. Knopf, 1985.

Miller, Emma Gene. *Clatsop County, Oregon*. Portland, Oregon: Binfords and Mort, 1958.

Netboy, Anthony. *The Columbia River Salmon and Steelhead Trout, Their Fight for Survival*. Seattle: University of Washington Press, 1980.

Nelson, Earl M., ed. *Pioneer History of North Lincoln County, Vol. 1*. McMinnville, Oregon: The Telephone Register Publishing Company, 1951.

Peterson, Emil R. and Alfred Powers. *A Century of Coos and Curry: History of Southwest Oregon*. Coquille, Oregon: Coos-Curry Pioneer and Historical Society, 1977.

Pojar, Jim and Andy MacKinnon. *Plants of the Pacific Northwest Coast: Washington, Oregon, British Columbia & Alaska*. Redmond, Washington: Lone Pine Publishing, 1994.

Ricketts, Edward, et al. *Between Pacific Tides, Fifth Edition*. Stanford, California: Stanford University Press, 1985.

Schultz, Stewart T. *The Northwest Coast: A Natural History*. Portland, Oregon: Timber Press, 1990.

Smith, Dwight A., et al. *Historic Highway Bridges of Oregon*. Portland, Oregon: Oregon Historical Society Press, 1989.

Underhill, J.E. *Coastal Lowland Wildflowers*. Surrey, British Columbia: Hancock House Publishers Ltd., 1986.

Weinmann, Fred, et al. *Wetland Plants of the Pacific Northwest*. Seattle: U.S. Army Corps of Engineers, 1984.

Wiedemann, Alfred M., et al. *Plants of the Oregon Coastal Dunes*. Corvallis, Oregon: Oregon State University Press, 1969.

Wyatt, Steve. *The Bayfront Book*. Newport, Oregon: Lincoln County Historical Society, 1999.

Bibliography

Index

Entries in bold type refer to **Must Stop** sites